FABRE D'OLIVET (1768–1825)

Hermeneutic Interpretation

of the

Origin of the Social State of Man

and of the

Destiny of the Adamic Race

Hermeneutic Interpretation

of the
Origin of the Social State of Man
and of the
Destiny of the Adamic Race

From the French
L'histoire philosophique du genre humain
by

Fabre d'Olivet

Done into English by

Nayán Louise Redfield

Hermetica

San Rafael, Ca

Second, facsimile edition
Hermetica, 2007
First edition, G. P. Putnam's Sons, 1915

For information, address:
Hermetica, P.O. Box 151011
San Rafael, California 94915, USA

Library of Congress Cataloging-in-Publication Data

Fabre d'Olivet, Antoine, 1767–1825.
[Histoire philosophique du genre humain. English]
Hermeneutic interpretation of the origin of the social
state of man and of the destiny of the Adamic race /
Fabre d'Olivet; translator, Nayán Redfield.—Reprint ed.

p. cm.
Originally published: New York: Putnam, 1915.
ISBN-13: 978-1-59731-200-4 (pbk.: alk. paper)
ISBN-13: 978-1-59731-230-1 (hardcover: alk. paper)
1. Human beings. 2. Sociology. 3. Political science.
4. History—Philosophy. I. Title.
HM 588.F3313 2007
301.0944—dc22   2007027041

*Those on
the Path of Knowing, seek
the signs of guidance. Out
of the Universal, Truth calls its
own, lighting its beacon-fire upon
the mountain top, to attract the
way-faring pilgrim in the valley.
To all who can see that
beacon-light, I, as a fellow
pilgrim, lovingly dedicate
this volume.*

TO THE READER

THE Translator offers no apology for the peculiarities or eccentricities of the literary construction of the Author, and after many months of conscientious work and faithful research decided to adhere strictly to the subject-matter contained in this volume of Fabre d'Olivet and translated it without separating or re-arranging the Author's plan. (Referring here to the division of the various books, parts, explanatory notes, foot-notes, or any obsolete form of spelling of foreign words.)

The Translator cannot ask the readers' indulgence in more fitting words than in those in which the Author craves their leniency: " If, after mature reflections, they judge that I have been in error, I shall still rely upon the equity of their judgment that they will at least believe in my sincerity which makes it impossible for me to wish to deceive any one."

N. L. R.

TRANSLATOR'S FOREWORD

FABRE D'OLIVET, the great metaphysician of Esotericism of the nineteenth century, who penetrated far into the crypt of fallen sanctuaries to the tabernacle of the most mysterious arcanas, was born Dec. 8, 1768, at Ganges, Bas-Languedoc.

At an early age he came to Paris, and soon began to devote himself with ardour to the study of ancient as well as living languages, and the better to become initiated into the mystical doctrines of the East, acquired Chinese, Sanscrit, Arabic, and Hebrew, for he had already a profound knowledge of the sciences, philosophies, and literatures of the West.

This man of genius, now almost forgotten—whom France will one day be proud to honour when esoteric or religious science is established upon its own irrefragable foundation —this man who, transcendental in his intelligence and with his attributes of seer, has "cleared the luminous path," has penetrated the mysteries of the Bible, and given to us not only the visions of a lost past, but has esoterically interpreted its symbols.

He was never understood by his contemporaries, for he was a century in advance of his day, and among them, when he died in 1825, had but the reputation of a visionary or a fool.

Of honourable and independent character, he worked unreservedly, and while confined in a studious retreat he saw the Revolution pass before him. In his researches of the languages he rejected what was clear, precise, and logical, seeking always for the mystic, throwing himself into shadowy regions where he sought to find unknown revelations.

Durozoir writes of him: "He pretends to have found the key of the hieroglyphics, and also the means of restoring hearing to deaf-mutes after a method borrowed from the priests of ancient Egypt. . . . He attaches so great faith to the power of the will, that he assures having often made rays come from a volume of his library, by placing himself in front of it and imagining strongly that the author in person was before his eyes; this, he said, happened often to Diderot."

His *Les Vers dorés de Pythagore*, translated for the first time in *eumolpique*[1] French,—that is to say, in harmonious cadence,—precedes his *Discours sur l'essence et la forme de la poésie chez les principaux peuples de la terre*; this was published in 1813. The next work of this wonderful seer of the prehistoric past of humanity, was *La Langue Hebraïque restituée*, published in 1815. It is in two parts, the first being a dissertation on the origin of Speech, in which he restores and proves the real meaning of the Hebrew words, by root analysis; and the second part, a translation of the Cosmogony of Moses, allegorically depicting the creation of the world in general and Adam in the generic sense; Eve as a faculty; and Noah, universal repose. This work was placed on the *Index* at Rome by the papal decree March 26, 1825.

Fabre d'Olivet, in his *Hermeneutic Interpretation of the Origin of the Social State of Man and of the Destiny of the Adamic Race*, sums up all his works. It is the history of the White or Borean Race—ours; and is a condensation of the destinies of this race, whose progressive development he traces across time and space.

His Introductory Dissertation is a veritable *chef-d'œuvre;* it contains the motives by which he has been urged to write

---

[1] εὐμολπος, sweetly singing.

this work; he shows that the knowledge of man is indispensable to the legislator and of what this knowledge consists; he then defines the metaphysical constitution of man and demonstrates that the latter is one of the three great powers that rule the universe. In defining the other two, he establishes between them a distinction, to wit: the Will of man, Destiny and Providence. Its occult sense has reference to the first chapter of the Sepher of Moses.

What is remarkable in this study is the prophetic power of the laws which are at stake. This is exercised not only upon the past, but even upon our present; and all politicians, all sociologists, all patriots ought, by meditating profoundly upon the essence of the principles which d'Olivet describes, to put themselves within reach of logically foreseeing the solution of the national, international, and world-wide problems which today occupy all intelligences.

NAYÁN LOUISE REDFIELD.

HARTFORD, CONN.
July, 1915.

INTRODUCTORY DISSERTATION

I

PREAMBLE—PURPOSE OF THIS WORK

THE work that I am publishing on the social state of man was destined at first to become part of a more considerable work that I had planned upon the history of the world and its inhabitants, and for which I had collected much material. My intention was to present from the same point of view, and in effective arrangement, a general history of the globe that we inhabit, under all the relations of history, natural and political, physical and metaphysical, civil and religious, from the origin of things to their last developments, in such a way as to describe without any prejudice the cosmogonical and geological systems of all peoples, their religious and political doctrines, their governments, customs, and diverse relations; the reciprocal influence which they exercise upon civilization, their movements upon the earth, and the fortunate or unfortunate events which describe their existence more or less agitated, more or less long, more or less interesting; in order to draw from all this, knowledge more extensive and more sure than has hitherto been obtained upon the intimate nature of things, and, above all, that of Man, whom it is most important to understand.

When I conceived this plan, I was still young and full of

that hope that characterizes a presumptuous youth; I saw
no obstacles that could prevent my carrying through this
great plan.   Proud of a certain moral force and determined
upon persistent labour, I believed that nothing could resist
the two-fold ascendancy of perseverance and the love of
truth.   I devoted myself, therefore, to study with an insa-
tiable ardour, and I increased unceasingly my store of learning, not concerning myself with the use to which I might
one day put it.   It must be said that I was forced somewhat
by my political position into the seclusion which necessitated
such devotion.   Although I had not played a conspicuous
part in the course of the Revolution, and although I had held
myself equally apart from both factions, a stranger to all
intrigue, to all ambition, I had such relations with affairs
and men that my opinions and my personality could not
remain wholly in obscurity.   Circumstances independent
of my will had caused my opinions to become known to
Bonaparte, exaggerating further in his eyes anything that
might have been contrary to his designs; so that since his
admittance to the Consulate, he had held against me a hatred
strong enough for him to determine to proscribe me without
motive, by expressly inserting my name among those of
two hundred unfortunates whom he sent to perish upon the
inhospitable shores of Africa.   If by a signal favour of Providence I survived this banishment, it would be necessary
for me to act with great prudence, as long as the reign of
Napoleon lasted, to evade the snares, which he might have
set for me.

My taste and my situation coincided therefore to make
me cherish the refuge and to devote my attention to study.

When resting a moment from my exploratory labours to
glance upon the results of my exploration, I beheld, however,
with some surprise that the greatest difficulties were not
where I had first magined them and that it was not so much
a question of collecting the materials to construct the edifice that I meditated as of understanding well their nature,

in order to arrange them, not according to their form, but according to their homogeneity; their form depending almost always upon time and exterior circumstances while their homogeneity belonged to the very essence of things. This reflection having brought me to examine profoundly many doctrines which the savants have classed ordinarily as incongruous and contrary, I convinced myself that this disparity and this opposition consisted solely in the forms, the basis being essentially the same. I presented henceforth the existence of a great Unity, the eternal Source whence all issues, and I saw clearly that men are not so far from the truth as they generally believe. Their greatest error is in searching for it where it is not, and in attaching it to forms, whereas they ought, on the contrary, to avoid form in order to dwell upon the essence; it should be borne in mind also that these forms are very often their own creations, as was the case with literary monuments of the highest importance such as the cosmogony of Moses. I beg the liberty of pausing a moment upon this extraordinary fact, because it will explain many things that without this would later on appear obscure.

If when one wishes to write a history of the earth, one takes this cosmogony according to its vulgar forms, such as are given by erroneous translations, one suddenly finds a shocking contradiction with the cosmogonies of the most illustrious, the most ancient, and the most enlightened nations of the world. Therefore it is wholly necessary either to reject immediately the scheme first accepted or to consider the sacred writers of the Chinese, Hindus, Persians, Chaldeans, Egyptians, Greeks, Etruscans, and the Celts our ancestors, as impostors or imbeciles; for all, without exception, give to the earth an antiquity incomparably greater than this cosmogony. It would be necessary to overthrow all the chronology of nations, to mutilate their history, to belittle all the great things they had seen, to magnify all that which to them had been imperceptible, and to renounce that wisdom so extolled by the Egyptians,—that wisdom for which the greatest men have searched at the peril of their lives and of which Pythagoras and Plato have transmitted to us incontestable monuments. But it is impossible to reject such a cosmogony; since it serves as a basis for three of the most powerful cults of the earth, whether by their antiquity, their brilliancy, or their extent,—Judaism, Christianity, and Islamism—it is evident for whoever can perceive divine things, that even through the thick veil which the translators of Moses have spread over the writings of this able theocrat, he will discover there unequivocal traces of the inspiration by which it was animated. However, ought one, in sanctioning this cosmogony such as is contained in the vulgar translations, to continue to isolate it from the rest of the world, regarding as impious or false all that which is not comformable with it and treating the rest of the earth as sacrilegious, as does enlightened and powerful Europe, and behaving as she behaved some thousand years ago, in regard to the small, ignorant, and poor country called Judea? This would be still less possible.

Perhaps someone may say, why fret concerning a thing that ought to be left to fall peaceably into oblivion? Books, such as those written by Moses, were for times of obscurity. The best thing to do in radiant ages such as ours is to abandon them to the people who reverence them without understanding them. The savants have no need of being instructed in what the law-maker of the Hebrews thought four thousand years ago in order to build the cosmogonical and geological systems; our encyclopædias are full of admirable things on this subject. Admirable indeed, if one judges by the number; but so vain, so futile, that whereas the book of Moses has sustained itself for forty centuries and held the attention of peoples, a few days suffice to overthrow those with which one attempts to oppose him and to extinguish the trifling sparks which are raised against this imposing meteor.

Be assured, savants of the world, it is not in disdaining

the sacred books of nations that you show your knowledge; it is in explaining them. One cannot write a history without monuments and that of the world is no exception. These books are the veritable archives wherein its deeds are contained. It is necessary in exploring the venerable pages to make comparison between them and to understand how to find the truth, which often languishes there covered by the rust of ages. I saw that if I wished to write a history of the world, I ought to know the monuments which it contains and above all to make sure that I was in a position to explain them thoroughly. Now, that the cosmogony of Moses is one of these monuments is assuredly beyond doubt. It would, then, be ridiculous to pretend to ignore it while passing along a route of which it occupies the whole extent. But if the historian is forced, as I have said, to stop before this colossal memorial and to adopt its principles, what will become of all the other monuments which he will encounter and whose principles, equally imposing and venerable, will be found contradicted? What will he make of all the modern discoveries which cannot adapt themselves to it? Will he say to evidence that it is deceiving and to experience that it has ceased to demonstrate cause and effect? No; unless ignorance and prejudice had previously tied a double bandage over his eyes. This historian will without doubt reason as I have reasoned in his place.

I say to myself: Since the Sepher of Moses, which contains the cosmogony of this famous man, is evidently the fruit of a sublime genius led by divine inspiration, it cannot but contain true principles. If this genius has erred sometimes, it is only perhaps in the matter of inferences, in overstepping the intermediary ideas or attributing to a certain cause effects that belong to another; but these trifling errors which result often from hastiness of peculiar phrasing and the *éclat* of representations are mere nothings in comparison with the fundamental truth which is the soul of the writings and which must be found essentially identical in all the sacred books of the nations, emanating as his from the unique and fecund Source whence flows all truth. If it does not appear thus, it is because the Sepher, composed in a language long since ignored or lost, is not longer understood and because its translations have voluntarily or involuntarily altered or perverted the sense.

After reasoning thus, I passed in order to its application. I examined with all the care at my command the Hebrew of the Sepher, and I was not long in perceiving, as I have remarked elsewhere, that it was not expressed in the vulgar translations, and that Moses said in Hebrew scarcely a word of what his Greek and Latin translators made him say.

It is utterly useless for me to repeat here at length, what one can find entirely developed in the work that I have expressly written upon this subject[1]; suffice it to say, for the understanding of the latter, that the time which I had planned for writing the history of the world, after I had collected the material, was almost entirely employed in explaining a single one of the monuments which contained the material in part, so that this monument of irrefutable authenticity should not contradict, by its formal opposition, the ordinance of the edifice nor cause it to give way upon its base, in refusing it its fundamental support. This explanation even, made in the usual manner, did not suffice. It was necessary to prove to others, with much labour and difficulty, that which was so easy to prove to myself, and to restore a language lost more than twenty-four centuries ago, to create a grammar and a radical dictionary to support the verbal translation of some chapters of the Sepher from a mass of notes drawn from all the languages of the Orient, and finally to increase twenty pages of the text to the extent of two quarto volumes of explanations and proofs.

---

[1] *La langue hébraïque restituée*, etc., in which is found the cosmogony of Moses, such as is contained in the first ten chapters of *Berœshith*, vulgarly called *Genesis*.

This was not all: in order to draw these two volumes from the obscurity of my portfolio, where they would have undoubtedly remained for want of means to meet the considerable expense of printing them, it was necessary to attract attention to them, and this I could not do without taking a stand which displeased Napoleon, at that time all powerful; and this again made me the victim of a persecution, secret it is true, but none the less painful, since it deprived me of the only means I had of subsistence.[1] My two volumes were indeed printed, but much later and through the co-operation of particular circumstances which I can justly regard as providential.

The publication of my book upon the Hebraic language, far from giving me the facilities upon which I was counting in order to pursue my design for the history of the world, seemed on the contrary to deprive me of them, by laying myself open to metaphysical and literary discussions which changing into dissensions carried their venom into the very precincts of my domestic fireside.

The time, however, is passed and although favoured with all the vigour of life, I have vainly tried to accomplish a plan perhaps out of proportion to my physical and moral power. Ought I to hope further for its attainment today, since the autumn of my life is daily losing its ardour? It would be presumption to believe it. But that which I shall not be able to do, another may, under more fortunate conditions, succeed in doing. My glory, if I obtain any, will be in having traced and smoothed the way for him. Already I have given him in my translation of the Sepher of Moses an absolutely sure foundation. If I can ever finish the commentary, I will show that the cosmogony of this great man is conformable, on account of the essence of things, with all the sacred cosmogonies admitted by the nations. I will do for it what I did for the *Vers dorés* of Pythagoras,

---

[1] See a small brochure entitled: *Notions sur le sens de l'ouïe*, etc., in which it speaks in detail of these annoyances.

in the examinations of which I have proved that the philosophical and theosophical ideas therein contained have been the same in all time and among all men capable of conceiving them. I had previously pointed out the origin of poetry and shown in what the essence differs from the form: this pertains always to the history of the world; for the first oracles were rendered in verse, and it is not without cause that poetry has been named the language of the gods.

Among the fragments over which I had worked in order to enter upon the great work of which I have spoken, the most noteworthy are those dealing with the social state of man and the diverse forms of government. Even if I had not been urged to publish them, in order to furnish useful material to those who wished to devote themselves to the same studies as I, it seems to me that the threatening circumstances in which we are would have made me take that resolve. All the world is occupied with politics; each one dreams of his Utopia, and I do not see, among the innumerable works that appear on this matter, that any one touches the real principle; the greater part, far from throwing a light upon this important mystery of human society, upon the bond which strengthens it and the legislation which conducts it, seem destined, on the contrary, to cover it with thickest gloom.

Those in general who write upon this serious subject, more occupied with themselves and their particular passions than with the universality of things of which the whole escapes them, circumscribe their views too much and show too plainly that they know nothing of the history of the world. Because they have heard of the Greeks and Romans, or because they have read the annals of these two peoples in Herodotus or Thucydides, in Titus Livius or Tacitus, they imagine that all is known; deluded by their guides, intoxicated with their own ideas, they trace in turn by a thousand ways the same road in the shifting sands; they imprint without cessation new steps upon effaced tracks and end always by wandering in the deserts or by losing themselves in the pitfalls. That which they lack is, I repeat, the knowledge of the true principles, and this knowledge, which depends upon that of the universality of things, is always produced by it, or produces it irresistibly.

I have pondered long upon these principles and believe I have penetrated them. My object is to make them known; but this enterprise is not without some difficulty; for although these principles have a name well known and extensively used, it is more necessary that this name should give the just idea of the immense thing that it expresses. It does not suffice therefore to name these principles in order to give even the vaguest knowledge concerning them; neither does it suffice to define them, since any definition of principles is incomplete for the reason that it defines that which is undefinable and gives limits to what has none. It is most necessary to see them in action in order to comprehend them and to try to distinguish them in their effect, since it is absolutely impossible to understand them in their cause. These considerations and others which will reveal themselves easily in the course of this work, have actuated me to lay aside at once the didactic or dogmatic form, substituting for it the historic form, so that I might present in a narrative many things whose development would otherwise have been prohibited or would have been impeded by interminable delays.

This historic form which I have adopted in essence affords many advantages, permitting me not only to put often *en scène* and to personify likewise the political principles, thereby making the action better felt; but it has given me opportunity to present compendiously a particular picture of the history of the world in its political relation, such as I had originally conceived and already outlined in order to make it form an integral part of the general picture with which I was engaged. I dare to flatter myself that a reader, curious to go back from effects to causes and to become acquainted with prior events, will pardon me the well-known details into which I am forced to enter, in favour of those little known or completely ignored which I will demonstrate to him for the first time. I think he will also permit me several indispensable hypotheses in the transcendental movement which I have taken towards the origin of human societies. I assume that he will not ask of me historic proofs of an epoch where no history exists and that he will content himself with the moral or physical proofs which I will give him—proofs drawn from rational deductions or from etymological analogies. It will be sufficient for him to see, when the historic proofs come, that they in no wise contradict these primary hypotheses which they on the contrary sustain and by which they are sustained. It only rests now for me, in terminating this preamble, to say one word and this word is perhaps the most important. We are about to speak of *Man;* and this being is not yet known to us either in his origin or in his faculties or in the hierarchical order which he occupies in the universe. To recognize him in his origin, that is to say, in his ontological principle, is useless for us at the moment, since we have no need to know what he has been outside the actual order of things, but only to understand what he is in this order; thus we can leave to cosmogony, of which ontology, properly speaking, constitutes a part, the task of teaching us the origin of man as it taught us the origin of the earth; it is in the writings of Moses and other hierographical writers that we can learn these things; but we cannot dispense with questioning the anthropological knowledge if it exists or creating it if it does not exist, in order to instruct ourselves concerning what Man is, considered as Man, what his moral and physical faculties are, how he is constituted intellectually and physically, in the same manner as we question geological or geographical science, if we could occupy ourselves with the interior and exterior forms of the earth. I assume that these last two sciences are known to my readers, at least in general, and that there are as many positive ideas upon physical man as is necessary in reading an ordinary history such as is commonly written. But my intention in treating of the social state of Man and of the political and philosophical history of Mankind is not to repeat what one finds everywhere, but, on the contrary, to disclose new things and raise myself to heights but little frequented. I must in advance make known the intellectual and metaphysical constitution of Man, such as I have conceived it, so that I can make myself understood when I will speak of the successive development of the moral faculties and of their action.

II

THAT THE KNOWLEDGE OF MAN IS INDISPENSABLE TO THE LEGISLATOR—OF WHAT THIS KNOWLEDGE CONSISTS

I beg here a little more attention than one would ordinarily accord to a preliminary discourse, because it is not so much a question of preparing the mind to receive certain ideas as of putting it in condition to comprehend them well before receiving them.

Since it is of Man and for Man that the political writers and the legislators have written, it is evident that the first and most indispensable knowledge for them ought to be, Man; and nevertheless it is a knowledge that the majority do not possess, that they do not seek to acquire, and that they would have been often incapable of finding even if they had sought it. They accept such a man as the naturalists and the physicists present to them according to anthropographical rather than to anthropological science, as an animal making part of the animal kingdom and differing from other animals only by a certain principle of reason, which God or rather Nature, dignified by this name, had given him, even as feathers had been given to the birds and fur to the bears—that principle which causes him to be designated by the epithet of *rational animal*. But considering that the principle of reason, according to the most profound physiologists, appears not to be foreign to certain classes of animals, of dogs, horses, elephants, etc., and that one has seen parrots learn even a language and avail themselves of a word to express reasonable ideas, whether in replying to questions or questioning one another, as Locke relates, it follows from this observation that man enjoys this principle only more or less in comparison with other animals, and that he owes this accidental superiority only to the suppleness of his limbs, to the perfection of his organs, which have permitted his entire development. For example, to the form of his hand has been attributed all the progress in sciences and arts, and it is quite possible to imagine that a horse might have equalled Archimedes as geometrician, or Timotheus as musician, if he had received from nature limbs as supple and fingers as propitiously suitable. The prejudice in this respect was so profoundly rooted that a modern historian has even dared to assert that the only real difference he had seen between animal and Man was that of apparel. Another writer even more celebrated—considering that superiority of reason which Man manifests at times, as a false light which weakens the force of his instinct, deranges his health, and troubles his repose to such a degree that he becomes sick and troubled—stated that if nature had destined us to be healthy, the man who meditates is a depraved animal.

Now if by meditating only, Man becomes depraved, how much the more if he contemplate, if he wonder, and, above all, if he adore!

When, after having assumed similar premises, one reasons upon the social state and, when seeing in Man only animal more or less perfect, he is set up for a legislator, it is evident that without being inconsistent, one can only offer instinctive laws, the certain effect of which is to draw the human race towards a rude and savage nature from which his intelligence ever tries to separate him. It is indeed what other

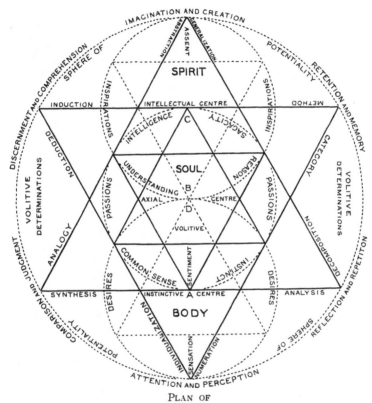

PLAN OF

THE CONSTITUTION OF MAN

ACCORDING TO FABRE D'OLIVET

writers see who, uniting a very great exaltation of ideas
to the same ignorance of principles and finding themselves
frightened at the consequences, into which these dismal
preceptors have dragged them, throw themselves with violence to the opposite side and overleap the golden mean so
recommended by the sages. The former made of Man pure
animal; the latter made him pure intelligence. Some place
their basis upon his most physical needs; others upon his
most spiritual hopes, and, whereas the first confine him in a
material circle from which all the forces of his being urge
him to escape, the second lose themselves in the vaguest
abstractions, throwing him into a limitless sphere, at the
aspect of which even his imagination recoils terrified.

No; Man is neither an animal nor an intelligence; but an
intermediary being placed between matter and spirit, between heaven and earth as a link for them. The definitions
which one has tried to give him all fail through want or
excess. When one calls him a reasonable animal, one says
too little; when one designates him as an intelligence served
by the organs, one says too much. Man, even assuming
that his physical form is like that of an animal, is more than
reasonable; he is intelligent and free. Granting that he
may be an intelligence in his purely spiritual part, it is not
true that this intelligence is always served by the organs,
since these organs, visibly independent of it, are often carried
away by blind impulses and produce acts which are dis-
owned by it. If I were asked myself to give a definition of
Man, I should day that he is a sentient being, elevated to
the intellectual life, susceptible of admiration and of adoration; or an intellectual being subject to the organs, susceptible of degradation. But definitions, whatever they may
be, will always represent imperfectly a being so complicated;
it is better to try to understand him.

Let us examine for a moment the sacred archives of
Mankind.

The philosophers, naturalists, or experimentalists who

have classed Man with animals, have committed an enormous error. Deceived by their superficial observations, by their trifling experiences, they have neglected to consult the voice of centuries, the traditions of all peoples. If they had opened the sacred books of the most ancient writers of the world, those of the Chinese, Hindus, Hebrews, or Parsees, they would have seen that the animal kingdom existed *tout entier* before Man existed. At the time when Man appeared upon the scene of the universe, he formed alone a fourth kingdom, the *Kingdom of Man*. This kingdom is called *Pan-Kou* by the Chinese, *Pourou* by the Brahmans, *Kai-Ormuzd* or *Meschia* by the followers of Zoroaster, and *Adam* by the Hebrews, and by all the people who accept the Sepher of Moses, whether they link themselves with the Gospel as Christians or trace their origin there by the Koran and the Gospel, as Mussulmans. I know well that the interpreters of these books, those who confine themselves only to the literal and vulgar forms, who remain strangers to the manner of the writings of the ancients, assume alike today *Pan-Kou, Pourou, Kai-Ormuzd,* or *Adam* as a sole man, the first individual of the species; but I have proved sufficiently in my interpretation of the cosmogony of Moses, contained in the first ten chapters of the Sepher, that it should be understood by *Adam* not man in particular, but Man in general, universal Man, Mankind complete, in short, the *Kingdom of Man*. If circumstances permit me some day to give the commentary upon the cosmogony which I have promised, I will prove in the same manner that the first man of the Chinese, Hindus, or Parsees, *Pan-Kou, Pourou,* or *Kai-Ormuzd*, must be universally equal and conceived not as a sole man, but as the union of all men who have entered, are entering, or will enter the composition of this great whole that we call the *Kingdom of Man*.

But supposing, finally, in spite of the many proofs brought to the support of my interpretation, proofs which no one has yet dared to attack seriously since they were issued and recognized five years ago—supposing, I say, that one accepted Adam and the different cosmogonical beings which correspond to him in the sacred books of all nations for an individual man, it will remain always certain that all these books agree in distinguishing these beings from the animal kingdom, making them appear alone at a different epoch, and making them the object of a special creation; and this authorizes me sufficiently, not to confuse man with animals by including him among them in the same category, but, on the contrary, to make of the human race a superior kingdom as I have done.

Besides, when one questions the most learned geologists, those who have penetrated most deeply into the material knowledge of our globe, they will tell you that, having attained a certain depth, one finds no vestige, no trace announcing the presence of man in the first ages of the world, whereas the débris and bones of animals are encountered in profusion; and this accords perfectly with the sacred traditions of which I have spoken. [1]

I have already had occasion in my *Examens sur les Vers dorés* of Pythagoras to speak of Man, and to unite as in a sheaf the sacred traditions preserved in ancient mysteries, the thoughts of the most celebrated theosophists and philosophers, in order to form a whole which may enlighten us as to the intimate essence of this being, so much more important and more difficult to understand since he does not belong to a simple nature, material or spiritual, nor even to a double nature both material and spiritual, but, as I have shown in this work, to a triple nature, itself linked

---

[1] If it had been my intention to write a work of erudition, I should have been able to crowd it with citations and to call all antiquity in testimony not alone of what I say here, but of what I shall say later on; but as this scholastic display would tend to retard my progress in a work destined to present thoughts rather than facts, I abstain and will abstain from citing any. I pray only that the reader believe that all the authorities upon which I lean are unimpeachable from the side of science and stand upon the most firm historic bases.

with a fourth power which constitutes it. I shall reproduce shortly the result of my earlier studies and I shall compare with it traits disseminated elsewhere, adding some developments which meditation and experience have suggested to me since.   First let me lay down some general ideas.

At the time Man appeared upon earth, there existed three kingdoms, which formed the whole and divided it. The mineral, vegetable, and animal kingdom had been the object of three successive creations, appearances, or developments. Man, or rather the Kingdom of Man, was the fourth. The interval which separated these diverse appearances is measured in the Sepher of Moses by a word which expresses a *phenomenal manifestation;* so that, taking it in its most restricted sense, one is able to make it signify, *a day;* but this sense is evidently unnatural and one cannot refuse to see here a period of time undetermined, always relative to the existence to which it is applied.   Among the nations of which I have spoken, where the several developments of nature are found expressed very nearly as in the Sepher of Moses, one ordinarily measures this period by the duration of the great year, equivalent to that astronomical revolution called today the precession of the equinoxes, or by one of its divisions; so that one can conceive it as nine, eighteen, twenty-seven, or thirty-six thousand of our ordinary years. But whatever may be the temporal length of this period, called by Moses a manifestation, an immensity, a sea, or a day, is not the question here; the important point is to have demonstrated by the agreement of all the cosmogonies that Man was never included in the animal kingdom. This kingdom as well as the other two inferior kingdoms, the vegetable and mineral, were comprised in his and were entirely subordinate to him.

Man, destined to be the link which unites Divinity to matter, was, according to the expression of a modern naturalist, a chain of communication between all beings. Placed on the confines of two worlds he became the means of exal-

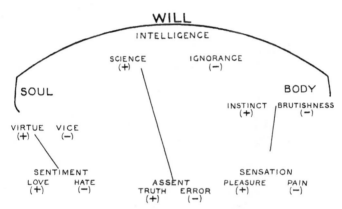

EXPLANATORY PLAN BY PAPUS OF
THE CONSTITUTION OF MAN
ACCORDING TO FABRE D'OLIVET

tation in the body and that of abasement in the divine spirit. The perfected essence of the three kingdoms of nature is united in him to a will power, free in its scope, which makes him the living type of the universe and the image of God Himself. God is the centre and the circumference of all that which is; Man, the image of God, is the centre and the circumference of the sphere which he inhabits; nothing else exists in this sphere, which may be composed of the four essences; it is he whom Pythagoras thus designates by his mysterious verse:

> *Immense et pur symbole,*
> *Source de la nature, et modèle des Dieux.*

The conception of all things is congeneric with Man; the knowledge of immensity and of eternity is in his understanding. Often, it is true, thick darkness deprives him of its use and discernment; but the assiduous exercise of his faculties will suffice to change this darkness into light and to render unto him the possession of its treasures. Nothing can resist the power of his will, when this will, moved by divine love, principle of all virtue, acts in accord with Providence. But without engaging further in these ideas which will better find their place elsewhere, let us continue our researches.

III

INTELLECTUAL, METAPHYSICAL CONSTITUTION OF MAN

Man, as I have said, belongs to a triple nature; he can therefore live a triple life: instinctive, animistic, or intellectual. When these three lives are developed, they become blended in a fourth which is the individual and volitive life of this wonderful being whose immortal source is in life and the divine will. Each of these lives has its particular centre and appropriate sphere.

I shall try to present to the mind of the reader a meta-physical view of the intellectual constitution of Man; but I forewarn him that he must think of nothing material in what I shall say regarding this. Although I may be obliged, in order to make myself understood, to use terms that will recall physical objects, such as those of centre, sphere, circumference, radius, etc., one must not think that anything physical, and above all anything mechanical, enters into these things. These words, which lacking others I shall employ, should be understood by the mind alone and abstraction made of all material conceptions.

Man, then, spiritually considered, in the absence of his physical organs, can be conceived under the form of a luminous sphere, in which three central fires give birth to three distinct spheres, all three enveloped by the circumference of this sphere. From each of these three fires radiates one of the three lives of which I have spoken. To the inferior fire belongs the instinctive life; to the median fire, the animistic life; and to the superior fire, the intellectual life. Among these three vital centres, the animistic is to be regarded as the fundamental point, *premier mobile* upon which rests and moves all the edifice of the human spiritual being. This centre in unfolding its circumference touches the other two centres and unites with itself the opposite points of the two circumferences which they unfold, so that the three vital spheres in moving one in the other communicate their diverse natures and carry from one to the other their reciprocal influence.

As soon as the first potential movement is given to the human being and as it passes into action by an effort of his nature, determined by the first Cause of all beings, the instinctive fire attracts and develops the elements of the *body;* the animistic fire creates the *soul,* and the intellectual perfects the *mind.* Man therefore is composed of body, soul, and mind. To the body belong the *necessities;* to the soul, the *passions;* to the mind, the *inspirations.*

In proportion as each central fire grows and radiates, it unfolds a circumference which, being divided by its own rays, presents six luminous points, each of which manifests a faculty, that is to say, a particular mode of action according to the life of the animistic, instinctive, or intellectual sphere.

In order to avoid confusion, we shall name only three of these faculties upon each circum'erence, which will give us nine in all, namely;

For the instinctive sphere: *sensation, instinct, common sense.*

For the animistic sphere: *sentiment, understanding, reason.*

For the intellectual sphere: *assent, intelligence, sagacity.*

The origin of all these faculties is first in the instinctive sphere; it is there that they have birth and receive their first forms.

The other two spheres, which are not developed until later, acquire their relative faculties only secondarily and by transformation, that is to say, that the instinctive sphere being entirely developed and bearing by its circumferential point, *sensation* for example, to the animistic centre, this centre is agitated and, unfolding itself, takes possession of this faculty which excites it and transforms sensation into *sentiment.* This sentiment, carried in the same way to the intellectual centre and when all the conditions are fulfilled for this, is seized in its turn by this centre and transformed into *assent.* Thus instinct, properly speaking, passing from the instinctive sphere into the animistic, is there transformed into *understanding;* and understanding becomes *intelligence* in consequence of its course from this last sphere to the intellectual. This transformation takes place for all the other faculties of this kind, whatever the number may be.

But this transformation which takes place upon the faculties of the sensation class—which I consider as circumferential affections, and consequently exterior—acts also upon the necessities which are central interior affections; so that necessity, carried from the instinctive centre to the animistic centre, there becomes or can become passion, and, if this passion passes from the animistic centre to the intellectual centre, it can there assume the character of an inspiration and react upon the passion as passion reacts upon necessity.

At present, let us consider that all circumferential affection of the sensation class excites a movement more or less vigorous in the instinctive centre and that it is immediately represented there as *pleasure* or *pain*, according as the movement is agreeable or disagreeable and whether it has its source in physical *good* or *evil*. The intensity of pleasure or pain is relative to that of the movement excited and to its nature. If this movement has a certain force, it produces, according as it is agreeable or painful, two inevitable effects: the *attraction* which attracts it or the *fear* which repels it; if it is weak and doubting it produces *indolence*. In the same manner as the instinctive centre perceives by sensation the physical good or evil under the name of *pleasure* or *pain*, the animistic centre develops by sentiment the moral good or evil, under the name of *love* or *hatred*, and the intellectual centre represents the intellectual good or evil under the name of *truth* or *error*. But these inevitable effects of attraction or fear, which attach themselves to the instinctive sensation, according as it excites pleasure or pain, do not survive this sensation but disappear with it; whereas in the animistic sphere the sentiment which brings forth love or hatred, drawing likewise two certain effects, *desire* and *terror*, far from disappearing with the cause of the sentiment which has produced them, persists, on the contrary, a long while after with this same sentiment, assuming the character of passions and inviting or repelling the cause which brought them forth. The notable difference of instinctive life and of animistic life is there; the attentive and curious reader should take notice of this and reflect upon it.

Instinctive sensations are all actual and their effects instantaneous; but animistic sentiments are durable, independent of the physical movement which produces them. As for intellectual assents which affirm truth or error, they are not only durable as sentiments, but are influential even more after they have passed.

Indolence, which excites a movement weak or doubtful in the physical sensation, is transformed into *apathy* in the moral sentiment and into a sort of *indifference* in the intellectual assent which confuses truth and error and leaves one as unconcerned as the other. This condition, habitual in the infancy of the individual as in the infancy of the kingdom, rules equally in that of society.[1]

This triple form existence of man—although it may appear already very complicated on account of the many actions and reactions which operate incessantly some with regard to others: the instinctive necessities, the animistic passions, and the intellectual inspirations—would still be very simple and would offer scarcely more than a being acting under necessity if we had not to consider this fourth life which includes the other three and gives to man the liberty which he could not have without it.

Let us redouble our attention here, for the subject is important and difficult.

In the very centre of the animistic sphere, primal cause of the spiritual human being, is another centre which is inherent there, the circumference of which, in unfolding,

---

[1] As it has not been my intention to give here a complete system of anthropological science, but only to establish the principles of it, I shall neither enter into the detail of all the transformations which take place in the necessities, passions, or inspirations of all sorts, which bring them forth and perfect them; nor into that still more considerable detail of the innumerable vibrations, which are brought into sensations, sentiments, or assents by the six senses with which man is endowed: touch, taste, smell, hearing, sight, and the mental sense; which uniting all the others, conceives, compares, and restores them to the unity from which their nature has estranged them. Such a labour would require alone a long work which would of necessity go beyond the limits of a simple dissertation.

touches the extreme points of the instinctive and intellectual spheres and likewise envelops them. This fourth sphere, in the interior of which the three spheres of the instinct, soul, and mind are moved into place according to the mode which I have tried to describe, is that of the efficient and volitive power, whose essence, emanated from the Divinity, is indestructible and incontestable as It. This sphere whose life incessantly radiates from the centre to the circumference, can expand or contract itself in the ethereal sphere, to bounds which might be called infinite, if *GOD* were not the sole infinite Being. And this is the luminous sphere which I mentioned in the beginning of this article.

When this sphere is sufficiently developed, its circumference, determined by the extent of its rays, admits of a great number of faculties, some primordial, others secondary, weak at first, but which gradually strengthen in proportion as the ray which produces them acquires force and grandeur. Among these faculties we shall enumerate only twelve, six primordial and six secondary, commencing with the most inferior and finishing with the highest.

These twelve faculties are: *attention* and *perception, reflection* and *repetition, comparison* and *judgment, retention* and *memory, discernment* and *comprehension, imagination* and *creation*.

Volitive power, which carries its faculties everywhere with it, places them where it wills in the instinctive, animistic, or intellectual sphere; for this power is always where it wills to be. The triple life which I have described is its domain; it uses it as it wills, nothing being able to attack its liberty but itself, as I shall relate in the continuation of this work.

As soon as a sensation, sentiment, or assent is manifested in one of the three lives which are submissive to it, it has *perception* by the *attention* that it gives to them, and, using its faculty to procure *repetition* even in the absence of their cause, it examines them by *reflection*. The *comparison* that it makes according to the type of what it approves or disapproves determines its *judgment*. Afterwards it forms *memory* by the *retention* of its own labour, reaches the point of *discernment*, and consequently *comprehension*, and finally assembled and brought together by *imagination*, the ideas disseminated, it arrives at the *creation* of its thought. It is indeed wrong as one sees, that in the vulgar language one confuses an idea with a thought. An idea is the simple effect of a sensation, sentiment, or assent; whereas a thought is a complex effect, a result sometimes immense. To have ideas is to feel; to have thoughts is to act.

The same operation that I have just described concisely, takes place in the same manner, in the necessities, passions, and inspirations; but in this last case the labour of the volitive power is central; whereas in the first case, it was circumferential. It is here that this magnificent power, shown in all its splendour, becomes the type of the universe and merits the name of microcosm, which all antiquity has given it.

Just as the instinctive sphere acts by *necessity*, the animistic by *passion*, the intellectual by *inspiration*, the volitive sphere acts by *determination*, and upon that depends the liberty of Man, his force, and the manifestation of his celestial origin. Nothing is so simple as this action which the philosophers and the moralists have had so much trouble to explain. I shall endeavour to make it understood.

The presence of a necessity, a passion, or an inspiration excites in the sphere, where it is produced, a rotary movement more or less rapid, according to the intensity of the one or the other; the movement is ordinarily called *appetite* or *appetence* in the instinct, *emotion* or *consent* in the soul and in the mind; often these terms are substituted for each other and are changed by synonyms, the sense of which expresses more or less the force in the movement. The volitive power which is disturbed has three determinations of which it is free to make use: first, it yields to the movement, and its sphere turns to the same side as the agitated sphere; secondly, it resists and turns to the opposite side; third, it remains in repose. In the first case it allows itself to be compelled by the instinct, drawn along by the soul or stirred by the mind, and connives with necessity, passion, or inspiration; in the second it resists them and deadens their movement by its own; in the third it suspends or rejects acquiescence and considers what is most fitting to do. Whatever may be its determination, its efficient will, which is manifested freely, finds the means of serving its diverse appetites, of resisting them or meditating upon their causes, their forms, and their consequences. These means, which are in continuous radiation from the centre to the circumference and from the circumference to the centre, are very numerous. I shall here describe only those which attach themselves most particularly to the twelve faculties already named:

Attention and perception act by *individualization* and *numeration*.

Reflection and repetition, by *decomposition* and *analysis*.

Comparison and judgment, by *analogy* and *synthesis*.

Retention and memory, by *method* and *category*.

Discernment and comprehension, by *induction* and *deduction*.

Imagination and creation, by *abstraction* and *generalization*.

The employment of these means and of many others that would be too long to name is called *meditation*. Meditation constitutes the force of the will which employs it. The acquiescence of this will or its resistance, according as they are well or badly applied, according as they are simultaneous or a long time debated, makes of man a being either powerful or weak, elevated or base, wise or ignorant, virtuous or vicious; oppositions, contradictions, storms of all sorts which arise in his breast have no cause other than the movements of the three vital spheres, instinctive, animistic, and intellectual, often opposed to each other and more often still contradictory to the regular movement of the volitive will, which refuses its definite adherence or which gives it only after violent combats.

When the determinations of the will take place upon objects of the source of sensation, sentiment, or assent, acquiescence or resistance follows simultaneously the impulse of instinct, understanding, or intelligence and bears their name: when they are preceded by meditation,they assume the character of common sense, reason, or sagacity and are said to belong to them and even to be their own creation.

After having traced this rapid outline of the intellectual and metaphysical constitution of man, there is no need, I think, to say that it is only sketched and that it demands, on the part of whoever would grasp it in its entirety or in its details, a concentrated attention and repeated study. I should indeed have liked to spare my readers so much trouble, and perhaps they will think that I should have succeeded, if I had gone into more details myself; but they are mistaken; I should only have lengthened my description with no result other than lessening the clearness of it. I have said all that was essential to say; I have exercised great care in the examination of the subject as a whole. As to the details, it is necessary to avoid them as much as one can in a subject where they are infinite, as is precisely the case here. Besides, in the work which follows, there will be many opportunities of applying and developing the principles which I have laid down. All that remains for me now to do is to anticipate several difficulties which might be found in their application.

Man, never having been analysed before as vigorously in his *ensemble*, and his metaphysical anatomy never having been so plainly presented, one is accustomed very often to take for the whole, only one of his parts and call it *soul*, for example, not only the soul, properly speaking, but also the three vital spheres and even the volitive sphere which envelops them.   Other times one is content to name this *ensemble, mind*, in opposition to body, and then, again, *intelligence*, in opposition to *instinct*.   Sometimes one has considered *understanding* alone as the union of all the faculties, and reason as the universal rule, true or false, of all the *determinations* of the will.   This abuse of terms will not be dangerous when it can be appreciated.   What we have done by force of habit, we can continue for the convenience of the discourse and to avoid the prolixity of disconcerting verbosity; but we must take care not to do it through ignorance.   If we would know Man in himself, we must consider him such as I have just described, for he is thus.

When I say, however, that Man is thus, it ought to be understood only as Man in general, considered abstractly in the possibility of his essence.   Even today when the kingdom of Man enjoys great power in nature, the individual man is very rarely developed in all his mental modifications. In the infancy of the kingdom, the mass of humanity was far from being that which it is at present; the preponderating life in the individual was the instinctive life; the animistic shed only feeble lights, and the intellectual existed as yet only in the germ.   Just as one sees an infant, born with weak organs, deprived even of the greater part of his physical senses, without any sign of the imposing faculties which he is one day to have, develop himself little by little, gather strength, acquire hearing and sight which he lacked, grow, understand his needs, manifest his passions, give proofs of his intelligence, instruct himself, enlighten himself, and become at last a man perfect through the use of his will, so must one consider the Kingdom of Man, passing through all the phases of infancy, adolescence, youth, and manhood. An individual man is to a great nation what a great nation is to the kingdom in general.   Who knows, for example, how many men have completed their career from the earliest dawn of life to its extreme decline among the peoples of Assyria or of Egypt, during the long existence of these two peoples? And who knows how many similar peoples are destined yet to shine and to become extinct upon the scene of the world before universal Man reaches caducity?

In tracing this metaphysical picture, I have considered Man in the greatest development that he can attain today. This same development does not belong to all men; it does not belong even to the majority of them. Nature does not make men equal; souls differ still more than bodies. I have already announced this great truth in my *Examens des Vers dorés* of Pythagoras, in showing that such was the doctrine of the mysteries and the thought of all the sages of antiquity. Equality without doubt is in the volitive essence of all, since this essence is divine; but inequality insinuates itself into the faculties by diversity of employment and difference of exercise; time is not measured equally for all; positions have changed, courses of life have become shortened or lengthened, and, although it is certain that all men having proceeded from the same principle must arrive at the same end, there are many, and indeed the greatest number, who are very far from arriving; whereas some have already done so, others are about to, and many, obliged to recommence their course, could not have escaped the nothingness which would have engulfed them if the eternity of their existence had not been assured by the eternity of its Author.

The animistic equality is then in the actuality of things a chimera still greater than the equality of the instinctive forces of the body.

Inequality is everywhere and in the intelligence still more than in all the rest, since it is among existing men and above all among a great number of men whose civilization is only sketched, whose intellectual centre is not yet on the path of development. As for political inequality, we shall see, further on in the work which follows, what one should think regarding it.

IV

MAN IS ONE OF THE THREE GREAT POWERS OF THE UNIVERSE —WHAT THE OTHER TWO ARE

Let us avoid the mistake which nearly all philosophers have made, especially in these modern times, and let us consider that if it is ridiculous to pretend to write upon Man without knowing him, it is both ridiculous and odious pretending to trace a course for him without being perfectly informed about his starting point, the goal for which he strives, and the purpose of his journey. Let us, above all, understand his position, and, since he himself is a power, let us try with attention to find what are the superior or inferior powers with which he must come in contact.

That universal Man is a power is averred by all the sacred codes of nations; it is felt by all the sages; it is even avowed by all true savants. I read in a *Dictionnaire d'histoire naturelle*, printed quite recently, these remarkable phrases: "Man possesses the essence of organizing power; it is in his brain that the intelligence that governs the formation of beings is confined. . . . He is born the minister and interpreter of the divine Will over all that which breathes. . . . The sceptre of the earth is entrusted to him." About fifteen centuries before our era, Moses had put these words in the mouth of the Divinity addressing Man: "Be fruitful and multiply and replenish the earth and subdue it: and have dominion over the fish of the sea and over the fowl of the air and over every living thing that moveth upon the earth." And, a long time before Moses, the legislator of the Chinese had said, in suitable words without figures of speech, that Man is one of the three powers which rule the Universe.

It would be better, without doubt, to receive these texts and an infinite number of others that I could cite in the same sense, than to believe with Anaxagoras, whose belief was followed by Helvetius, that man is an animal whose whole intelligence comes from the conformation of his hand, or with Hobbes, followed by Locke and Condillac, that there is nothing innate in him, that he can use nothing without practice, and that he is born wicked and in a state of warfare with his fellow creatures.

But, although it be very true, as all sages and theosophists affirm in attesting the name of the Divinity, that Man is a power destined by the eternal Wisdom to dominate inferior nature, to restore harmony in the discord of its elements, to render co-ordinate its three kingdoms, and to raise them from diversity to unity, it is, however, not true, as men more enthusiastic than judicious have believed without reflection and without examination, that this power should appear upon the earth all made, provided with all its forces, possessing all its developments and, so to speak, descending from heaven surrounded by a glory gathered without trouble and with knowledge acquired without pain. This exaggerated idea which issues from the golden mean, so recommended by the sages, issues also from the truth. Man is a power without doubt, but a power in the germ, which, in order to manifest his properties so as to attain the height to which his destiny calls him, has need of an interior action stimulated by the exertion of an exterior action upon it.   He is a celestial plant whose roots attached to the earth can suck up the elementary forces so as to perfect them by a particular process; and which, raising little by little its majestic trunk, covering itself in its season with flowers and intellectual fruits, matures them in the rays of the divine Light, and offers them in sacrifice to the God of the Universe.

This comparison, which is very just, can be continued. A tree, while it is still young, bears as yet no fruits, and the husbandman does not expect it, for he knows that its greatest importance and usefulness exact a longer elaboration and render its fruits less forward; but when the time has come to reap the harvest he does so and each season which renews it must augment the quantity of its fruits, if the excellence of the tree responds to the excellence of the cultivation. When, without injury to its fruitfulness, by exterior accidents, tempests, or destructive winds, the harvest fails many times in succession, the tree is reputed bad and defective and it is as such, following the forcible expression of Jesus, torn up and cast into the fire.

Now, cultivation is to the tree what civilization is to Man. Without the former, the plant, abandoned to a poor and degraded Nature, would bear only ordinary flowers without lustre, only fruits lacteous or resinous, insipid, or bitter and often poisonous; without the latter, Man, delivered to a cruel sort of Nature, severe with him because she does not recognize him as her own child, would develop only savage faculties and would offer only a character of a being out of place, suffering and ferocious, greedy and unfortunate.

It is therefore upon civilization that all in Man depends; it is then upon his social state that the edifice of his grandeur is established. Let us look carefully at these important points; let us not fear to make a study of them. There is no object more worthy of our examination, no study whose results promise us more advantages.

But if Man is, at first, as I have just said, only a power in germ which civilization must develop, whence will come to him the principles of this indispensable culture? I reply that it will be from the two powers to which he finds himself linked and of which he must form the third, according to the tradition of the Chinese theosophist already cited. These two powers, between which he finds himself placed, are Destiny and Providence. Beneath him is Destiny, *nature necéssitée et naturée;* above him is Providence, *nature libre et naturante.* He is himself, as Kingdom of Man, the mediatory will, the efficient form, placed between these two natures to serve them as a link, a means of communication and to unite two actions, two movements, which would be incompatible without him.

The three powers, which I have just named—Providence, Man, considered as the Kingdom of Man, and Destiny— constitute the universal ternary. Nothing escapes their action; all is subject to them in the universe; all except *God* Himself who, enveloping them in His unfathomable Unity, forms with it the Sacred Tetrad of the ancients, that immense quarternary, which is All in All and outside of which there is nothing.

I shall have much to say in the following work concerning these three powers, and I shall describe as much as is possible for me, their respective action and the part that each of them takes in the diverse events which vary the scene of the world and change the face of the universe. They will be seen appearing together for the first time as motive causes independent one of the other, although equally bound to the unique Cause which rules them, acting according to their nature, jointly or separately, and giving thus sufficient cause for all things. These three powers considered as primal causes are very difficult to define; for, as I have already announced, one would never be able to define a principle; but they can be known by their acts and grasped in their movements, since they do not leave the sphere in which individual man is included as an integral part of Universal Man. What opposes the idea that *God* may be known and grasped in the same manner as these three powers which emanate from Him is the fact that this absolute Being contains them without being contained and enchains them without being enchained. He holds, according to the beautiful metaphor of Homer, the golden chain which envelops all beings and which descends from the heights of brilliant Olympus to the centre of shadowy Tartarus; but this chain which He moves at His pleasure leaves Him always immobile and free. Let us content ourselves to adore in silence this ineffable Being—this *God* besides whom there is no other god and, without seeking to sound His fathomless essence, search to understand the powerful ternary in which He is reflected: Providence, Man, and Destiny. What I am about to say here will be in substance only what I have already said in my *Examens sur les Vers dorés* of Pythagoras or elsewhere; but in a subject so exacting it is impossible not to repeat oneself.

Destiny is the inferior and instinctive part of Universal Nature which I have called *nature naturée*. Its own action is called *fatality*. The form by which it manifests itself to us is called *necessity ;* it is this which links cause and effect. The three kingdoms of the elementary nature, mineral, vegetable, and animal, are the domain of Destiny; that is to say, everything comes to pass in a manner fatal and forced, according to laws determined beforehand. Destiny gives the principle of nothing but takes possession of it as soon as it is given in order to dominate the consequences. It is by the necessity of these consequences alone that it influences the future and makes itself felt in the present; for all that it possesses personally is in the past. Thus by Destiny we understand that power by which we conceive that the things created are created, that they are thus and not otherwise, and that once placed according to their nature they have forced results which are developed successively and necessarily.

At the time when Man appears upon the earth he belongs to Destiny, which for a long time involves him in the vortex of fatality. But, although plunged in this vortex and at first subject to its influence as all elementary beings, he carries in him a divine germ which never could entirely be confused with him. This germ, reacted upon by Destiny itself, develops to oppose it. It is a spark of the divine Will which, participating in the universal life, comes into the elementary nature to restore harmony in it. As this germ develops, it operates according to its energy upon forced things, and operates freely upon them. Liberty is its essence. The mystery of its principle is such that its energy augments proportionably as it exerts itself and that its force although indefinitely restrained is never vanquished. When this germ is entirely developed, it constitutes the Will of the Universal Man, one of three great powers of the Universe. This power, equal to that of Destiny which is inferior to it and even to that of Providence which is superior to it, is quickened only by God Himself to whom the others are equally subjected, each according to his rank, as I have already said. It is the Will of Man, which, as powerful medium, unites Destiny and Providence; without it, these two extreme powers not only would never unite, but they would not even understand each other. This Will, in revealing its activity, modifies the coexistent things, creates new ones which become immediately the property of Destiny, and prepares for the future mutations in that which was made and necessary consequences in that which is about to be.

Providence is the superior and intellectual part of Universal Nature, which I have called *nature naturante*. It is a living law emanating from the Divinity, by means of which all things are determined with power to be. All inferior principles emanate from it; all causes draw from its depths their origin and their force. The aim of Providence is the perfection of all beings, and this perfection it receives from *God* Himself, the irrefutable Type. The means that it has to attain this end is what we call *Time*. But time does not exist for it according to our ideas. It conceives it as a movement of eternity. This supreme power acts only immediately upon universal things; but this action by a chain of consequences can make itself felt as a mediator for particular things; so that the smallest details of human life can be interested in it, or can be deducted from it, according as they are bound by invisible bonds to universal events. Man is a divine germ which it sows in the fatality of Destiny, so as to change it and to render it master by means of the Will of this mediatory being. This Will, being essentially free, can exercise itself as well upon the action of Providence as upon that of Destiny; but with this difference, however, that, if it really changes the event of Destiny which was fixed and necessary and that by opposing necessity to necessity and Destiny to Destiny, it can do nothing against the providential event precisely because it is indifferent in its form and because it always reaches its goal by any route whatsoever.   It is time and form alone which vary. Providence is enchained neither by the one nor the other. The only difference is for Man, who changes the forms of life, shortens or lengthens time, enjoys or suffers, according as he accomplishes good or evil; that is to say, according as he unites his particular action to the universal action or as he discriminates it.

This is what I can say in general of these three great powers which compose the universal ternary and of the action upon which all things depend. I feel certain that the reader, indifferently attentive, will find what I have just said somewhat unsatisfactory and will probably complain of the vagueness and obscurity of my expressions; but it is not my fault if the material is in itself vague and obscure. If the distinction to be made between Providence, Destiny, and the Will of Man had been so easy, if one had been able to arrive without painful efforts at the understanding of these three powers, and if to the evidence of their existence one could have joined the clear and precise classification of their attributes, I know no reason why in these modern times, any savant could not have described their respective action, or have tried to establish upon it the bases of their systems, physical as well as metaphysical, political as well as religious. There should necessarily be some difficulty in making the distinction which I am attempting for the first time since Pythagoras or Kong-Tzée, as the majority of the writers who have preceded me have seen only one principle where there are three. Some, as Bossuet, have attributed all to Providence; others, as Hobbes, have made all proceed from Destiny; and still others, as Rousseau, have wished to re-

cognize everywhere only the Will of Man.   Many men have
gone astray following the coldness of their reason or the
rage of their passions, and have believed that they saw the
truth as much in the writings of Hobbes as in those of Rousseau, and this, because Destiny and the Will, which both
have chosen for the unique motive of their meditations, are
easier to grasp than Providence, whose course more lofty
and almost always covered with a veil, demands, in order
to be perceived, a more calm intelligence, and, in order to
be admitted, a faith less bound by the instinctive reason
and less troubled by the tempests of the animistic passions.

I should like very much to be able to respond to the
expectations of my readers in the manner of the geometrician,
to be able to demonstrate to them the three powers in question, and to teach them to understand these directly, wherever their own action manifests itself; but that would be
an enterprise as vain as ridiculous.   Such a demonstration
cannot be contained in a syllogism; a knowledge so extensive
cannot result from a dilemma.

Whatever words I employ, the meditation of the reader
must supply the insufficiency of the discourse.   I should
regard myself very fortunate if, after having reached the end
of the work in which I am about to engage, this demonstration was found in the *ensemble* of facts and this knowledge
in their comparison and in the application that a judicious
reader will not fail to make.   I shall neglect nothing in
order to facilitate this labour for him, and I shall seize all
occasions which present themselves to retrace the general
ideas that I have given and to strengthen them by examples.

This Introductory Dissertation could be terminated
here, since, after having explained the reason and the subject of my work, and after having presented the analysis
of the faculties of the being, who ought to be the principal
object, I have revealed in advance the motive causes of the
events which I am about to describe in it; however, to reply
as much as is possible to the desire of several friends whose

approbation is precious to me and who have pressed me to enter into several new details in regard to what I understand by the three great powers which rule the universe, I shall add, to what I have said in general, an example in particular, taken from the vegetable kingdom—that one of the three inferior kingdoms where the action of these three powers, more balanced and more uniform, appears to offer more influence in the examination.

Let us take an acorn. In this acorn is contained the life proper of an oak, the future germination of the tree which bears this name, its roots, trunk, branches, arborization, fructification, all that which constitutes the oak, with the incalculable succession of oaks which can arise from it. Here are two powers clearly manifest to me. First, I perceive an occult power, incomprehensible, impossible to grasp in its essence, which has infused in this acorn the potential life of the oak, which has specified this life as the life of an oak, and not the life of an elm, a poplar, a walnut, or any other tree. This life which manifests itself under the vegetable form and under the vegetable form of the oak pertains nevertheless to universal life; because all that lives, lives through this life. All that is, is; there are not two verbs *to be*.[1] Now this occult power which gives the power of being and which specifies the life in the power of being is called *Providence*. Secondly, in the acorn is an obvious power, comprehensible, seizable in its forms, which, manifesting itself as the necessary effect of the vital infusion of which I have spoken and which has been accomplished, one knows not *how*, will irresistibly show *why*, that is to say, it will result in an oak, every time that the acorn finds itself in a condition suitable for this. This power which appears always as the consequence of a principle or the result of a cause is called *Destiny*. There is this notable difference between Destiny and Providence: that Destiny has need

---

[1] One can see what I have written upon this unique verb, in my *Grammaire de la langue hébraïque*, ch. vii., § i.

of a condition as we have just seen, in order to exist; whereas Providence has no necessity for being. *To exist* is therefore the verb of Destiny; but Providence alone, *is*.

However, the moment that I examine this acorn I have the sensation of a third power which is not in the acorn and which can dispose of it; this power, which belongs to the essence of Providence because it *is*, depends also upon the forms of Destiny because it *exists*. I perceive this power free, since it is in me and nothing prevents me from developing it according to the extent of my strength. I hold the acorn, I can eat it and assimilate it thus with my substance; I can give it to an animal that will eat it; I can destroy it by crushing it beneath my feet; I can sow it and make it produce an oak. I crush it beneath my feet; the acorn is destroyed. Is its Destiny annihilated? No, it is changed; a new Destiny, which is my work, commences for it. The débris of the acorn decomposes according to fatal, fixed, and irresistible laws; the elements which were united in order to enter into its composition are dissolved, each returns to its place, and the life, for which they served as covering, unalterable in its essence, carried anew by its appropriate vehicle in the nourishing channels of the oak, will fertilize another acorn and once more offers itself to the chances of Destiny. The power which can thus take possession of the principles given by Providence and act effectively upon the consequences of Destiny is called *Will of Man*.

This Will can act in the same manner upon all things, physically as well as metaphysically, subject to the sphere of activity; for nature is everywhere alike. Not only can it interrupt and change Destiny, but, by modifying all the consequences, it can also transform the providential principles and that is without doubt its most brilliant advantage. I will give an example of this modification and of this transformation in following the comparison which I have made in the vegetable kingdom as the easiest to grasp and to generalize.

Suppose that, instead of examining an acorn, it is an apple that I examine, a sour, wild apple, which has as yet received only the influences of Destiny; if I sow a seed of this apple and if I cultivate with care the tree which springs from it, the fruits which are brought forth will be perceptibly improved, and by cultivation will be improved more and more. Without this cultivation, the effect of my will, nothing could improve it; for Destiny is a stationary power which carries nothing to perfection; but once I possess an apple-tree improved by cultivation, I can, by means of grafting, make use of this apple-tree in improving many others, modifying their destiny, and sour as they are, make them sweet. I can do more; I can by conveying the principle of another species into these seedlings thus transform sterile shrubs into fruitful trees. Now that which operates in one régime by means of cultivation operates in another by means of civilization. The civil and religious institutions accomplish here what the diverse cultivations and graftings accomplish there.

It seems to me, after what I have said, that the respective actions of Providence, Destiny, and the Will of Man, are very easy to distinguish in the vegetable kingdom; it is much less so in the Kingdom of Man; but it does not escape to such an extent that the mind's eye cannot grasp it readily, when the mind can once admit its existence. The action of Destiny and that of the Will move quite openly, that of Providence is, I admit, more shrouded and more veiled; it must be thus, so that it can never be comprehended. If man could foretell what the designs of Providence are, he might, in virtue of his free will, oppose their execution and this must never be, at least directly.

However, there is a last question which one can address to me upon the essence of the three universal powers, the action of which I am about to try to explain for the first time. I have said that it emanates from God Himself and forms a ternary which the divine Unity envelops; but are we to conceive them as three distinct beings? No; but as three distinct lives in the same being; three laws, three modes of being, three natures comprised in one single nature. Man, whose metaphysical constitution I have given, is an abstract image of the universe; he lives equally the three lives which his volitive unity envelops. In comparing the universe to Man, we can conceive that Providence represents there the intellectual sphere, Destiny the instinctive sphere, and the Will of Man itself, the animistic sphere. These spheres are not three distinct beings, although, to avoid lengthy phrasing, and paraphrasing, I will personify them often in describing their action; they are, as I have said, three different lives, living the universal life and giving particular life to a multitude of providential, instinctive, and animistic beings, that is to say, which follow the law of Providence, Destiny, or the Will; thus when I say further on, that Providence, Destiny, or the Will act, that will signify that the providential, prophetic, or volitive law unfolds itself, becomes efficient cause, and produces such or such effect, such or such event. This will signify also, according to the occasion which will be easily perceived, that any beings whatever, subject to one of these laws, serve or provoke this movement; and to cite one example among a thousand, when I say that Providence conducts Moses, the phrase will signify that the providential law is the law of this divine man and that he lived chiefly in the intellectual life of which it is the regulator. When I say that Destiny provokes the taking of Constantinople by the Turks that will signify that the taking of this city is a fatal consequence of anterior events and that the motive of the Turks who take possession of it holds to the prophetic law to which they are obedient. When I say finally that Luther is the instrument of the Will of Man which provokes a schism in Christianity, that will signify that Luther, drawn along by very strong animistic passions, makes himself the interpreter of all the passions analogous to his own, and presents to them a focus wherein their rays, coming to meet and to be reflected, cause a moral conflagration which tears the Christian cult into shreds.

After having given these explanations and interpretations, I do not believe that I have yet clearly explained all; but I am, in short, obliged to rely upon the sagacity of the reader which will supply what I may have omitted. Determined to reveal what my studies and my meditations have taught me regarding the origin of human society and the history of Man, I have dared, in a few pages, to run through an interval of twelve thousand years.   I have found myself in the presence of a mass of facts which I have tried to classify and a host of beings whose character I have rapidly sketched. My pen, consecrated to truth, has never flinched before it; I have always told it with the strong conviction of telling it; if my readers can recognize it, by the indelible sign with which Providence has marked it, their approbation will be the kindest recompense for my labours.   If, after mature reflections, they judge that I have been in error, I shall still rely upon the equity of their judgment that they will at least believe in my sincerity which makes it impossible for me to want to deceive any one.

TABLE OF CHAPTERS

CONTAINED IN PART FIRST

li

TABLE OF CHAPTERS

CONTAINED IN PART SECOND

FOURTH BOOK

SIXTH BOOK

Hermeneutic Interpretation

of the

Origin of the Social State of Man

and of the

Destiny of the Adamic Race

Part First

FIRST BOOK

CHAPTER I

IN this work I shall treat not of the origin of Man, but of that of human society. History is occupied solely with the second of these origins. Cosmogony reveals the first. History takes Man from the moment of his appearance on earth, and, without concerning itself with his ontological principle, seeks to find the principle of sociability which inclines him to approach his fellow-creatures and to come out of the state of isolation and ignorance where nature seems to have confined him in scarcely distinguishing him, so far as form is concerned, from several other animals. I shall tell what the divine principle is which Providence has implanted in his breast; I shall show by what necessary circumstances, dependent upon Destiny, this principle of perfectibility finds itself *réactionné*; how it is developed and what admirable succour it receives from itself when man, whom it enlightens, can make use of his will to mitigate more and more by the cultivation of his mind whatever is rigorous and savage in his destiny, in order to carry his civilization and welfare to the highest degree of perfection of which they are capable.

I shall transport myself for this purpose to an epoch

sufficiently remote from this in which we are living, and, fortifying my mental vision, which a long prejudice may have weakened, I shall fix across the obscurity of centuries the moment when the White Race, of which we are a part, came to appear upon the scene of the world. At this epoch of which I shall seek later to determine the date, the White Race was still weak, savage, without laws, without arts, without cultivation of any sort, destitute of memories, and too devoid of understanding even to conceive a hope. It inhabited the environs of the Boreal pole where it had its origin. The Black Race, more ancient than the White, was dominant upon the earth and held the sceptre of science and of power; it possessed all of Africa and the greater part of Asia, where it had enslaved and restrained the Yellow Race. Some remnants of the Red Race had languished obscurely upon the summits of the highest mountains of America and had survived the horrible catastrophe which had just struck them; these weak remnants were unknown; the Red Race to whom they had belonged had not long since possessed the Occidental hemisphere of the globe; the Yellow Race, the Oriental; the Black Race then sovereign, spread to the south on the equatorial line, and, as I have just said, the White Race which was only then springing up, wandered about the environs of the Boreal pole.

These four principal races and the numberless varieties which result from their mixture compose the *Kingdom of Man*.[1] They are, properly speaking, what the species are in the other kingdoms. One can understand nations and diverse people as particular species in these races. These four races clashed and fought together, turn by turn, distinguished and confused. Many times they disputed among themselves the sceptre of the world; they wrested or shared

---

[1] If one has read the Introductory Dissertation at the head of this work, which is necessary to give understanding, one knows that I mean by the *Kingdom of Man* the totality of men, which is called ordinarily *Mankind*.

it over and over again. My intention is not to enter into these vicissitudes anterior to the actual order of things, the infinite details of which would overpower me with a useless burden and would not lead me to the end that I purpose to attain. I shall devote myself only to the White Race to which we belong and to outlining the history, from the epoch of its last appearance at the environs of the Boreal pole: it is from there that they descended in swarms at diverse times to make incursions as much upon other races when they were still dominant as upon themselves when they had seized the dominion.

The vague memory of this origin, surviving the torrent of centuries, has caused the Boreal pole to be named the nursery of Mankind. It has given birth to the name of Hyperboreans and to all the allegorical fables which have been recited concerning them; it has furnished, in short, numerous traditions which have led Olaüs Rudbeck to place in Scandinavia the Atlantis of Plato and which authorized Bailly to discern upon the rocks, deserted and whitened by the hoarfrost of Spitzbergen, the cradle of all sciences, all arts, and all mythologies of the world.[1]

It is assuredly very difficult to say at what epoch the White Race, or the Hyperboreans, began to be united by any form of civilization, and it is still less easy to say at what more remote epoch they began to exist. Moses, who speaks of them in the sixth chapter of *Berœshith*,[2] under the name of Ghiboreans, whose names have been so celebrated in the depths of time, traces their origin to the first ages of the world. One finds a hundred times the name of Hyperboreans in the writings of the ancients, and never any positive light upon them. According to Diodorus of Sicily their

---

[1] One can see in the writings of these two authors the numerous proofs which they bring to the support of their assertions. These proofs, insufficient in their hypotheses, become irresistible when it is merely a question of fixing the first abode of the White Race and the place of their origin.

[2] This is the first book of the Sepher commonly called *Genesis*.

country was the nearest to the moon; which can be understood from the elevation of the pole which they inhabited. Æschylus, in his *Prometheus*, placed them upon the Rhipæan mountains. A certain Aristeas of Proconesus, who, it is said, had made a poem upon these people, and who claimed to have visited them, affirmed that they occupied the country north-east of upper Asia which we call today Siberia. Hecate of Abdera, in a work published in the time of Alexander, placed them still further back, and lodged them among the white bears of Nova Zembla on an island called *Elixoïa*. The pure truth is, as avowed by Pindar more than five centuries before our era, that no one knew in which region was situated the country of this people. Herodotus himself, so curious to collect all antique traditions, had in vain interrogated the Scythians about them and had been unable to discover anything certain.

All these contradictions, all these uncertainties, arose from confusing a single people with a race of men from which issued a host of peoples. At that time, they made the same mistake which we today should make if, confusing the Black Race with one of the nations which draws its origin from it, we wished absolutely to circumscribe the country of the entire race in the country occupied by this single nation. The Black Race certainly originated in the vicinity of the equatorial line and has spread from there over the African continent, whence it afterward extended its empire over the entire earth and over the White Race, before the latter had the strength to dispute this domination. It is possible that at such a very remote epoch the Black Race may have been called *Sudéenne* or *Suthéenne* as the White Race is called Borean, Ghiborean, or Hyperborean, and that from these may have come the horror which is generally attached to the name of *Suthéen* among the nations of white origin. We know that these nations have always placed at the South the abode of the infernal spirit, called for this reason *Suth* or *Soth* by the Egyptians, *Sath* by the Phœnicians, and *Sathan* or *Satan* by the Arabs and the Hebrews.[1]

[1] This name has served as a root for that of Saturn with the Etruscans and of Sathur, Suthur, or Surthur with the Scandinavians, terrible or beneficent divinity according to the manner of considering it. It is from the Celtic-Saxon *Suth* that the English *South*, the Belgian *Suyd*, the German and French *Sud* is derived, designating the part of the terrestrial globe opposite the Boreal pole. It is to be observed that the word, which generally is rendered by that of Midi, has no etymological relation to it. It designates properly all that which is contrary to elevation, all that which is low, all that which serves as basis or seat. The word *sediment* is derived from the Latin *sedere*, which comes itself from the Celtic-Saxon *sitten*, in German *sitzen*, to sit down.

CHAPTER II

LOVE, PRINCIPLE OF SOCIABILITY AND OF CIVILIZATION OF MAN

LET us resume now the thread of my ideas, which this necessary digression has slightly interrupted, and see what were the beginnings of civilization in the Borean Race concerning which I shall occupy myself exclusively.

It is presumable that, at the epoch in which this race appeared upon the earth under forms very similar to those of many species of animals, it could, notwithstanding the absolute difference of origin and the contrary tendency of its destinies, remain mingled with them for some time. This resulted from the dulness of its faculties, even the instinctive ones; the two superior spheres of the soul and mind, being in no wise developed in Man, he lived therefore only by sensation and, always compelled by it, he had instinct only for perception without attaining even attention. Individualization was his only means; attraction and fear were his only motives and, in their absence, indolence became his habitual state.[1]

But Man had not been destined to live alone and isolated upon earth; he possessed a principle of sociability and of perfectibility which could not always remain stationary; now the means by which this principle was to be drawn from

[1] The reader should turn back to the Introductory Dissertation, if he does not recall what I said about the metaphysical constitution of Man.

10

its lethargy had been placed by the high wisdom of its Author in the companion of man, in woman, whose organism different in very important points, physical as well as metaphysical, gave her inverse emotions. Such had been the Divine Decree, even from the origin of things, that this universal being, destined to put harmony into the elements and to dominate the three kingdoms of Nature, would receive his first impulses from woman and would owe to love his first developments. Love, the origin of all beings, was to be the fecund source of his civilization, and was to produce thus so many opposite effects, so much happiness, so many troubles, and such a great mixture of knowledge and of blindness, of virtues and of vices.

Love, principle of life and of fecundity, had therefore been destined to be the conservator and legislator of the world. Profound truth, which the ancient sages had known and which they had even announced clearly in their cosmogonies, attributing to it the disentangling of chaos. Isis and Ceres, so often called legislators, were only the deified type of feminine nature,[1] considered as the living focus whence this love was reflected.

If Man had been only pure animal, always forced in the same way, and his companion, like the females of other animals, had felt in the same manner the same necessities as he; if they had both been subject to the regular crises of the same desires, equally felt, equally shared; if, in short, to express it in proper terms, they had had periodical seasons of amorous ardour or heat and the like, never would man have been civilized. But it was far from being thus. The same sensations, although proceeding from the same causes, did not produce the same effects in the two sexes. This is worthy of the highest attention, and I beg the reader to concentrate his mental view for a moment upon this almost

---

[1] The name Isis comes from the word Ishah, which signifies *woman, lady.* The name Ceres, from the same root as the word *herê*, that is to say the *sovereign.* This word *herê* forms the name of Juno in Greek, Ἥρη or Ἥρα.

imperceptible point of the human constitution. Here is the germ of all civilization, the seminal point whence all must come to light, the powerful motive from which all is to receive movement in social order.

To enjoy before possessing is the instinct of man; to possess before enjoying is the instinct of woman. Let us explain this; but let us set aside for a moment the passions which the Social State has brought forth and the sentiments which the imagination has excited. Let us restrict ourselves to instinct alone and see how it acts under the sole influence of its needs; let us consider the Man of Nature and not of society.

At the moment when an agreeable sensation comes to disturb the instinct of this man, what does he feel? This: he will attach to the attraction proceeding necessarily from the sensation the actual need of enjoying his object and that more distant one of possessing it; that is to say, supposing it be some sort of fruit which has struck his view and excited his appetite, the instinctive man will feel the need of eating it before making sure of its possession and this fact will carry him quickly forward at any risk; so that if an intervention of fear, an unforeseen noise, the sight of an adversary should strike him, his first idea would be to brave the cause instead of fleeing from it. Whereas if the purely instinctive woman finds herself placed in a parallel situation, she will feel precisely the contrary. She will attach to the attraction proceeding from an agreeable sensation the actual need of possessing the object and that more distant one of enjoying it in all security; at the sight of some fruit which she desires to eat, her first thought will be possession, and this will keep her in suspense; so that if a sensation of fear seizes her, her first idea will be to flee from the cause instead of braving it.

This contrary disposition in the moral constitution of the two sexes established between them from the beginning a striking difference which prevented their passions from manifesting themselves under the same forms, brought forth from the same sensation another thought, and impressed upon them in consequence, a movement wholly opposed. To enjoy before possessing and to fight before fleeing constituted then the instinct of man; whereas to possess before enjoying and to flee before fighting constituted that of woman.

Now if one cares to examine for a moment the principal consequences which proceeded from this notable difference when it was decided between the two sexes, that is to say, when a woman was found happily enough organized to but push perception as far as attention, one will see that it was inevitable that she should not show a real and unexpected resistance to the man, led to her by sexual attraction; for, much more occupied with the idea of possessing than with that of enjoying and not at all forced by the appetite which mastered the man, she could instinctively examine what real advantage the sensation which he proposed would procure for her. Since there was no pleasure attached to this sensation for her and no advantage to be gained, overcome with fear, she decided suddenly to flee.

The nature of man is not, as I have said, to recoil before an obstacle. His first impulse is, on the contrary, to brave and conquer it. At the sight of the woman who flees from him, he does not therefore remain fixed, he does not turn his back, but urged by the attraction which subjugates him he precipitates himself upon her tracks. Often, swifter than he, she escapes him; sometimes he seizes her, but whatever may be the issue, the attention of the man is awakened. The very combat which takes place makes him feel that his aim is not accomplished whether the result be happy or unhappy. Then he reflects, but the woman has reflected before him. She has seen that it is not good for her to let herself be conquered, and he has felt that it would have been better for him if she had submitted. Why then did she flee? His reflection, still weak, does not permit him to understand that one may resist an inclination, and that there should above all be an inclination other than his. But the fact exists and is renewed. The man reflects again. He succeeds by the inward repetition of his own idea in retaining it and, memory forming, his mind takes an enormous step. He finds that he has several needs and for the first time perhaps he counts as many as three, and distinguishes them. Thus enumeration and individualization act in the sphere of his will.

If the woman towards whom an irresistible inclination drew him has fled, doubtless another inclination has forced her flight; what could be this inclination? Hunger perhaps! This terrible need which shows itself in the instinctive part of his being, in the absence of the sensation itself, produces an important and sudden revolution; for the first time the animistic sphere is disturbed and pity manifests itself. This gentle passion, the first by which the soul may be affected, is the true character of humanity. It is that which makes man a being veritably sociable. The philosophers, who have believed that this passion could be first awakened or produced by the aspect of a being suffering, are mistaken. The aspect of pain awakens fear, and fear, terror. This transformation of sensation into sentiment is instantaneous. There is in pity the impression of an anterior idea which is transformed into sentiment without the aid of sensation. Pity is likewise more profoundly moral than terror and pertains more intimately to the nature of Man.

But, as soon as Man has begun to feel pity, he is not far from understanding love. He reflects already upon the means which he can take to prevent the woman fleeing at his approach, and, although he is mistaken absolutely concerning the motives of this flight, he attains none the less the aim of his desires. He seizes the moment when he has a double supply of fruit and game or an abundance of fish, and when he finds the object of his desires, he offers her his gifts. At this sight the woman is touched, not in the way in which her lover believes her to be, by the satisfaction of an actual need, but by the innate inclination which urges her to possess.   She feels immediately all the advantages she can gain from this occurrence for the future, and, as she attributes it with reason, to a certain charm which she inspires, she instinctively experiences an agreeable sensation which disturbs the animistic spirit within her and vanity is awakened.

From the moment that the woman has received the gifts from the man and has extended the hand to him, the conjugal tie is woven and society has commenced.

CHAPTER III

MARRIAGE, BASIS OF THE SOCIAL EDIFICE; WHAT ITS PRINCIPLE
IS, AND WHAT ITS CONSEQUENCES ARE

HOWEVER little one may be instructed in the knowledge of ancient traditions, one should have no trouble in recognizing the two pictures which I have drawn, because they are in reality true, although the forms may vary in a thousand ways at diverse epochs and in diverse places. Greek mythology, so brilliant and so rich, offers a great number of examples of these amorous struggles between the gods or the satyrs pursuing nymphs who fled from them. Sometimes it is Apollo who runs upon the track of Daphne, Jupiter who presses on the steps of Io, Pan who seeks to seize Syrinx or Penelope. In the most ancient nuptial ceremonies, one always sees the husband making gifts to the wife and these constitute a dowry for her. This dowry, which the man gave formerly and which he still gives among some peoples, has changed place among us and among the greater part of modern nations, and must be offered principally by the woman, on account of reasons which I will show later. This change does not prevent, however, the ancient usage from still surviving in the wedding gifts, which one calls in French *corbeille de mariage*, or marriage-basket, as if by this word basket one wished to recall that this present first consisted of fruits or some sort of food.

However this event to which I have just attributed the

beginning of human society was repeated simultaneously or at very near epochs, in different places; so that centres of civilization were established in great number throughout the same country. These were the germs which Providence had sown in the heart of the Borean Race and which were to develop there under the influence of Destiny and the particular Will of Man.

The sentiments which had united the two sexes, not at all by the effect of a blind appetite but by that of a deliberate act, were not the same, as I have said, but their difference, ignored by the young couple, disappeared in the identity of the aim. The pity which the man had felt led him to think that his companion had chosen him as a tutelar support, and the woman, touched by vanity, saw her work in the welfare of her spouse. On the one side pride was born and on the other compassion. Thus the sentiments were opposed and enchained in the two sexes.

From the moment that instinct alone had no longer prepared the nuptial couch and an animistic sentiment, nobler and more elevated, had presided over the mysteries of Hymen, a sort of pact had been tacitly established between the young couple, from which it resulted that the stronger was pledged to protect the weaker and the weaker to remain attached to the stronger. This pact, in augmenting the welfare of the man, making him understand pleasure of which he was ignorant, increased also his labours. It was necessary that he should provide not alone for his own nourishment, but for that of his spouse, when her pregnancy had reached such an advanced stage that it did not permit her following him any more, and afterward for that of their children. Instinctive reason, another name for which is common sense or good sense, was not long in making him understand that the ordinary means, sufficient up to that time, were adequate no longer and that it was necessary to devise others. This reason reacting upon instinct caused ruse to be born. He set traps for the game on which he

2

lived. He invented the arrow and the boar-spear of the hunter; he discovered the art of catching more fish by means of hook and net. Necessity and practice doubled his forces and his skill. His wife, endowed with more finesse, added to a ruse greater than his, an observation more sure and a presentiment more prompt. She learned soon to set up rushes forming a kind of basket which, after having served as a cradle for her children, became the first article of furniture in her household. Spinning roughly the hair of many kinds of animals, she easily made cords, which were used to stretch the bow and to fashion nets. These cords, interlaced in a certain manner, were soon changed under her fingers into coarse stuffs, and this invention appeared to her no doubt as admirable as the usage seemed to her convenient, as well for her children as for herself and her husband. These stuffs, which a rigid climate often rendered necessary, were supplanted by skins of beasts with which it was not always easy to provide themselves.

It is useless, I think, to pursue further these details, which any one can continue at his pleasure and embellish with the colours of his imagination. When the principles are fixed, the consequences become easy. Only, I beg the reader to guard against falling here into an error whose imputation would be unfortunate for me. Although I obviously give marriage as the principle of the Social State, that is to say, the free and mutual consent of man and woman being united by a tacit pact to endure and share together the sorrows and joys of life, and although I make the existence of this bond spring from opposed sensations of the two sexes and the development of their instinctive faculties, I must of course, as I think I have been careful to make clear, regard the formation of this tie as fortuitous.

Those animals which nature has never joined since the origin of the species never do join; it is because man is not an animal and above all because he is susceptible of improvement, that he can pass from one estate to another and become from generation to generation more and more instinctive, animistic, or intellectual. Marriage, upon which rests the whole edifice of society, is the very work of Providence, which has determined it in principle. When it passes into action, it is a divine law which is accomplished by means determined upon in advance in order to attain an aim irresistibly fixed.

Still if one should ask me why this pact, being an indispensable necessity to the civilization of the Kingdom of Man, so eminently necessary itself, has not been arranged in advance, as is noticed in some species of animals, I shall answer that it is because Providence and Destiny have a contrary mode of operation appropriate to their opposed essence. That which Destiny makes, it makes complete at once, constrained in all its parts, and leaves it such as it has made it, without ever urging it further forward with its own movement; whereas Providence, producing nothing except in principle, gives to all things which emanate from it a progressive impulse, which, carrying them unceasingly with potentiality in action, brings them by degrees to the perfection of which they are susceptible. If Man belongs to Destiny, he would be what short-sighted philosophers have attributed him to be: without progression in his course and consequently without future. But, as the work of Providence, he advances freely in the route which is traced for him, perfecting himself in proportion as he advances, and tends thus to immortality.

This is what one must certainly believe, if one wishes to penetrate into the essence of things and to comprehend the word of that profound enigma of the universe which the ancients symbolized by the figure of the Sphinx. Man is the property of Providence which, considered as the living Law, as expression of the Divine Will, determines his potential existence; but as this being must draw all the elements of its actual existence from the domain of Destiny, whose productions he is entrusted with dominating and regulating, he must do it by the display of his efficient will, absolutely free in its essence. Upon the usage of this will depends his ulterior fate. Whereas Providence calls and directs him by its inspirations, Destiny resists and arrests him by its needs. His passions which belong to him incline him with force to one side or the other, and, according to the determinations which they arouse, deliver his future to one of these two powers; for he cannot be its absolute property except as he avails himself of the elementary life, transient and limited.

His social state depends therefore, as I have shown, upon the unfolding of his faculties which lead to marriage, and the social state, once constituted, gives birth to property from which results political right. But, since the social condition finds itself the work of three distinct powers— Providence, which gives the principle; Destiny, which furnishes the elements; and the human Will, which finds the means—it is evident that the political right which emanates from it must receive equally the influence of the three powers, and, according as the one or the other dominates it, separately or jointly, takes forms analogous to their action. These forms, which after all are confined in these three principles, can nevertheless vary and become modified in many ways by their fusions and their oppositions, and can bring about almost endless consequences. Later in this work I shall point out diverse forms, simple or mixed, after having clearly established the order, nature, and action of the three powers which create them. I shall show in the following chapter the origin of one of the most glorious results and the most brilliant phenomena which are attached to the formation of human society: speech.

CHAPTER IV

THAT MAN IS FIRST MUTE AND THAT HIS FIRST LANGUAGE
CONSISTS OF SIGNS—OF SPEECH—TRANSFORMATION OF
MUTE LANGUAGE INTO ARTICULATE LANGUAGE AND THE
SEQUEL OF THIS TRANSFORMATION.

MAN endowed in principle with all the strength, all the
faculties, all the means with which he can be vested
in time, does not actually possess any of these things when
he is born. He is weak and feeble and destitute of everything. The individual gives us in this respect a striking
example of what the kingdom is in its origin. Some who,
in order to extricate themselves from perplexities upon very
difficult points, state that man arrives on earth as robust
of body as enlightened of mind, say a thing which experience
denies and which reason condemns. Others who, accepting
this admirable being such as nature gives him, attribute to
the conformation of his organs and to his physical sensations alone, so many sublime conceptions which are foreign
there, fall into the most absurd contradictions and reveal their ignorance. And, finally, those who believe
themselves obliged, in order to explain the least phenomenon, to call God Himself upon the scene to make
Him the Preceptor of a being so often rebellious in his
lessons, announce plainly that they find it easier to cut
the Gordian knot than to untie it. They act as the
authors of ancient tragedies, who, not knowing what to do

with their actors, exposed them for this reason to a stroke
of lightning.

Man is a divine germ which is developed by the reaction
of his senses. All is innate in him, all; that which he receives from the exterior is only the occasion of his ideas;
not his ideas themselves. He is a plant, as I have already
said, which bears thoughts as a rose-bush bears roses, or an
apple-tree, apples. Each has need of reaction. But has
the water or air from which the rose-bush or the apple-tree
draws its nutriment any relation with the intimate essence
of the rose or the apple? Not any. They are indifferent
and can cause nettles or berries of deadly nightshade to
grow with equal ease, if the germ is offered to their action in
a suitable situation. So then although man has received
at his beginning a spark of the Divine Word, he does not
bring with him a language wholly formed. He indeed
contains within him the principle of the power of speech in
potentiality but not in action. In order to speak it is necessary that he should have felt the need of speaking, that he
should have wished it strongly, for it is one of the most
difficult operations of his understanding. As long as he
lives isolated and purely instinctive he does not speak, he
does not even feel the necessity of speech, he would be incapable of making any effort of the will to attain it; plunged
in absolute dumbness he delights therein; whatever disturbs
his hearing is noise; he cannot distinguish sounds as sounds
but as shocks, and these shocks, analogous to all his other
sensations, excite in him only attraction or fear according
as they awaken the idea of pleasure or pain. But from the
moment that he enters the social state, by the means of the
event which I have related, a thousand circumstances which
are accumulated about him make some sort of language
necessary for him; he needs a means of communication between his ideas and those of his companion. He wishes to
make her understand his desires and above all his hopes, for
since he has pride he has also hopes, and his companion is

still more eager to communicate her desires to him, as her vanity more active and more circumscribed suggests them to her more often and in greater number.

Scarcely is this will determined in them than means of satisfying it are presented. These means are such that they employ them without seeking them and as if they had always had them. They do not suspect in employing them that they are establishing the foundations of a most admirable edifice. These means are *signs* which they effect by a movement of instinctive intention and these they understand in the same way. This is extremely remarkable, that signs have no need of an anterior agreement to be understood; at least those that are radical, as, for example, signs which express approval or refusal, affirmation or negation, invitation to approach or order to withdraw, menace or accord, etc. I invite the reader to reflect a moment on this point, for it is here that he will find the origin of speech so long and vainly sought. Let us transport ourselves among some people, whether they be civilized or savage, inhabiting the North or the South of the earth, the Old or the New World; let us not listen to the diverse words which they use to express the idea of affirmation or of negation, *yes* or *no*, but let us consider the signs which accompany these words; we will see that they are everywhere the same. It is the inclination of the head in a perpendicular line which expresses affirmation and its double rotation on a horizontal line which indicates negation. If we see the arm extended and the open hand turned toward the breast, that invites us to approach. If we see, on the contrary, the arm at first folded, unfolded with violence in extending the hand, this orders us to leave. If the arms of the man are folded, the fists closed, he menaces. If he lets them fall, gently opening the two hands, he accedes. Let us take with us a person mute from birth; the more savage and near to nature people are the better they will understand him and the better they will be understood by him, and this for the simple reason that they will both be nearer to the primitive language of Mankind.

Let us not fear to announce this important truth: all the languages which men speak and which they have spoken on the face of the earth, and the incalculable mass of words which enter or have entered into the composition of these languages, have been derived from a very small quantity of radical signs. In searching some years ago to restore the Hebrew tongue in its constitutive principles, finding in my hands a language whose astonishing simplicity rendered analysis very easy, I saw the truth which I announce, and I have proved it as far as it has been possible for me, in showing, first, that the written characters or letters in the origin of this tongue had been only the very signs which had been indicated by a sort of hieroglyphic, and afterwards that these characters, drawing near to one another in groups of two or three, had formed monosyllabic roots and these roots, joining a new character or uniting together themselves, a mass of words.

This is not the time to enter into grammatical details which would be out of place here. I must offer only principles. The reader, curious concerning these sorts of researches, can consult, if he judges it apropos, the grammar and vocabulary which I have given to the Hebrew tongue.

The first language known to man therefore was a mute language. One cannot conceive of another without admitting an infusion of the Divine Speech in him, which, supposing a like infusion of all other sciences, is proved false by the fact. The philosophers who have recourse to an earlier convention for each term of the tongue fall into a shocking contradiction. Providence, I have frequently said, gives only the principles of all things; it is for man to develop them.

But the moment when this mute language was established between the young pair, the moment when a sign, issued as an expression of a thought from the heart of the

one into that of the other, was comprehended, it excited in
the animistic sphere a movement which gave rise to understanding. This central faculty was not long in producing
its circumferential, analogous faculties, and from that time
man could, up to a certain point, compare and judge, discern
and comprehend.

Soon he perceived by making use of these new faculties
that most of the signs which he used to express his thought
were accompanied by certain exclamations of voice, certain
cries more or less feeble or strong, more or less sharp or soft,
which seldom failed to present themselves together. He
noticed this coincidence which his companion had noticed
before him, and both judged that it would be convenient,
either in the darkness, or at a distance, or when an obstacle
had hidden them from each other, to substitute these diverse
inflections of the voice for the diverse signs which they accompanied. Perhaps they did so in some urgent circumstance, moved by some fear or by some vehement desire,
and they saw with keenest joy that they were heard and
understood.

It is needless to say how important this substitution was
for humanity. The reader perceives that nothing greater
could have taken place in nature and that if the moment
when such an occurrence presented itself for the first time
could have been fixed it would have merited the honours of
an eternal commemoration. But it was not so. Ah well!
who can know when or how, among what people, and in what
country it came? Perhaps it was sterile many times in
succession, or the unformed language to which it had given
birth disappeared with the humble cave which sheltered it.
For while to save time I refer to the same pair, can one doubt
that several generations should have passed away between
the smallest advances? The first steps which man makes in
the course of civilization are slow and painful. He is often
obliged to repeat the same things. Mankind as a whole is
without doubt indestructible, the race itself is strong; but

individual man is very feeble, particularly in the beginning.
It is, however, upon him that the foundations of all the
edifice rest.

Nevertheless, as I have said, many marriages, being
formed simultaneously or at slight intervals one from the
other in the same country and in several countries at the
same time, had given birth to a great number of families,
more or less drawn to one another, who followed nearly the
same course and developed themselves in the same manner,
thanks to the providential action which had thus determined
it.   These families whose existence I have placed designedly
in the Borean or Hyperborean Race inhabited consequently
the environs of the Boreal pole and received necessarily
the influences of the rigorous climate in which they were
obliged to live.   Their habits, their customs, their ways of
nourishing, clothing, and lodging themselves, everything
affected them; everything around them took on a particular
character.   Their caves resembled those of the people of
today who still inhabit the most septentrional regions of
Europe and Asia.   These were hardly anything more than
holes dug in the earth while a few branches covered with
skin closed the opening.   The name *tanière* [cave] which is
perpetuated even to our time, signified in the primitive
language of Europe a fire in the earth, and this proves that
the use of fire, very quickly understood by a race of men
to whom it was so necessary, goes back to most remote
antiquity.

No subject of discord or of hatred could spring up in the
midst of these families, no particular interest divided them,
whose chiefs or hunters or fishermen had found it easy to
provide subsistence.   The profound peace which reigned
among them, drawing them near to each other by their
common leisures, facilitated alliances which brought them
still nearer each day, uniting them by family ties which the
women were the first to understand and make respected.
The authority which they maintained over their daughters

and the benefit which they derived from it made the force and utility of these ties. The language, at first mute and consisting of signs only, then becoming articulate by the substitution for the sign itself of the inflection of the voice which was made at first unconsciously and which ordinarily accompanied the sign, extended quite rapidly. It was at first very poor, as are all savage languages; but the number of ideas being very limited among these families, it sufficed for their needs. It must not be forgotten that the richest tongues of today commenced by being composed of only a small quantity of radical terms.

Thus, for example, the Chinese tongue which is composed of more than eighty thousand characters offers hardly more than two hundred and fifty roots, which form scarcely twelve hundred primitive words by the variation of the accent.

I shall not relate here, how the sign being first changed into a noun by means of a vocal inflection, the noun was changed into a verb by the affiliation which it made with the sign; nor how this verbal sign itself, being again vocalized to express it, was thus changed into a sort of affix or inseparable preposition which verbalized the nouns without the aid of signs. I have elsewhere given ample details on this subject.[1]

All that I must add incidentally is that when the language was vocalized, the radical terms were generally admitted in a tribe formed by a certain number of families united and bound to each other by all the kindred ties, the one who found or who invented a new thing gave it necessarily a name which characterized it and remained attached to it. Thus, for example, *rân* or *rên*, being applied to the sign which indicated the movement of running or flight, was given to the reindeer, which is a septentrional animal very swift in running. Thus the word *vâg*, being likewise substituted for the sign which expressed the movement of

[1] In my work *La Langue Hébraïque* and in *La Langue d'Oc*.

going ahead, was given to any conveyance for transportation and particularly to the wagon, of which the Borean Race made great use, when, having increased considerably in numbers, they spread afar and fell in swarms upon Europe and Asia.[1]

[1] The word *rên*, not being able to be applied in the more temperate climates to the reindeer (*rêne*) which does not exist there, it is applied for the same reason by the French to *renard* (fox). From the word *vag*, which signified a *wagon*, the French have drawn the word *vaguer* (to wander about). All the people of the North have named *veg* the route traced by the chariot *vag* and this word, changed through pronunciation, became the Latin *via*, the French *voie*, and the English *way*, etc.

I restrain myself in order not to fall into a useless and fatiguing prolixity, where my inclination and favourite occupation might lead me. I desire only that the reader may be convinced when I present later on any etymology whatever, that the root upon which I support it, of Borean or Sudeen origin, Celtic or Atlantean, is really authentic and cannot be attacked by science. If I do not always give proof, it is to evade the delays and the useless display of scholastic erudition out of place. However, the most of my readers will see it quite easily. Who does not know, for example, that the root *rân* or *rên*, that I just quoted, expresses the sense of running or of flowing, in all the Celtic tongues? The Gallic Celt said *dho runnia ;* the Armorics *redek ;* the Irish *reathaim* or *ruidim ;* the Saxon *rannian ;* the Belgian *runne ;* the German *rennen* etc. The Greek ρεῖν signifies *to flow, to run.* It is to this root that is attached the Oscitanic *riu*, a stream, a river and all its derivatives, and thence come the names of the *Rhine* and the *Rhone*, etc.

CHAPTER V

DIGRESSION ON THE FOUR AGES OF THE WORLD AND RE-
FLECTIONS ON THIS SUBJECT—FIRST REVOLUTION IN THE
SOCIAL STATE AND FIRST MANIFESTATION OF THE
GENERAL WILL.

THE poets, and after them the systematic philosophers,
have spoken much of the four ages of the world known
in the ancient mysteries under the names of golden, silver,
bronze, and iron ages, and, disregarding the fact that they
had reversed the order of these ages, have given the name of
Golden Age to that epoch when man, scarcely escaped from
the influences of instinct alone, began to make the first
trials of his animistic faculties and to enjoy their results.
It was without doubt the infancy of Mankind, the dawn of
social life. These beginnings were not without advantage,
especially when compared with the state of absolute apathy
and darkness which had preceded them. But it would be
strangely deceiving oneself to believe that this was the culminating point of felicity, the point where civilization was
to stop. An infancy beyond natural limits would become
an imbecility; a dawn which would never bring the sun
would strike the earth with sterility and stupor.

A modern author has already remarked with much
sagacity that men, inclined naturally to embellish the past
especially when they are old, have acted in a national body
precisely as they act as private individuals; they have al-

ways given praise to the first ages of the world without
adequately reflecting that these first moments of their social
existence were very far from being as agreeable as they
pretend. The volatile and almost puerile imagination of
the Greeks has singularly confused this picture, in transporting it purposely and to please the multitude from the
end to the beginning of time. That which they have named
the Golden Age ought to be called the age of Iron or Lead,
since it was that of Saturn, represented as a suspicious and
cruel tyrant, mutilating and dethroning his father in order
to succeed him, and as devouring his own children so as to
deliver himself from the fear of a successor. Saturn was the
symbol of Destiny. According to the doctrine of the mysteries, the passing of the kingdom from Destiny to that
of Providence was prepared by two median kingdoms: that
of Jupiter and that of Ceres called Isis by the Egyptians.
One of these kingdoms served to repress the audacity of the
Titans, that is to say, to subjugate the animal species and
establish harmony in Nature, by straightening the river
courses, draining the marshes, inventing works of agriculture, arts, etc. The other served to regulate society by
establishing civil, political, and religious laws. These two
kingdoms were called the ages of Bronze and Silver. The
name of the Golden Age which followed was reserved for the
kingdom of Dionysus or Osiris. This kingdom which was
to bring happiness upon earth and maintain it there a long
time was subjected to periodical returns which were measured by the duration of the great year—the Platonic year.
Thus, according to this mysterious doctrine, the four ages
were to succeed each other immediately on earth like the
four seasons, until the end of time, commencing with the age
of iron or kingdom of Saturn—compared to winter.

The system of the Brahmans conforms in this respect
with that of the Egyptian mysteries whence the Greeks
have taken theirs. The *Satya-youg*, which corresponds to
the first age, is that of physical reality. According to what

is said in the Pouranas, it is an age filled with frightful
catastrophes where the conspiring elements declare war;
where the gods are assailed by demons; where the terrestrial
globe, at first engulfed by the seas, is every instant menaced
with total ruin.   The *Tetra-youg* which follows it is no more
fortunate.   It is only at the epoch of the *Douapar-youg* that
the earth begins to present a picture more smiling and more
tranquil.   Wisdom, united to valour, speaks by the mouth
of Rama and Krishna.   Men listen and follow their lessons.
Sociability, arts, laws, morals, and religion flourished there,
vying with each other.   The *Kali-youg*, which has commenced, is to terminate this fourth period by the appearance
of Vishnu, whose hand, armed with a glistening sword, will
strike the incorrigible sinners and make the vices and evils
which defile and afflict the universe disappear forever from
the face of the earth.

The Greeks, however, were not the only ones guilty of
having reversed the order of the ages and so brought confusion into this beautiful allegory.   The Brahmans themselves advocate today the *Satya-youg* and slander the present
age, and this despite their own annals which describe the
third age, the *Douapar-youg*, as the most brilliant and most
fortunate.   This was the age of their maturity; they are
today in their decrepitude; and their attention as that of
old people is turned often toward the time of their childhood.

In general, the men whom pride makes melancholy,
always discontented with the present, always uncertain of
the future, love to reflect upon the past from which they
believe they have nothing to fear; they adorn it with smiling
colours which their imagination dares not give to the future.
They prefer, in their sombre melancholy, superfluous regrets
without fatigue to real desires which would cost them some
efforts.   Rousseau was one of these men.   Endowed with
great talents by nature he found himself misplaced by
Destiny.   Agitated by ardent passions which he could not
satisfy, constantly seeing the end which he desired to attain

receding from him, he concentrated upon himself the activity of his soul, and, turning the impulses of the imagination of his heart into vain speculations, into romantic situations, he brought forth only political paradoxes or sentimental exaggerations. The most eloquent man of his century he declaimed against eloquence; he who was able to be one of the most learned, disparaged the sciences; loving, he profaned love; artist, he calumniated the arts, and, fearing to be enlightened as to his own errors, he fled from the knowledge which had accused him; he dared not try to extinguish it. He would have extinguished it if Providence had not opposed his blind transports, for his will was a terrible power. In declaring the sovereignty of the people, in placing the multitude above the laws, in overpowering its magistrates and its kings as representatives, in throwing off entirely the authority of the priesthood, he tore up the social contract which he pretended to establish. If the system of this melancholy man had been followed, the human race would have rapidly retrograded towards that primordial nature which his clouded and disordered imagination represented to him under an enchanting form, whereas it concealed in reality nothing but what was discordant and savage.

A man, attacked with the same malady but more cold and more systematic, failed to put into action what Rousseau had left with potentiality. He was called Weishaupt and was a professor in a small town in Germany. Impressed by the ideas of the French philosopher, he clothed them in the mysterious forms of Illuminism and propagated them in the lodges of the Freemasons. One could have no idea of the rapidity with which this propagation took place, so eager are men to welcome that which flatters their passions. In a moment European society was menaced by an imminent danger. If the evil had not been arrested, it is impossible to say to what point these ravages might have extended. It is known that one of the adepts of this subversive society was struck by lightning in the street and carried fainting into a private house; upon him was found a pamphlet which contained the plan of a conspiracy and the names of the principal conspirators, and this was nothing less than a conspiracy to overthrow everywhere the Church and State, in order to return all men to that primitive nature, which, according to these visionaries, makes sovereign pontiffs and kings without distinction.

What a dreadful error! To Weishaupt has been given the title of Illuminated! He was, on the contrary, a blind fanatic who, with the best faith in the world, believing that he was working for the welfare of the human race, was pushing it into a frightful abyss.

It is because I know that at the admittance of many initiates to the mysteries of this extravagant policy, a description of the Golden Age was read, that I have wished to destroy the false idea which might still exist in some minds. Weishaupt, even as Rousseau, had only an indifferent learning. If both had known the true traditions, they would have known that the idea of placing the Golden Age at the beginning of society among men wanting in government and culture had only appeared plausible to certain Greek and Latin poets because it was in harmony with the erroneous opinion of their times. At the opening of the ancient mysteries, no doubt much above those of Weishaupt, it was not so brilliant a description that one read, but the beginning of the cosmogony of *Sanchoniathon*, which, as one knows, presents a picture very different and very gloomy.

That one may not be surprised at my devoting such a long digression to oppose an idea so trifling as that of the Golden Age, it is necessary to consider that those who today write the most coldly regarding politics, and who would laugh with pity if they were accused of indulging a like idea, only obey, however, a movement of which politics has been the occasion. If Rousseau had not been moved by it, he could not have said in his *Discours sur l'Origine de l'Inégalité*, that man who meditates is a depraved animal; and in his *Émile*, that the more men know the more they deceive themselves; that the only means of evading error is ignorance. It is never the men whom reason counsels or whose pen is guided by interest who are dangerous in politics in whatever party they range themselves; it is those who, possessed by a fixed idea, whatever it may be, write with persuasion and enthusiasm. I return to my subject.

Man, such as I left him in terminating the last chapter, had arrived by the successive development of his faculties at the first degree of social state; he was established in families united by bonds of kinship; he had invented many useful things; he was lodged; he was coarsely dressed; he had domesticated many kinds of animals; he understood the use of fire, and, above all this, he possessed an articulate language which, although unformed, sufficed for his needs. This state, that many complaisant poets and some mediocre statesmen have believed to be the Golden Age, was anything but that; it was in fact a first step made in civilization, which was to be followed by a second and by a third. The course had been opened, and it was as impossible for man to stop there at his first appearance as it would have been impossible for him not to enter there; the action of Providence and that of Destiny acted in concert in this event.

In the meantime, woman, who could justly take pride in all the good which had resulted, did not understand how to profit by it; she committed a very grave mistake in this beginning of civilization, a mistake whose consequences, terrible for her, almost brought about ruin for the entire race. Content with the change which was made in her lot, she thought only of fixing it, and, considering only her individual interest, forgot the general interest of society. As her instinct inclined her to possess rather than to enjoy, and as her vanity showed itself always before that of any other sentiment, she became attached to her husband more through interest than through pleasure; and she made use of her vanity, rather to be assured of possession by it than to make her own more agreeable to him. She wished always to be loved before loving, so as never to risk her empire. Man, inclined by a contrary instinct to enjoy rather than to possess, and making his pride yield to what his pity had first pointed out to him as weakness, facilitated the interested projects of his companion. As his outdoor labours excited her sedentary indolence, he raised no obstacles to the daily usurpation of the woman, who soon found herself, according to her desires, absolute mistress of all the household; she made herself the centre of it, arranged everything, and commanded him whom Nature had destined to be her master. The education which she gave to her daughters conformed to her ideas, increased in them the force of instinct, and made them more and more disposed to follow the perverted route which she had opened; so that at the end of several generations feminine despotism was established.

But what instinct had done on the one hand instinct had to undo on the other; the movement begun there could not be arrested; it was necessary that Destiny should take its course. Man, subject to the woman by a kind of proud indolence, soon perceived that it was easier to renounce possession than to enjoy. He encountered beyond his cave some young maiden who awakened his desires, and, as perhaps his wife had passed the age of fruitfulness, he wished to associate with another of her kind. At these tidings, jealousy, a passion heretofore unknown, was awakened in his wife; wounded vanity and alarmed interest caused it. The most frightful troubles were the consequence. What occurred in one family disturbed all; for the first time trouble became general; for the first time the Borean Race felt that it could have general interests. The men on one side, the women on the other, discussed in their way this point of legislation, the first that had been discussed: could a man have several wives?

As there had not been up to that time any exclusive cult

which could dominate their reason, and, as the hopes of another existence could not be born in their torpid intelligence, the men decided that this could be. Assembling for the first time in great masses away from their caves, they realized that their strength, being mingled, was increased in intensity and that their resolutions had something solemn. The more timid were astonished at their audacity. Such was the occasion and such the result of the first use that man made of his general will.

The women, irritated to the last degree by a decision so contrary to their dominion, resolved to impede the execution of it by all means possible. They could not conceive how these same men, so weak when with them, had been able to show such a great audacity. They hoped to bring them back, but in vain; because the act which had just happened had created a thing hitherto unknown, a thing whose results were to be immense: *opinion* which, by impressing upon pride a new direction, changes it into *honour* and places it a step beyond pity. In this situation, the women ought to have let themselves be inspired by compassion; but, their vanity not permitting this ascending movement which might have been able to stir their intelligence, they trusted in their instinct, which ruined them. Ruse having persuaded them that they could oppose weakness with force and that their husbands being frightened would not dare combat them, they imprudently provoked them, but hardly had they raised their arms, when they were vanquished; Destiny which they had invoked had overpowered them.

CHAPTER VI

SEQUEL—DEPLORABLE LOT OF WOMAN AT THE BEGINNING OF SOCIETY—SECOND REVOLUTION—WAR AND ITS CONSEQUENCES—OPPOSITION OF THE RACES

THE calamitous event which I have just related in very few words is not at all an idle hypothesis imagined only to support a system; it is a real fact which unfortunately has left too many traces. The torrent of ages has not been able to efface them yet; everywhere they engross the attention of the historian and observer. Consider the savage people who, adhering nearest to the Borean Race, have preserved their original customs, the *Samoyèdes*, for example; you will still find there in all its force the fatal cause of the evils which during a great lapse of time have weighed upon woman. She wished to dominate by ruse, she was crushed by force. She wished to master all, and nothing was left to her. One cannot think without shuddering of the horrible state to which she was reduced. It is only too natural for man to pass from one extremity to the other in his sentiments and to break with disdain the objects of his love or his veneration.

There still exists in our day peoples whom local situations or fatal circumstances have estranged from the benefits of religion and civilization, among whom the wretched condition of woman is perpetuated. The manner in which she is treated there cannot be related without disgust. She is less the companion of man than his slave, less a human being than a beast of burden. The most beautiful half of mankind, whom Nature seems to have taken pleasure in making for *le bonheur*, has lost there even hope. Her fate there is so deplorable that it is not rare to see mothers, whom compassion renders unnatural, suffocating their daughters in order to spare them the horrible future which awaits them.

O women, women, objects dear and fatal! if this writing falls into your hands do not hasten to assume prejudice against its author. He is the most sincere of your friends, he was perhaps the tenderest of your lovers! if he points out your faults he points out also your benefits. He has already pointed them out when he said that the beginnings of civilization were your work. Defend yourselves from puerile vanity, production of your instinct, and search in your heart, and above all in your intelligence, for the gentler sentiments and more generous inspirations. You will find them there easily, since the Divinity who is the Source of it has wished that all should be developed in your breast with exemplary promptitude. You offer the charms of adolescence at an epoch when man is still but a child, and your tender glances betray already the emotions of your soul when he is ignorant of their existence. How admirable you would be if, always on guard against the movements of an exclusive vanity, of a jealous interest, you would turn to the profit of man and of society the enchanting means which you possess! Assuredly would you then be called the tutelary genius of infancy, the charm of youth, the support and counsel of the man; thus would you embellish the dream of life.

The mistakes that I have shown and those that I shall yet show, you will find foreign to you, and they are in fact, both in time and form; but the substance exists and you can commit them in a different way; your education badly understood and badly conducted drives you to it; be careful.

Europe is in a secret fermentation. If you do not conduct yourselves with discretion I tell you with sorrow that the fate of the women of Asia surely awaits you.

But let us return to the history of bygone ages.

While the Borean Race was becoming civilized, and while it was increasing in numbers from year to year and spreading over greater extent of territory, the centuries rolled on in silence. All inventions were being perfected, and one could observe already among the different tribes of which the entire race was composed some beginnings of pastoral and agricultural life. Canoes had been hollowed out to traverse the arms of the sea and to navigate rivers, and wagons had been made to penetrate more easily into the interior of the country. When the pastures were exhausted in one country they passed into another. The earth, which never failed the inhabitants, sufficed for their needs. The deep forests abounded in game, the seas, the rivers offered inexhaustible and easy fishing. Any private discords which arose, quickly extinguished, never became general, and the people, destined to be the most warlike in the world, were then the most pacific. This people might have enjoyed at this epoch a happiness as great as their position would have permitted if a part of them had not groaned under the weight of oppression. Women were everywhere reduced to the state in which one sees them today among the *Samoyèdes.* Very nearly servants, they were burdened with the most painful labours. When they became aged, which was rare enough, so that they could serve no further, they were often barbarously drowned. The groans of these unfortunate victims awakened at last the solicitude of Providence which, tired of so much cruelty and wishing besides to advance this stagnant and roughly formed civilization, determined a potential movement, which Destiny brought into action.

At that time the Black Race, which I shall call always *Sudeen* on account of its equatorial origin and in opposition to the White Race which I have named *Borean*, the Black

Race I say, existed in all the pomp of social state. It covered entire Africa with powerful nations sprung from it; it possessed Arabia and had planted its colonies over all the meridional coasts of Asia and very far into the interior. An infinity of monuments which bear the African characters still exist in our day in all these latitudes and attest the grandeur of the peoples to which they have belonged. The enormous constructions of Mahabalipouram, the caverns of Ellora, the temples of Isthakar, the ramparts of the Caucasus, the pyramids of Memphis, the excavations of Thebes in Egypt, and many other works, which the astonished imagination attributes to the giants, prove the long existence of the Sudeen Race and the immense progress that it had made in the arts. Regarding these monuments an interesting observation can be made. It is that the type, after which they are all constructed, is that of a cavern hollowed out in a mountain, and this gives rise to the thought that the first habitations of the African tribes were sorts of crypts formed in this manner and that the name of troglodytes must have been their first generic one. The type of the primitive habitation of the Borean nations which has been the wagon is recognized in the lightness of Grecian architecture, in the form of ancient temples, and even in that of the houses. As for the intermediate races which have dominated or which still dominate in Asia and which still belong to the Yellow Race, the Oriental Tartar and the Chinese, very numerous although very advanced in its old age, it is evident that all their monuments trace faithfully their form from the tent which was their first dwelling.

Now the Sudeen Race, very powerful and widely spread throughout Africa and the south of Asia, was but imperfectly aware of the septentrional countries of this part of the world, and had of Europe only a very vague idea. The general opinion was, no doubt, that this vast extent, occupied by sterile lands and stamped with an eternal winter, must be uninhabitable. The contrary opinion was held in

Europe in respect to Africa, since the Borean Race, having attained a certain degree of civilization, began to have a geographical science. However that may be, the north of Europe and Asia came to be known by the Sudeens at the moment when this event was to take place. Whatever were the circumstances which brought it about and the means which were employed for this, it matters not; Providence had willed it and it was.

The white men perceived for the first time by the light of their burned forests men of a colour different from theirs. But this difference alone did not strike them. These men covered with extraordinary garments, resplendent with cuirasses, handled with dexterity redoubtable arms unknown in these regions. They had numerous cavalry; they fought from chariots, and like colossi, advancing with formidable manœuvres, flung death on every side. They were stupefied. Some white women, of whom these strangers had taken possession and whose good will they strove to win, were not difficult to seduce. They were too unhappy in their own country to have nourished any love for it. Returning to their caves they showed the brilliant necklaces, the pleasing and delicately shaded stuffs which they had received. Nothing more was needed for them to raise their heads above all others. A large number profiting by the shadows of night fled and rejoined the newcomers. Fathers and husbands, thinking only of their resentment, seized their feeble weapons and advanced to reclaim their daughters or their wives. Their movement had been anticipated and was awaited. The result of the combat which ensued was not doubtful. Many were killed, a great number taken prisoners; the rest fled.

Alarm, gaining by degrees, spread itself in a short time throughout the Borean Race. The tribes assembled in great numbers and deliberated upon what was to be done, without having considered in advance what they would deliberate, without even knowing what a deliberation was.

Common peril awakened the general will. This will manifested itself, and they issued a decree in form of a plebiscite, but its execution was not so easy as it had been formerly. The general will no longer acted. The assembled people felt it and they saw that the intention of making war was not sufficient and they would undoubtedly be vanquished if the means of directing it was not found. Thereupon a man, whom Nature had endowed with a mighty stature and extraordinary force, advanced in the midst of the assembly and declared that he would undertake to disclose these means. His imposing aspect, his assurance, electrified the assembly. A general cry arose in his favour. He was proclaimed the *Herman* or *Gherman*, that is to say, the chief of men. Such was the first military chief.[1]

The important decree which established one man above all the others had no need to be written or promulgated. It was the energetic expression of the general will. The force and the truth of the movement were engraved upon all minds. When it has been necessary to write laws has been when laws were no longer unanimous.

At first the Herman divided the men into three classes. In the first he placed all the venerable men not able to endure the fatigues of war; he called in the second, all the young and robust men, of whom he made up his army, and placed in the third the weak and old, but still active, whom he destined to provide for all its wants. The young women and children were sent off beyond the rivers or into the depths of the forests. The aged women and young boys were employed to carry the provisions or to guard the wagons. As the old men were entrusted with distributing to each of the combatants his daily rations and as they looked after the provisions they were given the name of *Diet*, that is to say the subsistence, and this name is preserved even to our

---

[1] It is from the name of *Herman* or *Gherman* that the names *German* and *Germany* are derived. The root here signifies in its literal sense an *eminence*, figuratively speaking, a *sovereign*, a *master*.

day in that of the German *Diet*,[1] not that it occupies itself
as at other times with subsistence properly speaking, but
with the existence of the political body.   This Diet was the
model of all the senates which were instituted afterwards
in Europe for the purpose of representing the general will.
As for the two other classes established in the mass of the
population, to the one which contained the warriors was
given the name of *Leyt*, that is to say the *élite*, and to the
other, that of *Folk* or *Volg*, that is to say, the one who
follows, the one who serves, the crowd, the vulgar. [2]

This is the origin of the inequality of conditions so much
sought for and which was established so early among the
septentrional nations.   This inequality was neither the
result of caprice nor oppression; it was the necessary result
of the warlike state in which these nations found themselves
engaged.   Destiny which provoked this condition determined
all the consequences of it.   It divided the people irresistibly
into two classes: those of the strong and those of the weak;
the strong ones called to fight and the weak reserved for
feeding and serving the combatants.   This state of war,
which by its long duration had become the habitual state of
the Borean Race, consolidated these two classes and in the
course of time caused fixed demarcation and hereditary occupation in them.   There, in the heart of this race, were born
nobility and plebeianism with all their privileges and their
attributes, and when, after having been a long time enslaved
or restrained, this same race became at last superior to the

---

[1] This word signifies the manner of feeding upon or providing subsistence,
in the Greek word δίαιτα as well as in the Latin *diæta*, in the French *diète*, in
the English *diet*, etc.   Even today it is said in English *to diet one*, to express
the care that is taken in nourishing someone.   This word preserves the ancient
root *æd*, the nourishment, united to the article *de*, in the English *the*, in the
German *die*.   From this root *æd* have emerged the verbs *edere* in Latin, *ætan*
in Saxon, *to eat* in English, *essen* in German, etc.

[2] The words *Leyt* and *Volk* are still used in German.   The Attic Greek word
λεώς is attached to the word *leyt*.   The Latin *vulgus* is derived from the word
Volg, as the French word *foule* (crowd).

Sudeen Race and when it subjugated the diverse nations, it still kept the existence of these two classes in the titles of Borean and Hyperboreans,[1] or the Barons and the High Barons, which the conquerors, having become sovereign or feudal masters, claimed.

[1] It is necessary to consider as a thing worthy of attention that whereas the word *Borean* became a title of honour in that of *Baron* in Europe, in Asia and in Africa the word *Sudeen* held the same sense in that of *Syd* which was written very inappropriately *Cid*.

CHAPTER VII

A T the time when the Herman had made the division,
which I mentioned in the preceding chapter, he considered extending this warlike constitution as much as he
was able, and chose to this effect several lieutenants, whom
he sent away among the Borean tribes in order to inform
them of what was taking place and to engage them in the
name of the common welfare to unite themselves according
to the same principles, and to come in all haste to fight the
enemy. This embassy, whose necessity suggested ways
and means, had all the success that could be expected. The
different tribes, alarmed by the accounts which they had
heard and drawn on by the impressed movement, all became
constituted on the same plan and created as many *Hermans*
as there were congregations. These different *Hermans*,
uniting, formed a corps of military chiefs, who were not
long in feeling, guided always by the force of things, that
it was useful, as much for them as for public matters, to
give themselves a supreme chief. This chief proclaimed on
his own presentation and because he was evidently the
strongest and most powerful was called *Heröll*, that is to
say, the chief of all.[1] The Diets of the various tribes re-

[1] This name in changing from the guttural inflection into that of *Hercöll*
or *Hercules* has become celebrated throughout all the earth. It has been

45

cognized him and the different classes of *Leyts* and of *Folks* swore to obey him. Such was the first emperor, and such was the origin of feudal government; for in Europe, and among the Borean Race, imperial or feudal government does not differ. An emperor who does not rule over military chiefs, sovereigns of the people whom they govern, is not a veritable emperor. He is not at all a *Heróll*, properly speaking he is a Herman, a military chief more or less powerful. An emperor, such as Agamemnon of Homer, must reign over kings.

But, besides the two primordial classes which divided the entire tribes into men-at-arms and serfs, there were formed two other classes superior to those which were composed of chosen men who were attached principally to the Heróll or the Herman and who formed his guard, his suite, and, in short, his court. These two classes, to which in time were attributed great privileges, gave their name to the entire race, especially when this race, having seized the dominion, spread afar their conquests and founded powerful nations. From these sprang the Heruli and the Germans.

And as in imitation of the Herólls, or Hermans, the inferior chiefs rendered powerful by conquest had also their followers called *Leudes*, on account of the class of men-at-arms from whom they came; they gave their names likewise to entire peoples, when these peoples conducted by them succeeded in distinguishing themselves from the nation, properly speaking, by establishing themselves at a distance.[1]

---

applied in the course of time to the Universal Divinity, to the sun, as that of *Herman* has been given to the God of War. The symbol of this God which was represented by a lance, was called *Irminsul*, or rather *Herman-Sayl.*

[1] It is necessary to note with care that all the peoples, whose names are found in the ancient writers ordinarily included under the generic name of Celt or of Scythian, were in reality only the divisions of one and the same people issued from one and the same race. The name of *Celts*, which they gave in general to themselves, signified the males, the strong, the illustrious; it was derived directly from the word *held*, a hero, a master. The name of

But whilst the Borean Race was thus preparing itself for combat, the combat had continued. The Sudeens profiting by their advantages had advanced into the interior of the country. Fire and sword had opened for them routes through the forest hitherto impassable. They crossed rivers with facility by means of bridges of boats which they understood how to build. In proportion as they advanced, they raised inaccessible strongholds. The Boreans notwithstanding their number and their valour could not hold out against these redoubtable enemies, so far above them in their discipline, their tactics, and difference in arms. If they tried to fall upon their enemies unawares, or to surprise them under cover of the night, they found them enclosed in fortified camps. Everything betrayed this unfortunate race, and seemed to conduct it to its absolute ruin. Even the women of the Boreans abandoned them for their conquerors. The first women who freed themselves, having learned the dialect, served the Sudeens as guides and showed them the most hidden retreats of their Borean fathers and husbands. These unfortunates, surprised, surrounded on all sides, cut off, dexterously thrown upon the banks of the rivers or driven back against the mountains, were obliged to surrender themselves or to die in misery. Those who were made prisoners in the combats or who surrendered to evade death submitted to slavery.

However the Africans, already masters of a great part of the country, had had the natural riches of it explored by their savants. They had discovered mines of copper in abundance, tin, lead, mercury, and above all iron, whose great utility rendered it so precious to these peoples. They found immense forests rich in timber. The plains offered

---

Scythians, which their enemies gave to them, signified, on the contrary, the impure ones, the reprobates; it came from the word *Cuth* or *Scuth* applied to all things which one sets aside or which repels one or which one repels. It designated properly spittle. It was by this offensive word that the Black Race characterized the White, on account of the colour of spittle.

to the tillers of the soil who would clear them the hope of splendid harvests of grain.   Rivers in great numbers presented their slopes of rich pasturage capable of receiving and nourishing a large number of cattle.   These tidings carried into Africa and Asia drew a host of colonists.

They began to exploit the mines.   The miserable Boreans, whom they had taken, and whom they continued to take, were given over to grasping masters who employed them at this coarse work.   They were skilled only in roughly digging the earth; they were taught to do it methodically, using suitable implements.   They penetrated into the interior of the mountains and drew from them in great masses, minerals of copper, iron, and other metals.   They were obliged to work and to smelt them.   Buried alive in mephitic abysses, attached to wheels, forced to keep up enormous fires and to beat the fiery masses on the anvil, what suffering they had to endure!

Others, during this time, dragged the plough and watered with their sweat the furrows from which their conquerors were to reap the harvest.   The women even were not spared. After the victory was decided and when their help was not needed further they were treated no better than their husbands.   They were sold as slaves, and were sent with the men pell-mell into Africa, where their posterity was speculated upon while they were employed in the vilest labours.

If the Borean nations instead of being still nomadic had been fixed, if they had inhabited cities as those which the Spaniards found in America, they would have entirely perished.   But it seemed that Providence, desiring their preservation, had impressed upon their minds an invincible horror for all that had the appearance of a walled enclosure. This horror, augmented without doubt by the numberless calamities which they experienced in the prisons of their tyrants, lasted a great number of centuries after their deliverance, even in the midst of their triumphs.   And, notwithstanding the *mélange* which had many times taken place between the peoples of the South and the North, one still finds many hordes of Borean origin, whose repugnance for fixed dwellings nothing has ever been able to conquer, even after having settled in the mildest climates.

What saved the White Race from utter destruction was their facility in fleeing from their conquerors, after they had recognized the impossibility of resisting them. Remnants of the different tribes gathered together by the hermans, who since their creation had not ceased to be renewed, took refuge in the north of Europe and Asia and reaching those immense regions which had served as their cradle, they made there a stronghold of the ice accumulated by long winters. Their oppressors strove at first to follow them there, but after many fruitless attempts were repulsed by the asperity of the climate.

4

CHAPTER VIII

FOURTH REVOLUTION—PEACE AND COMMERCE

IN the meanwhile an implacable war continued between the two races: on one side, the vanquishers wished to obtain slaves to exploit the mines and cultivate the lands, on the other the vanquished wished, first, to avenge the evils which they had suffered and which they still suffered, and, afterwards, to appropriate what they could plunder of the chattels of the Sudeens. There were among these chattels, besides cattle and grain, numberless objects whose great util'ty the Boreans had recognized, and especially weapons of copper and iron, and instruments of all kinds made of these two metals.

Often at a moment when least expected, a deluge of Boreans inundated the settlements of their enemies; everything that they cou'd they took away and what they could not bear off was destroyed. These incursions generally took place in the heart of winter, while a sheet of ice was over the rivers and lakes. All the precautions of the Africans were useless against the first violence of the torrent; less accustomed to the rigours of the climate they could not leave their strongholds so easily, and the country without defence became the prey of their ancient possessors. The Boreans fell into ambuscades, and often left men dead and prisoners, but the spoils which they carried away always compensated them beyond their losses; in seizing certain mines, certain forges, they often rescued a great number of their compatriots and so took with them many skilful workmen of the Sudeens. The advantage which they succeeded in deriving from these captures was of incalculable importance; one of their hermans, who perhaps had been a slave of their enemies, persuaded them to use their prisoners for the same labours, so as to procure equal arms in sufficient quantity. Their success was at first mediocre, but they learned finally the art of smelting copper and iron and this was an enormous step that they took. Their lances, their arrows, their hatchets, although badly shaped and badly tempered, became no less redoubtable in hands so strong as theirs; for it is well to observe here that as to physical force they were infinitely superior to the Sudeens. Their lofty stature had at first caused them to be taken for giants, and it appears even certain that the fable of the Titans, although having in view a cosmogonical object, has been materially conceived from them, when having succeeded in clearing Europe of their adversaries they carried the war into Africa and menaced the temple of Jupiter Ammon.

As soon as the season became less vigorous, the Sudeens again took the offensive; but it was in vain that, during six or eight months of the year, they covered the country with their armies; the Boreans, accustomed to evade them, turned back into the vast solitudes of the north of Asia and seemed to disappear from their sght. At the first approach of winter, at the moment when the frosts obliged their enemies to retreat, they were seen emerging again from their shelters and recommencing their depredations.

This hostile condition, which lasted a long time no doubt, had the inevitable result of developing in the minds of the Boreans a warlike valour, by changing to a permanent passion the instinct of courage which they had received from nature. Trained by their numerous defeats, they learned from their very enemies the art of fighting them with fewer disadvantages. Happily relieved of all prejudices, without

other stubbornness than that of resistance, they easily changed
their bad tactics for better and did not keep their rude and
less dangerous arms, when they had found occasion to procure more formidable ones. At the end of some centuries
these men, whom the proud inhabitants of Africa and of
Asia regarded as contemptible savages, whose life was at
their mercy, became warriors whose attacks could not as
at other times be disdained. Already the extreme frontiers
had been crossed more than once, the forts razed and destroyed, settlements too far buried in the interior of the
country pillaged or devastated, and soon the very towns
built along the shores of the Mediterranean Sea from the
Euxine to the Atlantic Ocean did not feel themselves
safe, notwithstanding the ramparts with which they were
surrounded.

At that time, the Sudeen nations to which these colonies
belonged, reflected on this critical situation and judged that
it would be better to seek means of living in peace with the
natives of the country than to be compelled to sustain an
eternal war against them, from which they would receive
only harm without benefit. One of these nations, the first
perhaps to which the idea had come, determined to send an
embassy to the Boreans; it was again necessity which determined this act. Destiny, in developing the consequences
of a first event, placed the Will of Man in opposition with
them and furnished it with occasions to try its strength.

No doubt this was a spectacle as novel as extraordinary
for men whose natural state was a warlike one, who had
understood no other manner of existing than that of braving
the enemy or fearing him, and who, born in the midst of
alarms, had never conceived the idea of repose or of seeing
the disarmed enemy coming to them preceded by a great
number of their compatriots whose chains were not only
broken but replaced by brilliant emblems. These compatriots appointed as interpreters, having asked to speak to the
herman, began to spread out before him the rich presents

of which they were the bearers and afterwards explained to him the desires of the Sudeens; but as a word expressing the idea of *Peace* did not exist in the Borean tongue, they used one which expressed *Liberty*,[1] and they said that they had come to ask for liberty and to offer it.

I am convinced that the herman had at first much difficulty in understanding what was demanded of him, and that he had to turn to the old men to know if anything like that existed in the traditions. Nothing existed to which this could be compared. From time immemorial there had been war; could this condition cease? Why and how? The interpreters of the Sudeens interested in making the embassy successful did not lack good reasons; they easily showed to the Diet that the cessation of hostilities would offer to both peoples a great advantage in leaving them more leisure to attend to their labours and more security to enjoy them. Instead of seeking to pillage from one another the objects which they needed, instead of carrying them off dripping with the blood of friends and brothers, would it not be better to exchange them without peril? Limits could be arranged for this, which they would reciprocally pledge never to overstep; a place could be determined where they could make the exchanges. If they wished iron, arms, stuffs, why not give them in exchange for cattle, grain, and furs?

The Diet composed of old men liked these reasons. The warrior-class instinctively feeling that peace would diminish its influence had much difficulty in consenting. They yielded finally, but without surrendering their arms. Among the other tribes the greater part followed the example of the first; but there were some who would not agree to it. For the first time it was seen possible for a nation to be divided, and also for the first time it was felt that the smaller number should yield to the greater. The Heröll, having assembled his hermans, counted the voices and, perceiving that the

---

[1] In German the word *frey* still signifies *free* and the word *frid* signifies *peace*.

majority was for peace, used his authority to constrain the minority. This act of the greatest importance took place without its importance being realized. The Borean Race was already governed without suspecting that it had a government; it obeyed the law without knowing what law was. Events brought forth events and the force of things inclined the Will.

Thus the first treaty of peace which was concluded was also a treaty of commerce. Without the second motive, the first could not have been conceived.

But two acts which followed greatly amazed those of the Boreans who saw them. The first, which was made without preparation, consisted of tracing with the point of a stiletto on a sort of prepared skin several characters to which the Sudeens who traced them seemed to attach great importance. Some of the old men, having asked of the interpreters what they signified, learned with astonishment mingled with admiration that these black men represented in this manner all that had just taken place, so as to remember it and to be able to give account of it to their hermans when they returned home to them. One of the old men, greatly impressed by this idea, judged that it was not impossible to adopt it for his tribe, and, as soon as he had conceived the thought and had merely tried to trace with his stick upon the sand simple lines straight or crossed to express the numbers, it was sufficient; the art of writing was born and entered the domain of Destiny which developed it.

The second act which was performed with great solemnity had as its object a sacrifice which the Sudeens made to the sun, their great Divinity. The general worship of all the nations of African origin was Sabeanism. This is the most ancient form of worship whose remembrance has been preserved on earth.[1] The pomp of the spectacle, the raised

---

[1] The word *Zaab* designated the sun in the primitive tongue of the African people. It signified properly the Father, living or resplendent. Thence the Hebrew word *zehb*, gold.

altar, the sacrificed victim, the extraordinary ceremonies, the men clothed in magnificent robes invoking on their knees the Star of light, all this struck with admiration the mass of Boreans gathered to enjoy so unique a spectacle. The interpreters, interrogated anew on this matter, responded that it was thus that the Sudeens conducted themselves when they wished to give thanks to the sun for some great benefit, or to persuade it to grant one. Although the old men understood well the words which the interpreters used, they could not, however, comprehend the idea which these words contained. What they did receive seemed to them extravagant. Was it possible to believe that the sun which rose every day to lighten the world might grant other benefits? Was it possible that it favoured one people more than another, and could it be less good today than tomorrow? The intelligence of these men still apathetic was not susceptible of rising to anything spiritual; the instinctive and the animistic spheres alone were developed in them; their only emotions came to them through their needs or passions. They had no inspirations; the moment was not far off when they would begin to feel their influences; but it could not be by any other perceptible means. Everything has its principle and there can be but one; forms alone can vary. When the philosophers of all ages have sought for the origin of intellectual things in that which is not intellectual, they have testified to their ignorance. Like produces only like. It is not fear that has caused the gods to be born; it is the divine spark confided to our intelligence, whose radiance manifests all that is divine. Who would not sigh to hear one of the greatest philosophers of the past century, Voltaire, the *coryphée* of his time, say seriously: "It thunders; who makes it thunder? it might perhaps be a serpent in the vicinity; this serpent must be appeased. Hence the cult." What pitiable reasoning! How could he so forget himself! How does a man who arrogantly pretends to enlighten Mankind dare to express such an hypothesis?

I do not wish to forget before terminating this chapter to say, that one can trace back to the first treaty of peace which was concluded in Europe, the first generic name which was given to the autochthonous nations inhabiting it. It appears certain that up to that time they had taken only that of *man*.[1]   But having learned through their interpreters that the Sudeens gave themselves the title of *Atlanteans*,[2] that is to say, masters of the Universe, they chose that of *Celts*, heroes, and knowing besides, that on account of the white colour of their skin they had been given the offensive name of *Scythians*, they designated their enemies by the expressive name of *Pelasgians*,[3] that is to say, tanned skins.

[1] The word *man* which is still used to designate man in nearly all of the septentrional languages signifies pre-eminently Being. It comes from the root *ân* or *ôn*, expressing in Celtic the verb *to be*, thence the Greek ὦν, the Latin *ens*, the English *am*, etc.

[2] This well-known name is composed of two words *atta*, the master, the ancient, the father, and *lant* universal space.

[3] Already having explained the name of the *Celts*, I mention here only that it should be pronounced *Kelts*, being formed from the Greek Κελτοί. I have also explained the name of *Scythians*. As for the name *Pelasgian* it can also signify the Black People because the word *ask*, which designated a wood, designated also a people. One could see likewise without much difficulty seafaring people, since they were really that.

CHAPTER IX

CONCERNING PROPERTY AND THE INEQUALITY OF CONDITIONS —THEIR ORIGIN

UP to this time the Boreans had possessed many things of their own without the abstract idea of property entering into their mind. It did not any more occur to them to doubt the possession of their bow and their arrows than that of their arms or their hands. Their cave belonged to them because they had dug it out, their wagon was theirs because they had made it. Those who possessed reindeer, elk, or any other cattle enjoyed them without trouble because they possessed them. The pains they had taken in raising them, the pains they continued to take in feeding them assured their possession. Everyone had them or could have them at the same price. As the earth failed no one, no one had the right to complain. Property was such a consequence of the social state and the social state such a consequence of the nature of man that the idea of fixing and confirming it by law could not be conceived. Besides how could any law be made? All political right was then founded only upon customs, and these customs were linked together with the same force as other acts of life. Now, each associated the consciousness of his life with that of his property, and it would have seemed as strange to seek to live the life of another as to wish to enjoy the fruit of another's labour; and this was nothing else than living his own life.

The political writers who do not see what I have said are tormented trying to find the origin of the right of property and are lost in absurd hypotheses. One may as well question the right of man to possess his body. The body of man is not man entire; it is not he, properly speaking, but only that which belongs to him. His property is not his body either, but is that which belongs to his body. To steal his body is to take away his life; to steal from him what belongs to his body is to carry off the means of life. Force can no doubt deprive him of both; but force can also preserve them, and man has as much right to defend his l'fe, as to defend the means of his life, that is to say, his body and that which belongs to his body or his property.

Thus from the moment that Providence determined a principle of social state among men, there was necessarily a principle of property; for the one could not possibly exist without the other. The first instinctive sensations of which the Kingdom of Man may have consciousness are to enjoy and possess for the man and to possess and enjoy for the woman; it is even from this very contrast, as I have shown, that the first emotion which causes all the rest issues.

Property is then a need as inherent in man as pleasure. The sensation of this need transformed into sentiment in the animistic sphere, becoming permanent as all the other sentiments in the absence of the need itself which brought it forth, produces there a multitude of passions whose force is revealed and spread in proportion as civilization makes progress. From the sentiment of property, right is born; from the passions that accompany it are born the means of acquiring this right and preserving it. There is by no means need of an agreement for that; the law which established it is engraved beforehand in the hearts of all.

I do not mean to say by this, that it could not possibly happen in the beginning of society that a man deprived of his bow, for example, would not try to appropriate that of another; that he would not take away if he could the game that the other had hunted, the reindeer that the other had raised; I only say that in doing this, he would know that he was acting against a right that he recognized for himself and that he wished to be respected in him; a right for the preservation of which he knew in advance that the man whom he wished to despoil would fight in the same manner as he himself would fight on a similar occasion. If he had not known this the social state would not have existed, the bow would not have been cut, the game would not have been taken, and the reindeer would not have been tamed. From this consciousness is born a situation unfortunate for the refractory, for his strength is diminished all the more as he feels his wrong, and that of his adversary is augmented all the more as he feels his right.

Therefore man would choose to make a bow in peace rather than to steal one all made at the peril of his life. He would prefer to go hunting or fishing on his own account rather than to fight constantly, and he would judge rightly that the least fatigue and the least danger were on the side of labour. Unless, however, dire necessity urged him irresistibly to brave death in order to preserve his life, in that case, he would momentarily re-enter the state of nature whence he had come and would expose himself to the danger of losing his life in order to attain the means of preserving it. Sometimes he would succeed, but more often he would perish, and his death, which would be known throughout the tribe, would be a lesson by which the social state would profit.

Such was the general situation of the Borean Race relative to the right of property at the epoch of the appearance of the Sudeens. This appearance and the state of war of which it was the consequence brought to this right important changes. At first, the tribes were divided into two distinct classes and were given several kinds of chiefs. The division which was made was in the nature of things. For it is in no wise true as certain political writers, either indiffer-

ent observers or systematically impassioned, have advanced,
—that all men are born strong and warlike.   Men are born
unequal in all ways and more inclined towards certain faculties than towards others.   There are the weak and the strong,
the small and the great, the warlike and the pacific, the
indolent and the active.   Whereas some love excitement,
noise, dangers, others, on the contrary, seek repose and calm,
and prefer the calling of the shepherd and the farmer to
that of the soldier.   The labour of the plough suits them
better than the fatigues of war and the shepherd's crook has
more attractions for them than the lance or the javelin.

Now, the division which was made between them was
not at all arbitrary.   It was freely, and by an instinctive
movement, that each took his place.   There was not yet
any point of honour which forced men to appear what they
were not, and still less a conscriptive law which ordered them
to follow, in spite of themselves, a calling for which some
would feel an invincible aversion.   Thus, as soon as the
herman had announced his intention of forming a class of
men-at-arms destined to fight the enemy, and a class of
labouring men reserved to maintain this class, and to furnish it with all the things which it could not provide for
itself, the formation took place without the least difficulty.
I must say that not any of these men who entered one or the
other of these classes foresaw, the enormous consequences
which his choice could have in the future.   How were they
able to foresee that a simple, natural inequality of strength
or inclinations would afterwards be transformed into political inequality and would constitute a right?   This, however,
was what did happen.   This social form, freely consented
and confided to Destiny, had the result that it must necessarily have, and gave birth to the most ancient government
that Europe has known, the feudal government.

CHAPTER X

BUT perhaps the attentive reader will ask me how a simple physical inequality can constitute a moral right, and above all how the choice of parents can bind the children. For it seems that the first division consisting of two classes —that of men-at-arms and that of labouring men,—the children of each remain, in general, in one or the other of these classes; so that at the end of a certain time, and when the Celtic nations were definitely constituted, it was found that those of the first class were superior to the others, and they enjoyed certain honorary privileges which caused them to be considered nobles while the others were plebeians. The reply to this question is so simple that I cannot conceive how so many of the political writers to whom the question has been put have not solved it. It is thus: the class of men-at-arms, by the mere fact of its free formation is found entrusted not only with its own defence, but also with the defence of the other class; so that it could not perish unless the other perished likewise. All the destinies of the Borean Race rested upon it. If it had been conquered the entire race would have disappeared. Its triumph assured them more than its existence; it assured the existence of all the race and its perpetuity. The children that were born in one class as well as in the other were born because it had triumphed. Therefore they owed their life to it and this life could be classed without any injustice, according to the political inequality in which and by which this life was favoured to manifest itself. It is thus that this inequality, first physical and then political, could constitute a legitimate and moral right, and pass from fathers to children, since without it the fathers would have died or would have been condemned to slavery and the children would not have been born.

The triumph of the Borean Race to which I now give the name of *Celtic* was assured by the treaty of peace and of commerce concerning which I have spoken; but this triumph which guaranteed its existence was very far from giving it repose.

Until then, as I have tried to show in the beginning of the preceding chapter, property had been a fact rather than a right among the Celts, and it would never have occurred to any one to dwell upon the fact. But when commerce was opened with the Sudeens, now known under the name of Atlanteans, and when exchanges had been made between the two nations, it happened that the tribes nearest to the frontiers had a greater advantage than the others farther away, and they found themselves able to make better traffic. On the other hand, the furs which the Atlanteans desired were in the hands of tribes most remote in the North, whence they could be obtained only by making many exchanges. Relations became complicated, interests were thwarted, and unequal riches caused envy. These causes of misunderstanding came to the ears of the Africans who cleverly profited by them. These men, far advanced in all physical and moral sciences, were not ignorant of that of politics; it is a probability that they put to use their most secret means in order to foment this misunderstanding which was favourable to them. The ferments of discord which they aroused had all the success that they could have expected. The Celtic tribes, irritated against each other, ceased to consider themselves as the inseparable parts of a unique whole, and conducted themselves face to face as simple individuals would have done. Now the only way that these individuals had known of settling their differences up to that time had been private combats. There had never been any jurisprudence other than that of the duel.

The Celts fought for all manner of reasons, for private interests as well as for general interests. When a tribe had assembled to elect a herman, the one who presented himself to fill this military post carried, by the mere fact of presenting himself, a challenge to all his competitors. If one was found who was judged more worthy than he to command the others, he accepted the challenge and the victor was proclaimed. When these hermans of all the tribes were united to elect a Heröll, the same method was followed. It was always the strongest or most fortunate who received this dignity. If some difference arose among the partisans, the Diet had no other means of judging it than to order a combat between the contestants. The one who was declared vanquished was condemned. The men-at-arms fought with their weapons and nearly always to the death. The labouring men fought each other with the cestus or armed only with a club. The combat was terminated as soon as one of the two was thrown to the ground.

It is clearly seen that it was Destiny alone that still dominated this race and that the intellectual sphere was not open to any moral idea of justice or injustice, of truth or error. For them justice was triumph and truth the exercise of force. Force was everything to these instinctive and impassioned men; it was for them *the naked truth* as a man energetically expressed it not long ago.

When in consequence of the change which was made in the manner of living it was no longer the partisans alone who had opposed interests, but the numerous tribes who believed themselves to be wronged by other tribes, they had no means of terminating the differences that arose between them other than by invoking the force of arms.

War was declared in the same manner and almost in the same form as one would be challenged to a duel. The tribes fought often for very frivolous objects, and even for simple offences. The Atlanteans, witnesses of these bloody contests, excited them secretly; adroitly making the balance incline to one side or the other by the secret interventions they always found means of gaining where their allies lost. I do not fear to advance the hypothesis too far, in saying that their political astuteness went so far as to buy as slaves the prisoners whom the miserable Celts had made from one another. If this is, as I believe it and as I perhaps might find it in the written traditions, the fatality of Destiny had been pushed as far as possible. For, considered from a certain view-point, death is not so cruel as slavery. And here is the reason: death only puts man under the power of Providence which disposes of him according to his nature; whereas slavery delivers him to Destiny which draws him into the vortex of necessity.[1]

It is certain that this epoch was most disastrous for the Celts. Their calamities became aggravated by the faults which they did not cease to commit and because the perfidious peace which had been given them, more dangerous than war itself, would have brought about their downfall, if the moment indicated by Providence, where their intelligence was to acquire its first development, had not arrived.

[1] Nevertheless, it is here only a question of that kind of slavery which results from force of arms and which weighs upon the vanquished enemy. This slavery, which is purely a fact without being a right, in no way obliges the slave to remain a slave; for as it is force alone which has made him such, force can also unmake him. There exists two other kinds of slavery of which I will speak later: domestic slavery, which was established in the republic, and feudal serfdom, which had place in the feudal states. The most terrible of these three conditions of slavery is without doubt domestic slavery, because it is not only a fact but a right; because it becomes legitimate on account of the law which establishes it, and because it obliges the slave to remain a slave by duty and to rivet his own chains by the virtues of the slave with which he has been inculcated since childhood. Feudal servitude is less rigorous, because it is based upon an agreement and it can be considered legal rather than legitimate. I shall explain later what I can only indicate here.

CHAPTER XI

BEFORE reading this chapter and above all before passing any judgment upon the idea which it contains, I should like the reader to be convinced of a fundamental truth beyond which are only error and prejudice, namely: that nothing in elementary nature is formed at once; that all comes from a principle, of which the developments, subject to the influence of time, have their beginning, their middle, and their end.

The most vigorous tree or the most perfect animal issues from an imperceptible germ; they grow slowly and attain their relative perfection only after having submitted to an infinite number of vicissitudes. What happens to physical man also happens to instinctive, animistic, or intellectual man, and what takes place for the individual also takes place for the entire race and for Mankind itself which comprises many races.

We have already seen develop in one of these races, which I have called the Borean Race, the instinctive and the animistic sphere, and we have been able to follow the diverse movements of their respective faculties, as well as the rapid course which I have adopted would permit. I have not wished to write a voluminous work but a useful one; it is not the number of pages that is of conse-

quence, it is the number of thoughts. Now, the development of the two inferior spheres, the instinctive and the
animistic, all important as it is, would have remained un-
fruitful, if that of the intellectual sphere had not come in
time to strengthen it. Man, whose needs influence and
whose passions draw him unceasingly on, is far from having
attained the perfection of which he is susceptible. It is
necessary that a purer light than that which is born of
excitement of the passions should come to his aid, in order
to guide him in the career of life. This light, which springs
from the two great torches of religion and law, can be born
only after the first perturbation of the intelligence has taken
place. But this perturbation is not such as some men of
more enthusiasm than sagacity imagine; this light does not
appear abruptly in all its splendour; it opens out of twilight
as that of the day, and passes through all the degrees of
dawn and morning before arriving at its midday. Nature,
I repeat in other terms, shows in nothing sudden transi-
tions; she passes from one extreme to the other by almost
imperceptible modifications.

It is not astonishing to see among infant peoples obscure
intellectual notions, superstitious beliefs, cults, and ceremonies which appear to us sometimes ridiculous, sometimes
atrocious and extraordinary laws, to which one could assign no moral end; all these things depend upon a still disordered movement of the intellectual sphere and of the
shadowy planes which the providential light is obliged to
cross; these planes more or less dense breaking this light,
refracting it in many ways, often denature it and transform
the most sublime images into frightful phantoms. The
individual imagination of children among the most advanced nations still offers an accurate picture of the general
imagination of people at the dawn of their civilization.
But a danger presents itself here to the observer and I will
describe it.

In the same way as old people attaining a state of decrepitude have many traits of resemblance with children, likewise nations in their old age ready to disappear from the face of the earth are not unlike those who are just commencing their career. To make the distinction between them is difficult but not impossible. A man accustomed to observation does not confuse the last days of autumn with the first days of spring although the temperature may be the same. He feels in the air a certain tendency which announces to him in the one the close of life and in the other its exaltation; thus, although there was much resemblance, for example, between the cult of the Peruvians and that of the Chinese, the position of the peoples was far from being the same.

The Celts, at the epoch in which I examine them, were not far from the age of the Peruvians when these were discovered and destroyed by the Spaniards; but they had over them incalculable advantages, that is, the physical part in them was completely developed before the intellectual had begun its work; they were strong and robust, and their passions were already aroused when the Africans encountered them. Their bodies hardened by the bitterness of the climate, their wandering life, the absence of all civil and religious obstacles, gave them the advantage of which I have already spoken. Among the Peruvians, on the contrary, the intellectual development had been precocious, and the physical development had been tardy and stifled. I have reason to believe that among this last people the disturbance of the intellectual sphere had occurred too soon, in consequence of an accident. It is probable that some Chinese navigators driven by a tempest, having landed among certain people of the bay of Panama, undertook their civilization, and succeeded in carrying it very far in many respects. Unfortunately they acted like imprudent preceptors who, to make a pupil shine for a moment, render him an idiot for the rest of his life. With the exception of morals and politics, the Peruvians had made very little progress in the other sciences. They were fruits of a hot-house, brilliant to look upon, but to the taste flaccid and without savour. While comedies and tragedies were represented at Cuzco, magnificent fêtes celebrated there, they were ignorant of the art of war, of which they had had but one experience in a civil dissension of short duration. A few avaricious brigands, armed with ruse and ferocity, sufficed to annihilate this people too early occupied with things beyond their comprehension. The Celts, more fortunate, had resisted entire nations, warlike and powerful, by the sole opposition of their instinctive strength. Their ideas were developed slowly and consistently. At present their too much excited passions placed them in danger; their superabundant strength was turned against themselves. It was necessary to place a restraint upon them. This was the work of Providence.

Again this time the movement impressed upon the minds of the women began to manifest itself. Weaker, and therefore more accessible than the men to all impressions, it is always they who take the first steps in the course of civilization. Fortunate if, to profit honourably by it, they knew how to mingle their own interest in the general interest; but it is this that rarely happens.

War was kindled between two tribes, and the two hermans, violently angry, at the head of their men-at-arms, challenged each other; they were about to settle their differences by a single combat. Already the weapons gleamed in their hands, when suddenly a woman all dishevelled threw herself between them at the risk of her life. She cried for them to stop, to stay their blows, and to hear her. Her action, her tone, the ardour of her eyes astonished them. She was the wife of one and sister of the other. They stopped; they listened. Her voice had something supernatural which moved them notwithstanding their anger. She told them that, while overpowered with grief in her wagon, she felt herself about to swoon without however entirely losing consciousness and that then being called by a loud voice, she had raised her eyes and had seen before her a warrior of colossal stature, all resplendent with light who had said to her: "Descend, Voluspa, gather up thy robe and hasten to the place where thy spouse and thy brother are about to shed Borean blood. Tell them that I, the first Herman, the first Hero of their race, the Vanquisher of the Black People, have descended from the palace of clouds, where resides my Soul, to order them by thy voice to cease from this fratricidal combat. It is a ruse of the Black People which divides them. They are there hidden in the denseness of the forest. They await until death shall have destroyed the most valiant, to fall upon the rest and enrich themselves with their spoils. Dost thou not hear the cries of victory which they already shout at the feet of their idol? Go! lose no time. Surprise them in the intoxication of their ferocious joy and strike them with death. My soul will tremble with joy at the sound of thy exploits. Carried on thy steps by the breath of the storm, I shall feel myself wielding again the strong lance and bathing it in the blood of the enemy."

This discourse uttered with a vehement voice easily opens the way to their soul; it penetrates and causes an emotion hitherto unknown. The sensation that they experience is impetuous and sudden; they do not doubt the veracity of Voluspa.[1] They believe her; all is accomplished. Sentiment is transformed into assent and admiration takes the place of esteem. The intellectual sphere is stirred for the first time, and imagination establishes its empire there.

Without taking time to reflect, the two warriors clasp hands. They swear to obey the *first* Herman, that Herman whose memory has been perpetuated from age to age as a model to heroes. They do not doubt at all that he exists still in the clouds. Neither the principle nor the mode nor the aim of this existence disturbs them. There they add

[1] Voluspa signifies one who sees the universality of things.

faith by an intuitive emotion which is already the first
of the reaction of their admiration for warlike valour, their
favourite passion.

With all haste they harangue their men-at-arms. They
inform them of the event that has just taken place. The
men are impressed; their enthusiasm is passed from one to
another. No one doubts that the first Herman may, though
invisible, be at the head of their battalions. They call him
their *Heröll*[1] and this name which remains consecrated to
him alone becomes their war-cry. They reach the camp of
the Africans. They find them in the attitude that the prophetess has indicated, awaiting the issue of the combat of
the two tribes to profit by it. The tribes precipitate themselves upon their enemies and massacre them. The hastiest
flight can scarcely save from death a small number who go
spreading terror afar.

Meanwhile the Celts return triumphant. At their head
was the same woman whose inspired voice had prepared their
triumph. In passing through the forest she is obliged by
fatigue to rest at the foot of an oak. After a few moments
the tree appears in the midst of a great calm to agitate its
mysterious foliage. Voluspa herself seized with an inexpressible excitement stands up crying that she feels the spirit
of Herman. They assemble about her, they listen. She
speaks with a force that impresses even the most savage
men. In spite of themselves they feel their knees give way;
they bow down with respect. A holy terror penetrates
them. They are religious for the first time. The prophetess
continues. The future unrolls itself before her eyes. She
sees the Celts, vanquishers of their enemies, usurping all the
kingdoms of the earth, dividing the riches, and trampling

---

[1] I have already said that this name with the guttural inflection became
that of *Hercules*. It is by the suppression of the first syllable that *Röll* or
Raoul results. By adding to it the word *land*, borrowed from the Atlanteans
to signify an extent of ground, is formed *Herolland*, *Orland*, or *Roland*, that is
to say the master of all the earth.

under foot these Black People of whom they had long been the slaves. "Go," she said at last, "valiant heroes, march to your glorious destinies, but forget not Herman, chief of men, and above all respect Teut-tad, the Sublime Father!"[1] Such was the first oracle pronounced among the Boreans and such was the first religious impression which they received. This oracle was pronounced by a woman beneath an oak in a forest and this tree became sacred to them and the forest served as their temple. From this moment women took a divine character in their eyes. This woman was the model of all the pythonesses and all the prophetesses which became known in the course of time in Europe as well as in Asia. At first they prophesied beneath the oaks, and it was this which rendered so famous the oaks of the forest of Dodona.

When the Celts had become masters of the world, and had acquired from the conquered nations the taste for arts and for magnificence, they raised for their pythonesses superb temples, where the symbolic tripod placed over an aperture, real or artificial, was substituted for the oak and caused it to be forgotten.

But long before this epoch the Borean tribes thought only of consecrating the place where the first oracle had been uttered. They raised an altar after the model of those which they had seen among the Atlanteans, and, placing above it a lance or a sword, dedicated it to the first Herman, under the name of Herman-Sayl.[2]

---

[1] I translate *Teut-tad* as *Sublime Father*, but it can also signify *infinite, universal Father*. The Greeks and Latins changed this name to that of *Teutates*. From the word *Teut-Æsk* which signifies the people of *Teut* the French have made *Tudesque;* of *Teut Sohn*, the son of Teut, *Teuton*. The Germans still call their country *Deutschland*, that is to say, the land of Teut.

[2] I have already explained this word; it signifies literally *the Pillar of Herman*.

CHAPTER XII

IN the first book I have made known the principal object of this work, and, taking Man at the moment of his appearance upon the stage of the world, still reduced to the most simple perceptions of instinct, a stranger to all kinds of civilization, I have brought him by the development of the principal faculties of his soul to the threshold of the social edifice, to that age which has been inappropriately called the Golden Age; after having destroyed this error and contested several false theories attached to it, I herewith continue my course.

Established in families, possessor of an articulate language, Man had reached a point where are found even in our day a great many of his fellow creatures. He did not yet know laws, government, or religion. I have been obliged to lead him to the consciousness of these important objects, and to show that only by their means could he become moral, powerful, and virtuous, make himself worthy of his high destinies, and attain the end for which he has been created. I have chosen for this the historical form so as to evade either dryness of citations or tediousness of abstract reasonings. I hope that the reader will pardon me this boldness. I beg him to believe, although he may take this beginning of history as an hypothesis, that it is really an hypothesis only in relation to details. It would not be at all difficult for me, if the case required, to prove the substance by a great number of authorities, and even to give the secular date for the principal events. But this would be quite useless for the object of this work.

First, I have presented the Will of Man, still feeble, struggling against itself, and afterwards, stronger, having to resist the power of Destiny. I have shown that the results of this struggle and this resistance have been the development of the two inferior spheres, the instinctive and the animistic, from which development depended a great number of his faculties.

I have attached to this same development the principle of political right, and I have shown that this principle which is *Property* is a need as inherent in man as that of possession, without which he could neither live nor propagate.

After having proved that property is a need, I have made clear that the inequality of strength, given by nature to satisfy this need by establishing a physical inequality among men, determines necessarily there the inequality of conditions, which constitutes a moral right and which passes legitimately from fathers to children.

Now from the political right, which is property, and from the moral right, which is the inequality of conditions, result the laws and diverse forms of diverse governments.

But, before distinguishing any of these forms by its constitutive principle, I have wished to arrive at the development of the intellectual sphere, so as to conduct man as far as the threshold of the temple of the Divinity. There I have stopped a moment; content with having sketched so vast a subject and having indicated in passing a multitude of things whose origin has been until now little known.

SECOND BOOK

The principal object of this book will be to describe the effects of the first disturbance given to the intellectual sphere, and to conduct Man as far as the entire development of his faculties.

CHAPTER I

THE providential event which manifested itself among
the Celts revealed to their meditations two great
truths—the immortality of the soul, and the existence of
God. The first of these truths took hold of them more
than the second. They understood well enough how the
invisible part of themselves which felt, became animated,
thought, and finally willed, could survive the destruction
of the body, since it could even watch while the body slept,
and could offer in its dreams pictures more or less filled with
sensations, passions, thoughts, and pleasures whose actual
effect no longer existed; but they could with difficulty comprehend the idea of a universal Being, Creator, and Preserver
of all beings. Their feeble intelligence had still need of
something perceptible upon which it might support itself.
The power of abstraction and of generalization was not
strong enough to sustain them at this metaphysical height.
It is not that they did not admit the name of *Sublime Father*
that Voluspa had given to this unknown Being for whom
she had commanded respect; but this very name of Father,
instead of raising them to Him, persuaded them rather to
make Him descend to them, in presenting this Being to them
only as the first Father of the Borean Race and the most
ancient of their ancestors. As to the first Herman he was

77

clearly revealed to them. They saw him such as memory had preserved in the traditions—terrible, indomitable in combat, their support, their counsel, their guide, and above all the implacable enemy of the Black People.

So that one can surmise, without fear of erring much, that the first worship of the Celts was that of the ancestors or rather that of the divine human Soul, such as it exists from time immemorial in China and among the greatest number of Tartar people. The Lamaic cult, whose antiquity yields only to Sabeanism, is the same cult as the ancestors perfected, as I will show further on.

The first effect of this worship, whose establishment was owing to the inspiration of a woman, was to change suddenly and completely the fate of women. As much as they were humiliated on account of their weakness, so much were they exalted on account of the new and marvellous faculty which was discovered in them; from the lowest place which they held in society, they passed all at once to the highest. They were declared law-makers; they were regarded as interpreters of heaven; their orders were received as oracles. Invested with supreme sacerdotal power, they exercised the first theocracy that may have existed among the Celts. A college of women was intrusted to regulate all in the cult and in the government.

This college, however, whose laws were all received as divine inspirations, was not long in perceiving that to make them understood and executed, it was necessary to have two coercive bodies possessing knowledge and power with the right of reward and punishment both moral and civil. The voice of Voluspa made itself understood, and the college named a sovereign pontiff on the one hand under the name of *Drud* or *Druid* and a king on the other, under the name of *Kanh, Kong,* or *King.*[1] These two supreme magistrates

---

[1] The word *Drud* signifies the radical instruction, the principle of science. It comes from the word *rad* or *rud*, which means a root. Thence the Latin *radix*, the English *root*, the Gallic *gredham*, etc. The word *kanh* expresses

regarded themselves justly as delegates of heaven, appointed to instruct and to govern men, and in consequence were entitled pontiff or king, by divine right. The *Drud* was the chief of the Diet in which he formed a sacerdotal body, and the *Kanh* established himself in a like manner at the head of the Leyts and the Folks or men-at-arms and labouring men among whom he chose officers who were to act in his name.

He was not, however, at first confused with the herman, who was always elected by his peers after the trial of combat, and carried upon a shield according to the ancient custom; but this military chief ceased to bear the name of *Herman*, in order to leave it wholly to the first divine Herman, and contented himself with the name of *Mayer*, that is to say, the strongest or the most valiant.[1]

It is well known that violent rivalries were raised in the course of time between the kanh and the mayer, or the king vested with civil power reigning by divine right and the mayor possessor of the military force and commanding the men-at-arms by right of election; often the king had united in him the two functions and more often still the mayor had deprived the king of his crown which he had placed upon his own head. But these details, which properly speaking belong to history, do not belong to my subject. I shall be content to reveal the origins later so as to draw inductions relative to the important matter with which I am occupied.

---

the moral power. It belongs to the root *anh*, which develops the sense of breath, of spirit, of soul; thence in Teutonic *konnen* and in English *can*.

[1] The word *mayer* comes from *mah* or *moh*, motive force. They say in English *may*, in German *mühe*. In French the word is changed from *Mayer* to that of *Maire*.

Thus by the word *Drud* the Celts understood a radical *Principle*, a guiding Power, upon which depend all other powers. They attached to the word *Kanh* the idea of moral force and to the word *Mayer* that of physical force. The *Drud* was then among them the head of the religious doctrine; the *Kanh* the civil legislator, the high judiciary, and the *Mayer* the military chief.

CHAPTER II

SIXTH REVOLUTION—POLITICAL AND RELIGIOUS SCHISM—
ORIGIN OF THE CELTS, BEDOUINS OR NOMADS,
AND THE AMAZONS

LET us retrace our steps for a moment. We have seen
that, after the development of his instinct, Man lived
in absolute anarchy; he had not even that sort of instinctive
government that is observed in several species of animals,
and this for the very reason I have shown when speaking of
marriage. Nothing was made in advance with him, although everything was determined there in principle. Providence, whose work he was, willed that he should develop
himself freely and that nothing should be forced in him.

This absolute anarchy ceased as soon as he had reflected
upon his condition, and as soon as his marriage, the result
of this reflection, had constituted a family. Several families, drawing together, formed a sort of domestic government of which the feminine will usurped little by little the
exclusive dominion. We have seen how Destiny broke
this unnatural government by the sudden opposition of the
Will of Man. Woman, until this time mistress, became slave;
all the burden of society fell upon her; a sort of masculine
tyranny took place. The people obeying were composed
of mothers and daughters; the people commanding, the
heads of families, of which each was a despot in his own
hut. It was a kingdom of the instinctive force alone.

An event which Providence and Destiny brought about jointly in opposing the animistic force to the instinctive modified this state of things. The Borean Race, suddenly attacked by a powerful and warlike race, was obliged to search outside of instinct a means of resistance; their animistic faculties keenly excited by danger were developed; the necessity of self-defence together with that of procuring food suggested the happy idea of dividing themselves into two classes: the one destined to fight and the other to work; the strongest were chosen to guide the combatants and the wisest to watch the labourers. Special chiefs were created, all dependent on a general chief; a Diet was established. This was a military government where the principles of feudalism were found united to those of imperial rule.

At first, the Will acted in the instinct, afterward it operated in the understanding, now it is about to be placed in the intelligence. But the same danger which had already presented itself at the epoch of the development of the instinct presents itself anew under other forms and menaces the social structure with an even greater disturbance.

As it is by woman that the movement has begun, is it not to be feared that, drawn on by her character, seduced by interest or by vanity, she only seeks to turn to her sole profit an event which Providence has destined for the general advancement of the race? Heaven has spoken through her voice, but is it true that it will always? And when it no longer speaks will she not make it speak? Although these considerations did not generally strike the minds of the Celts, they were sufficiently valued by some among them to raise great difficulties. All had not been witnesses to the first movement of Voluspa; the greater number had not heard her oracle; many refused to believe it; those who did judged it extraordinary that any one could doubt a thing which they had affirmed as truth. None of these knew that this effect is produced from the essence of providential events. They had wondered at a thing which

6

constitutes the most excellent concomitant of Man; if Providence had drawn him into an irresistible movement, it would not differ from Destiny and the same necessity would direct them equally. The Will of Man, forced in all directions, would have no other choice to make, and its actions, indifferent in respect to him, would be susceptible neither to praise nor censure. The mental liberty that an event allows proves whether it is providential or not. The more it is elevated the more it is free; the more it is forced, the more it inclines toward the fatality of Destiny.

The mental liberty, inherent in providential events, was felt here for the first time and felt with force. The Celts saw with astonishment, perhaps, but they saw at last that it was possible that they should not think the same thing on the same matters. Whereas the greater number of tribes received with respect the order of the feminine college and submitted without any resistance to the sovereign pontiff and to the king that it had nominated; whereas the sacerdotal teachings and the civil and military government spread in their midst and threw out deep roots; whereas at last the oracles of Voluspa were received there as sacred laws, there were other tribes that, holding with obstinacy to their ancient forms, rejected all innovations. That which shocked them the most, and to which it seemed that the feminine college held with utmost force, on account perhaps of a little private interest which began to mingle with the general interest, was the fixing of abodes and the circumscription of families; and this tended to establish territorial property, which up to that time had been unknown. This innovation was apparent pretext for the schism which occurred; it was violent; both sides came to blows; but as the dissenters were a very weak majority in comparison to those who directly wished the innovations or who received them without debate, they saw themselves obliged to submit or to retire. They preferred this last expedient, and marching ever onward from the north to the south of Europe they arrived on the shores of that sea which has since been aptly called the *Black Sea*, although this name belonged formerly to all the extent of waters in general which bathed the south of Europe, on account of the Black People who possessed it; as by a contrary reason, that part of the ocean which surrounds Europe and Asia on the side of the Boreal pole is called the *White Sea*.

Having come to the shores of this interior sea, the dissenting Celts skirted it to the east and penetrated to that part of Asia which bears the name of Asia Minor. The weak colonies which the Sudeens had pushed thus far were easily overthrown. The conquerors encouraged by the first success advanced rapidly, increasing their spoils and the number of their slaves, and soon it was rumoured that a deluge of Scythians was inundating the septentrional countries of Asia. The efforts made to arrest the torrent only tended to increase its impetuosity, and gave further opportunity for depredations. The Celts finding it impossible to retreat were obliged to advance or perish. They advanced.

Owing to the reasons which had forced them to abandon their fatherland they were given the name of *Bodohnes*,[1] that is to say, without fixed habitations, and this name, which exists still in that of the Bedouins, has been famous. After many vicissitudes, upon which it is altogether useless for me to dwell, these Bodohnes Celts, having become masters of the borders of the Euphrates so celebrated later, conquered Arabia, where the greater part finally settled, after having assumed many of the customs and habits of the people whom they had subjugated, and having adopted

---

[1] It is remarkable that this name, Celtic and Phœnician alike, is still perfectly intelligible in German and Hebrew. The Celtic root *bod* or *bed* signifies properly a bed, and the same Phœnician root *beth* or *beyth* signifies a habitation. The root *ohn*, preserved in German, and *ain* or *oin*, which is found in Hebrew, expresses an absence, a negation. The French verb *habiter* is derived from the first root, *bed* or *beyth*, as is the Saxon *abidan* and the English to *abide*, *abode*, etc.

their laws and their cults. The Arabs issued from this fusion of Borean and Sudeen blood. All the cosmogonies where woman is presented as the cause of evil and the fecund source of all the misfortunes which have afflicted the earth have come from there. Even in the time of Mohammed, woman was considered as impure by the people of Yemen who, as their prophet reproaches them for it in the Koran, wept at the birth of daughters and often buried them alive.

I do not wish to leave these Celtic dissenters, whose lot became afterward so brilliant, since it was from them that the Assyrians and Arabs had their origin, without relating a fact whose singularity has greatly embarrassed the savants of all ages. This fact is relative to the Amazons. I shall guard against details of endless controversies caused by the existence of this people of warrior-women. All that has been said either or or against proves that such a people has indeed existed; at first in Asia near Thermodon and afterwards in some of the islands of the Mediterranean and even in Europe. The Hindus who have preserved a memory of them call the country of the Amazons *Stri-radjya* and place them near the mountains of Coulas on the borders of the sea. Zoroaster said in the *Boun-dehesh* that they inhabited the city of Salem. Pausanias speaks of their invasion of Greece and of their fighting to the very walls of Athens. Apollonius relates in his *Argonauts* that they dwelt in the island of Lemnos and on the mainland near Cape Themiscure. What appears most probable is that these extraordinary women first existed in Asia Minor. No doubt some hordes of Bodohnes, having advanced without precaution, fell into an ambuscade where the men were cut to pieces. The women having had time to seek a shelter, whether on the other side of a river or on some island, seeing themselves stronger, thanks to this event, resolved to profit by it and seize the dominion. Among them probably was a woman of firm and decided character, who inspired them with the plan and placed herself at their head. According

to tradition they massacred the old men who had remained
with them and even some men who had escaped from the
enemy. However that may be, it appears certain that
they formed a monarchical government which was maintained for a considerable time, since the names of several of
their queens have come down to us. The historians are
not agreed upon the manner by which they admitted men
among them; all that can be inferred as true is that they
reduced to slavery those whom they made prisoners and
that they gave to those who were born of their transient
union an education conforming to their views.

Moreover the name of the Amazons, under which
antiquity has made us know these warrior-women, proves
at the same time their Celtic origin and their abode in
Asia by its composition.[1] It signifies properly those who
have no males or husbands.

One feels indeed, without weighing the subject further,
that if such women existed, it must have been excessive misfortune that changed their nature and drove them to this
act o despair. Now, in the position that I have represented
the women of the Bodohnes Celts, their misfortune must
have been excessive since it was the result of a schism both
political and religious. Their husbands, unheedful of the
voice of Providence which called them to gentler manners
by laying without reason a heavy arm of iron upon a sex
already too much punished for its faults, del vered to Destiny
the germs of calamity, which could not fail to produce fatal
fruits, as soon as occasion favoured the development.

---

[1] This word is composed of the root *mâs* preserved purely in Latin and
recognizable in the old French *masle*, in the Italian *maschio*, in the Irish *moth*,
etc.; this root joined to the negation *ohne* constitutes the word *mâs-ohne*,
to which adding the Phœnician article *ha*, in *ha-mâs-ohne*, offers exactly the
sense I have indicated.

CHAPTER III

FIRST GEOGRAPHICAL DIVISION OF EUROPE

WHILE these events were occurring in Asia, the Celts having remained in Europe continued to follow there the movement impressed by Providence. A royal and theocratic government was established and promised the most favourable results. Already a considerable number of Druids instructed by the care of the sovereign pontiff, called *Drud*, spread in all directions and added to the two classes already existing among the Boreans, a class eminently useful since it tended to maintain harmony between the two others in preventing oppression on the one side and revolt on the other. This class composed of men called *Lœhr*, that is to say, the enlightened ones or the savants, has become among us today the clergy. Even more anciently, at the time when theocracy dominated Europe, and in the absence even of royalty, the theocratic sovereigns, whose principal seats were in Thrace, in Etruria, and in the Britannic isles, took the title of *Lar*.[1]

Thus the Borean Race was divided into three classes, and what is worthy of the greatest attention is that each class represented one of the three constitutive spheres of Man and followed its development, so that the sphere of *Folk* or labouring men was analogous to the instinctive

---

[1] The Greek word κλῆρος which makes destiny out of anything whatever; among the Latins *lares* and in modern English, *lords*.

sphere, that of *Leyt* or men-at-arms, to the animistic, and that of *Lœhr* or enlightened men, to the intellectual. This progress although disturbed by occasional shocks was admirable till then.

As the whole of the Celtic nation tended to settle itself, the division of lands had to be considered, but, before coming to the decisive point, it was necessary first to understand and to establish boundaries. From the providential event which I have related, war was rekindled more actively than ever between the White and the Black races. The Celts, penetrated with a religious and warlike enthusiasm, showed prodigious valour. The Atlanteans, pressed on all sides, could no longer hold the field against them. Time had effaced the differences which had previously existed. Arms had become nearly equal, and the Celts, now instructed in military tactics, found in their physical force an advantage more and more noticeable. All the interior of the country was already swept. The Sudeens, relegated to the meridional extremities of Europe on the shores of the sea, could only maintain themselves under cover of their fortified cities which the Celts were incapable of besieging and which, furthermore, a powerful marine force rendered impregnable to famine.

The possession of Europe was thus assured to them with the exception of the meridional coasts; the Druids divided the interior into three great regions. The central region was called *Teuts-land*, that is to say, the land elevated, sublime, or the land of the *Teut ;* that of the Occident received the name of *Hôl-land* or *Ghôl-land*, the land inferior; that of the Orient took that of *Pôl-land*, the land superior. The countries placed to the north of these three regions were called *D'ahn-mark*, the limit of souls, and those of the south, still occupied by the Atlanteans from the Tanaïs to the Pillars of Hercules, were known under the generic name of *d'Asks-tan*, the dwelling of the *Asks* or Black Peoples.[1]

[1] The word *ask* sometimes written with a *c*, sometimes with a *q*, sometimes varying the vowel, is found in a multitude of names of peoples in these lati-

This geographical division, although altered by a multitude of subdivisions, has survived all the political and religious revolutions, and is still recognized in our day in its principal points.   As to the immense countries which extended beyond the Borysthenes, regarded as the limit of the Borean Empire, [1] as its name indicates sufficiently, it was believed to be absolutely deprived of people, and to be inhabited only by savage animals among which the horse was the most esteemed. It was also on account of this warlike animal that the name of *Rossland*, the land of horses, was given to these countries. [2]

In believing the countries situated beyond the Borysthenes and the Duna entirely uninhabited, the Celts were greatly deceived. This erroneous opinion showed only that they had lost sight of the place of their origin and that they no longer remembered that they were themselves descended from these glacial regions. Whereas they had made enormous steps in civilization and whereas ready to march to the conquest of the world, they already constituted a numerous and powerful nation; unknown tribes hardly passed over the first limits of the social state had formed in silence, increased in number, and awaited only a favourable moment in order to descend in their turn from the boreal heights and enter a milder climate to demand from them a share of it.

---

tudes, the *Thraskes, Osques, Esques, Tosques* or *Toscans, Etrusques, Baskes* or *Wasques,* or *Vascons* or *Gascons*, etc. I have written at length my ideas on all these people in my *Grammaire de la Langue d'Oc.* By *Traskes* we understand Oriental Asks, by *Tosques* meridional Asks, and by *Vasques* Occidental Asks. The name *Pelasges* or *Pelasks* designated the Black People in general and the seafaring ones in particular. The name *d'Asks-tan* is preserved in those of Oscitania and Aquitania.

[1] The name of this river is composed of the words *Bors-stein*, the limit of Bor.

[2] The word *Ross* signifies still a *horse* in German, the French word *rosse* is a corruption.

CHAPTER IV

CONCERNING THE FIRST DIVISION OF LANDS AND TERRITORIAL PROPERTY

IN the meantime, the Druids, always obedient to the oracles of Voluspa and subject to the decrees of the Sacred College, continued their division. They gave to the men-at-arms general property of a vast extent of land, and to the labouring men private property of a small extent within the greater. So what was possessed by ten or a hundred families of *Folk* belonged as a whole to a family of the *Leyt* who, without being obliged to till the soil or to be occupied in any other calling than that of men-at-arms, enjoyed a certain part of the revenues, labour, and industries of the small landowners charged with turning to account the great estate.

As several small estates formed a great one, several great ones formed a greater, and these, being united, constituted another still greater, so that, if the first man-at-arms who ruled over certain labouring men assumed the title of baron, the second took that of great baron, and the third that of very great baron.

The king had dominion over all the barons, and enjoyed the honorary right of the universal estate; that is to say, that all the lands were reputed to belong to him and the great and small landowners recognized that their respective rights depended upon him. All unoccupied lands belonged to him; he gave them to new families, according as they were formed, and likewise he disposed of domains vacant through the extinction of old families. Besides that, he possessed as his own a very extended domain whose revenues were set apart for the crown.

It appears that, in the beginning of this legislation, the Druids had no other estates than those of the sanctuaries where they dwelt with their wives and children. Their principal revenue consisted in a sort of tithe levied upon all the wealth of the State, but the gifts which they received in the course of time made them proprietors of a great quantity of lands attached to these same sanctuaries, and put into their hands immense treasures.

After this rapid sketch, it can be seen that the territorial landowners were at first of a triple nature, as it were, instinctive, animistic, and intellectual. Those who imagine that it sufficed for a man first to enclose a space of land and then to say "*this is mine*," in order to possess it, commit the greatest blunder. The real possession of man, his instinctive possession, does not go beyond his efforts. The earth belongs to all or it belongs to no one. A providential concession is necessary to assure the ownership of property, and this concession can only be the effect of a theocratic legislation. Providence does not manifest itself immediately and does not come in person to dictate its laws to man; it has always need of a human organ to make its wishes understood. It is only when this organ is found that theocratic legislation commences.

This legislation, as I have said, had begun among the Celts at the epoch determined for this. It had added to force the only power which then existed: two other powers destined to serve as a mutual support—the civil law and the religious law. The military chief who up to that time had been in the first rank had to yield his place to two new chiefs appointed to be his superiors—the king and the sovereign pontiff. The king, by the sole fact of his coronation, had been declared the temporal representative of Providence, and consequently the universal proprietor of the earth. He could then, as universal proprietor, create general proprietors, and these general proprietors could in their turn establish particular proprietors. This was precisely what was done. But as Providence, represented temporarily by the king, preserved nevertheless its spiritual action, with which the sovereign pontiff was invested, it followed that the king owed homage for his universal property to this sovereign pontiff through whom his right had been promulgated, and the latter justly claimed for himself, as well as for the sacerdotal body, a legal portion of all the products.

If one will give attention to the laws, and above all to the customs which are attached to the right of territorial property, notwithstanding the infinite number of revolutions of which Europe has been the theatre, it will be seen that they all tend to prove what I advance, to wit—that this right has been originally only a concession.

What I say here regarding territorial property must not, however, be confused with what I have said elsewhere of industrial property. These two ownerships do not at all resemble each other by right. Industrial ownership constitutes a natural right inherent in man, a need from which the social state draws its principle; whereas the territorial ownership is based on the contrary, upon an unnatural concession, foreign to man, which did not take place until a long time after the social state was constituted. There is no need of any law, as I have said, to establish the right of industrial ownership, because each feels instinctively that the product of man's work belongs to him just as does his body; but it is only in consequence of a law, and of a strong one, that the right of territorial property can be admitted; because instinct rejects the existence of such a right, and it would never take place if the intelligence in which it has its principle had not sanctioned it. Thus, one sees impassioned men, whose will is placed in the instinct, violently objecting to the exclusive possession of lands, and ever demanding why a great portion of the people is disinherited. The only answer to make to these men is: because Providence has willed it. Now without presuming audaciously to interpret the ways of Providence, the motives of such a will can be easily explained. These motives are evidently to give to the social edifice an elevation and a splendour which otherwise it might never have obtained.

CHAPTER V

ORIGIN OF MUSIC AND POETRY—INVENTION OF OTHER SCIENCES

ABOUT this epoch, and perhaps a little earlier, several things came to pass which influenced in a perceptible manner the civilization of the Celts.

The Druids, in listening to the oracles of Voluspa, perceived that these oracles were always contained in measured phrases of regular form, drawing with them a certain harmony which varied according to the subject so that the tone with which the prophetess pronounced her sentences differed much from the ordinary language. They examined attentively this singularity, and, after becoming accustomed to imitate the diverse intonations which they heard, they succeeded in reproducing them, and saw that they were harmoniously adjusted according to fixed rules. These rules, reduced to a system by dint of hard work, gave them the principles of two of the most beautiful conceptions with which men have been able to honour themselves—music and poetry. Such was the origin of melody and rhythm.

Until then, the Celts had been little affected by music. That of the Atlanteans, which they had heard in combats or in ceremonies, seemed to them only noise more or less loud, shrill, or low. Seeking to outstrip their enemies they had duly invented instruments warlike and monotonous, such as drums, the cymbal, the horn, and the *bucine,* by means of

which they indeed filled the air with noises or formidable
sounds but without any melody.   It was not until their
priests had received from Voluspa the principles of musical
and poetical harmony that they began to find any charm in
it.   The flute, whose inventor was a favoured genius, caused
a revolution in the ideas.   They saw with inexpressible
rapture that they could follow with this instrument the
voice of Voluspa and, as it were, recall her words by the
sole repetition of the sounds which she had attached to them.
The repetition of these sounds constituted the poetic rhythm.
This rhythm, presented to the nation as a gift from heaven,
was received by it with an enthusiasm difficult to express.
It was learned by heart, chanted on all occasions, inculcated
at an early age in the minds of the children; so that in a very
short time it became instinctive, and by means of it one was
able to spread with the greatest facility the text of all the
oracles or all the laws which Voluspa always uttered in the
same measure.   Such was the reason for which in antiquity,
music and poetry were never separated and were likewise
called the language of the gods.

Notwithstanding the pleasure that I would take in ex-
patiating upon subjects so pleasing, and towards which my
particular tastes have often drawn me, I can here merely
touch upon them lest I retard too much my progress; and,
moreover, I have in other works written at greater length
upon them.[1]

The invention of music and poetry in electrifying the
minds gave rise to observations, researches, and meditations
whose results were most useful.   For the first time this
brilliant phenomenon of speech, to which as yet no attention
had been given, was examined.   The Druids, whom Voluspa
had made musicians and poets, became grammarians.
They examined the language which they spoke, and dis-

---

[1] Principally in my *Examens sur les Vers dorés de Pythagore* succeeding my
Discours sur l'Essence et la forme de la Poésie, in my *Considérations sur le
Rhyme*, and finally in my work on *La Musique*.

covered with surprise that it was supported by fixed principles. They distinguished the substantive from the verb and found the relation of number and gender. Drawn on by the spirit of their cult, they pronounced the feminine gender the first, and thus they stamped the Borean language with an indelible character, a character entirely opposed to that of the Sudeen language. Having to design, for example, objects whose gender exists only in forms of language, they applied the feminine or masculine gender in a manner opposed to the unvarying opinion of the Kingdom of Man, attributing feminine gender to the sun and masculine to the moon, thus placing themselves in contradiction with the nature of things.[1]

This mistake, which was one of the first where the animistic vanity of the woman involved the spirit of the prophetess, was unfortunately neither the last nor the greatest. I shall mention presently the most terrible of all, the one which again nearly ruined the entire race. I wish beforehand to say a word upon the invention of writing which coincided with that of grammar.

The Celts, as I have said, had acquired by association with the Atlanteans a vague knowledge of writing, but their mind, not well developed, had not felt all the usefulness of so admirable an art and was but slightly concerned with it. It was only when the Druids came to reflect upon their original tongue that they felt the necessity of fixing by writing its fluctuating forms. The greatest difficulty in this art is the conception of the first idea; once this idea is conceived and the metaphysical object grasped by the mind, the rest has nothing perplexing.

It would be presumption to say at this time, that the first

---

[1] This contradiction has disappeared in a great many of the Celtic dialects, on account of the ascendancy of the Atlantean dialects with which they are mingled, but in the centre of Europe the German dialect has preserved this singularity. In this dialect the sun, *die Sonne;* air, *die Luft;* time, *die Zeit;* love, *die Liebe,* etc., are of feminine gender, and the moon, *der Mond;* death *der Tod;* water, *das Wasser;* life, *das Leben,* etc., are of masculine or neuter.

inventor of literary characters had only copied something
that he had been able to distinguish from those of the
Atlanteans, or that the forms which he gave to the sixteen
letters of his alphabet were absolutely his own work; what is
certain is that these sixteen letters took, under his hand, a
direction absolutely opposed to that which the Sudeen
characters followed; that is, whereas among the Atlanteans
the writer traced his characters on a horizontal line going
from right to left, among the Celts he placed them adversely,
proceeding from left to right. This notable difference, for
which no one as far as I know has ever given the cause,
depended upon what I am about to relate.

At the very remote epoch when the Atlantean characters
were invented, the Sudeen Race, still near to its beginning,
inhabited Africa beyond the equator towards the South pole;
so that the observer having turned towards the sun, seeing
it rise at the right and set at the left, naturally followed its
course in the movement of his writing. But what was
natural in this position, which might even be considered as
sacred by peoples worshippers of the sun, ceased to be so on
the opposite side of the globe for septentrional peoples
placed very far from the tropics. Among these peoples, the
observer turned towards the sun saw it, on the contrary,
rise at the left and set at the right, so that in starting from
the same principle which had directed the Sudeen writer,
the Celt, in following the course of the sun, must naturally
trace a line of opposite direction and give to his writing the
movement from left to right.

The knowledge of this cause, so simple in appearance,
gives to the observer an historical key which will be of
great use to him, for any time he sees any writing following the direction from right to left, as that of the
Phœnicians, Hebrews, Arabs, Etruscans, etc., he can attribute the origin to the Sudeen Race, and, on the contrary,
when he sees this writing follow the opposite direction
from left to right, as the Runic, the Armenian, Tibetan,

Sanscrit, etc., he will not be mistaken in considering the origin Borean.

The Celts distinguished their alphabetical characters by the epithet *runic*, and this word convinces me that they imitated Atlantean characters. For this reason: the Atlanteans had two kinds of writings, the one hieroglyphic and the other cursive, as is sufficiently proved by the testimony of Egypt, the last place on the earth where their power had flung its final splendour. Now the word *runic* signifies in a great number of dialects, *cursive*,[1] so that it can be conjectured that the runic characters were only the cursive characters of the Atlanteans, slightly altered in their form and turned the opposite way.

This opinion receives, besides, a great degree of probability by the striking resemblance between the cursive Phœnician characters and the runic, or cursive, characters of the Etruscans and the Celts.

But, even before poetry and music, grammar and writing were invented, the mathematical sciences had made some progress. Numeration had no need for the development of the intelligence to give the first elements to arithmetic, and one cannot but believe that the division which was made of the territorial possessions soon furnished them with practical geometry, as the needs of agriculture led to those of astronomy.

These sciences, no doubt, were still far from their perfection, but it sufficed that they had begun to be cult vated, in order that the aim of Providence might be fulfilled. I have frequently said that Providence gives only the principles of things. It is to the Will of Man that culture belongs, under the influence of Destiny.

---

[1] The Celtic root *ran* or *run* develops the idea of course and of flight as I have already shown. The word *runig* or *runik* expresses then the disposition to run.

CHAPTER VI

DEVIATION OF THE CULT: THE CAUSE OF IT—SUPERSTITION AND FANATICISM: THEIR ORIGIN

IF the principles given by Providence had continued to be developed w.th the same rectitude, the Borean Race, having rapidly attained the culminating point of the social edifice, would have offered a spectacle worthy of admiration. Europe, which it had made illustrious early, would not have been the victim of so many vicissitudes, and, without having need of becoming the slave of Asia during so long a train of centuries, would have held much sooner the sceptre of the world. But Destiny, which determined a series of events wholly opposed, would have demanded a Will as pure as it was strong, to prevent this realization or to resist their efforts, and this Will not only does not exist, but the one which existed, instead of following the movement with which Providence had impressed it, resisted it, wished to make itself the centre, to be its own motor, and, far from evading Destiny, allowed itself to be dominated by it and to bend beneath its law.

A single passion badly governed caused all the evil. It was vanity which, being exalted in the bosom of Voluspa in particular, and in all women generally, brought forth egotism whose cold inspirations instead of extending the intellectual sphere restrained it and produced in the soul an ambition devoid of love of glory.

In the different countries occupied by the Celts, several colleges for women were established, at the head of each of which was a Druidess who was under the orders of Voluspa only; these Druidesses presided over the cult and uttered the oracles; they were consulted in special affairs, as Voluspa was consulted in general affairs. At first, their authority was widely extended; the Druids did nothing without taking their advice, and even the kings obeyed their orders; in proportion as the sacerdotal class became enlightened, in proportion as sciences and arts began to flourish, the Druidesses perceived that their influence diminished, that authority was leaving them, and that they were revered less for themselves than for the Divinity whose instruments they were.

It was evident that Man, astonished by the magnitude of the movement which had taken place, recovered imperceptibly from his astonishment and endeavoured to regain his real place which this movement had caused him to lose. The same thing which had happened on the occasion of the first development of the instinctive sphere happened in other respects. It was a question, then as before, of knowing which of the two sexes would be the master.

If woman had been wise, she would have consented to let herself be considered the instrument of the Divinity, the means of communication between the Divinity and Man. This position was assuredly glorious enough to satisfy her vanity. Her vanity was not, however, satisfied, because the awakened egotism persuaded her that there was nothing in this for her. When she spoke, was it she whom they heard? No; it was the Divinity who spoke through her voice. When she was silent, what authority had she? None; it was the Druid, it was the king, it was the mayor who commanded. Was she to conceal herself in her insignificant rôle? Was it sufficient for her ambition? Did not her faculties call her to highest destinies? Her faculties! Ah! who could appreciate them better than she? Did not all that had happened depend on her? The Divinity was sought in the heavens because her voice had placed it there. Oracles were demanded of her because her intelligence had conceived them. If the future had been penetrated, was it not the force of her will that had realized the visions of her imagination? Would it not be possible that the future should depend on her, even as the existence of the Divinity had depended on her?

Hardly is this impious idea conceived than Providence, dismayed, withdraws, and Destiny takes its place. Voluspa is no longer the organ of Divinity, she is a prophetic instrument of whom Destiny will dispose. Henceforth it is in vain that you will search for the real future of any verb in the language she will use. The verb in her tongue will be deprived of a future.[1]

The necessity of Destiny alone will bring forth the future in developing the consequences of the past.

Thus woman, no longer able to reign by truth, and wishing to preserve absolutely her sway, sought to rule by error. All the oracles which proceeded from the sanctuaries were equivocal and mysterious; one heard only of calamities, of sins committed, of expiations demanded, of penances to be done. The supreme Divinity, *Teutad*, formerly represented by the beautiful image of a father, appeared only in the austere traits of a tyrant. The first Herman having become the God of War under the name of *Thor*[2] was no longer their protecting ancestor, always occupied with the welfare of the nation; this was a god terrible and severe, who gave to himself the most formidable titles; he was named the Father of Carnage, the Depopulator, the Incendiary, the Exterminator. His spouse Friga or Freya, *dame par excellence*, who, quite as cruel as her husband, designated in advance those

---

[1] The Celtic languages, which have not felt the mixing of the Atlantean tongues, such as the Saxon, the German, the English, etc., have not the simple future.

[2] The word *thor* which signifies properly a bull was the emblem of strength. The bull was later the emblem of the Celts as I will relate.

who were to be killed in combat and, in bizarre contrast, held in one hand the cup of voluptuousness, in the other the sword dedicated to death.

A frightful superstition succeeded the simple cult which had been followed until then; religion became intolerant and savage, all the passions which agitated the soul of Voluspa inflamed the souls of the ancestors; they became like her jealous, greedy, and suspicious, and the innocent sacrifices, which one had been accustomed to make to them, could no longer content them. Animals were sacrificed, libations of milk were replaced by libations of blood, and, as it became necessary to establish a difference between the special ancestors and those of the nation, they were led to sacrifice to Teutad, to Thor, to Freya human victims, believing that the purest and noblest blood would be to them the most precious.[1]

And one must not imagine that these victims were taken from among the captives or among the slaves, no; the most noble heads were often the most menaced. The Druidesses, inspired by Voluspa, succeeded in filling the minds with such religious furor that those were regarded as favoured of the gods whom fate designated to be buried alive, or to shed their blood at the foot of the altars. The victims themselves congratulated each other when they were chosen. No one was excepted; blindness reached the point where it was regarded as the most favourable sign when the king himself was called to this honour and, without respect for his rank,

---

[1] From the name *Thor*, the God of War, are derived the words *terror* and *terrible*. The words *fright*, *frightful*, *fear*, attach themselves likewise to the impression made by the cult of Freya. One says still in Saxon *frihtan*, in Danish *freyeter*, in English, *frighten*. And what is strange is that from the same Goddess Friga or Freya the word *frigan* to *make love* is derived; in *Langue d'Oc*, *fringer* and in French, *fringuer*. Hence also the words *frai* and *frayer* in speaking of fish. This singular contrast gives rise to the thought that according to the doctrine of the Celts, this goddess was conceived under a double nature; sometimes presiding at love and birth under the name of Friga, and sometimes over war and death under the name of Freya. I will return later to this contrast upon which no one has commented sufficiently.

he was sacrificed in the midst of applause and shouts of joy of all the nation.

The fêtes, where these atrocious sacrifices were offered, were often repeated; every nine months a fête was celebrated, during which nine victims a day were sacrificed for nine consecutive days.   On the slightest occasion the Druidesses demanded a messenger to go to visit the ancestors and carry to them news of their descendants.   Sometimes the unfortunate was thrown headlong upon the lance of *Herman-Sayl;* sometimes crushed between two stones; sometimes drowned in a whirlpool; more often they caused his blood to spurt forth, drawing a more or less favourable sign by the more or less impetuosity with which it spurted.   But it was when the fear of an imminent evil agitated the minds that superstition displayed what was most horrible.   If I should relate the many instances which come to my mind, I would never finish.   Here an army sacrifices its general; there, a general decimates his officers.   I see a sexagenarian monarch who is burned in honour of Teutad; I hear the cries of the nine children of Haquin, whose throats were cut upon the altar of Thor; it is for Freya that these deep pits are dug where the victims who are her devotees are buried alive.

Wherever I glance in Europe I see traces of these hideous sacrifices.   From the glacial shores of Sweden and of Iceland to the fertile shores of Sicily, and from the Borysthenes to the Tagus, I see everywhere human blood smoking about the altars.   Europe does not suffer alone from this destructive scourge; the calamitous epidemic crosses the borders with the Celts and their trail infects the opposite shores of Africa and Asia.   It comes even from Iceland and carries its venom into the other hemisphere.   Yes, it is from Iceland that Mexico has received this abominable practice.   In whatever place one sees it established, in the North or the South, in the Orient or the Occident, its origin can without doubt be traced to Europe; it originated in the sombre horror of its forests; its beginning has been, as I have said, wounded vanity and weakness which wished to command. This weakness was often punished by its own faults; often the sword which the women held suspended over a sex which they knew how to govern only by terror fell upon their own breasts. Without speaking here of the young virgins who were buried alive or were thrown into the rivers in honour of Freya, one must not forget that the wives of kings and princes of the State were forced by superstitious opinions, which they had created themselves, to follow their husbands to the tomb by strangling themselves at the funerals or by throwing themselves upon the flames of the funeral pyre. This barbarous custom, which exists still in certain places in Asia, was brought there by the Celtic conquerors.

CHAPTER VII

SEVENTH REVOLUTION IN THE SOCIAL STATE—ESTABLISHMENT OF THEOCRACY

THE ferocious and superstitious cult to which a fatal deviation from the providential laws had subjected the Celts, the terror which was the natural consequence of it, and that habit of always feeling death hovering over their heads made them inaccessible to pity. Intolerant by system and valorous by instinct, they dealt death with the same facility as they received it. War was their element; it was only in the midst of battles and whilst fatigue overpowered their bodies that their spirit, assailed on all sides by phantoms, found a sort of repose. In whatever place victory guided their steps, devastation followed them. Implacable enemies of other religions, they destroyed the symbols, overthrew the temples, broke the statues, and, often, on the point of going to a decisive battle, they made a vow to exterminate all men and all animals which might fall into their hands; and this they did in a forbidden manner, even as the Hebrews did a long time after. They believed thus to honour the terrible Thor, the most valiant of their ancestors, and did not imagine that there were other means for Teutad himself to show his force and power than carnage and destruction. The sole virtue for them was valour; the sole vice, cowardice. They named the infernal region *Nifel-*

heim,[1] the sojourn of cowards. Convinced that war was the source of glory in this world and that of salvation in the next, they regarded it as an act of justice, and thought that the strength that gives the incontestable right over the weak established the obvious mark of Divinity. When they were unfortunately vanquished, they received death with a savage intrepidity and forced themselves to laugh, when dying even in the midst of agony.

They had already had more than one occasion to exercise their favourite passion. The Atlanteans, being attacked in the very heart of their cities, had been vanquished on all sides. The coasts of the Mediterranean ravaged from the shores of the Black Sea to the ocean belonged to the Celts. The few remaining Sudeens had been reduced to slavery. Masters of many ports, the conquerors were not long in creating a sort of navy, with which, gaining without trouble the opposite coasts of Africa, they had settled colonies there. Conducted by one of their mayors, whose great valour had given him the name of Heröll, they overran Spain, and even pillaging and devastating the settlements of the Atlanteans, came as far as the famous strait, since called the Pillars of Hercules. I think I am quite right in advancing the opinion that it was on account of this event that this strait was thus named, for as I have already observed, the name of Hercules does not differ from that of Heröll. There is elsewhere preserved an ancient tradition on this subject. The surname of this Hercules of Celtic origin was *Ogmi;* now the word *Ogmi* signifies the great power or the grand army.[2]

Thus, the Celts, possessing entire Europe at this epoch, pushed their hordes as far as Africa, menaced the Temple of

[1] The word *nifel* expresses the snorting of horses when they are frightened. The French verb *renifler* is derived from it. In the *Langue d'Oc* today is *niflar*, to blow with the nose, and, figuratively, to bleed from the nose.

[2] This word composed of two others should be written *Hug müh;* the first *huge* preserved in English means very vast; it has served for the Latin *augere*, for the French *augmenter;* the second, *müh*, preserved in German, is analogous to the English *may*, whence comes *mayer*, a powerful one, a *mayor.*

Ammon, and caused Egypt to tremble. It was to be feared that this savage power would conquer the world; and indeed it would have, had it made itself mistress of this ancient realm whose foundation, according to Herodotus, goes back at least twelve thousand years before our era. This event, if it had taken place, would have been most calamitous for humanity. Providence prevented it, not by directly changing the perverted Will of the Borean Race, but by chastising it; and this is what was done.

Some Celts returning from Africa to Europe brought with them the germs of an unknown malady, so much the more terrible in its effects as it destroyed the very hopes of the population by attacking the generative principles. It was called *elephantiasis*, perhaps on account of the elephant which appeared to be subject to it. In a short time, this cruel malady, spreading from south to north and from west to east, made frightful ravages. The Celts who were attacked lost suddenly their strength and died of exhaustion. Nothing could counteract its venom. When Voluspa was interrogated she ordered in vain expiatory sacrifices. The human victims which were immolated by thousands did not turn aside the curse. The nation was perishing. For the first time in a long while, these indomitable warriors, whose only resource was their strength, felt that strength was not everything. The weapons fell from their hands. Incapable of the least action, they dragged themselves into their solitary camps, more like spectres than soldiers. If the Atlanteans had been prepared then with means of attacking them they would have perished.

There was at that time among the Druids a wise and virtuous man whose knowledge and peaceful virtues had been little observed until then. This man, still in the flower of his youth, groaned in secret over the sins of his compatriots, and believed justly that their cult, instead of honouring the Divinity, had offended it. He understood the traditions of his country and had studied nature deeply.

When he saw the fatal malady extending its ravages, he did not doubt that it was a scourge sent by Providence. He examined it with care, he understood the principle of it; but it was in vain that he sought the remedy. Desperate and being unable to work the good that he had hoped, wandering one day in the sacred forest, he sat down at the foot of an oak and there fell asleep. While he slept it seemed to him that a loud voice called him by name. He thought himself awake and saw before him a man of majestic stature clothed in the robe of the Druids and carrying in his hand a wand around which a serpent was entwined. Astonished at the phenomenon he asked the Unknown the meaning of it, when this one taking him by the hand made him arise and showing him, under the same tree at the foot of which he had been lying, a beautiful branch of mistletoe, said: "O Rama! the remedy thou seekest is here." And suddenly drawing from his breast a small golden pruning knife, cut the branch and gave it to Rama. After having added a few words, as to the manner of preparing the mistletoe and using it, he disappeared.

The Druid awoke with a start, profoundly agitated by the dream which had just come to him; he did not doubt that it was prophetic. He prostrated himself at the foot of the sacred tree where the vision had appeared to him and thanked from the depths of his heart the protecting Divinity that had sent it to him. Then, having seen that in truth this tree bore a branch of mistletoe, with reverence he detached it and carried it to his cell, carefully enveloped in the end of the scarf which served him as a girdle. After having prayed, in order to invoke the blessing of heaven upon his work, he began the operations which had been indicated to him and accomplished them successfully. When he believed his mistletoe sufficiently prepared, he approached a man hopelessly diseased, and having made him swallow a few drops of his divine remedy in a fermented liquor, saw with inexpressible joy that life about to become extinct was reanimated

and that death forced to abandon its prey had been vanquished. All the experiments that he made had the same
success, so that soon the rumour of his marvellous cures
spread afar.

From all sides they hastened to him. The name of Rama
was on all lips accompanied by a thousand benedictions.
The sacerdotal college assembled, and the sovereign pontiff
having asked Rama to disclose by what means a remedy so
wonderful and to which the nation owed its salvation had
come into his possession, the Druid had no difficulty in telling
him, but, wishing to give to the sacerdotal corps a proper
power which it had not had up to that time, he made the
Drud realize that in causing the plant indicated by the
Divinity to become known to the nation, in offering it even
for its veneration as sacred, the preparation of it ought not to
be divulged, but, on the contrary, to be concealed with care
in the sanctuary, so as to give to religion more splendour
and more force by a means less violent than those employed
until then. The sovereign pontiff felt the value of these
reasons and approved them. The Celtic nation knew that
it was to the mistletoe of the oak, designated by the Divine
Goodness, that it owed the cessation of the terrible plague
which was devouring it, but learned at the same time that
the mysterious property of this plant, the manner of gathering and preparing it, were reserved for the *Lœhrs* alone, to
the exclusion of the other two classes, the *Leyts* and the
Folks.

This was the first time, in reference to the sacerdotal
caste, that the other two castes of men-at-arms and of
labouring men were blended in a single one, and this gave rise
to a new idea and a new word. In considering the *Leyts* and
Folks as a single people over whom the *Lœhrs* had dominion,
the two words were contracted into one and formed the word
Leyolk, the French *laique* or layman. If the Leyts experienced some trouble from this confusion they were not at all
prepared to oppose it. Conditions influenced them. As in

the principle of society the Folks who had owed their preservation to the Celts had rightfully been placed under their
dependence, it was equally just that the Folks themselves,
who owed them their preservation should recognize their
dominion.

This change, which did not seem of much importance at
the moment when it was effected, had the most important
consequences afterwards, when pure Theocracy, being established and every line of demarcation effaced, degenerated
into absolute despotism or into anarchistic democracy,
according as the power was usurped by the force of a
single one or by that of a multitude.

Thus, in the Universe, evil is often born of good and good
of evil, as night succeeds day and day night, so that the laws
of Destiny may be accomplished and the Will of Man,
choosing freely the one or the other, may be drawn along by
the very force of things to the light and the truth which
Providence constantly presents to him.

CHAPTER VIII

APPEARANCE OF A DIVINE MESSENGER

MEANWHILE, a solemn fête was established to celebrate this auspicious event. They wished the commemoration of the discovery of the mistletoe of the oak to coincide with the commencement of the year, which was placed at the winter solstice. As obscure darkness covered the Boreal pole at this epoch; they were accustomed to think of night as the beginning of day and they called the first night after the solstice, *Night-Mother*. It was at the middle of this mysterious night that the *New-heyl* was celebrated,[1] that is to say, the new welfare or new health. The night became then sacred among the Celts, and they were accustomed to count by nights. The sovereign pontiff regulated the duration of the year by the course of the sun, and that of the month by the course of the moon. One can imagine from all the traditions which have come down to us from these remote times that this duration was established after very exact calculations, announcing an already extensive knowledge of astronomy.[2]

[1] It is, I think, unnecessary to say that the French festival of Noël, unknown to the early Christians, is derived from it.

[2] The month it appears was composed of thirty days, the year of three hundred and sixty-five days and six hours, and the cycles of thirty and sixty years. The festival of *New-heyl*, which ought to take place the first night of the winter solstice, is found put back forty-five days in the time of Olaüs Magnus in the year 1000 A.D., and for the reason that the Celtic year, being

As I am forbidden details in this work, I shall refrain from describing the ceremonies observed in gathering the mistletoe of the oak. All that can be desired on this subject may be found in many places.[1] Only I must not neglect to say, however, that the mysterious Being who had shown the mistletoe to the Druid Rama, honoured as one of the ancestors of the Borean Race, was known by the name of *Æsculapius*,[2] that is to say, the hope of salvation of the people, and considered as the Genius of Medicine.

As for the Druid Rama himself, his destiny was not to be confined there. The Divinity who had chosen him to save the Celts from an inevitable downfall in arresting the terrible plague which was destroying them had likewise elected him to tear from their eyes the bandage of superstition and to change their homicidal cult. But in this respect his mission was not so easy to fulfil. The physical epidemic was evident to all, it menaced all; none had any motives for preserving it, whereas the moral epidemic not only did not seem such to all, but was considered sacred by some, and was for others an object of interest or of vanity. Accordingly, as soon as the Druid had made known his intentions, as soon as he had said that the same Genius who had appeared to him to show him the mistletoe of the oak had appeared again to command him to dry the traces of blood which had inundated the altars, as soon as he had condemned human sacrifices as useless, atrocious, horrifying to the gods of the nation, he was regarded as a dangerous innovator whose ambition sought to profit by a propitious event to assure his power.

---

longer than the revolution of the sun, gave the mistake of a day in one hundred and thirty-two years. These forty-five days which remained correspond to five thousand nine hundred and thirty years, and, even supposing there had been no other change, carry back consequently the establishment of the Celtic calendar to nearly five thousand years before our era.

[1] Particularly in Pliny's *Nat. Hist.*, lxvi., c. 44.

[2] The word *Æsc-heyl-hopa*, whence the name Æsculapius, can also signify, the hope of salvation is wood, or the wood is the hope of salvation; because the word *Æsc* signified likewise a people and a wood.

Voluspa, being consulted at first, dared not accuse him of impiety and rebellion; the ascendancy which he had acquired over a great part of the nation by the immeasurable service which he had rendered them did not yet permit such expressions; but after having praised him and having thanked heaven for the favour he had done, she was moved to pity by the weakness of his soul and showed him as a pusillanimous man, full indeed of gentleness and good intentions, but utterly incapable of elevating his thoughts to the austere height of the divine thoughts. This explanation of the pythoness found at first many adherents. Although they did not cease to love the good Rama, they sincerely regretted that he lacked courage, and as his enemies saw this inclination they cleverly profited by it by adding ridicule to pity. His name *Rama* signified a ram; they found it too strong for him and by a malicious softening of the first letter changed it to *Lam*, in other words, a lamb. This name of *Lam* which he retained became celebrated throughout the earth as we shall shortly see. Man can reject the benefits of Providence, but Providence goes on none the less to its end. The Celts, by disdainfully ignoring its voice, by persecuting its messenger, lost their political existence, and allowed Asia to take a glory which they should have been able to have kept for Europe. Destiny was again too strong for the blind Will of Man to resist it.

CHAPTER IX

CONSEQUENCES OF THIS EVENT—THE DIVINE MESSENGER IS
PERSECUTED—HE SEPARATES HIMSELF FROM THE CELTS

NOTWITHSTANDING the decision of Voluspa regarding
him, Rama none the less continued his movement; he
manifested boldly his intention of abolishing blood sacrifices
of any sort, and announced that such was the Will of Heaven
as revealed by the great ancestor of the nation, *Oghas*.[1] This
name, which he substituted for that of Teutad, obtained the
effect which he desired. The Celts, according as they
adhered to his opinions, or as they discarded them, found
themselves suddenly divided into Oghases or Teutads, and
one can judge in advance the success which the schism made.
In order to give his party a rallying point more fixed and
more evident, the Druid innovator seized upon the allusion
which had been made to his name and took for his emblem a
ram, which he allowed his followers to call *Ram* or *Lam*,
according as they wished themselves under the relation of
force or gentleness. The Celts being attached to the ancient
doctrine, on account of *Thor*, their first Herman, opposed the

[1] The word *as*, *ans*, or *hans* signified *ancient* and as I have already said *og*
meant *very great*. The French *ancêtre* holds to the root *ans;* this root which
first furnished the name of the god *Penates* of the Celts, *As, Æs,* or *Esus,* finally
became a simple title of honour, given to distinguished men in addressing
them: *Ans-heaulme, Ans-carvel, Æs-menard, Ens-sordel,* etc. This title pronounced singly signified *sovereign ;* from there the German Hansa and the
name of Hanseatic towns.

bull to the ram and took that vigorous and furious animal as symbol of their strength and their audacity.[1] Such were the first emblems known among the Borean Race, and such was the origin of all armorial bearings which later were made use of to distinguish nations from nations and families from families.

Each setting up according to his own opinion the Ram or the Bull, it was not long before the partisans went from abuses to menaces and from menaces to combats. The nation found itself in a situation eminently dangerous. Rama saw it, and as violent means were foreign to his peace-loving disposition, he tried to persuade his adversaries. He showed them with as much sagacity as talent that the first Voluspa, in founding the cult of the Ancestor, had given fewer proofs than he of her celestial mission, since speaking only in the name of the first Herman she had but arrested partial evils, had only given special laws, often calamitous; whereas he, guided by the supreme Ancestor, Father of the entire race, had had the felicity of saving the nation from total ruin, and he had presented to it, in the Father's name, general and propitious laws, by means of which it would be forever delivered from the odious yoke which the bloody sacrifices had imposed.

These reasons, although they influenced peace-loving and sincere men, found an invincible opposition in the interest, pride, and warlike passions of the others. Voluspa, who felt her authority wavering, had the need of a *coup d'éclat* to reinforce herself, and seized the opportunity during a festival to call Rama to the foot of the altar. Rama who perceived the snare refused to come, not wishing to present his head to the axe of the priests. He was anathematized. In this extremity, since it was necessary either to fight or to expatri-

---

[1] As I have already remarked that the words *terror* and *terrible* were attached to the cult of *Thor*, symbolized by a bull, I need only say here that by a contrary sentiment, the cult of the lamb, *Lam*, produced the words *lament, lamentable, lamentation*, etc.

ate himself, and being resolved not to bring upon his fatherland the scourge of a civil war, he determined upon the latter.

An immense crowd of followers of all classes attached
themselves to his fortune.   The nation, shaken to its foundations, lost through its stubbornness a great part of its inhabitants.   Before leaving, Rama made a last effort; he
uttered in the name of Oghas, the supreme Ancestor, an
oracle in which the Celts were threatened with the greatest
evils if they continued to shed blood upon the altars.   He
sent it by a messenger to the sacerdotal college.   Voluspa
who was informed of it and who feared its effect upon the
minds anticipated the arrival of the messenger by a contrary oracle dedicating him to the merciless Thor; and upon
the messenger's arrival had his throat cut.

Doubtless the Borean Race never before found itself in
such difficulties.   It seemed as if the very gods, divided in
opinion, fought from the depths of the clouds a battle of
which unfortunate mortals were to be the victims.   It was
in fact Providence and Destiny that were struggling together.
The Will of Man was the battlefield where these two formidable powers carried their blows.   The different names which
this Will gave them mattered not.   The ancient poets felt
indeed this truth, and Homer particularly has rendered it
with a magnificence no other has equalled.   It is, nevertheless, in the understanding of this truth that real poetry
exists.   Outside of that, there is only versification.

At last, deprived of all hope of an agreement Rama
departed, taking along with him, as I have said, the healthiest
and most enlightened part of the nation.   He followed at
first the same route that the Bodohnes Celts had taken; but
when he came in sight of the Caucasus instead of following
the sinuosities of this famous mountain between the Black
Sea and the Caspian, he ascended the Don, and passing
afterwards the Volga, he reached, in skirting this last sea,
that elevated plain which looks down upon the Aral Sea.

Before arriving at this country, which in our day is still

occupied by hordes of nomads, he had encountered several of those tribes belonging ostensibly to the Borean Race. He was entirely ignorant of their existence, and was not a little surprised to find these places, which he believed deserts, fertile and inhabited. These tribes, at first frightened by the aspect of so many armed warriors, became easily calmed when they saw that these men, who had almost the same colour and language,[1] did not try to do them any harm and did not belong to the Black People with whom they were forced to be in continual warfare in order to avoid slavery. Some even became united with the Celts and served them as guides in these new regions. Their dialect was soon understood, and it was learned from them that the country in which they were was called *Touran*, in contrast to the less elevated country, more level, more agreeable, situated beyond the mountains, called *Iran*, from which they had been driven by conquering people who had come from the southern coast. From the description which Rama obtained of these peoples, he was not long in recognizing them as belonging to the Sudeen Race, and he resolved immediately to oust them from this country which they had usurped and to establish himself there. He remained, however, some time in Touran, in order to take a census of the people who had submitted to his doctrine, to regulate the different classes which so sudden a movement had confused, and to give to the theocratic government which he was planning the beginning of whatever improvement circumstances might permit. He neglected nothing in order to draw to him all the Touranian tribes of which he had knowledge; as he knew that there existed an immense country towards the north, which these tribes called the paternal land, *Tat-ârah*,[2]

---

[1] It is remarkable that still in our day the Tartar Oighouri has very close relation with the Irish Celts; it is known that the Persian and German have also many roots in common.

[2] It is from the word *Tat-ârah* that the name *Tatâre* is derived, which we have for a long time written *Tartary* in opposition to the synonym of all the Asiatic people.

because it had been the abode of their first Father, he did not fail to make them understand that it was in the name of their great Ancestor Oghas[1] who was also his, that he had come to deliver their fatherland from the yoke of strangers. This idea, which flattered their pride, gained their confidence without trouble. Several phenomena which had not struck them until then were called to their mind. One remembered a dream; another a vision. This one related the speech of a dying old man; that one spoke of an ancient tradition; all had reasons for regarding the present event as a marvellous thing. Their enthusiasm increased as they talked together. Soon it reached a high pitch. It is the nature of man to believe in the action of Providence upon him; in order that he should not believe it, it is necessary either that his passions blind him or that anterior events may have caused his will to bend the laws of Destiny, or that his own will influencing him takes the place of Providence.

[1] The Tartars of our day revere still *Oghas* or *Oghous* as their first Patriarch; those who call themselves *Oighours* on account of that are the most learned and the most anciently civilized.

CHAPTER X

WHO RAMA WAS—HIS RELIGIOUS AND POLITICAL THOUGHTS

SEVERAL messengers were dispatched into upper Asia to carry the news of what had come to pass; the rumour reached to the remotest countries; from all parts were seen tribes issuing, curious to see the messenger of their Great Ancestor and envious to take part in the war which was being prepared. On several important occasions Rama showed himself worthy of his exalted reputation. His active wisdom anticipated all needs, it smoothed all difficulties; whether he spoke or whether he acted, one felt in his words as in his actions something supernatural. He penetrated their thoughts, he foresaw the future, he healed the sick; all nature seemed to submit to him. Thus Providence, which destined the Borean Race to rule the earth, willed it, and threw before their steps the luminous rays which were to lead them. Rama was therefore the first man of this race whom it inspired immediately. It is he whom the Hindus still honour under his own name of *Rama*; it is he whom Tibet, China, Japan, and the vast regions of northern Asia, know under the name of *Lama, Fo, Pa, Pa-pa, Padi-Shah,* or *Pa-si-pa.*[1]

[1] I have said that the word *Rama* signified properly a *ram ;* thus it is by the symbol of the ram that Osiris, Dionysus, and even Jupiter have been designated. The lamb as most particularly applied to the word *Lam* has not been less famous. The white or the black lamb still designates in our day the diverse hordes of Tartars. From the same *Fo, Pa, Pa-pa* is understood the Father pre-eminent. *Padi-shah* signifies the Paternal Monarch and *Pa-si-pa,* the Father of Fathers.

It is he whom the first ancestors of the Persians, the Iranians, named *Giam-Shyd*, because he was the first monarch of the world, or the first ruler of the Black People; for this People was called the *People of Gian*, or the *Gian-ben-Gian*, as the Arabs say. One sees in the *Zend-Avesta* that the last Zoroaster renders Rama homage, in placing him long before the first prophet of this name, and designating him as the first man whom Ormuzd favoured with his inspiration.[1] He is everywhere called the Chief of the people and the flocks, the most powerful and the most fortunate Monarch. It was he who made agriculture the first of the sciences, and who taught men the cultivation of the vine and the use of wine. He founded the city of *Ver*, the capital of *Var-Giam-Gherd*. "Admirable city," said Zoroaster, "like unto Paradise, whose inhabitants were all happy."

The sacred books of the Hindus express themselves somewhat in these same terms; they have represented Rama as a mighty theocrat, instructing savage men in agriculture, giving new laws to a people already civilized, founding cities,

[1] This is what is written in the *Zend-Avesta*, page 108: "Zoroaster consulted Ormuzd saying to him: 'O Ormuzd, absorbed in excellence, just Judge of the World . . . who is the first man that has consulted you as I have done? . . .' Then Ormuzd said: 'The pure Giam-Shyd, chief of the tribes, and of the flocks, O holy Zoroaster, is the first man who has consulted me as thou art doing now. I said to him in the beginning, I who am Ormuzd, submit thou to my Law . . . meditate upon it and bear it to thy people. . . . Afterwards he reigned. . . . I put into his hands a golden sword. He advanced towards the light, towards the country of the south and he found it beautiful. . . .'" Anquetil-Duperron has written *Djemschid* but the orthography is bad. *Giam-Shyd* can signify the Monarch of the World or the universal Sun, that which returns to itself; it may also signify the Ruler or the Sun of the Black People, because this people at the time of his power bore the name of *Universal* and had itself called *Gian, Gean, Jan,* or *Zan* according to the dialect; but as the word *Gian,* which signifies properly the World, is applied to the intelligence which moves it, to the universal Spirit, to all that which is spiritual or spirituous and finally to Wine, it has happened that Rama, Osiris, Dionysus, or Bacchus, who are but the same personage under different names, have been considered sometimes as Universal Intelligence, sometimes as the Spiritual or Spirituous Principle of all things and at last, by an absolute materialization of the primitive idea, as the God of Wine.

overthrowing perverse kings, and spreading felicity on all
sides.

Arrian, who gives to Rama the name of Dionysus, that is
to say, Divine Intelligence, relates that this prince taught
these men, who before his coming led a wandering, savage
life, to sow the lands, to cultivate the vine, and to make
war.

However Zoroaster whose object was the reformation of
the Persian cult accuses Giam-Shyd of pride, and said the
end of his reign did not correspond with the beginning.
Some commentators add that this theocrat offended the
Divinity in trying to put himself in his place and in usurping
the divine honours. This reproach would have been better
founded, indeed, if Rama had announced as the object of his
cult, the Being of Beings, the Most High God Himself in
His Fathomless Unity; but his ideas could not rise to that
height, and, supposing that they had been able, those of the
people whom he conducted could not have followed him
there. Whatever great developments the intellectual sphere
had before acquired among the Borean Race, it had nevertheless not reached the point of attaining such heights. The
idea which it seized most easily was, as I have said, that of
the immortality of the soul; that is why the cult of the
Ancestors was the most suitable for it. The idea of the
existence of God, which was connected with it, only struck
it in a vague and confused manner.

The Celts saw in Teutad or in Oghas only the same thing
as these words expressed in the most physical sense: the
Universal Father or the Great Ancestor of their nation.
Rama, in setting himself up as the representative of the
Father or this common Ancestor, in affirming that their will
was reflected in his, in clothing himself, so to speak, with
sacerdotal immortality, and in persuading his followers that
he would leave his actual body only to take another, so as to
continue to instruct and govern them, from body to body till
the end of time; Rama, I say, did not do such an audacious

thing as did Krishna, Fo-Hi, and Zoroaster himself a long time after. He did not leave the sentient and comprehensible sphere of things, whereas the others did. The immortality of the soul being recognized, his doctrine was simply a consequence. He affirmed of the Great Ancestor only what he affirmed of himself; and when he said that he would be born again in order to continue his ministry, he did not say anything else, except that the immortality of his soul, instead of acting elsewhere in an invisible manner, would act in a visible manner here on earth; so that his doctrine and the forms of his cult profit mutually by support and proofs.

When one judges the Lamaic cult after the ideas acquired during many centuries, it is not astonishing to find great mistakes in it, especially if one cannot separate from it the rust of superstitions which ages have attached to it and by which its splendour is tarnished; but, if it is examined without prejudice, one will feel that this cult was the most suitable which could have been offered at this epoch to the intelligence of man. It succeeded Sabeanism which, already stricken with age, shaken from all sides, could only be sustained by its means. It was the cult of the Ancestors restored to its highest relative perfection. It was simple in its dogmas, innocent in its rights, and very pure in the morals which resulted from it. It did not elevate the minds greatly, it is true, but neither did it cause them violent disturbances. Its principal virtue, which was filial piety, offered to the civil institutions an almost unshakable base. I am persuaded that if anything on earth could have claimed indestructibility, this cult could have claimed it above any other. Observe how, after so many vanished centuries,[1] Japan, the whole of

---

[1] I hardly dare say here how many centuries the chronologists count. I have already shown how one can by means of astronomical calculations go back nearly five thousand years before our era, to the epoch of Rama, supposing that there were no corrections in the runic calendar; but who will assure that there were none? Arrian, who no doubt wrote according to the original traditions, relates that from Theocritus to Sandrocottus, who was conquered by Alexander, was reckoned 6402 years. Pliny agrees perfectly

China, Tibet, and the immense regions of Tartary are still dominated by the Lamaic cult, notwithstanding the multitude of revolutions which have taken place in these countries.

Rama, escaped from persecution, endowed with a gentle and compassionate character, banished all persecution from his cult and prohibited all idols and all bloody sacrifice. He divided the nation into four classes, thus adding a class to the three which existed already among the Celts. The classes which have survived in India are those of Priests, Warriors, Labourers and Artisans; thus he divided into two, those of *Folks* and gave to both the independence of territorial property. The sovereign pontiffs belonged to the class of priests and were considered immortal, their soul never left one body but to inhabit another and always that of a young child dedicated for this purpose. The royal dignity was hereditary in a single family of the military class, and this family, held sacred, became inviolable. The civil magistrates were chosen by the king from the class of labourers and duly held their judicial powers from the sovereign pontiff. The artisans furnished workmen and servants of all kinds. Slavery was abolished.

After having laid these simple foundations for his cult and his government, Rama, surrounded by the veneration of an immense people devoted to his orders, left Touran where he had remained until that time and entered Iran to make the conquest and establish there the seat of his theocracy.

---

with Arrian, although he does not appear to have copied from him. Now every one knows that Alexander's expedition to India took place in 326 B.C., from which it results that from Rama up to the present year, 1821, a duration of 8550 years is established.

CHAPTER XI

ESTABLISHMENT OF A UNIVERSAL EMPIRE, THEOCRATIC AND ROYAL

AS I am forbidden purely historical details I shall continue rapidly through this part of the history of Rama. All that is preserved of it in tradition seems allegorical. The poets who have sung his triumphs long time after, without doubting that he had ceased to be, have ostensibly confused him, not alone with the Great Ancestor of the Borean Race whose cult he established, but even with the entire race which they have personified in him. This is evident in the *Ramayana*, the greatest poem of the Hindus, work of the celebrated Valmiki, and in the *Dionysiacs* of Nonnus.[1] In these two poems, Rama and Dionysus are equally persecuted in their youth, given over to the hatred of an artificial and cruel woman who forced them to desert their fatherland. After several adventures more or less *bizarre*, both finished by triumphing over their enemies and by making the conquest of India where they obtained divine honours.

Without stopping, then, at this tissue of allegories, which would here be of little interest, let us continue our historical

---

[1] The English savants who have read *Le Poème de Valmik* affirm that it infinitely surpasses in unity of action, magnificence of detail, and elegance of style, the polished, erudite but cold work of Nonnus. There are, however, remarkable points of similarity to be made between these two poems.

observation, so as to draw from it in the course of time useful inferences, in order to attain to the moral understanding and true politics founded upon the very nature of things. What has most bewildered modern philosophers is the lack of positive and traditional erudition. Not only did they not know Man in himself, but they ignored also the course which he had already travelled and the diverse modifications which he had undergone. Among a multitude of situations, they have never fixed but two or at most three, and they truly believed, when their imaginations had made several flights among the ancient Romans and among the Greeks, and perfunctorily among the Hebrews, that all was said, that they knew the history of the human race and everything that was most wonderful in that history. They did not know that Rome and Athens presented only small political incidents of a certain form, whose generalization was impossible, and that the Hebrews, bearers of a tradition that they did not comprehend, could offer to their meditations only a book closed with seven seals, more difficult to break than those mentioned in the *Apocalypse*.

We shall touch upon all of these things in their place; let us first finish running through with a general description the centuries which separate us from it.

The Sudeens, established long since in Iran, opposed the Celtic theocracy with a vigorous resistance; but nothing could arrest the religious enthusiasm with which Rama had imbued his army. The sacred city Isthakar was taken by storm.[1] A general and decisive battle having been fought at

---

[1] The name of this ancient city should be written *Ysdhan-Khatr*, that is to say the divine City. It is curious that in the ancient tongue of Iran, *Isdhan* signifies God of Genius, as it still signifies it in Hungarian. This city is believed to be the same that the Greeks named *Persepolis*. It is today in ruins. One finds upon several monuments and especially upon the one that the modern Persians call the *Throne of Giam-Shyd* inscriptions traced in characters entirely unknown. These characters, obviously written from left to right, indicate a Borean origin. Several Persian poets and among others Nizamy and Sahdy have covered with moral sentences the ruins of Istha-Khar; the

a short distance from this capital, they were utterly vanquished. All those who refused to submit were obliged to
leave Iran, and they retreated in disorder, one part towards
Arabia and the other towards Hindustan, where the rumour
of their defeat had preceded them.

Rama, having built a city to establish the seat of his
sovereign pontificate, consecrated it to the Truth which he
proclaimed and named it in consequence *Vahr*.[1] In the
meantime, he dreamed of consolidating and extending his
empire. The Grand Khan, whom he had consecrated,
established his residence in Isthakhar and was subject to
him alone. The inferior khans obeyed his orders. One of
them, at the head of a powerful army advanced towards
Asia Minor, then called *Plaksha*, while another, marching
from the opposite side, arrived at the borders of the Sind, the
Indus of today, and, notwithstanding the formidable opposition which he encountered there, he crossed the water
and penetrated into Hindustan. These two khans had
different success. The one who advanced towards the
north, having encountered the Bodohnes Celts with whom
he made alliance, had first to fight the Amazons whose entire
dominion he overthrew. These warrior-women, obliged to
submit or to leave the continent of Asia, took refuge in
small numbers in the islands of Cyprus, Lesbos, and some
others of the Archipelago. The conquest of Plaksha being
achieved, both the Tigris and the Euphrates flowing henceforth under the laws of Rama, the city of *Nineveh* was built
as the capital of a kingdom which bore the name of Chaldea,

---

following sentence is one of the most remarkable: "Among the sovereigns of
Persia, since the ages of Feridoun, of Zohak, of Giam-Shyd, dost thou know
among them any one whose throne has been sheltered from destruction, and
which has not been overthrown by the hand of chance?"

[1] One finds in the *Zend-Avesta* that the city of *Vahr* was the capital of
Vahr-Giam-Ghard, that is to say, the universal precincts of Truth. It
believed that the lovely city of Amadan rests today upon the ruins of the
ancient Vahr. In explaining in Chaldean the name *Amah-dan*, it is found to
signify the metropolis of Justice.

as long as the sacerdotal caste ruled there, and later took the name of Syrian or Assyrian empire, when the military caste came to gain the upper hand.[1] The Arabs, who at this epoch were already a mixture of Celts and Atlanteans, easily contracted an alliance with the followers of Rama and received his doctrine.

The Sudeens who did not want to submit to the law of the vanquisher advanced towards Egypt, where, embarking upon the Persian Gulf, they gained the southern part of Asia where their greatest forces were gathered. It is there that the struggle was severe. The khan who had passed the Sind safely, being beaten afterwards by his enemies, was obliged to recross it in disorder. The rumour of his defeat having come to the ears of the Grand Khan, he marched to the aid of the khan but vainly. A power greater than his was needed here. Rama felt it; he saw that it was a question now of more than ordinary conquest, and that upon the contest which was beginning in Hindustan depended the future of the Borean Race and the triumph of his cult. It was upon the borders of the Ganges that this great question was to be decided: to which of the two peoples, the black or the white, would belong the empire of the world. He advanced therefore in person and collected about him all the forces that he had. Tradition relates that a great number of women called *Thyiads* fought under his orders, likewise a great multitude of savage men called *Satyrs*. These were, no doubt, a part of the Amazons whom he had subdued, and those tribes of wandering Tartars whom he had united and civilized.

---

[1] One can notice that the words *Chaldea* and *Syria* are equally interpretable by the Celt or by the Hebrew, as the greater part of those which go back to a great antiquity. In the words *Chaldea* and *Syria* are found the roots *Oald*, an old man; and *Syr*, a master, a lord.

The foundation of the city of *Ask-chaldan*, called today *Ascalon*, proves what I advance; the name of this ancient city, celebrated as the birthplace of Semiramis, can signify the Celtic People, as well as the Chaldean People; the primitive root of these two words being the same. It is worthy of attention that the Hindus still consider today the city of *Askchala* as sacred.

According to the same tradition, the war lasted for seven years, and was marked by the most astonishing phenomena. Rama used on many occasions supernatural means. In the midst of most arid deserts, while his troops were consumed by a burning thirst, he discovered copious springs which at his voice appeared to rise from the depths of the rocks. When food failed, he found unexpected resources in a sort of manna, of which he taught them the use. A cruel epidemic having broken out, he received again from his Genius a remedy which arrested the ravages. It appears that it was from a plant named *hom*[1] that he extracted its salutary juice. This plant which remained sacred among his followers replaced the mistletoe of the oak and caused them to forget the latter. But the most astonishing thing was to see that this powerful Theocrat, finding himself transported by the events of a long war into the midst of a nation long since arrived at the highest degree of civilization, industrious and rich, equalled it in industries and surpassed it in riches.

Among the things that I should have related in their place, I find that I have omitted one, whose oversight the sagacity of the reader could hardly supply. It is the invention of money. This invention like all those of greatest importance is lost in the night of time. Those of the writers who have believed it modern, as Wachter or Sperling, have testified indeed to little knowledge of antiquity. At the epoch when the Chinese Empire was founded, it was already used. It is known that the Emperor Kanghi, having collected pieces of money of all the dynasties, possessed some that dated back to the time of Yao. Even to the French missionaries he showed some of Indian origin struck as a coin and anterior by far to those of the first Chinese monarchs.

It cannot be doubted that certain metals, particularly gold, silver, and copper, have been chosen from time im-

---

[1] This is thought to be the same that the Greeks called *Amomos* and the Latins *Amomum*. The Egyptians who knew it named it *Persea*, perhaps owing to its origin.

memorial as representative tokens of all other objects, on account of the facility with which one can divide them without losing any of their value. There are cases, as Court de Gébelin well observes, where one has need of a very small representative value, and where can one find this value in a thing which, without altering itself at all, can be presented *en masse* and offer divisions as small as any one could wish? A sheep, an ox cannot be divided without being destroyed. Leather, cloth, a vase once divided can never be united *en masse*. Metals alone have this faculty, and it is also why they are used in the composition of this token called money; wonderful token, without which neither real commerce nor perfect civilization can exist.

I believe that it was at the epoch of the first alliance which the Celts contracted with the Atlanteans that they received the first knowledge of money, a knowledge at first somewhat confused, as all other things, but which adjusted and perfected itself little by little. The imminent conditions in which Rama found himself must have greatly extended the use of it. He had to traverse countries where a long habit rendered gold and silver an indispensable necessity. These two metals he never lacked; one could say he had a Genius at his orders, who disclosed treasures and mines on all sides wherever there were any.

The mark with which this Theocrat struck his moneys was a ram; this is why the figure and name of the symbol are alike preserved among many nations. It appears that the type used by the autochthonous Celts was a bull. As to the money of the Atlanteans which had circulation then in India, everything leads to the belief that it had as impress the figure of a winged serpent called Dragon.[1] The Dragon was the ensign of these peoples. Their supreme sovereign

---

[1] The antique word, *Drach-mon*, a drachma, comes from it, that is to say a dragon of silver. If one wishes to see some curious details concerning moneys, he can consult my *Vocabulaire de la langue d'Oc*, the words *Mouneda, Dardena, Escud, Piastra, Sol, Deniar, Liard, Patac, Pecugna*, etc.

bore the title of *Rawhan* or *Rawhôn*, that is to say, Universal Guardian, the Great King; whereas like those in Egypt, the inferior sovereigns who were subject to him were called *Pha-rawhôn*, which signifies the voice, the echo or the reflex of Rawhôn.

In the poem of *Ramayana*, it speaks in detailed length of the terrible battles which Rama and the Rawhôn fought to determine to whom the empire should belong. Nonnus in his *Dionysiaca* has devoted twenty-five cantos describing them. He calls the Rawhôn *Deriades*, no doubt his own name, and speaks of him always as the Black King, chief of the Black People. After many vicissitudes, which it is needless to discuss, the Rawhôn, forced to abandon his capital Ayodhya[1] and to leave even the continent, retired to the island of Lankâ, the Ceylon of today, and expected to find there a shelter from his enemies, considering the water that surrounded it an insurmountable obstacle; but he learned soon to his cost what real courage can do when supported by religious enthusiasm. Tradition reports that the companions of Rama, whom neither dangers, nor labours, nor fatigues could dishearten, used stones scattered about to hold back the waves, and, fastening together many rafts, they formed an immense bridge, upon which they passed over.[2] The Grand Khan, by means of this, carried fire into the very palace of Rawhôn, and Rama, who followed him closely, decided the victory. The Rawhôn was killed in the battle, and his vanquisher remained sole master of Asia. It is said that in this memorable combat a woman

---

[1] Today *Aoud* or *Haud*, on the meridional border of Gagra or Sardjou, which empties into the Ganges about latitude 26°. If one can believe the narratives of Pouranas, this ancient city was one of the greatest, most celebrated, and holiest on earth; it was fifteen leagues in length.

[2] The Hindus still show the remains of this famous bridge in a series of rocks which they call the *Bridge of Rama*. The Mussulmans believed it their duty, in a spirit of piety, to change the name of *Rama* to that of *Adam*. Besides one reads in the *Ramayana* that the chief of the companions of Rama was called *Hanouman;* this name, of Celtic origin, signifies the King of Men, *Khan-of-man*.

was happily delivered. Suspected of having yielded to the desires of Rawhôn, she proved her innocence by submitting to the trial of fire. This event has provided and still today provides the subject for a great number of dramas among the Indians. It is even from there that the art of the theatre has had its origin, as I have endeavoured to show in another work.[1]

After the conquest of Lankâ, nothing more resisted the Celtic Theocrat. From the South to the North, from the Orient to the Occident all submitted to his civil and religious laws.

[1] *Discours sur l'Essence et la Forme de la Poésie*, en tête des *Vers Dorés*.

CHAPTER XII

RECAPITULATION

SUCH were the effects of the first intellectual disturbance. These men whom I have left at the close of the last book hardly escaping from a hostile race have become in a few centuries masters of an immense empire and the legislators of the world. It is true that this has not been without trouble, without error, without accidents of any kind. But is there anything great on earth that is founded without pain and executed without peril? If the most mediocre edifices have caused fatigue, how much more must have been involved in the strongholds of the Caucasus, in the pyramids of Egypt, or the great wall of China?

Modern politicians, accustomed to read histories edited in miniature, see all on a small scale. They imagine that a law only put down on paper is a law, and that an empire is constituted because a constitution has been written. They do not concern themselves as to whether Providence, Destiny, or the Will of Man enters into these things. They declare simply that the law must be atheistic, and they believe that all is said. If they name Providence, it is as Epicurus does, perfunctorily, and only to say that they have named it. But it is not in this manner that the vast decrees which rule the Universe reveal themselves.

Listen, Legislators, or Conquerors, and remember this. Whatever your plans may be, if at least one of the three great powers which I have mentioned does not sustain them, they will vanish into air as vain smoke. And do you want to know what kind of support each of these powers will give them, if they are isolated? Destiny will lend them force of arms; the Will of Man, force of opinion; Providence, moral force which bears religious or political enthusiasm. The union of these three forces alone gives stability. As soon as one gives way, the edifice is shaken.

With Destiny alone, one makes conquests more or less rapid, more or less disastrous, and one astonishes the world with it, as Attila, Genghis, or Tamerlane. With the Will alone, one institutes republics more or less stormy, more or less transitory, as Lycurgus or Brutus; but it is only with the intervention of Providence that one founds regular States, Theocracies, or Monarchies whose *éclat* covers the earth, and whose duration fatigues time, as that of Taôth, Bharata, Rama, Fo-Hi, Zeradosht, Krishna, or Moses.

THIRD BOOK

Nations resemble individuals, as I have said several times; and entire races conduct themselves as nations. They have their beginning, their middle, and their end. They pass through all the phases of adolescence, virility, and old age. But, as among individuals, the greater part die in childhood without even attaining adolescence, it is the same with nations. It is their nature to swallow up one another and to aggrandize themselves by conquest and aggregation. Rarely do they attain old age.

I have explained in the preceding book the first triumph of the Borean Race. This triumph marked its adolescence. It founded the Lamaic Theocracy and gave to the Indian Empire a new splendour. Asia dethroned Africa and took in hand the sceptre of the world, but Europe, which had produced the movement, was still nothing and this for reasons which I have clearly indicated: that instead of adhering to the movement of Providence, it strove to stifle it.

In this third book, I shall examine the consequences of this first triumph, following the most noticeable phases, and shall describe the important events which decided the destiny of Europe.

CHAPTER I

DIGRESSION UPON THE CELTS—ORIGIN OF THE SALIANS AND
THE RIPUARIANS—THEIR EMBLEMS—SALIC LAW

THE Celts of Europe who persisted in the cult of Thor and
who, notwithstanding the opposition of Rama continued to offer to their savage Divinity human sacrifices,
regarded at first the schism which had taken place among
them as a small matter; they even gave to the followers of
Rama a name which designated less hatred than pity. It
meant to them a wandering people, *Esk-wander*.[1] This
name, illustrious through success and used in the course of
time by all people for a particular chief, became the generic
name for all heroes who distinguished themselves by glorious
exploits. There are few nations that do not boast of a
Scander. The first of all, Rama, has been designated as the
Scander of the two horns, on account of the ram which he

---

[1] I have already said that the root *ask, osk, esk* designated a people in
relation to a multitude or army. The root developed also by the same reason
the idea of woods, on account of the multitude of trees of which it is composed;
thence the verb ἀσκεῖν, *to exercise, to plan a manœuvre*, and also *to stir, to swarm;*
from these again the words ἄσκιος, *bushy*, and σκιά, *shade*. From the word
ost in old French an army is derived, the word *wander*, united to the radical
esk to signify a people wandering or misled, came from the primitive *wand*,
a whirlwind; from this last root are formed the Saxon, English, and German
Wind, the French *vent* and the Latin *ventus*.

Besides it is from the radical *osk*, a people, that the modern French ter-
mination *ois* is derived. Formerly was said *Gôl-land-osk*, for *Gauls* or *Hollanders*, the People of the Low Countries; *Pôl-land-osk*, for *Polacks*, the People
of the High Countries, etc.

135

took for an emblem. These two horns have since been
singularly celebrated. They were put upon the head of all
theocratic personages. They gave the form of the tiara and
the mitre. Finally it is noteworthy that the last of the
Scanders, Alexander the Great, bore the name by which
these ancient heroes had been designated.[1]

In the sacred books of the Hindus, called *Pouranas*, the
greatest details touching the conquests of Rama are found.
These conquests extended over all the inhabited earth. As
it does not seem possible that the life of a single man may
have been sufficient for so many events, it is probable that,
according to the manner of writing history at this remote
epoch, the first founder of the cult was credited with all that
was done by· his lieutenants or his successors. However
that may be, one finds in these books, that Rama, under the
name of *Deva-nashousha*,[2] the Divine Spirit, after securing
the sacred island of Lankâ, returned to the septentrional
countries of Asia and took possession of them. The holy
cities of Balk and of Bamiyan[3] opened their gates to him and
submitted to his cult. From there, crossing Iran, he went
towards Arabia which received him with homage. After
having visited Chaldea, which belonged to him, he retraced
his steps and appeared upon the frontiers of Egypt. The
Pharaoh who reigned there, judging that resistance would
be useless against a power so formidable, declared himself his tributary. The ruler of Ethiopia imitated the
Pharaoh's example. So that from the borders of the Nile
to those of the Ganges and from the island of Lankâ to

[1] The name Alexander is formed from the ancient *Scander* to which the
Arabic article *al* is joined.

[2] It seems certain that it is from this name, vulgarly pronounced *Deo-naush*,
that the Greeks have derived their *Dio-nysus*.

[3] The city of Bamiyan is one of the most extraordinary cities in existence;
like the famous Egyptian Thebes it is hewn entirely in the rock. Tradition
traces the construction of it to the people of *Gian-ben-Gian*, that is to say, the
Black People; two colossal statues are seen at the portico of this temple in
which an entire army with all its baggage could be lodged.

the mountains of the Caucasus all were subject to Rama's laws.

The Occidental part of Europe, which the Hindu books name *Veraha*, and the Oriental part which they call *Kourou*, were likewise visited by the armies of Rama, and colonies were there founded. The autochthonous Celts, forced to recede towards the septentrional countries, encountered wandering tribes with which it was necessary to dispute the territory. A murderous struggle ensued. Equally pressed on both sides, the Celts found themselves in a most painful situation. Sometimes vanquished, sometimes victors, they passed many centuries fighting to preserve their existence. Almost always repulsed from the meridional coasts, ceaselessly harassed by hordes of Tartars who were accustomed to cross the Borysthenes, they enjoyed not a moment of repose. Playthings of a pitiless Destiny, instead of advancing in the course of civilization, they receded. All of their institutions deteriorated. Hiding their sanguinary cult in gloomy forests, they became savage and cruel. Their virtues even took on an austere character. Impatient of any kind of yoke, irritated by the least constraint, they made of liberty a sort of savage idol to which they sacrificed all, even themselves. Always ready to expose their life or to take away that of others, their courage became ferocity. A sort of veneration for the women, whom they continued to regard as divine, softened a little, it is true, the harshness of their manners, but this general veneration did not last long. An inevitable event came to divide their opinion in this regard.

For a long time, as I have said, the women shared the priesthood, and even dominated it, since it was from their lips that all the oracles issued; the Druidesses presided at the ceremonies of the cult and even at the sacrifices, and immolated the victims as their husbands did; but no woman had as yet ascended the throne. As long as the military chiefs were elective this was impossible, for the election involved almost always trials by combat, but when they became hereditary by taking the place of civil chiefs the case was absolutely different.

It happened that a khan dying without male issue left only a daughter. The question was to know if this daughter should inherit the crown; some favoured the idea; others opposed it. The nation was divided. It was observed that in this quarrel the inhabitants of the fertile plains, those who lived on the borders of rivers and seas, were of the first party and sustained the absolute legitimacy of birth; whereas the inhabitants of the mountains, who had to struggle against the wildest nature, wanted the legitimacy of birth only in the males. This was the reason that the first were called *Ripuarians* and the second *Salians*. The Ripuarians passed for effeminate and soft, and were given the name of *Frogs* on account of their marshes. The Salians, on the other hand, were called rustic and lacking in spirit, and were designated by the epithet of *Cranes*, on account of the heights which they cultivated. The two parties seized these allusions and took as emblems these different animals; so that the bull no longer appeared alone upon the Celtic ensigns, but accompanied by frogs at its feet or cranes on its back, the frogs to express that it belonged to the Ripuarians and the cranes that it designated the Salians. The bull finally disappeared and frogs and cranes alone remained. The Ripuarians and Salians fought a long time and their partisans vowed implacable hatred.[1] The

---

[1] The *Ripuarians* were thus called from the word *ripa* or *riba* which signified a bank, and the *Salians*, from the word *sal* or *saul*, which expressed an eminence. It is from this word that the French words *sault*, leap, *seuil*, threshold, *saillant*, projecting, and the ancient verb *saillir*, come; they all hold to the root *hal*, *hel*, or *hil* designating a hill. At the epoch of the Etruscan dominion, of which I shall speak later, the Salian Celts provided certain priests of Mars, whose custom was to leap while chanting the hymns to this god. Their ensign, which was a crane, was ennobled, in the course of time becoming the Roman eagle. The same thing happened to the frogs of the Ripuarians, which, as is well known, became the *fleur de lis* of the Franks.

miserable Celts, having abandoned the ways of Providence, went from division to division, from misfortune to misfortune. The Celtic nation, properly speaking, existed no more. Scattered about in the septentrional countries of Europe, only fractions of the great whole were seen. Each fraction wished to command; none wished to obey. Anarchy, which was in each division, was also in each individual. The names which they gave themselves expressed invariably their independence. They were the Alains, the Germans, Vandals, Frisons, Quades, Cimbri, Swabians, Allobroges, Scandinavians, Franks, Saxons, etc., whose signification may be found in the note below.[1]

The movement of Providence was then in Asia. It was there that the Borean Race had transported its force. We shall now transport ourselves there for a while, before returning to Europe.

[1] The *Alains* or *All-ans* equals in sovereignty; the *Allemands* (Germans) equals in virility; the *Vandals*, those who separate themselves from all; *Frisons*, the children of liberty; *Quades*, the speakers; *Cimbrians*, the shadows; *Swabians*, the haughty; *Allobroges*, the breakers of all ties; *Scandinavians*, those who wander about in ships; *Franks*, the roysterers, those who stop at nothing; *Saxons*, the children of nature, etc.

CHAPTER II

A T the epoch when Rama made the conquest of Hindustan, that country did not bear this name. Even today, although it is generally received there, the Brahmans only use it with repugnance. This name signifies the abode of the Black People; it had been given by the first tribes of Iran who derived it from a word in their dialect which signified black.[1] At this remote epoch, the name *Bharat-Khant* or *Bharat-Versh* was used by the whole of India. This name expressed in the African dialect the possession or tabernacle of Bharata.[2] Now this Bharata, a very celebrated personage among the Hindus, is claimed to have been one of the first legislators, one from whom they received their cult and their laws, their sciences and their arts, prior to the arrival of Rama. The god which Bharata offered to the adoration of the people was named *Wôdha*, that is to say, Eternity or the type of all that which is Eternal; Eternal Bounty, Eternal Wisdom, Eternal Power, etc. The Hindus of today still recognize him under the name of *Buddha*, but greatly degenerated from his ancient grandeur on account of many innovators who have usurped his name. The name of this

---

[1] Consequently a *Hindu* signified a negro. It is from this word that the word *indigo* is derived and perhaps the English and Belgian word *ink*.

[2] The name of Bharata may signify the son of the tutelary ruler.

ancient Wôdha is found in all cults and all mythologies of the earth. Ordinarily the surname most given to him by Bharata was *Iswara*, that is to say, the Supreme Being.

Thus, before the conquest of India by Rama, Divine Unity was taught and understood there. This mighty Theocrat did not destroy it; but as it appeared that this Unity was presented in its incomprehensible immensity, he united to it the cult of the Ancestors, which he considered as an intermediary hierarchy, necessary to unite Man to the Divinity; and he conducted in this manner the intelligence of his people by the knowledge of a Particular Being to that of an Absolute Being. He named these intermediary spirits *Assour*, from two words of his language which might equally signify an Ancestor or a Prince.[1] As to the visible objects of Sabeanism, such as the sun, moon, and other planets, he banished them from his cult and would admit there nothing perceptible, neither any idol, nor any image, nor anything which could assign any form whatever to that which had none.

When he arrived in India, this country was subject to two dynasties which the Atlanteans had doubtless established there and which reigned conjointly under the name of *Solar* or *Lunar Dynasty*. In the first were the children of the Sun, descendants of Ikshaûkou, and in the second the children of the Moon, descendants of the first Buddha. The Brahmans said that this Ikshaûkou, chief of the Solar Dynasty, was son of the seventh Menou, son of Vaivasouata who was saved from the Deluge.[2]

[1] These are the words *As* and *Syr*, which I have already cited several times.

[2] By *Menou* is understood the legislative intelligence which presides over the earth from one deluge to another. It is like a providential constitution which comprehends many phases. The Hindus admit the successive appearance of fourteen *Menous;* according to this system, we have arrived at the seventh *Menou* and at the fourth age of this *Menou*. If, as I believe, one can date the establishment of the Atlanteans in Asia from the reign of Ikshaûkou, it should go back to about 2200 years before *Daçaratha*. Nonnus names this last Indian monarch, dethroned by Dionysus, *Deriades*, a name which is not far removed from that given him by the Brahmans.

The Rawhôn, dethroned by Rama, was the fifty-fifth solar monarch since Ikshaûkou; he was called Daçaratha.

The throne of the Solar Dynasty was established in the sacred city of Ayodhya, today Aûdh, and that of the Lunar Dynasty in that of Pratishthana, today Vitora. Rama wishing, as I have said, to remove from his cult all that which could recall the idols of Sabeanism, united these two dynasties in a single one. Thus it is that in the chronology of the Hindus, no trace is found of the Lunar Dynasty, from Rama to Krishna, who re-established it after many generations.

The first khan whom Rama consecrated to be the sovereign king of the world was named *Kousha*. He reigned over a great number of kings, such as those of Iran, Arabia, Chaldea, Egypt, Ethiopia, Libya, and even Europe, who were dependent on him. The seat of his immense empire was in the city of Ayodhya. Rama established his supreme priesthood upon a mountain near Balk and Bamiyan. As he was given immortality, according to the Lamaic system of which I have before spoken, the names of any of his successors were not known. The Brahmans fill the long interval which has passed between Rama and Krishna, by the sole name of *Youdhistir*,[1] which signifies nothing else than the divine representative.

Just as the supreme king reigned over a host of feudatory kings, the supreme pontiff dominated a number of sovereign pontiffs. The ordinary title of these sovereign pontiffs was that of father or *papa*. The supreme pontiff bore that of *pa-zi-pa*, the Father of Fathers. Wherever there was a king, there was a sovereign pontiff, and the place where he always lived was reputed sacred. Thus Balk or Bamiyan became the place pre-eminently sacred, for the reason that the supreme pontiff had fixed his residence there, and the country round about these two cities was called *Para-desa*, the deified land. One can still, when searching the places which tradition has consecrated, recognize in the ancient

---

[1] This name should be written *Wôdh-Ester*, he who is in place of God.

continent traces of the Lamaic cult, and can judge of the vast extent of the Indian Empire.[1]

I allow myself to be drawn into historical details, which perhaps will appear out of place, but I cannot, however, refrain before the close of this chapter from relating an hypothesis which I believe not to be devoid of foundation.

Thus, as I have related above, the Celts had already made some progress in astronomy in order to have a regular calendar; but it does not appear that they had arranged the stars of the heavens by groups called asterisms, so as to form the Zodiac and the system of constellations which we know today. Court de Gébelin said that it was principally from the observation of the ebb and flow of the septentrional ocean that this people owed the regularity of their year. When Rama achieved the conquest of India and his sacerdotal authority was recognized by all the earth, he examined the calendar of the Atlanteans and saw that it was superior in many points to that of the Celts. He resolved therefore to adopt it, especially in that which had reference to the form of the celestial sphere; but, using his right as supreme pontiff, he took away the greater part of the figures which these earlier peoples had applied to the different constellations, and designed them anew with such incomparable sagacity and talent that he presented the zodiacal constellations, which the sun passed through in a year, in a series of

[1] The most celebrated of the sacred places in India are the island of Lankâ today Ceylon; the cities of Aûdh, of Vitora, the places called Guyah, Methra, Devarkash, etc.; in Iran, or Persia, the city of Vahr, today Amadan; those of Balk, Bamiyan, etc.; in Tibet, Boutala Mountain, the city of Lassa; in Tartary, the city of Astrakhan, the places called Gangawaz, Baharein, etc.; in ancient Chaldea, the cities of Nineveh, of Babel; in Syria and Arabia, the cities of Askchalâ, today Ascalon; those of Balbec, of Mambyce, of Jerusalem, of Mecca, of Sana; in Egypt, the city of Thebes, of Memphis, etc.; in ancient Ethiopia, the cities of Rapta, of Meroë; in ancient Thrace, Mount Hæmus, and the places called *Balkan* and *Caucayon;* in Greece, Mount Parnassus and the city of Delphi; in Etruria the city of Bolsene; in ancient Oscitania, the city of Nîmes; in the Occidental Asques, the city of Huesca, that of Gades; in Gaul, the city of Perigueux, that of Bibracte, today Autun, that of Chartres.

emblematical figures perfectly distinct; the first having relation to the progress of this planet and to the influence of the seasons; the second containing the history of his own journeys, his labours, and his success; and the third enveloping, under most ingenious hieroglyphics, the means which he had received from Providence in order to attain an end as extraordinary as elevated.

This celestial sphere thus conceived was received among all the people subject to the dominion of Rama, and he delivered to them a wonderful book for their meditations, which, after a long course of centuries, still causes in our day astonishment or study for a host of savants.[1]

[1] The signs of the Zodiac, twelve in number, are the most remarkable of anything in the celestial sphere; the others serve no further than to develop in it the triple expression. It is in the invention of these signs that Rama has put all the might of his genius. That which bears his name, the ram, must without doubt be considered as the first. But to what part of the year ought it to correspond? If at the beginning, as it seems certain, it is necessary to place it at the winter solstice, to this very night called by the Celts *Modra-Nect*. Then, in examining the condition of the heavens, we shall see today that this night falls upon Sagittarius, which gives a retrogradation of nearly four signs, or 120 degrees. Now in calculating these 120 degrees, at the rate of seventy-two years a degree, we find by the antiquity of the Zodiac precisely 8640 years; and this does not differ greatly from the chronology of Arrian, which I have already cited. In following this hypothesis, it is found that the sign of the balance, Libra, fell in the summer solstice and divided the year into two equal parts. As Rama has been confused with the Sun, which is also designated by the symbol of the ram, it has been quite simple, as many writers have made it, to see the course of this planet and its diverse influences characterized by the twelve signs through which it passes; but, in reflecting upon the history of this celebrated Theocrat, such as I have described it, one sees that it is well enough expressed by the figures which accompany these signs. First, it is the ram, Aries, which flees, the head turned backwards, the eye fixed towards the country it is leaving. That is the situation of Rama abandoning his fatherland. A furious bull, Taurus appears desirous of opposing its flight, but half of its body, buried in the mire, prevents the execution of its plan, it falls upon its knees. These are the Celts designated by their own symbol, who notwithstanding their efforts end by submitting to Rama. The twins, Gemini, which follow, express quite clearly his alliance with the Turanians. Cancer signifies his meditations and his self-examinations; the lion, Leo, his combats and particularly the island of Lanká, designated by this animal; the winged virgin, Virgo, carrying a palm in her hand, indicates his

It does not enter into my plan to dwell upon the secret mysteries which this book may disclose to the curiosity of all; it is sufficient for me to have shown that it is neither the result of hazard nor of a frivolous imagination, but, on the contrary, of the intelligence of man in the vigour of his first development.

---

victory. By the balance, Libra, is not the equality which he established between the victors and the vanquished characterized? The scorpion, Scorpio, can tell of some revolt, some treason, and Sagittarius the vengeance which he drew. The goat, Capricorn, the water-bearer, Aquarius, and the fish, Pisces, relate more to the moral part of his history; they trace the events of his old age and perhaps by the two fishes he has wished to express the manner in which he believed his soul would be linked to that of his successor.

As it was in the environs of Balk about thirty-seven degrees latitude that these emblematical figures of the celestial sphere have been invented, the astronomers can see that a circle drawn from the side of the austral pole by the constellations of the Ship, the Whale, the Altar, the Centaur, and the space left below them, in the most ancient spheres, show exactly the horizon of this latitude and give in consequence, the place of their invention.

CHAPTER III

THUS the Borean Race had definitely taken dominion over the Sudeen. The remnants of the latter, repulsed on all sides towards the deserts of Africa, were about becoming extinct. The Indian Empire extended over all the inhabited earth. With the exception of a few rejected peoples at the extremities of the South and the North, there existed for all men but a single cult, of which a sole supreme pontiff maintained the dogmas and regulated the ceremonies, and a single government, of which a sole sovereign king had the jurisdiction. This supreme pontiff and this sovereign king, bound to one another by the strongest ties, free without being independent, lent each other a mutual support and co-operated to preserve everything in a wonderful unity.

An edifice so majestic was not at all the work of hazard; it had its foundation in the nature of things and received its principles, forms, and developments from the simultaneous action of the three great powers which rule the Universe. Even as two metals become stronger when amalgamated, the two races gave to the materials of the edifice more solidity, by mingling the one with the other.

It is useless to say how much splendour this epoch of human civilization had, and how much happiness it procured. The Brahmans, who described it as their third age, did not weary of praising it; their Pouranas, vying with each other, resound with the most magnificent descriptions. Many centuries passed without leaving the least trace. The happiness of man is like the calm of seas; it presents fewer pictures and leaves fewer memories than calamities and tempest.

But then, this was only the youth of the race; although all was brilliant and ostentatious, nothing was as yet profoundly beautiful; passions moreover were to be feared; and this came to pass. Man had still need of lessons; he received them.

I have described in another work the singular cause which disturbed the harmony existing in the greatest and most glorious empire that had ever appeared on earth; and regarding this, I have entered into most minute details which would be forbidden me here. This cause, who would believe it! had its faint beginning in music. To understand this, it is necessary to make a momentary truce to the prejudices of our childhood and understand what Pythagoras, Zoroaster, Kong-tzée, Plato, and all the sages of antiquity have said, that music is the universal science, the science without which one cannot penetrate the intimate essence of anything. This science was here, however, only the pretext of the overthrow which occurred. The real cause was the nature of Man which, constantly pushing him ahead in his course, can leave him stationary on the same point but a short time. His intelligence once shaken can no longer be stopped; a profound truth moves him even unawares; he feels that he is not in his place and that he must attain it. Intellectual men are not long in becoming contemplative; they wish to know the reasons of everything; and, as the Universe is linked with their exploration, it is felt that they have much to do and many opportunities to be mistaken.

I have already said that, at the epoch when the Celts made the conquest of India, they found established there a complete system of physical and metaphysical sciences. It appears certain that, at that time, the Atlantean cosmogony carried all back to the Absolute Unity and made all emanate from and depend on a sole Principle. This unique Principle, named *Iswara*, was conceived purely spiritual. One cannot deny that this doctrine does not present great advantages; but one must agree that it involves some disadvantages, particularly when the people, to whom it is given, do not find themselves in proper conditions to receive it. It is necessary, in order that the dogma of Absolute Unity may rest in pure spiritualism and not draw the people, whose cult it is, into materialism and abject anthropomorphism, that this people be enough enlightened to reason always justly, or that it be shallow enough not to reason at all. If it possesses only half-intellectual intelligence, then, as its physical learning leads it to draw just inferences from certain principles, the fallacies of which it cannot perceive, its deviation is inevitable; it will become atheistic or it will change the dogma.

Since it is proved that the Atlanteans had admitted the dogma of a sole Principle, and that this Principle had been until then in harmony with their situation, one cannot refuse to believe that they had arrived at the highest degree of social state. Their empire had embraced the earth, but, doubtless, after having shed their greatest brilliancy the lights had begun to be obscured when the Celts conquered them. The Hindus, who had succeeded them in another part of the globe, although their most learned disciples, were far from possessing the same means. Their government still progressed, thanks to the impulse which it had received, but already the means were worn out and the principles of life which had animated it had not reappeared.

Such was the condition of things many centuries indeed before the arrival of Rama. It is evident that if this Theocrat had not found the Empire of the Atlanteans in its decline and tottering upon its base, not only would he not have so easily taken possession of it, but he would not even have tried to do it, for Providence would not have willed it so. He adopted, as I have said, the Divine Unity to which he joined the cult of the Ancestors, and, finding all the sciences founded on a unique Principle, offered them thus to the consideration of his people.

But it came to pass, after a lapse of time more or less long, that one of the sovereign pontiffs, examining the musical system of Bharata, which was believed founded upon the sole Principle, as everything else, perceived that it was not thus with it and that it was necessary to admit two Principles into the generation of sounds. [1]

Now, that which made music such an important science for the ancients was the faculty which they had recognized in it, of being able easily to assist the transition from the physical to the intellectual; so that in transporting the ideas that it contributed from one nature to another, they believed themselves authorized to pronounce by analogy—from the known o the unknown.   Music was therefore a sort of proportional measure in their hands that they applied to spiritual essences.

The discovery which this sovereign pontiff had just made in the musical system, having been divulged and recognized throughout all the Empire, the contemplative savants did not delay in taking possession of it and in employing it, according to the custom, to explain by its means the cosmogonical laws of the Universe; and soon they saw with astonishment, that what they had heretofore considered as the product of an Absolute Unity was that of a Combined Duality.   They would have been able, doubtless, without being alarmed at this idea, to set all in its place, regarding the two Principles whose existence they were forced to admit as primordial substance, instead of regarding them as relating to principles, even as Zoroaster did some centuries later; but

---

[1] I have given great details on this subject as well as on all those which I only indicate here, in a work on *La Musique* which will be published shortly.

it would have been necessary to raise them to heights which were still beyond their intelligence. Accustomed to see everything in Iswara, they had not the force to dispossess it of its supremacy, and they preferred rather to double it, as it were, by joining to it a new Principle which they called *Pracriti*, that is to say, Nature. This new Principle possessed the *sakti*, or the conceptive power, and the ancient Iswara, the *bidja*, or the generating and vivifying power.

The result of this first step, which was of rather long duration, was therefore to consider the Universe as the product of two Principles possessing, each in its own particular, one the faculty of the male, and the other, that of the female. This system, whose implicity attracted at first, was generally adopted. One finds among most peoples these two Principles invoked by a multitude of names. Sanchoniathon called *Hipsystos*, the Most High, and his wife *Berouth*, the Creation, or Nature. The Hindus possess more than a thousand names, which they have given at various times to these two cosmogonical Principles. The Egyptians, Greeks, and Latins have an infinity of epithets to designate them. Those that we use today most generally in poetry are included in the mythological names of Saturn and Rhea, corresponding to those of Iswara and Pracriti.[1]

---

[1] The names of *Saturn* and *Rhea* signify the fiery Principle and the watery Principle. The two roots which compose them are recognized in the names of the two races, the Sudeen and the Borean.

CHAPTER IV

EIGHTH REVOLUTION—DIVISION OF THE UNIVERSAL PRINCI-
PLES—INFLUENCE OF MUSIC—QUESTIONS REGARDING
THE PRIMARY CAUSE: IS IT MALE OR FEMALE?—SCHISM
IN THE EMPIRE FOR THIS REASON

BUT as soon as the dependent nations of the Indian
Empire were authorized to consider the Universe as
the product of two Principles, one male and the other female,
concerning the nature of these same Principles, they were
unconsciously moved to put forth questions which the circumstances necessarily brought about. Since the Universe
is the result of two powerful Principles, of which the one
acts with the faculties of the male and the other with those
of the female, they asked, how can the relations which link
them be considered? Are they independent of each other?
Equally innate and existing from all eternity? Or ought one
to see in one of them the pre-existing cause of its companion?
If they are both independent, how are they united? And,
if they are not, to which of the two ought the other to be
submissive? Which is the first in rank, whether in order of
time, or in the comparative order of influence? Does Iswara
produce Pracriti, or Pracriti, Iswara? Which of the two
acts more necessarily and more actively in the procreation
of beings? Which is to be named first in the sacrifices, in
the religious hymns, when a vast multitude of people ad-
dresses them? Ought one to mingle or separate the worship

that is rendered them? Ought men and women to have separate altars for each, or one for both together?

It is said, they continue, that sacred music presents sure and facile means of distinguishing the two universal Principles; yes, as to their number and their opposed faculties, but not as to their rank and still less as to their sexual influence.[1] Thereupon, they interrogated the musical system of Bharata, which, far from throwing light upon all these difficulties, perplexed them only the more.

If the reader will recall what I said in the first book of this work, and if he will consider the obstacle which arrested the consolidation of the first age of civilization, he will see that it is here, under the highest relations, the same difficulty is presented. It was then only the question of governing a miserable cave; at present it is a question of the Universe. The forms are very varied; the basis is always the same.

Still, if persons little accustomed to reading the annals of the world find trifling and even ridiculous these questions whose calamitous consequences caused so much blood to flow, may they kindly believe that these questions are of tremendous depth in comparison to those which, a long time after, and in the centuries not far from ours, have caused ravages proportionate to the extent of the country which they were able to invade. For, at the epoch when the Indian Empire covered the whole earth, to what have these difficulties which have tended to divide it been reduced? To know whether the Primary Cause of the Universe, in admitting that it had in it but one, acted in the creation of things according to the faculties of the male or the female, and in the case where this Cause was double, as the analogies which were drawn from the musical science indicated, which of the two Principles was to be placed first, whether in the order of time, or in that of power, the masculine or the feminine? And when this empire, divided, torn in every way,

[1] One can see what I have said in regard to this in my work on *La Musique*, book iii., ch. 3.

was on the point of expiring in its last shreds in what was called the Greek Empire, or more justly the Lower Empire, to what end did the questions come, which for a thousand years had ravaged the Roman Empire? To know whether the light which certain fanatical monks, named *Hesicartes*, had seen about their navel—compared to that which shone forth on Mount Tabor—was created or uncreated? It is known that several councils, assembled to decide upon this singular difficulty, were divided, and by their dissensions facilitated the progress of the Tartars, who under the name of Turks took possession of Constantinople and put an end to the Empire. I am silent,—as much for the honour of humanity as to evade the prolixities, the numberless questions, each more ridiculous than the other, that I could relate. A learned reader will easily make up for my silence. Therefore it is not according to any particular opinion that one would have, that it is necessary to appreciate the questions of which I have just spoken, but according to the general condition of the mind, at the epoch in which they took place.

At first, these questions circulated surreptitiously through the Empire and were propagated there by strengthening themselves with anything irrefutable that their very nature presented. The supreme priesthood whether it feigned to ignore them, or examining, condemned them, equally irritated the authors. The disciples were multiplied on all sides; and, when forced to speak in favour of one or the other, the priesthood maintained the dominance of the masculine sex over the feminine, the priority of the male principle and its greater influence in the Universe; it was considered tyrannical and its orthodoxy, which it was obliged to strengthen with a certain legal force, became a deplorable intolerance. The irritated minds, fermented in secret, became excited and awaited only a favourable occasion to burst forth.

This occasion presented itself; for opportune occasions are never wanting when one desires and expects them. One reads in several Pouranas[1] that two princes of the reigning dynasty, both sons of King Ougra, having conceived intense hatred for each other, divided the Indian Empire, which, according to opposed opinions, was divided in their favour. The elder of these princes, called *Tarak'hya*, drew on his side the nobles of the State and citizens of the highest class; whereas the younger, named *Irshou*, had for himself the lowest class, as it were, the dregs of the people. This is why the partisans of Irshou were at first named in derision, *Pallis*,[2] that is to say, in Sanscrit, the Herdsmen.

These Pallis, or Herdsmen having become famous in history under the name of *Shepherds*, did not at first succeed in their projects; for Tarak'hya, having vigorously pursued them, destroyed their principal place of defence, which they had established on the borders of the river Narawind-hya and called from their name *Pallisthan*. It is very probable that if the movement caused by Irshou in the Indian Empire had been purely political, it would have remained such and would have been stifled at birth. But whether Irshou was really one of the zealous disciples of Pracriti, or whether he believed it useful to his interests to become so, he broke openly with the orthodox priesthood and declared that he adored the feminine faculty as pertaining to the Primal Cause of the Universe and that he accorded to it priority and pre-eminence over the masculine faculty. From that moment the aspect of things was changed. The war which had only been civil took on a religious form. His faction was strengthened by all those who had shared this doctrine, whatever their rank might be, and covered in a short time the entire face of the earth, of which nearly a half declared itself for him.

My plan is not to describe here the numberless combats

---

[1] Principally in the *Scanda-pourana* and in the *Brahmanda*.

[2] The Sanscrit word *Palli*, analogous to the Etruscan and to the Latin *Pales* the God or the Goddess of Shepherds, came from the Celtic *pal*, designating a long stick which serves as a shepherd's crook or a sceptre.

which were fought by the two parties; when, turn by turn victors or vanquished, rising again and destroying a hundred times the same trophies, they covered during many centuries, Asia, Africa, and Europe with bloody ruins. I feel that I have allowed myself to be led too much aside by the pleasure of retracing some extraordinary facts of this ancient history, so interesting and so little known! Let us come now to the principal results of the event of which I have spoken.

The disciples of the feminine faculty, called at first Pallis, the Shepherds, having taken for symbol of their cult the distinctive sign of this faculty, called in Sanscrit *Yoni*, were surnamed, in consequence, *Yonijas, Yawanas, Ionioi*, that is to say, *Ionians*, and as for mysterious reasons that it is useless to explain here, they had taken for ensign the colour red inclining to yellow, the name of *Pinkshas* or *Phœnicians*, which signifies *russet*, has been given them. All of these names, offensive in the mouths of their adversaries, became glorious in their own and were received or translated among all the nations where they triumphed and became quite as much titles of honour.[1]

On their side the Hindus, their antagonists, remaining faithful to the cult of the masculine faculty in the Divinity, had also their particular appellations; but as they triumphed

---

[1] The name of *Palli*, changed into that of *Bâlli* by the Chaldeans, Arabs, and Egyptians, who sounded with difficulty the consonant *p*, has signified according to the country and according to the times, governor, lord, sovereign, and even God. It exists still among the French in the title of *bailli* (bailiff). The name of *palace*, which is given to the dwelling of a sovereign, is derived from it. It is on account of this name that we have Pastor or Shepherd in many languages synonym of a lover or a man lovable with women. It is on account of the name *Yoni*, analogous to that of *Ioneh*, a dove, that this bird has been consecrated to the Goddess of Love, *Milydha, Aphrodite, Venus*, etc., and that all the arts of luxury, all the soft and delicate inventions have been attributed to Ionia. It is on account of the Phœnician colour called *ponceau* that the purple colour has been the emblem of sovereignty; lastly it is on account of the red dove which these people carried on their armorial bearings that the heraldic bird called the *Phœnix*, from the very name of the Phœnicians, has become so celebrated.

more rarely in Europe these appellations and symbols became much less common. However, one can recognize on certain monuments their most striking symbol, which was, by opposition to those of their enemies, the distinctive sign of the masculine faculty.[1] The colour of their ensign, white as that of the ancient Druids, caused the name of *Whites*, to be given them, and it is under this name, translated in diverse dialects, that one can distinguish in very ancient times the resistance which their adversaries—called sometimes *Philistines*, sometimes *Ionians*, sometimes *Phœnicians* or *Idumeans*, according as they were considered as Shepherds, adorers of the feminine faculty or bearing the red colour—encountered in different countries of Asia and of Europe.

---

[1] This sign called *Linga* in Sanscrit, *Phallos* or *Phallus* in Greek and Latin, is recognized although disfigured in the order of Doric architecture in opposition to the Ionic. This symbol transforms itself ordinarily into the head of a ram. The *Yoni* takes also the form of a violet and this is why this flower consecrated to Juno was so cherished by the Ionians.

The white colour which was that of the Druids, as it has since been that of the Brahmans, is the reason why in the greater part of the Celtic dialects, the word white is synonymous with sage, spiritual and savant. One still says in Germany *weis* white, and *wissen*, to know; *Ich weis*, I know, etc. In English *white* and *wit*, *witty*, *wisdom*, etc. It is presumable that the Argives and Albains, that is to say, the Whites, were the adversaries of the Phœnicians in Greece and Italy.

CHAPTER V

ORIGIN OF THE PHŒNICIAN SHEPHERDS—THEIR OPINIONS ON
THE PRIMAL CAUSE OF THE UNIVERSE—THEIR CONQUESTS
—NEW SCHISMS, WHENCE RESULT THE PERSIANS AND THE
CHINESE—ESTABLISHMENT OF THE MYSTERIES: WHY?

THESE dissenting Indians, as has been confirmed by
all the Sanscrit legends, never succeeded in making
great progress in India, properly speaking; but that did not
hinder them on the other hand from becoming extremely
powerful. Their first great settlement was effected upon
the Persian Gulf; from there they passed into Yemen,
which they conquered notwithstanding the powerful opposition which they encountered there. The Bodohnes
Celts, long time masters of Arabia, after having resisted
as much as they were able, preferred to be expatriated
than to submit, when finally obliged to cede to Destiny.
A large part passed into Ethiopia and the rest spread
about in the desert and became divided into wandering
peoples, who were called *Hebrews* for this reason.[1]   The
Phœnicians, however, having seized the dominion of the
sea which separated Arabia from Egypt, gave it their
name and came, as Herodotus said, to occupy the shores of

---

[1] The word *hebri*, from which we have made Hebrew, signifies transported,
deported, expatriated, passed on the other side.   It has the same root as the
word *harbi*, an Arab, but it has more force in that it expresses a greater
displacement.

157

the Mediterranean where they established the seat of their Empire.[1]

At this epoch, the Chaldean Empire was overthrown. One of the chiefs of the Phœnicians, known under the name of *Bâlli*, made the conquest of Plaksha in Asia Minor, and built upon the border of the Euphrates the celebrated city of Babel, to which he gave his name. This Bâlli, called *Belos* or *Belus* by the Greeks and Latins, was, then, the founder of the celebrated empire which has been called sometimes *Babylonian*, sometimes *Syrian* or *Assyrian*. The Hebrews, implacable enemies of the Phœnicians, because they were issued from the Bodohnes Celts, driven by these Shepherds from Blessed Arabia, and compelled to wander in the deserts, the Hebrews I say, gave to this Bâlli the title of *Nimrod* to express the violence and tyranny of his usurpation. But it was in vain that they tried to arrest the torrent which burst forth upon them. From the Nile to the Euphrates all submitted in a few centuries to the yoke of these formidable Shepherds who, although seated upon the throne, kept this name that had been given them in contempt. Upper Egypt resisted their efforts for a long period, on account of the vigorous partisans that the masculine faculty had there under the name of *Iswara*, *Israël*, or *Osiris;* but the opposed faculty finally took possession on all sides and the Goddess Isis, among the Thebans, and the Goddess Milydha, among the Babylonians, were likewise placed above Adonis. In Phrygia, the Great Mother *Mâ*, called *Dindymene* or *Cybele* by the Greeks, deprived *Attis*, the sovereign Father, of his virile force, and his priests could save themselves only by offering to him in sacrifice the same thing which the Orthodoxy had elsewhere made the emblem of his cult.

Such was in ancient times that influence of music, of which so much has been spoken, without ever seeking to

---

[1] The Pouranas of the Hindus gave it the name of *Pallisthan*, that is, Palestine, or properly speaking, Idumea or Phœnicia.

understand it.   Thence the severe laws promulgated against innovators in this science, and the efforts of the pontiffs to hide with care the essential principles in the depths of the sanctuaries.   It was this more especially that made the Egyptian priests, when forced to bow the head beneath the yoke of the shepherd kings and obliged to feign sentiments that they never had, dream of establishing those secret mysteries where Truth, buried and reserved for the initiates alone, appeared no more to the eyes of the profane except covered with the thickest veils.   It was in those mysteries that they consecrated the incidents of which I have just made mention, and because they could not openly testify their sorrow respecting the defeat of the masculine Principle in the Primal Cause of the Universe they invented that allegory so well known of Osiris betrayed, lacerated, whose scattered members stained Egypt with blood; whilst Isis, abandoned to the most terrible despair, although crowned by the hand of Anubis and suspected of having taken part in this cowardly treason, weeping gathers the members of her spouse and encloses them in a tomb, with the exception of one which was lost in the waters of the Nile.   This ingenious allegory, which was received in all the sanctuaries where orthodoxy was preserved by its partisans, is found with a few changes of name in all the mythologies of the earth. [1]

[1] The chronologists have experienced great difficulty in fixing the epoch of the Phœnician Shepherds in Egypt. This appears to me very easy, as one can consult facts and not be confined to limits that one cannot pass beyond. We know by the sacred books of the Hindus that the schism of Irshou, which gave birth to these Shepherds, took place before the beginning of the Kail-youg, about 3200 B. C.   Now these peoples, at first having settled in the Persian Gulf, required many centuries in order to establish themselves solidly in Palestine and to put themselves in a condition to attack a kingdom as powerful as Egypt.   They certainly began with the conquest of Arabia and Chaldea.   We know by the table of the thirty Egyptian Dynasties of Manetho, preserved by Julius Africanus, that the Phœnician Shepherds produced three of these Dynasties, from the XV. to XVII., of which the total duration was 953 years.   The Pharaoh Amos, who vanquished them, mounted the throne

In the meantime, the orthodox Hindus, justly alarmed
at the success of their adversaries, and seeing their subdivided empire collapsing abroad, put all their attentions
upon defending at least the centre, by collecting there all
their forces. There appeared upon the pontifical throne
an extraordinary man who was compared to the first Rama
and honoured by his name because of the force which he
manifested. For some time he upheld this edifice about to
fall, but it was reserved for a greater man to arrest the downfall. Meanwhile the Yonijas were declared impious, anathematized and banished for life. All commerce with them
was prohibited. It was forbidden the Hindus not only to
receive them, but even to go to see them in their own country. The red colour which served as their ensign was regarded as abominable. The Brahmans were obliged to
abstain from ever touching anything which bore this colour,
even in their greatest distress, and the river Indus was
designated as the fatal limit which none could pass without
incurring anathema.

These vigorous measures, perhaps necessary to preserve
the whole, had, nevertheless, the disadvantage of again
detaching several parties, which gave rise to a schism nearly
as great as the first. This new schism had birth in the heart
of the warmest partisans of the male principle and of the
most zealous defenders of its priority and pre-eminence.
Among the Iranians a man endowed with great force of
intelligence, named Zeradosht or Zoroaster, declared that

---

about 1750 years before our era and preceded by 130 years the famous Amen-
hotep III., who erected in honour of the Sun the colossal statue of Memnon.
So that, if one unites this 1750 years with the first 953 he will find that it was
about the year 2703 before our era that the Phœnicians entered Egypt, about
five centuries after the schism of Irshou.

According to the data, it can reasonably be inferred that the first Egyptian mysteries were celebrated twenty-five or twenty-six centuries before
Christ. A tradition exists, however, that, at the time when they commenced,
the equinox of the spring fell upon the first degrees of Taurus, and this shows
a remarkable coincidence.

they were deceived in conceiving the two cosmogonical Principles, Iswara and Pracriti, as relating to principles and possessing one the faculty of the male and the other the faculty of the female; that they ought, on the contrary, to be regarded as primordial substance, both males and both emanating from Eternity, Wodh; but the one acting in the spirit as Principle of good and the other in matter as Principle of evil; the first called *Ormuzd*, the Genius of Light, and the other *Ahriman*, the Genius of Darkness.

Among the peoples who dwelt beyond the Ganges, another not less audacious theosophist called *Fo-Hi* asserted that the first schism of the Pallis had had birth in a misunderstanding, and that it could easily have been averted if it had been examined; that the sexual faculties had been wrongly placed upon two cosmogonical Principles, Iswara and Pracriti, or Spirit and Matter; that it was Pracriti, or Matter, which possessed the masculine faculty, stable and igneous, whereas Iswara, or Spirit, possessed the feminine faculty, volatile and humid. So that, according to him, the Phœnicians were not schismatical in placing Matter before Spirit but only in attributing to it faculties opposed to those which it really has.

Zeradosht and Fo-Hi brought to the support of their reasons proofs drawn from the musical science, which seemed peremptory, but which would be quite out of place here.[1] They both flattered themselves to restore calm in the Empire by satisfying in a measure the pretentions of the refractory Pallis; their hope was equally deceived. The sacerdotal caste, seeing further than they themselves the consequences of their own idea, rejected and condemned them alike. Zeradosht, more irritated even than Fo-Hi, because he was more passionate, kindled a civil and religious war, whose definite result was the absolute separation of Iran. The peoples who recognized him as their theocratic sovereign took henceforth the names of *Parthes*, *Parses*, or *Perses*,

[1] They can be found in the work already cited.

because of the name *Paradas*, which the orthodox Hindus had given them in derision. These peoples, who later took possession of the dominion of Asia, became very celebrated there and very powerful. They had at different epochs diverse theocratic legislators, who took successively the name of the first Zeradosht[1] whom we call *Zoroaster*. The last, who appeared in the time of Darius, son of Hystaspes, is the one whose doctrine, recorded in the *Zend-Avesta*, is still followed by the Ghébres.[2]

The two opposed principles of light and darkness, Ormuzd and Ahriman, are therein presented as equal issues of Time-Without-Limit, otherwise Eternity, the sole *Principe principiant* to which they are submissive. The third Principle which unites them is called *Mithra*. This mediator Principle represents the Will of Man, as Ormuzd and Ahriman represent Providence and Destiny. This cosmogonical system is united to the cult of the Ancestors, as are all those belonging to the same origin. The Eternal *principe principiant* is worshipped there under the emblem of fire.

As to Fo-Hi,[3] endowed with a character more pacific and more gentle than Zeradosht, he did not wish to kindle a new civil war in the midst of the empire, but departed, followed by his partisans, and, passing through the deserts of India which bordered on the Orient, he established himself upon the banks of the Hoang-ho River, which he named thus Yellow River, on account of the yellow colour which he took for his ensign, to distinguish himself from the orthodox

---

[1] I believe that this name, whose signification has always been wanting, is perhaps derived from the two Celtic and Phœnician roots *Syrah-d'Osht*, the prince, or the chief of the aggression, or the army.

[2] The *Ghébres* are the remains of the celebrated peoples whom Moses called *Ghiborim* and whom the Greeks have known under the name of *Hyperboreans;* these are the sole descendants of the Borean People who have preserved the ancient name to our day. They called the prince in whose reign the last Zeradosht appeared, *Gustasps*. The *Zend-Avesta*, translated by Anquetil-Duperron, is only a sort of breviary of the work of this ancient Theosophist.

[3] The name of *Fo-Hi* signifies the Father of Life. It is worthy of attention that the two roots which compose this name are of Celtic origin.

Hindus, as well as not to be confused with the Phœnicians. He collected upon the borders of this river a few hordes of wandering Tartars, ancient *débris* of the Yellow Race, who united with his followers, and he gave to them his doctrine which strongly resembled in substance that of Zoroaster. According to him, the two *Principes principiés* are *Yn*, repose, and *Yang*, movement, both issues of a single *Principe principiant* called *Tai-ki*, Primal Cause. The two Principles *Yn* and *Yang* give birth by their reciprocal action to a third mediator Principle called *Pan-Kou*, the Universal Being; there existed then three powers called *Tieng-hoang*, *Ti-hoang* and *Gin-hoang*, that is to say, the Celestial Kingdom, the Terrestrial Kingdom, and the Kingdom of Man, or in other terms,—Providence, Destiny, and the Will of Man,—the same that I established in the beginning of this work. The cult of the Ancestors was admitted still more directly into the religion of Fo-Hi than into that of Zoroaster.

It is to this emigration that the Sanscrit books attribute the origin of the Chinese Empire, which they name *Tchandra-Douïp*, the region of the masculine moon, that is to say, the region where the feminine Principle has become masculine. The name of *Tchinas*, which the Brahmans give to the peoples who inhabited it, does not signify absolutely impious and reproved ones, as that of *Yawanas*, by which they signify the Ionians in general and the Greeks in particular, but only the schismatics. The Chinese whom we call by this offensive name have not accepted it; they name themselves and they name their own country *Tien-hia*, that which is the most precious under heaven.[1]

It is certain that of all the dismemberments of the Indian Empire which were made at this time, doubtless none equalled

---

[1] There exists a tradition important chronologically. One finds at the epoch of the first astronomical observations among the Chinese, that the polar star, called *Yeu-tchu*, *le pivot de la droite*, was in the constellation of the Dragon, which we designate as *Alpha Draconis*. This tradition, which we assign to about 2700 years before our era offers a new coincidence which corroborates all that I have said in a preceding note.

that of the Tchinas, either in extent or power; nor did any other nation observe with more inviolable respect the laws and customs of its ancestors, whose cult was never extinguished in its midst.   It is today a very beautiful fragment of the Universal Empire which has survived almost intact the torrent of ages.   Whereas Asia has experienced a host of revolutions; whereas the weak remnants of the Indian Empire have been the prey of thirty rival nations; whereas the sceptre of the Phœnicians, torn from their hands by the Assyrians, passed into those of the Egyptians, the Arabs, and even the Etruscans; whereas it returned again into the hands of the Assyrians to fall into that of the Medes, the Persians, the Greeks, and Romans; whereas, finally, its remains, escaped from the ruin of Constantinople, have been dispersed into all the countries of Europe,—China has survived these catastrophes, which have changed a hundred times the face of the world and has never been able to be conquered without the force of its constitution having immediately enslaved its own conquerors.

CHAPTER VI

REFLECTIONS UPON THE DISMEMBERMENT OF THE UNIVERSAL EMPIRE

BEFORE continuing this historical exploration, which assuredly gives to my first hypothesis a force more than hypothetical, it seems to me important to record here a reflection. One will ask, perhaps, why the empire of Rama, whose principle was evidently providential and whose foundations the Will of Man had laid in accord with Providence, was not more durable. If the difficulty were confined there, and it were not asked why it was not eternal, I should answer easily; and if the difficulty were pushed to the utmost bounds, I should answer still more easily. First, I should say to those who may not know, that whatever is of Absolute Eternity, *GOD* alone possesses it; for one cannot admit of two Absolute Beings without implicating contradiction. The eternity which God imparts can therefore be only a relative eternity the principle and the mode of which this Absolute Eternity determines. All forms are in the domain of time; time itself is but the succession of forms; essences alone are indestructible because they depend for their principle on Absolute Essence which can never pass: for to conceive of transition, space must be conceived, and how can space be conceived outside of Absolute Space?

One must then distinguish form from essence, time from space, and relative eternity from Absolute Eternity. Form,

Time, Relative Eternity are emanations; Essence, Space,
Absolute Eternity are divine identities. All that which
constitutes these identities is immutable; all that which
belongs to these emanations is mutable. Forms succeeding
one another beget Time; Time gives birth to Relative Eternity, but this eternity and the time which measures it and
the forms with which it is filled vanish alike in the Essence
which gives forms, in the Space which creates Time,
and in the Absolute Eternity which envelops Relative
Eternity.

Everything has its weight, its number, and its measure,
that is to say, its rank in the scale of beings, its own faculties,
and its relative power. Nothing can appear in elementary
life without submitting to the laws of that life. Now, the
first of these laws is to appear there under a form, subject
to the three epochs of beginning, middle, and end. All form
whose movement proper is not disturbed by foreign events
passes through these three epochs; but it is only the smallest
number that passes through without interruption. The
greater part of the forms are broken from the beginning,
few attain the middle of their existence, and still fewer arrive
at the end. The more forms are multiplied in a single
species, the more this species miscarries in its origin. Who
can count, for example, how many acorns an oak tree produces, all destined to become oaks, before another oak
grows from a single one of these acorns?

If among the three powers which rule the Universe,
Destiny obtained the sole dominion; if the Will of Man disappeared or were rendered inert; if Providence were absent,
can one conceive what terrible chaos would follow this state
of things? All species, struggling against each other, would
declare an endless war; all would desire to occupy the earth
alone and to bring to a successful issue all the germs which
they scatter; so that there would be no reason why, in the
vegetable kingdom for example, the species of the oak, the
elm, or any other tree should not stifle all the others and

cover all the earth.[1] But the Will of Man is there to maintain all in just limits, in the vegetable kingdom as well as in the animal, and to prevent noxious plants and dangerous animals from multiplying as much as their strength would permit. This Will, moved by its own interest, watches, on the contrary, to see that the weak but useful species are propagated and preserved, thanks to the care that it gives them.

But although the Will of Man may prefer one species to another and may cover with splendid harvests of corn or rice immense plains which would produce without it only thistles or some other sterile plants; although it may propagate the vine upon the hillsides, where only heather would otherwise grow, and may lead many herds of tame animals into desert p aces where only ferocious beasts would dwell; although it may bring all to a state of perfection by cultivation, this Will, however, can in no way change the intimate nature of anything nor take it away from the laws of Destiny, from whose domain it is obliged to draw its nutriment. All that which lives the elementary life must submit to its laws. The annual plant cannot live two winters; the sturdy oak must reach the stage of decomposition; and, whereas the ephemeral fly lives only a day, the elephant, that can live two centuries, is obliged like it to die.

Thus, then, Man can choose among the physical germs or the intellectual principles which Providence places at his disposition, those whose development he wishes to protect; he can understand their proper faculties, their diverse virtues, their vital force, their relative duration, and know in advance what will be the result of his care. An agriculturist

[1] Buffon made the judicious remark that Nature, which tends to organize bodies as much as possible, emits an immense quantity of germs. This naturalist has made the calculation that if nothing arrested the productive power of a germ, as the seed of an elm for example, after a huhdred and fifty years there would be more than a million million cubic leagues of organized elm timber; so that the entire earth would be covered with organized material of a single species.

knows well, for example, that if he sows a grain of corn he will grow a plant only frail and transient, whereas if he sows an acorn he will obtain a hardy and deep-rooted tree; but he knows also that the annual plant will give him a prompt and easy pleasure, whereas the centenary tree will make him wait a long time for its fruit. His choice then will be in either case influenced by his needs and will be founded upon his agricultural knowledge; he will intelligently make the decision. The position of the legislator will be exactly the same as that of the agriculturist, if the one could unite to the same degree the experience which enlightens the conduct of the other. This is almost impossible; however the legislator, quite blind and inexperienced, who will throw political principles haphazard without knowing beforehand either the nature of these principles or that of the people to whom he destines them, will not merit at all this title, and will resemble the ignorant agriculturist who would sow rice in an arid sand or who would plant the vine in a swamp. Both will be justly considered fools, worthy of all sorts of calamities that await them.

Now that I have thrown sufficient light upon the main point of the question that I propose to solve, I will say that Rama having received directly from Providence the intellectual principle of a theocratic empire, threw the germ into favourable conditions which hastened the development. But this germ, the hardiest and most deep rooted of all of its species, must submit, however, to the vicissitudes of all things confided to Destiny, and, inasmuch as it had a beginning of temporal existence, it must necessarily after having attained its prime decline toward its death. I have shown by several chronological allusions that the epoch of its beginning could date back about six thousand seven hundred years before our era. Now the first disturbance which was felt and of which history has preserved the memory dates from the year 3200 B.C. This empire remained then in all the splendour of its youth during thirty-five centuries. At this time, the passions began to make themselves felt and formed in its midst storms more or less violent. It survived, however, notwithstanding the defections and schisms of which I have spoken, and, for eleven or twelve centuries, possessed the whole of India. It was not until the year 2100 B.C. that the extinction of the Solar dynasty and even that of the Lunar dynasty which Krishna had established, as I shall presently relate, having brought about its political downfall, it concentrated itself in the sole religious existence and placed its principal seat in Tibet where it still survives, notwithstanding its great age, in the Lamaic cult.

If we consider that this cult, today more than eighty-five centuries old, still rules over a great part of Asia, after having enjoyed nearly forty-six centuries of the Universal Empire, thirty-five of which were enveloped in a splendour unmarred by any shadow, one will agree that its fate has been fairly good and that one must not be either astonished or distressed at its decline or at its impending disappearance.

CHAPTER VII

NOW let us return to the Phœnicians, and continue to
sketch in a general way the sequence of their history.
The schismatic Shepherds having caused the first division of the Indian Empire, soon were divided among themselves. The flame of the fire which they had kindled must,
lacking exterior fuel, necessarily react upon themselves.
Although, at first, they agreed upon the principal point of
the schism, which was the pre-eminence accorded in the
Universe to the feminine faculty, they were not long in
proposing difficulties quite as serious regarding the nature
of this faculty. Many sects were formed, the greater part
of which pretended that this faculty ought not to be considered as simply conceptive but as creative, and that it ought
to be designated by the name of *Hebe*, which in Phœnician
dialect signifies love of the feminine.[1] This sect asserted
that, from the origin of things, there existed two beings,
Love and Chaos; Love, the spiritual feminine Principle;

[1] The modern German word *Liebe*, love, has the same root as the Phœnician
word *hêbeh;* it is likewise feminine gender. This analogy is noticeable in all
words extending back to great antiquity. The word *chaos* opposed to that of
hebe develops the idea of all that which serves as basis of things, as dregs, waste
matter, the *caput mortuum.* Generally speaking all that which remains of a
being after the spirit has departed.

Chaos, the material masculine Principle.   According to the doctrine which spread, it was Love that brought order out of Chaos and gave birth to the Universe.

It is very certain that the Phœnician sect which adopted this cosmogony and recognized in Love, feminine Principle, Creator of all things, was very numerous and widespread. The fragments that remain to us of Sanchoniathon and the Greek theogony of Hesiod are manifest proof of it.   It is a matter worthy of attention that this doctrine was not very different from that of the ancient Celts from whom Rama had felt obliged to separate more than forty centuries before.   It also happened, as soon as the Phœnicians appeared upon the meridional coasts of Europe, that they took possession of the colonies placed there by the Hindus upon the ruins of those of the Atlanteans, and had no trouble in becoming allied with the rest of the Celts still existing in the interior of the land, on the septentrional coasts of Denmark, or in the isles of Britain.   So that they made a sort of fusion of the two cults which should be readily recognized in the mythological book of both peoples.[1]

The Phœnicians, possessors of various kinds of ethical and physical knowledge, but whose cult was destitute of rites, made then a most unfortunate exchange.   They taught the Celts their sciences and received in return a multitude of superstitions, among which human sacrifices were of the first rank.   As they had departed from the ways of Providence and had fallen into those of Destiny, they could only oppose it with a passionate and badly enlightened Will; they abandoned themselves to these new superstitions with more enthusiasm than those even who had delivered these superstitions to them.   Haruspices, augurs, divinations of all sorts found place in their new religion.   They adopted the cult of Thor with all its atrocities, and became infatuated to the extent of giving his name to one of the cities.   This

---

[1] It is sufficient to read the fragment which remains of Sanchoniathon and the fables found in the Icelandic *Edda* to be convinced of what I advance.

was the famous metropolis of Tyre, in which they raised a magnificent temple under the name of Herchôl.

This name, by a coincidence which should not escape the sagacity of the reader, is found to have the same meaning in Celtic as the Phœnician. However the words which composed it had already something too ancient; they translated them into the more modern, *Melicartz*,[1] the king of the Earth. As for Teutad, whom they borrowed also from the Celts, they gave him the name *par excellence* of *Moloc*, the king, or that of *Krôn*, the Crowned.[2] This became in course of time the famous *Kronos* of the Greeks, the Saturn of the Etruscans, from whom came all the other mythological gods of the ancient polytheists.

It is a very singular thing to see how these Phœnicians, after having taken nearly all the mythological divinities from the Celts, and having adapted them to their diverse cosmogonical systems, later gave them back to them under a variety of new names and presented them under an infinity of emblems which rendered them unrecognizable; for the thoughtlessness and the inconstancy peculiar to these peoples furnished them with the most incongruous and extravagant ideas, as is proved by the contradictions and remarkable incoherencies of their mythology, which is preserved for the most part by the Greeks and Romans, who sprang from them. Their instability in this regard is as striking as the tenacity and perseverance of the Chinese, their most decided antagonists. It seemed that the feminine faculty to which they had accorded the universal supremacy worked upon their versatile imagination. If it were a question of writing their history, it could easily be shown that the multitude of names which the Phœnician nations had at different times,

---

[1] We know it from the Greeks under the name of *Melicertes*.

[2] The word *Krôn* signifies properly a horn in Phœnician. But I have said this was originally on account of the horn of the *ram*, from which were designed all the sacerdotal and royal head-dresses. The Celtic word *Krohne*, a crown, is derived from it.

and which they had given to their colonies, have only characterized the versatility of their ideas and the enormous
quantity of their cosmogonical symbols.

But not only, as I have said, were the Phœnicians divided
into a great number of sects which weakened them; but they
also had to struggle against several nations attached secretly
to orthodoxy, and over whom they held sway rather by the
force of arms than by the justice of their arguments.   Among
the nations, the Egyptians were those who always bore most
impatiently the yoke of these Shepherd Kings, and who, as
their history attests, made the most frequent efforts to
throw it off.   I have already said, it was to this secret attachment to orthodoxy that those Mysteries of Isis owed their origin, so famous afterwards and which served as model for all
others, even to those which, on account of different changes
made in the cult, had quite another aim and quite another
form.   However, notwithstanding this interior opposition,
as much religious as political, it was by no means Egypt
that first had the glory of throwing off the yoke of the
Phœnicians.   The sacred books of the Brahmans state
expressly that it was upon the borders of the *Kamoud-vati*,
or the Euphrates, that the masculine faculty having retaken
dominion over the feminine faculty, its symbol was adored
anew under the name of *Bâl-Iswara-Linga*.[1]   The peoples
of these borders returned thus into orthodoxy, but they
did not unite with the Indian Empire; they formed a distinctive one, the duration and splendour of which were very
great.

It was from the heart of this empire that the first purely
political conqueror arose that had appeared in the Borean
Race.   Up to that time all the wars had had as object,
either the preservation of the race or civil or religious dis-

---

[1] This epoch can be dated from the erection of the famous tower of Babel,
which according to the observations of the Chaldeans sent by Callisthenes to
Alexander, dates back 1903 years before this conqueror, and places this epoch
2230 years before our era; about a thousand years after the schism of Irshou.

sensions. History names this conqueror *Ninus*, that is to say the son of the Lord[1]; which caused him to be considered in later times as the son of Belus; but Belus, or rather Bâl, was the name given to the supreme Being, to the one whom the Celts named *Teutad*, the Hindus *Iswara*, and the Phœnicians *Moloch*.

The first conquest of Ninus was that of Iran, which lost then its primitive name to take that of Persia, preserved by this country to this day. The dynasty, which the first Zoroaster had established there, nearly a thousand years before this event, was called *Mahabad*, that is to say, the Great-Wisdom[2]; it was purely theocratic. It was succeeded by that of the Pishdadiens, or Judges, kinds of Viceroys that the Assyrian monarch gave them. This last dynasty did not end until the accession to the throne of Kai-Kosrou, whom we call Cyrus.

Ninus, after having extended his conquests well into Scythia and as far as the Celts of Europe, turned his arms against India and attempted to take the Empire of Rama; but death surprised him in the midst of his vast projects, of which his wife, who succeeded him, accomplished a part. This celebrated woman, in order to testify that she took no part in the schism of the Shepherds, and in order to gain adherents among the orthodox Hindus, called herself *Semiramis*, that is to say, the Splendour of Rama,[3] and took for ensign a white dove.

But long before this epoch, there came to pass in India a very important event, which was to have the greatest influence over the destinies of the Universe. It is well to retrace our steps a moment.

----

[1] *Nin-Iah* signifies in Chaldean, as in Phœnician, the progeny of the sovereign Being.

[2] It should be written *Mâha-wôdh*, the eternal Power or the Great Eternity. Today the Parsees, called *Ghèbres*, give their priests the name of *Mobêd*.

[3] The word *Sem* or *Shem* signifies a sign, a place, a name, or a brilliant thing.

CHAPTER VIII

NEW DEVELOPMENTS IN THE INTELLECTUAL SPHERE—AN-
OTHER DIVINE ENVOY: KRISHNA—ORIGIN OF MAGIC
AMONG THE CHALDEANS AND OF THEURGY IN EGYPT—
NEW ASPECT OF THE UNIVERSE—ADMISSION OF A TRINITY
INTO THE DIVINE UNITY

IT was evident that the schism of the Phœnician Shepherds
brought about the division and the downfall of the Universal Empire of Rama; and that it was necessary to find a
means of preserving the central force as long as it would be
needed, in order that the truths which ought to survive the
catastrophe should not be swallowed up with it. Providence
willed it, and an extraordinary man appeared in the world:
this man, born among the Shepherds, as indicated by his
name *Gopalla*,[1] was afterwards called *Krishna*, celestial-
blue, on account of the colour which he took for his emblem.
The Brahmans regard him today as one of the most brilliant
Manifestations of the Divinity, and place him ordinarily
at the eighth incarnation of *Vishnu*. It was generally
agreed that this divine man, seeing the deplorable condition
to which the rival sects of the *Lingajas* and of the *Yonijas*
had reduced the Indian Empire, and groaning over numberless evils, which their fanaticism had caused, undertook
to make amends for the evil which had resulted from it, by

[1] *Gopalla* signifies properly the driver. The Hindus in making his apotheo-
sis place him among the constellations. It is the βούτης of the Greeks, which
the Arabs still name *Muphrid-al-Rami*, the one that explains Rama.

175

bringing their minds to an intermediary doctrine, tolerant in its principles, susceptible of satisfying the objections of all parties, and fitted to remove their doubts without incensing them against each other.

Krishna, they said, began by establishing that the two faculties, male and female, were equally essential, equally influential in the production of beings; but that these faculties would remain eternally separated one from the other and consequently inert, if a third faculty did not provide the means of uniting them. This faculty which he attributed to Vishnu was conceived by him as a sort of median bond between Iswara and Pracriti, so that if by the one was understood the spirit and by the other matter, the third faculty should be considered as the soul which operates the union of the two. That being stated this great man went further. He caused it to be conceived that the two faculties which are shown independent and isolated in physical and primordial beings, are not so in intellectual and spiritual beings; so that each male faculty possesses its inherent female faculty and each female faculty its male faculty. Thus, admitting a sort of universal hermaphroditism, Krishna taught that each cosmogonical principle was double. Therefore, leaving aside the Absolute Being, Wôdh,[1] as inaccessible to the human understanding and considering Iswara and Pracriti as the creative and inherent faculties, he established three principles of the Universe, emanated from this Ineffable Being, which he named *Brahma*, *Vishnu*, and *Siva*, to which he added as their inherent faculties Sarasvati, Lakshmi, and Bhavani.[2] Such was the origin

---

[1] The Brahmans named also the Absolute Being, *Karta*, the Primary Cause; *Baravastou*, the Great Being; *Parasashy*, the Sole Sovereign, etc. Its mysterious name that they never utter for fear of profaning it, is *O. M.* This name composed of three letters, A. U. M., represents Vishnu, Siva, and Brahma. These three divinities according to the doctrine of Krishna constitute but one and are only the manifested faculties of Absolute Eternity.

[2] The doctrine of Indian Theosophy, as I have just briefly explained, is contained in the Pouranas entitled *Bagwhat-Vedam*, and *Bagwhat-ghita*. One

of this Indian Trinity, which under different names and different emblems has been admitted or known by all the peoples of the earth.

Among the three persons of this Trinity, the Indian prophet chose Vishnu as the principal and offered him in preference to the adoration of his people. He set aside, in consequence, the symbols of *Linga* and of *Yoni*, which had caused so many troubles, and took for his the figure of the umbilicus, as uniting the other two and characterizing the doctrine of the Divine Hermaphroditism which he established. This doctrine had a prodigious success in India, properly speaking, where its first effect was to restore peace. Religious fanaticism became extinct there. Krishna conceived at that time the vast design of beginning again the Universal Empire. He dared to go even further than Rama and to reinstate the Lunar dynasty which that ancient Theocrat had judged fitting to interrupt and which had remained so for more than thirty-six centuries; but the providential movement did not go so far. The political ideas could not follow the course of moral ideas; and the schism which was made was too strong for the disunited parties ever to reassemble and be united.

The veritable good which resulted from the mission of Krishna after that of re-establishing religious peace, was to give to India a moral force capable of resisting all invasions, and of placing it at the head of universal civilization as worthy to teach and to rule its own conquerors. So that the conquest of this country was long considered as the aim of an immortal glory, rather intellectual than physical. All the heroes that a noble emulation urged into the career of conquest, from Ninus to Alexander, coveted the surname of vanquisher of India and believed thus to march

---

must understand by *Brahma*, the Spirit or Intelligence; by *Vishnu*, the Soul or Understanding, and by *Siva*, the Body or Instinct. *Sarasvati* represents the intellectual sphere; *Lakshmi*, the animistic, and *Bhavani*, the instinctive, and that as much in universal nature as in particular nature.

in the footsteps of Rama, the first Scander of the two horns.

Ninus and Semiramis attempted to triumph over India and after them Larthe Sethos made the conquest. This Sethos having come from Etruria, as I will relate further on, was seventeenth monarch after Amasis, the very one who put an end in Egypt to the Kingdom of the Shepherds. At about the same epoch, when these Shepherds were forced to leave the throne of Egypt, about eighteen hundred years before our era, they were likewise driven out of Arabia by peoples tired of their yoke. These peoples, after becoming independent, chose themselves kings from their nation, to whom they gave the affectionate name of *Tobba*, that is to say, he who does good. Thus the Phœnician Empire, equally pressed on all sides on the continent of Asia and Africa, was almost limited to the shores of the Mediterranean and could only maintain itself by means of its immense marine force and by its colonies, which subjecting the sea always to their power rendered the rest of the world tributary to its commerce. Tyre and Sidon were at this epoch the mart for the riches of the world.

Although it may appear strange that I allow myself to stray into the pleasure of writing history, I shall again enter here into some details. I do not wish to neglect, since the occasion presents itself so naturally, to show how far from the truth the wrong interpretation of the Sepher of Moses has placed us, and how this interpretation has forced us to mutilate the history of the ancient nations, in order to enclose them in the most ridiculous and most limited of chronologies, nearly in the same manner as the Greek mythology relates that a certain Procrustes cut off the legs of strangers so as to make them fit in his iron bed.

Here I believe are some important details. When the Assyrian Ninus made the conquest of Persia, he found there the doctrine of Zoroaster long since established, and thus it gave the Chaldean priests an opportunity to understand it. This doctrine founded on the two opposed principles of Good and Evil singularly pleases men who give themselves over to natural science, because it readily explains a great number of phenomena. The animistic men conform to it. One also finds that it made great progress in Babylonia. At this epoch the appearance is usually placed of the second Zoroaster, who was the creator of that sort of science called *Magic* on account of the *Magi*[1] who became savants in it. The Hebrews at the era of their captivity were initiated into this science, and also into the doctrine of the two principles, and they gave to each a place in their cult. It is through the Hebrews that we know about them. There is nothing in the Sepher of Moses that may have treated of the downfall of the rebellious Angel. Magic, which is a kind of result of it, is, on the contrary, severely forbidden there. This therefore is the reason why first the Chaldeans, and afterwards the Jews, have been mentioned among all ancient nations for their magical works and their occult knowledge.

This is why Egypt, on the contrary, was celebrated among these same nations for her theurgical knowledge and her wisdom, and why her mysteries, where the principles of things were revealed, were sought by the greatest men, who often risked their lives to become initiated into them.

Egypt, it must not be forgotten, was the last country which remained under the dominion of the Atlanteans. She always preserved, therefore, the memory of these peoples; and, even when she came under the power of the Phœnician Shepherds, she remained in possession of two important traditions: the first which came to her originally from the Sudeen Race, of which her inhabitants were considered a part, and the second which she had acquired from the Borean

---

[1] The word *Magian* signifies both great and mighty: this title was given to the Iranian priests at the time of their theocracy. Magic was then properly the great science, the knowledge of Nature.

Race, to whose cult and laws she had afterwards submitted. She was even able by means of the first tradition, to go back to an earlier one and preserve some idea of the Austral Race, which had preceded the Sudeen.   This first race, to which, perhaps, belonged the primitive name of Atlantean, had perished utterly in the midst of a terrible deluge, which, covering the earth, had ravaged it from one pole to the other and submerged the immense and magnificent island which this race had inhabited beyond the seas.   At the moment when this island had disappeared with all the peoples which inhabited it, the Austral Race held the universal empire and dominated the Sudeen, which was hardly beyond a state of barbarism, and was still in the childhood of social state. The deluge which annihilated it was so violent that it left only a confused memory in the minds of the Sudeens who survived there.   These Sudeens only owed their salvation to their equatorial position and to the summits of the mounta ns which they had inhabited; for only those who were fortunate enough to be upon the highest summits were able to escape the destruction.

These traditions, which the Egyptian sacerdotal body possessed almost exclusively, gave it a just superiority over the others.   The priests of Thebes had doubtless only laughed with pity when after a number of centuries they had heard the Greeks, new people, hardly beyond their infancy, boast themselves to be autochthonous; speaking of partial inundations as the Universal Deluge and giving Ogyges or Deucalion, mythological personages, as the ancestors of Mankind; calmly forgetting what they owed to the Sudeens, the Celts, the Chaldeans, the Phœnicians, and the Egyptians themselves, in order to boast of their high science; placing in Crete the tomb of Zeus, the living God; claiming Dionysus, the divine intelligence, to have been born in an obscure village of Bœotia; and Apollo, the Universal Father, in a small island of the Archipelago.   All these things, and many others that I could relate, were well calculated to authorize that priest to say to Solon: "You Greeks are like children who strike their nurses. You believe yourselves great savants and you do not yet know the history of the world."

CHAPTER IX

APPEARANCE OF THE POLITICAL CONQUEROR INVOLVING THE
DESPOTISM AND THE DOWNFALL OF THEOCRACY—SEQUEL
OF THESE EVENTS—MISSION OF ORPHEUS, OF MOSES, AND
OF FO-HI—FOUNDATION OF TROY

NINUS, the Assyrian, was, as I have said, the first political conqueror. Thanks to him, and to Semiramis
who succeeded him, Babylon held the sceptre of the world
until the accession of the Pharaohs, Amenophis and Orus,
who gave it to Egypt about six centuries later. But, during
this interval, several remarkable events came to pass.

The Phœnician Shepherds were dethroned in Egypt by
Amasis, and were driven from Arabia. Some drifted into
Palestine; others established themselves along the septen-
trional shores of Lybia, for then the name of Lybia was given
to all the African continent[1]; a large number remained in
Egypt and submitted to the dominion of the victor.

The successors of Ninus and Semiramis, however, seeing
all obedient to their orders, grew negligent of their royal
duties and gave themselves over to indolence. Aralios
and Armatristis were the first monarchs who lost sight of
their high destination, and who, forgetting that they were
the temporal representatives of Providence and that they

---

[1] This name was given it on account of its form. In the Atlantean language
the word *Lyb* meant *heart;* thence the French word *lobe.* Africa has received
its modern name from the Celt *Afri*, which signifies *savage, barbarous;* thence
the French word *affreux*, frightful.

owed the homage of their dignity to the sovereign pontiff, strove to render themselves independent and to govern their states despotically. Belochus, who succeeded them, had even the audacity to lay his hand upon the sacred tiara; and whether he profited by the death of the sovereign pontiff or whether he hastened the last moments of the pontiff in order to unite it to his crown, he declared himself absolute monarch. This profanation had the consequences that it should have had. The European colonies that he had crushed with the weight of his tyranny and his pride revolted. They heard the voice of their sovereign pontiff, in the sacred mountains of Thrace, of Etruria, and of the Hesperides, and refused to obey. The Anaxes of the Thracians, the Larthes of the Etruscans, the Reghes of the Basques, all dependent until then upon the supreme authority of the sovereign king, profiting by this occasion favourable to their ambition, threw off the yoke and declared themselves kings, instead of viceroys. All the strength of the Assyrian Empire, then very considerable, arose against them. The Phœnicians, obliged to keep up with the movement, furnished them with ships; but the Arabs and the Egyptians made a powerful diversion. The war kindled between Asia on the one hand and Europe on the other, having Africa as an auxiliary, was long and terrible. During more than three centuries blood flowed unceasingly. In the midst of these political troubles, it seemed as though nature herself, agitated by internal convulsions, desired to add to the horrors of war. The most terrible plagues broke out. Frightful deluges inundated many countries; the seas overflowed and covered Attica; lakes opened up ways through the mountains of Thessaly, and while whole peoples were carried away by the angry waves, a copper-coloured sky covered other countries and during the space of seven years left them without a drop of rain or dew. Volcanoes became active in many places. Ætna flung forth its first clouds of flame. A furious conflagration burst out in the forests of Gaul, without any one knowing whence came the first spark. Nearly all Italy burned. The mountains of Hesperia were ablaze and took on account of this event the name of *Pyrenees*. For the first time the blood of kings flowed about the throne. Unknown wretches raised impious hands against their princes and put themselves in their stead. The earth trembled. Mountains were thrown down and whole cities buried beneath their débris.

Wherever one glances, in whatever era one considers these deplorable times, from the reign of the Assyrian Belochus to that of the Egyptian Orus, one sees only disasters and calamities.[1] These are the fragments of people, who, clashing and fighting, pass from Asia into Europe and from Europe into Asia, soaking the shores with their blood. In the midst of this confusion, hordes of savage Boreans are seen descending from the septentrional heights. They come like birds of prey eager for carnage, to devour the remainder of the Phœnician Empire now falling to pieces.

The sacrilegious audacity of the impious Belochus had given the signal for all these evils.

Even India and China were not more tranquil than the rest of the world; already China had been the theatre of many revolutions. In India, the Solar and Lunar dynasties having become extinct, in consequence of the conquests of Semiramis, audacious warriors, with no other title than their courage, with no other right than their sword, had founded kingdoms more or less powerful. Without asking the consent of the supreme pontiff banished to the mountains of Tibet, they put the crown upon their own head and thus risked losing it by the same means by which they had acquired it. A certain Sahadeva in Magadha, a certain Bohd-Dhant in the city of Sirinagour, were thus declared

---

[1] If we place the reign of Ninus, according to the calculations of Callisthenes, at 2200 B.C., we shall have for the reign of Belochus the year 1930 B.C. and for that of Orus about 1600 B.C.; hence it follows that the interval between Belochus and Orus is about three centuries.

kings; but their weak posterity, playthings of political tempests, had frequently stained with blood the steps to the throne; sometimes the prime minister of one, sometimes the commander of the guards of the other had supplanted them. The venerable Nanda, assassinated at the age of more than a hundred years, was replaced by a man of basest extraction.

Such were the sequels of the schism of Irshou. The powerful genius of Krishna had indeed been able to stay the state of dissolution for twelve or fifteen centuries, but the suppressed movement only became all the more dangerous. The Will of Man delivered over to Destiny must needs follow its course. All that was possible to be done at that moment was to preserve the archives of ancient traditions and the principles of the sciences, so as to deliver them later, when the storm had passed, to new peoples who might be able to profit by them. Providence had conceived the thought, and this potential plan was not long in becoming action.

About fourteen or fifteen centuries before our era, three extraordinary men appeared on the earth: Orpheus, among the Thracians, Moses, among the Egyptians, and Buddha, among the Hindus. This Buddha was at first called *Fo-Hi* and afterwards named *Shakya*. The character of these men, wholly dissimilar, but of forces equal in their way, may be still recognized in the doctrine which they have left: its indelible stamp has braved the torrent of ages. Nothing is more beautiful in imagery, nothing more enchanting in details than the mythology of Orpheus; nothing more profound, more vast, nothing even more austere than the cosmogony of Moses; nothing more intoxicating, more capable of inspiring religious enthusiasm than the contemplation of Fo-Hi. Orpheus has clothed with most brilliant colours the ideas of Rama, of Zoroaster, and of Krishna; he has created the polytheism of the poets; he has inflamed the instinctive imagination of the people. Moses, in transmitting to us the divine Unity of the Atlanteans, in unfolding before us the eternal decrees, has carried human intelligence to a height where often it has difficulty in sustaining itself. Fo-Hi, in revealing the mysteries of successive existences, in explaining the great enigma of the Universe, in showing the aim of life, has spoken to the heart of man, has aroused all his passions, and above all has exalted his animistic imagination.   These three men, who share equally the same truth, but who devote themselves particularly to bringing out one of its aspects, if they had been able to be united, would perhaps have succeeded in making known the Absolute Divinity: Moses, in his unfathomable Unity; Orpheus, in the infinity of his faculties and his attributes; Fo-Hi, in the principle and the aim of his conceptions.

At the epoch when Orpheus appeared, Egypt dominated the earth; she had humbled the power of the Babylonians, had made alliance with the Ethiopians and Arabs, and had forced the arrogant successors of Ninus to recognize not alone the independence of the Phœnician colonies established in Europe, but also those of the Phœnicians properly so called existing in Africa and Asia, under the diverse names of *Numidians, Lybians, Philistines, Idumeans*, etc.   These colonies, having acquired their independence, were very far from being tranquil.

Although three principal centres could be recognized on the meridional coasts of Europe, from the Euxine to the Pillars of Hercules, because of the three sovereign pontiffs established on the Rhodope Mountains, the Apennines, and the Pyrenees, the Thracians, Etruscans, and the Basques were far from forming three distinct and perfectly united powers.   A number of small sovereignties were formed in the midst of them, as different in name as in pretensions, in extent as in force.   Anaxes, Larthes, and Reghes were endlessly multiplied.   All wished to command, none wished to obey; the sovereign pontiff was unable to make his voice heard; no one listened; anarchy was complete.[1]   Hardly had

[1] It is to this time that one dates the origin of the name *anarchy*.

these little sovereigns been freed from the cares of fighting the Assyrians, when they turned their arms against each other. From the Orient to the Occident, and from the Occident to the Orient, there was a continual movement of petty peoples, who, seeking mutually to dominate, clashed and fought turn by turn.

The historians and the chronologists who have sought to penetrate into this epoch of the annals of the world have lost themselves in an inextricable labyrinth.[1] In the midst of these movements, which are of too small importance for me to dwell upon, one, however, came to pass that I must relate on account of the singular influence which it afterwards acquired.

A certain Jasius, one of the Larthes of the Etruscans, declared war against another Larthe, named Dardanus, who, probably finding himself too weak to resist, invoked the support of the King of Babylon, Ascatade.[2] After several combats, wherein the two Larthes were sometimes vanquished, sometimes victors, Dardanus, not caring to return to Italy, ceded his rights to a certain Tyrrhenus, son of Ato, relative or ally of the Assyrian Ascatade, and received in exchange a part of the Mæonian field, where he established himself with those of the aborigines who had followed his colours. As for Tyrrhenus, he went by sea to Italy and there obtained, following a treaty, the city of Razène, where he founded a small kingdom.

This Dardanus was the first King of Troy, a small city which he found built at the foot of Mount Ida, and which he enlarged considerably. His successors, called *Dardanides*, although always dependent on the Assyrian monarch, gave great *éclat* to their name by leaving it to the strait of the Dardanelles over which they ruled. Their capital city,

---

[1] To evade perplexity they have called these times of tumult, *heroic times;* it was, on the contrary, the time of decadence, when the obscurity of the intelligence was beginning to make itself felt.

[2] I mention here that the name of this king, which is formed of two Celtic roots, signifies *Father of the People.*

embellished by three centuries of prosperity, became famous by the siege of ten years which it sustained against the Greeks, and its fall was sung and is still sung by all voices of Fame, thanks to the genius of Homer, who chose it for the subject of his epic poems and allegories.

CHAPTER X

ORPHEUS, MOSES, AND FO-HI; WHO THEY WERE—THEIR
DOCTRINE—ESTABLISHMENT OF THE AMPHICTYONS IN
GREECE—ORIGIN OF THE CONFEDERATIONS OF THE NA-
TIONAL REPRESENTATION—TENTH REVOLUTION IN THE
SOCIAL STATE

IN those times a very violent dispute having arisen in Egypt
between two brothers who were both pretenders to the
crown, a civil war of long duration ensued. The one, named
Rameses, was on account of his ostentatious manner surnamed
Gôpth, the Proud; and the other named *Armesis*, was on
account of his gentleness and modesty surnamed *Dônth*, the
Modest.[1] The former becoming victor, obliged his brother
to be expatriated; and the latter, followed by those who
remained attached to his cause, passed into Greece where he
established many colonies. It is he whom the Greeks have
called *Danaüs*, on whose account many mythological fables
were founded. Gôpth, whose name has been changed to that
of *Egyptus* according to the Greeks, gave his name to Egypt,[2]
which before this event had been called *Chemi* or *Mitzrah*.

[1] It is presumable that these two brothers were twins and that they reigned
at first together without quarrelling.

[2] It is here that the Phœnician article *ha*, rendered in Greek by the article
ά, which has been placed before the word *Gôpth* in order to make it *ha-Gôpth*,
was changed afterwards to Αἴγυπτος. The modern name of the Copts proves
this derivation. The ancient names *Chemi* or *Mitzrah* likewise express in two
different dialects, compression or incapable of expansion, and allude to the
geographical position of this country.

It was with one of these colonies that Orpheus, of Thracian origin but initiated in Thebes to the sacred mysteries of the Egyptian priests, passed into Greece. He found this beautiful country, as I have said, a prey to the double scourge of political and religious anarchy. Favoured, however, by the influence of the Egyptians, and sustained by his own genius, he accomplished in a short time what Providence exacted of him. Not being able to reconstruct upon the same plan a fallen edifice, he profited at least with rare ability by the materials which he found at hand. Since he saw Greece divided into a certain number of small sovereignties which would absolutely not recognize further the supremacy of the Thracians, he persuaded them to unite in a political and religious confederation and offered them an assembling place on Mount Parnassus, in the city of Pytho,[1] where he gave great fame to the oracle of Apollo which was already established there. The force and charm of his eloquence, together with the phenomena which he effected, whether in predicting the future or healing the sick, decided all minds in his favour, and they furnished him with means whereby to establish the Council of the Amphictyons, one of the most admirable institutions that has honoured human intelligence.

Nothing in antiquity has been more celebrated than this Council, raised above peoples and kings in order to judge them alike. It assembled in the name of all Greece twice a year, in the springtime and in the autumn, in the temple of Ceres, at Thermopylæ near the mouth of the river Asopus. The decrees of this august Tribunal had to be submitted to the sovereign pontiff, residing on the sacred mount, before possessing the force and dignity of law, and it was not until after being approved and signed by him that they were engraven upon the columns of marble and considered as authentic.

[1] It was the ancient name of the city of Delphi, so called because of the pythoness who uttered there the oracle of Apollo.

We see that Orpheus, no longer able to preserve the forms of monarchy which the kings themselves had helped to destroy, preserved at least those of theocracy, in order to raise an obstacle which might arrest the invasions of anarchy which excessive despotism and demagogy had equally provoked. This Amphictyonic Council offered the first example of the confederation of many peoples united under the dominion of one, that of the Hellenes, and created a political innovation of greatest importance—that of national representation, as its name readily expresses.[1] How fortunate it would have been could he have surrounded himself with a force sufficient to prevent the turbulent attempts of several cities, which, to give themselves an absolute liberty, oppressed others and gave rise to a new form of legitimate slavery, of which I shall have occasion to speak further on.[2] But the evil already conceived in the heart of man and served by all the power of Destiny, was inevitable. Orpheus could only retard the outbreak, and prepare at a distance the remedy which would arrest the effects of it.

I shall not expatiate further upon the doctrine of Orpheus; I have spoken sufficiently in other works of it, so that I may in this one dispense with useless repetitions. It is shown in all that the ancients have left us regarding this man, so justly admired, that he was the creator of the musical system of the Greeks and that he was the first to use the rhythm rendered illustrious by Homer. If Greece has surpassed all other nations of the world in the culture of the fine arts, if she has opened to us the course of moral, political, and philosophical sciences, it is to Orpheus that she has owed this advantage. Orpheus has produced Pythagoras and it is to Pythagoras that Europe has owed Socrates, Plato, Aristotle, and their numerous disciples. It appears

---

[1] This name is composed of two Greek words, Ἀμφί and χθών: it signifies properly that which makes one country of several or one people of many people.

[2] In the seventh book of this work, Chap. III. I do not think I ought here to break the historical thread.

that Orpheus taught, as Krishna, the divine Hermaphroditism and that he concealed the cosmogonical principles in a
Sacred Triad.[1]   His ideas were the same as those of the
Indian prophet; he abhorred, as the latter did, bloody sacrifices.   The attempts which he made to substitute the mysteries of Bacchus for those of Ceres became calamitous for
him.   It appears that even the Ionians, that is to say, the
ancient partisans of the feminine faculty, having gathered
their forces against him, succeeded in crushing him, that is
at least according to the tradition preserved in a collection
of fables, where it is related that Orpheus was torn by furious
women who were opposed to the innovations which he
desired to bring into their cult.   Be that as it may, his
institution survived him and his disciples, called *Eumolpides*,
that is, the perfect ones, rendered Greece illustrious for a
long time.

---

[1] Aristotle has preserved for us on the subject of the divine Hermaphroditism this beautiful verse from Orpheus:

Ζεὺς ἄρσην γένετο, Ζεὺς ἄμβροτος ἔωλετο νύμφη.
Zeus is the Immortal Bridegroom and Spouse.

This doctrine was received by all the earth, but each state, in receiving it,
proclaimed itself the sole and true possessor of the umbilicus, that is to say, of
the central point of which it was the emblem.   The city of Delphi disputed this
honour with that of Thebes in Egypt, as the latter had disputed it with the
famous temple of Shakanadam and with the sacred island of Lankâ.

As to the Sacred Triad of Krishna, *Brahma, Vishnu,* and *Siva,* it is evident
that the ideas varied greatly concerning the rank, attributes, and degree of
power of each of these three divinities.   Sometimes one saw in *Vishnu* an
aqueous fluid, aerial or fiery; sometimes *Brahma* was confused with light or ether,
and *Siva* with fire or earth.   *Osiris, Orus, Typhon* among the Egyptians; *Zeus,
Dionysus, Aïdes* among the Greeks; *Jupiter, Bacchus, Pluto,* or *Vejovis* among
the Latins have not by any means represented their models; they have frequently even been confused; but one has always been able to recognize their
common origin through the variations which they have experienced and to see
that produced by two opposed principles, male and female, they could be
brought back to an absolute principle, inaccessible to all research, called *Wôdh*
or *Karta* by the Hindus; *Kneph* or *Chnoun* by the Egyptians; *Phanes, Faunus,
Pan, Jan, Zan, Janus,* or *Jaô* by the Romans and the Greeks.   One finds sometimes the Indian Trinity represented by *Saturn, Jupiter,* and *Mars.*   The
three altars of these gods are often seen united in Rome.

The name of Orpheus, which signifies the Healer, the
enlightened Physician, indicates a title given to this theocrat
on account of the services that he rendered to his native
country. It is probable that it was the name of some mythological personage, perhaps that of Æsculapius, whose legend
in the course of time became blended with his history.
This remark applies equally to Moses, whose name signifies
on the contrary, the Rescued.

Moses, raised at the court of the Egyptian Pharoah,
initiated into the sacred mysteries, passed early into Ethiopia because of a murder that he had committed. It was
there that he learned the primitive tradition of the Atlanteans regarding Divine Unity and that he found a part of
those Arab tribes whom the Phœnician Shepherds had
driven from Yemen, as I have already related. These
Arabs, issues of a mixture of Atlanteans and of Bodohnes
Celts, had all manner of reasons for detesting these Shepherds
with whom they had preserved the name of Philistines.
Scattered through Ethiopia as in Egypt they were very
unhappy there. Moses had been born among them. He
was wandering, he was welcomed by them. Misfortune
drew them together. It is well known how this divine man,
called by Providence to such a high destiny, was reduced
to guard the flocks of Jethro, whose daughter Zephora he
espoused.

Jethro was one of the priests of the expatriated Arabs
of whom I have just made mention. They were named
Hebrews for the reason I have given. Jethro knew the
traditions of his ancestors and he taught them to Moses.
Perhaps he had preserved some genethlialogical books relative to the Atlanteans; he gave them to him. The book of
the *Generations of Adam*, that of the *Wars of Jehovah*, that
of the *Prophecies* are cited by Moses. The young theocrat
penetrated all these things and meditated long upon them.
At last, while in the desert, he obtained his first inspiration.
The God of his fathers, who named Himself *Jehovah*, the

Being of Beings, made him hear His voice from the midst of a burning bush.

I shall not insist at all upon the mysterious and secret meaning of the *Sepher* of Moses, since I have said elsewhere many things upon this subject.[1] What I shall add here as having particularly to deal with the matter I have in hand is that Moses after having related the legend of *Elohim*, the Being of Beings, related afterwards that of *Noah*, the Repose of Nature; that of *Abraham*, the Sublime Father; that of *Moses*, the Rescued, with which he skilfully mingles his own, leaving to *Joshua*, the Saviour, whom he chose theocratically to succeed him, the care of finishing his work. So that the origins, which he seemed to give to his people and which he gives to himself by the manner in which he links these legends to his own history, are purely allegorical; they attach themselves to cosmogonical subjects infinitely more important and go back to epochs infinitely more remote.

Such was the method which the ancient sages followed, and such was that of Moses. The Sepher of this extraordinary man having come down to us complete by favour of the triple veil, with which he has covered it, has brought us the most ancient tradition which exists today on earth. It reaches not only the epoch of the primitive Atlanteans, but going beyond the catastrophe of which they were the victims, transports itself through the immensity of centuries to the first principles of things, which is given in detail under the form of a divine decree emanated from the Eternal Wisdom.

The Hebrews were not at all a remnant of the Phœnician Shepherds, as some writers have believed, since these shepherds had no deadlier enemies. This people was the result of a first mixture made in Arabia between the Sudeen blood and the Borean. Their opposition to the Ionian doctrine constrained them at first to abandon their native land. Persecuted in Egypt and in Abyssinia, they became intolerant themselves there. The doctrine of Krishna

[1] In my work on *La Langue hébraïque restituée*.

having found them as refractory as that of Irshou, they were considered unsociable men whose stubborn character would not flinch, and they were relegated to the deserts as a sort of impure pariahs.[1] It was there that Moses found them, and, having seized them in their own ideas, he led them to the conquest of Palestine through a multitude of obstacles that his genius surmounted. This people, whom Moses calls stiff-necked people, were those whom Providence entrusted with the sacred archives of which I have spoken. These archives, of which the Hebrews have rarely known the true worth, have traversed intact the torrent of ages, have braved the effort of water, fire, and sword; thanks to the ignorant but sturdy hands which guarded them.

The names of Orpheus and Moses are, as I have announced, titles resulting rather from their doctrine than from their own names. Other men may have had these names before them, and that is what has thrown some confusion into their history. As to Fo-Hi, surnamed *Buddha* or *Shakya*, his original name is also known as is that of Krishna. I have said that the latter was called *Gôpalla*. The real name of Fo-Hi was *Sougot*. He did not take that of Fo-Hi until after his vocation. This is how the Hindus relate his first inspiration. The young Sougot, they said, while on Solitary Mountain where he had taken refuge to escape the wrath of his father, who wished him to marry, and while gazing upon the morning star, fell into a sort of ecstasy, during which heaven opened before his eyes. He saw then the Essence of the First Principle. Ineffable mysteries were revealed to him. Recovering from the astonishment into which this vision had thrown him, he took the name of Fo-Hi, the Living Father, and began to establish the foundations of his cult. He was surnamed afterwards *Buddha*, the Eternal Wisdom, and *Shakya*, the Being always existing.

---

[1] The *pariahs* constitute in India a caste of reprobate men who are forbidden to live in the society of other men.

The essential points of his doctrine are reduced to the following: the souls of men and animals are of the same essence; they differ from each other only according to the body which they animate and are likewise immortal. Human souls, alone free, are rewarded or punished, according to their good or evil actions.

The place where virtuous souls enjoy eternal pleasure is governed by Amida, the principle of Good, who regulates ranks according to the sanctity of men. Each inhabitant of this happy place, in whatever rank he may be, deceives himself with the sweet illusion of thinking that his lot is the best, and he in no wise envies the felicity of others. All sins are effaced there by the mercy and mediation of Amida. No distinction is made between women and men; the two sexes enjoy the same advantages according to the doctrine of Krishna.

There is no everlasting punishment in the place reserved for evildoers. Guilty souls are tormented there only in proportion to the crimes they have committed, and their torments are more or less long according to the intensity of their crimes. They may even receive some alleviation by the prayers and good deeds of their relatives and friends and the merciful Amida can appease *Yama*, the Genius of evil, supreme monarch of the infernal regions. When these souls have expiated their crimes, they are sent back to earth, passing into the bodies of unclean animals, whose inclinations accord with their former vices. Their transmigration is made then from the vilest animals to the noblest, until after perfect purification they are worthy to re-enter human bodies, when they pass through the same course which they have already gone over and submit to the same tests. [1]

[1] It was in order to spare themselves these reiterated tests, that the followers of Fo-Hi, being resolved not to live again upon the earth, have exaggerated the moral principles of their prophet and by a spirit of penitence have carried self-abnegation to an almost unbelievable excess. It is not a rare thing today, even after more than three thousand years of existence, to see fanatics of this cult, so tolerant and so gentle, become their own executioners and give them-

The cult of Fo-Hi is only a sort of corollary of that of Rama and is easily amalgamated with it. Nearly all the Lamas are today Buddhists, so that it can be admitted without error that it is one of the most diffused cults on the face of our hemisphere. The system of metempsychosis was born of it, and all those who have received it from Pythagoras have but followed the ideas of Fo-Hi.

---

selves up to a death more or less painful or violent: some with a stone at the neck throw themselves into the water; others bury themselves alive; some sacrifice themselves in the crater of volcanoes; others expose themselves to a slow death upon rocks arid and burned by the sun; the less fervent condemn themselves to receive, in the heart of the winter, on their naked bodies, one hundred pitchers of iced water; they prostrate themselves to the earth a thousand times a day, striking each time the pavement with their foreheads; they undertake barefooted, perilous journeys over sharp pebbles, among the brambles, along roads strewn with dangers; they suspend themselves over frightful abysses. It is not unusual to see in public ceremonies a throng of these devout Buddhists placing themselves to be crushed by the wheels of chariots or horses' feet. Thus do extremes meet. The merciless Thor and the gentle and beneficent Amida have both had their devout victims: how difficult it is to recognize the golden mean where alone reside Truth, Wisdom, Virtue!

CHAPTER XI

THUS Providence, in its inexhaustible goodness, being unable to prevent the dissolution of the Universal Empire that it had raised by the hands of Rama, desired at least to moderate its consequences and to preserve in its principal fragments as much force and harmony as was possible, in order to be able to employ them later when the time for it should arrive for the erection of a new edifice still greater and more beautiful than the first.

Here are the reasons which determined the mission of Orpheus, Moses, and Fo-Hi. These three men, very dissimilar, adapted themselves with wonderful sagacity to the peoples and circumstances which demanded them. These circumstances were such that the three great powers which ruled the Universe, having united their action during a long space of time in the empire of Rama, now separated it, but in such a way that while Destiny remaining almost sole master in Asia and in Africa, and the Will of Man ready to dominate all Europe, Providence, obliged to retire, could preserve here and there only a few circumscribed points hidden in obscurity. Orpheus, destined to restrain the passions of the Will, seized it by the imagination, and, offering it the enchanting cup of voluptuousness, induced it by the prestige of the fine arts, by the charm of poetry and of music, by the splendour and majesty of ceremonies to draw from its mysteries moral lessons and universal knowledge that could no longer be left to the multitude which would have profaned them. Since the political bond had become loosened, it was necessary that that of religion and philosophy should become proportionately tightened.

On the other hand Fo-Hi, whose intellectual influence was opposed to that which the fatality of Destiny held most rigidly, offered the compensations of a future life, and showed that the action of this power, so terrible in appearance, was closed within very narrow limits, and that the Will of Man, by yielding to it in the course of a passing life, could escape from it for eternity. He showed besides, that the men most favoured by this power were always the most exposed, and that the splendour and the pomp of its gifts concealed dangers so much the greater as their possessors were disposed to abuse them. As it was in Asia that absolute despotism established itself because the kings, not content in escaping everywhere from the sacerdotal dominion, had again usurped the power of the sovereign pontiff, it was necessary to lighten as much as possible the yoke with which they burdened the mass of the people and to show at the same time to these imprudent monarchs the perilous situation in which they were.

As for Moses, his mission was limited to preserving the cosmogonical principles of all the races and to conceal as in a holy ark the germs of all future institutions. The people to whom he confided the keeping of this ark were a plain but sturdy people, whose strength was still more augmented by his exclusive legislation. The forms of his government did not matter; it sufficed, in order that the views of Providence might be fulfilled, that its fusion with another government should not be able to take place.

If the reader has clearly understood what I have just said, he must realize how very important was this epoch of the social state. Three principles long blended in Unity, being divided, gave birth to three entirely new forms of government. In Asia, the mass of people, having submitted to the individual, suffered despotism under the laws of Destiny; in Europe, the individual, having submitted to the mass, gave way before democracy and followed the impulse of the Will of Man; in Arabia, Egypt, Ethiopia, and above all, in Palestine, a sort of intellectual power, deprived of force and of apparent means, governed invisibly peoples indiscriminately a prey to all forms of government, fluctuating between a thousand whims and a thousand diverse opinions, and changing at the will of these caprices the most sublime verities into superstitions and puerile practices.

After the civil war which broke out in Egypt between Armesis and Rameses, surnamed *Dônth* and *Gôpth*, or *Danaüs* and *Egyptus*, and whose result had been the expatriation of Danaüs and the passage into Greece of a great number of Egyptian colonies, this country had lost a great part of its strength; so that, after the weak reign of the second Amenophis, it fell under the dominion of the Etruscans. We know by a very curious fragment of Manetho that the famous Sethos was not of Egyptian origin, since he did not bear upon the throne the title of Pharaoh, but that of Larthe, which was the title that belonged to the sovereigns of Etruria. The dynasty of this Sethos, who reigned over Egypt and who made a temporary conquest of Arabia and India, furnished six Larthes, the last of whom, called *Thuoris*, died the same year that Troy was taken by the Greeks.

After some internal dissensions, the Egyptians succeeded, however, in resuming their sway, but they were soon despoiled of it by the Lydians who took possession of the Empire of the seas. These Lydians became for some time what the Phœnicians, from whom they were descended, had been; but as things were, nothing could last. At the end of several centuries, it was the Rhodians who had replaced them.

The same revolutions which took place at Memphis and at Sardis followed also at Babylon. The Empire of the Assyrians, heretofore so flourishing, had become so infirm, that Teutamos who still held the title of King of Kings, could not defend Priam against the Greeks, although this monarch had implored his assistance, according to what Diodorus relates. The siege of Troy was celebrated in antiquity for precisely this cause. It seemed astonishing that certain weak tribes hardly escaped from the yoke of the Thracians should dare to besiege a royal city, placed under the protection of the King of Kings, without either Nineveh or Babylon, although almost within sight, being able to oppose its conflagration. So this exploit inflated singularly the pride of these men whose imagination had already been exalted by the doctrine of Orpheus. They were seen pushing their military enterprises to possess in a few centuries all the islands of the archipelago,[1] and covering with their colonies nearly the entire shore of Asia Minor.

It was at this epoch that Rhodes became celebrated for its maritime commerce, and that Homer appeared.[2]

[1] This word is remarkable; it is an abridgment of the Greek 'Αρχιπέλαγος which signifies exactly that which rules over the Black Sea. This corroborates what I have said before that all the Mediterranean Sea bore formerly the name *Pelasgus* or Black Sea on account of the *Pelasgians* or Black People who possessed it.

[2] Certain rather injudicious writers sometimes represent this epoch as the dawn of civilization, whereas it was, on the contrary, the decline. They do not observe that the Greek tongue had already reached its highest point of perfection; that, first, the Lydians and, afterwards, the Rhodians had acquired by commerce, immense wealth; that the arts had made such progress that one had been able to model, cast, and set up the colossus of Rhodes,—that enormous statue of bronze representing Apollo placed at the entrance of the port in such a way that each of his feet rested on one of the extended moles and a sailing vessel full-rigged could pass between his legs,—which announced in the exact physical and mechanical sciences means that we have not yet renewed. It is

At that time, a general disturbance took place in all Europe. The Will of Man, raising itself above Providence and Destiny, pretended to dominate and was dominated by the multitude. All lines of demarcation disappeared. One distinguished among the peoples only free men and slaves, according as they were victors or vanquished. One would have said that the human race, carried along by a retrograde movement, was returning to the childhood of society and was recognizing no authority other than force.

In Athens, an oracle, dictated by this dominant Will, forces Codrus, its last king, to give himself up to death. In Lacedæmon, Lycurgus, likewise influenced by democratic opinion, abdicates royalty and forms the bold project of regulating this anarchistic movement by making Sparta a monastery of soldiers. Corinth drives out her kings. On every side royal power is overthrown. The kings who resist the torrent, or those who, after being overthrown, succeed in seizing again the authority, being obliged to employ an extraordinary force in order to preserve it, are called *tyrants*, and are compared with the despotic viceroys whom, during the power of the Phœnicians, Tyre sent afar to govern its colonies. Entire Greece is bristling with republics. This form of government passes from the islands of the archipelago into a part of Asia possessed by the Greeks and there is propagated. The Phœnicians themselves, profiting by the weakness of the Assyrians and the Egyptians who have held them enslaved, throw off the yoke and form many independent states whose influence is felt by Arabia. Two powerful tribes, those of the Hemyarites and those of the Koreishites, are divided in opinion. The first, which wished to preserve the monarchical forms, is attacked by the other which yields to the popular movement. Violent combats ensue in which the two tribes suffer equally.

---

generally believed that Homer has painted the customs of his century, but this is a mistake. This poet has retraced the imaginary customs of ancient times such as his genius represented them to him.

The tribe of the Hemyarites having triumphed momentarily, one of their kings believed himself strong enough to make an incursion into Persia and there founded the city of Samarkand, on the ruins of that of Soghd, capital of ancient Soghdiana.

In the midst of these troubles, the Greeks, having become more and more numerous and formidable, were sending colonies everywhere. Miletus in Asia Minor; Mytilene, on the island of Lesbos; Samos on the island of this name; Cumæ, in Italy, spring up under their dominion. Carthage, on the shores of Africa, receives a new lustre by the attentions of the Tyrians. The city of Syracuse is founded in Sicily, and, a short time after, Rome begins to appear upon the scene of the world.

In the meantime, the Empire of the Assyrians becomes dismembered. A prefect of Media, named Arbaces, seconded by a Babylonian priest, named Belesis, revolts against Sardanapalus, last King of Assyria, and compels him to set fire to his palace in Nineveh and to burn himself together with his wives and his treasures. Shortly after a king of Babylon, named Nabon-Assar, full of fanatical pride, irritated by the praises he had heard given to his predecessors, contrives to make all these annoying examples disappear in order to fill the universe with his name. He orders, in consequence, that all inscriptions be effaced, all tablets of bronze broken, and the bibliothecas burned. He wishes that all memories shall date from his accession to the throne.[1]

---

[1] This era of destruction dates from the year 747 B.C. It is stated that a similar idea came to the Romans after the establishment of the Republic, and that the consuls caused the Books of Numa to be secretly destroyed, and everything which could recall the ancient dominion of the Etruscans over them. It appears equally certain that the monuments of the Thracians and Basques met the same fate as those of the Chaldeans and Etruscans. The memory of a like event is perpetuated in India. It is quite well known what took place in China, and that the Emperor Tsin-che-hoang went further than Nabon-Assar, in forbidding, under pain of death, the keeping of any literary monument prior to his reign. At an epoch much nearer to us, Omar, the most passionate and most ignorant of the disciples of Mohammed had the famous library of Alex-

Thus, since there was no longer Unity in things, that is to say, since the Will of Man, either weakened or abandoned to an inordinate effervescence, no longer bound Providence to Destiny, things such as they were, good or bad, had only a precarious existence and appeared in continual flux. If, in the midst of the ever-growing darkness, some brilliant lights showed themselves at intervals, like meteors, they disappeared with the same rapidity. The general tendency, although stamped by two opposite causes—the despotism of an individual, or that of a multitude—was towards the extinction of knowledge. Everything inclined towards its decadence. Empires and republics carried equally in their midst the germs of destruction, which were not long becoming developed. Knowledge, insensibly enfeebled, became extinct; memories were effaced; allegorical history misunderstood, and mythology disfigured, had materialized, so to speak, in passing from moral to physical. Veils, precursors' of an obscurity more and more profound, had covered the intellectual world. Corruption made frightful progress in all classes of society. From the height of the thrones of Asia, where it first took possession, it stole into the sanctuaries, and if European republics, at their beginning, were able to escape from it, it was only by a violent effort, which, soon becoming fatigued, let them fall into a dissolution even more profound.

Providence, however, although not able to suspend entirely the disorganizing movement, checked at least its course and prepared a means of salvation for the future. In the space of a few centuries, it raised up a number of extraordinary men, who, inspired by it and endowed with different

---

andria burned. Before him several Christian popes, not less intolerant, had caused a great many antique monuments to be destroyed. The archives of Mexico and those of Peru have disappeared to satisfy the fanatical zeal of a Spanish bishop. Thus, from one end of the earth to the other, pride and ignorance were linked to stifle the voice of antiquity and to deprive men of their own history. One might have been able to evade these disastrous events by anticipating them.

talents, erected barriers against this excess of vice and error and introduced asylums for Truth and Virtue. Then appeared, within a short time of each other, the last of the Buddhas in India, Sin-Mou in Japan, Lao-tzée and Kong-tzée in China, the last of the Zoroasters in Persia, Esdras among the Jews, Lycurgus in Sparta, Numa in Italy, and Pythagoras for all Greece. All tending to the same end although by contrary roads.

At the time when Pythagoras appeared, rich in all the learning of Africa and Asia, about the ninth century after Orpheus, he found the memory of this theosophist almost effaced from the minds of men and his most beautiful institutions either unrecognized or attributed to most fantastic origins. The m serable pride in being considered autochthonous, in raising themselves above other nations, and in disowning their benefits received from them, caused the Greeks to be charged with great extravagances of which those I have already related are only the least part. Profiting by a certain analogy which was found between the name of their cities and those of the cities of Phœnicia or Egypt, an analogy which proved their origin, they claimed Bœotian Thebes as the birthplace of Hercules, the Universal Sovereign, without concerning themselves that numberless other places had claimed this signal honour. For them Menou of the Indians became Minos of the island of Crete and Scander of the two horns, the son of Semele. They affirmed that Perseus, son of Danaë, had been the legislator of the Persians. They attributed the discovery of iron to Dactyl, the invention of the plough to Ceres, that of the chariot to Erechtheus, and forged an infinity of fables of this sort each one more absurd than the other.[1] The people having become

---

[1] I have at hand a volume which treats of the *Science of History*, where chronology, founded upon that of Usserius is presented in a series of numerous pictures. One sees there among other things that Prometheus taught men the use of fire in 1687 B.C.; that Cadmus showed the art of writing to the Greeks in 1493 B.C.; that a fortunate hazard procured for Dactyl the discovery of iron in 1406 B.C.; that Ceres taught the use of the plough in 1385 B.C.; and all this

sovereign believed it, and arrogantly commanded the most obstinate to believe it also. The mysteries established to make Truth understood, being opened to too many initiates, lost their influence. The hierophants, intimidated or corrupt, either said nothing or sanctioned the deceit. Truth must necessarily be lost or another way of preserving it must be found. Pythagoras was the man to whom this way was revealed. He did for science what Lycurgus had done for liberty. Unable to arrest the torrent, he yielded to it, in order to take possession of and master it.

Lycurgus, as legislator, had instituted a sort of warlike fraternity, a curious mixture of despotism and democracy, in appearance consecrated to liberty, but secretly destined to restrain excesses of all descriptions. This formidable institution, against which Persian despotism came to break, overthrew the anarchistic haughtiness of the Athenians, and prepared the triumphs of Alexander. Pythagoras, as philosopher, instituted a sort of sacred congregation, a secret assembly of the wise and religious men, which, spreading itself in Europe, Asia, and even in Africa, struggled there against the ignorance and the impiety which were tending to become universal. The service which he rendered to humanity was very great. The sect which he created, and which today is not entirely extinct,[1] traversing like a streak of light the darkness gathered about us by the irruption of the barbarians, the downfall of the Roman Empire, and the

---

many centuries after the foundation of the kingdoms of Sicyon and Argos, while Phoronus had already given a code of laws to the Argives; Sparta had been built; gold coin had been struck in Athens; and Semiramis had astonished the world by the magnificent gardens that she had had constructed in Babylon. Indeed how wonderful, kingdoms without ploughs, codes of law without letters, gold money without fire, and cities built without iron!

[1] There still exist some forms and some precepts among the Freemasons who have inherited them from the Templars. These last received them in Asia, at the time of the first Crusades, from a remnant of Manichæans whom they found there. The Manichæans received them from the Gnostics and these imbibed them from the School of Alexandria where the Pythagoreans, the Essenes, and the Mithraicists were blended together.

necessary erection of a severe and lugubrious cult, has brought about the revival of learning a thousand times more easily than could have been done without it, and has spared us many centuries of labour. It has pushed ahead all sciences of natural philosophy, has reanimated chemistry, disencumbered astronomy of the ridiculous prejudices which have arrested its progress, preserved the principles of music, taught the importance of numbers, geometry, and mathematics, and has given points of support to natural history. It has equally influenced the development of the moral sciences, but with less success, on account of the obstacles which it has encountered in the metaphysics of the schools. I have spoken enough of this wonderful man in various other works of mine[1], so that I need not here dwell at length upon his noble deeds.

[1] Particularly in my *Examens sur les Vers dorés.*

CHAPTER XII

RECAPITULATION

I HAVE shown in this book, Human Intelligence attained to its highest development, vested with all the splendour which genius gives, like the orb of day arrived at the summer solstice, remaining as in suspense at the summit of its career, and reluctantly leaving that sublime station to descend slowly toward the inferior point whence it had risen.

I have told what the last Universal Empire had been, and I think I have made it understood that a similar empire could be only theocratic. There can be nothing universal, nothing durable, nothing veritably great, where Divine Force is not, that is to say, where Providence is not recognized.

But as all that has begun must end, I have endeavoured to explain in accordance with what Eternal laws this Universal Empire, after having blazed with a long splendour, had to tend towards its decline and lose by degrees its constitutive unity. The cause of its first division has been seen, and I believe I have said on this subject things but little known today. If the reader has observed the origin that I give to many things, I hope that he will experience some satisfaction in seeing with what fertility the simple principles laid down in the first book are developed. If, from the beginning of this work, he has considered merely as hypotheses the events that I have related, he must at least agree that it was difficult to find any more analogous to those which were to follow. At the point which we have reached, positive history has begun long ago, and I hardly know what hand would be bold enough to dare to place the line of demarcation. In a chain where all the links are joined, which shall it be necessary to regard as the first one? If half of this chain has been hidden for a long time in obscurity, is that any reason to deny its existence? If, when I show it by throwing light upon it, one says that I create it, let some-one take another torch and make me see, by throwing upon it a greater brilliancy, either that it does not exist or that it exists otherwise.

14

Part Second

FOURTH BOOK

The third book has explained the causes which brought about the decline of the last Universal Empire. I have shown how this decline, at first imperceptible, became accelerated little by little and had finished in a downfall more and more rapid. I shall relate in this book the result of the last struggles between Europe and Asia and I shall show that it was upon the débris of the Roman Empire that the Universal Empire of Rama expired.

As the sun, having reached the winter solstice leaves the Boreal pole plunged in darkness for some time, so moral obscurity rolling on with waves of barbarians, which inundated Europe at this epoch, took possession of the human mind for several centuries, and put back civilization. But, at last, the ascending movement recommenced, and knowledge, lost to view or enfeebled, showed itself anew and acquired an ever increasing brilliancy.

CHAPTER I

THE situation of the world was remarkable to the highest degree at the time when the great men, of whom I have spoken at the close of the last book, appeared. The fatality of Destiny, dominating Asia and creating there the despotism of kings, was face to face with the Will of Man which sanctioned the sovereignty of the peoples in Europe. Providence, unrecognized, although invoked by both parties, was in neither, except in form. The diverse cults degenerated everywhere into frivolous ceremonies or into superstitions, lugubrious when they were not ridiculous. With the exception of a few secret sanctuaries where Truth, having taken refuge, found shelter only beneath the thickest of veils; even Egypt offered in her sacred mythology only an inextricable chaos where bewildered reason was lost. The dragon of the Atlanteans, confused with the crocodile, received the adorations of an imbecile people. The ram of Rama usurped the altars of the sun, and the bull of the Celts was adored in place of the moon. As each star of the heavens was designated by an animal, a multitude of deified animals usurped the temples. This fatal epidemic, passing from Egypt into Arabia, carried its venom as far as India and even Persia. But as the moon, instead of being considered here as possessing the male faculty, was regarded, on the contrary, as representing the female faculty of the Universe, it was no longer a bull which served them as symbol but a cow and the cow became for the degenerate Hindus the object of a stupid veneration. The dog, attributed to Mercury, surnamed the *Prophet* or *divine Minister*, recalled the idea of all the providential emissaries, and, according to the country, received the name of *Boudh, Nabu, Job, Anubis*, etc. So that the people, becoming accustomed to see their prophet represented by the figure of a dog, or only with the head of this animal, gave to the dog the respect which they felt for the prophet. It was the same with the white or red dove which signified Venus; with the tortoise, which belonged to the earth; and the wolf, the bear, the wild boar, which was the symbol of Mars; with the crane, the hawk, the eagle which characterized Jupiter, etc.

At first Egypt, and then all the earth, was covered with religious practices as fantastic as puerile. The symbolic animals, deified by superstition, were passed on to the plants, and, as Juvenal amusingly says, household gods of some nations were seen growing among the vegetables in their gardens. Then was verified that prediction of an ancient Egyptian priest, who, seeing this deviation from the cult had said to his native country, that posterity in considering its idolatry would place in the category of lies and fables all that could be said of its ancient wisdom, of its knowledge, and of its virtues.

My intention is not to dwell here upon details which are found everywhere. It was only necessary, concerning the subject of which I am treating, to show that this condition of the earth, such as existed about six centuries before our era, was not at all habitual, as some writers have wished to point out, but that it was the almost inevitable result of the divisions which had taken place in the Universal Empire, and of the degeneration which had followed them in all moral and political institutions.

The great men who appeared then, although assisted by Providence, and although possessors of most powerful geniuses, could not change the state of things, because this condition had its principle in the Will itself of Man, which, as I have often said, is irrefutable. All that they could do was to preserve, in the midst of the disorganizing torrent, immobile centres where Truth might be maintained. One should observe, if one has not already done so, that after Orpheus, Moses, and Fo-Hi, no new religion was established upon earth. The last Buddhas, Sin-Mou, Lao-tzée and Kong-tzée, the last Zoroaster, Esdras, Lycurgus, Numa, and Pythagoras, all gave way to the established cult, conformed even to their exterior rites, and contented themselves with founding theosophical or philosophical sects more or less extensive. It was then that by their care were established almost everywhere two doctrines perfectly distinct, one common, conforming with the ideas of the multitude, the other secret, destined to give to a small number only the knowledge of the Truth and explanation of the thoughts of sages. Many new initiations were opened; the ancient ones took on a new character. With the cosmogonical traditions of the ancient mysteries were blended positive knowledge of the principle of things, of sciences, of arts, of morals, and even of politics. For the first time, there were secret societies whose members, united by the same principles, were sworn to an inviolable fidelity and recognized each other even among other initiates by certain signs. The Pythagorean Society was the most extensive and productive of great men. One recognized also, the Orphic, the Mithridatic, the Essenian, the Nazarene, the Isiac, the Shamanistic, the Taoistic, and innumerable other societies which it is unnecessary to name. The aim of all these societies was to arrest corruption wherever it was found, to offer refuge or help to virtue, and to place as much as possible a restraint upon the errors of despotism, royal, aristocratic, or popular.

It is very remarkable, also, that the societies multiplied principally in Europe, or upon the shores of Asia and Africa, where the rule of the populace was most strongly manifested. For, although it may be true that all despotism is pernicious whatever its form—and I mean here by despotism all power which is founded upon the arbitrary and unlimited will of those who exercise it without the intervention of the Divinity who regulates its use—it is, however, none the less true that the violence or the danger of despotism increases in proportion as it descends from the highest classes of society to the lowest, and as it spreads among the greater number.   In short, it is always upon the armed multitude that despotism is founded whether it be imperial or republican, whether this multitude receives the law from one alone or from many or whether it makes it for itself.   At any rate, there revolutions are more rapid and less profound; here more tenacious and more rancorous.

Moreover, at this epoch, while the evil had commenced to be great, it had however not reached the extreme point of breaking all forms and appearing openly in its hideous nudity.   The monarchs of Asia, although they had really thrown off the theocratic authority of sovereign pontiffs, preserved none the less an exterior respect for the Divinity. They always maintained priests to perform the sacrifices and the usual ceremonies, and thus kept the people in a sort of religious stupor favourable to their plans; but this stupor, lacking the principle of Truth, necessarily degenerated into stupidity or foolish superstition.   And it is very remarkable that while Asiatic despotism preserved certain exterior forms of theocracy which it had stifled, European anarchy believed itself obliged to preserve certain forms of royalty which it had abolished.   There was in Athens, as in Rome, and in all the other republican states, a king of sacrifices, so the people might legitimately communicate with the sacerdotal phantom which still existed. It seemed that, on the one side, Destiny fearing the force of the Will, tried to pacify it, and that, on the other hand, this force openly displayed, dreading the absolute abandonment of Providence, tried to deceive it.

CHAPTER II

ACCORDING to the situation of things which I have
just described, one can judge of the action of the three
great powers of the universe. Destiny dominated in Asia,
the Will of Man in Europe, and Providence, repulsed on
both sides, was obliged to conceal its course, in order not to
infringe upon those laws of Necessity and Liberty which it
had imposed upon itself.

But since there existed only two active and opposed
powers, it was evident that they had to fight. Necessity
and Liberty cannot remain indifferent face to face with
one another. As soon as the sole power which can maintain
harmony between them is ignored, discord must necessarily
arise. So Asia and Europe had to fight to determine to
which of the two should remain the Empire. Destiny on
the one side, and the Will of Man on the other, displayed
their most redoubtable forces.

Already Europe had invited the struggle by irruptions
more or less considerable; the taking of Troy, almost within
sight of the Assyrian monarch, who dared not oppose it
had been a great event. The establishment of several

Greek colonies upon the Asiatic littoral had been the result; Sicily, Corsica, Sardinia had been overcome and peopled with free colonies. The Cimmerians descending from septentrional heights had many times invaded Asia Minor and had established themselves there; they had made felt there the force of their cavalry, swifter and better trained for war than that of the Assyrians. The Greeks had imitated their example and, for the first time, chariot-racing was introduced at the Olympian Games.[1] All urged Asia to think of her defence; but neither the kings of Babylon, nor even those of Ecbatana, were in condition to resist Greece, if Greece united in a single people should attack them. This union, although still far distant, was preparing itself silently. The kingdom of Macedonia had just been founded.

The King of Media, Cyaxares,[2] however, after having driven the Celts from Upper Asia, which they had invaded, and after becoming master of all Assyria, of Palestine, and a part of Arabia, left a flourishing realm which fell, a short time after, into the hands of Cyrus. Thanks to this young hero, Persia, subject to the Babylonians for more than fifteen centuries, placed itself in the first rank of Asiatic powers and aspired to the Universal Empire. The conquest of Lydia opened to Cyrus immense treasures; he entered Babylon in triumph; he penetrated India. At his death, his son Cambyses pursued the course of his victories and conquered Egypt. The Jews, after having obtained from Cyrus permission to return to Jerusalem and there to rebuild their temple, made themselves tributaries of the Persian

[1] The Olympian Games established by Iphitus in honour of Olympian Zeus about the year 884 B.C. had as aim the maintenance of a religious unity in Greece which politics tended to destroy. These games were not used as a chronological epoch until towards the year 776 B.C. The era of the Olympiads dates from the victory of Corœbus which was the first inscribed on the public registers. The introduction of chariot-racing was in the year 645 B.C.

[2] This name which should be written *Kai-assar* signifies the supreme monarch. It was a title at that time, which the Median king took as King of Kings. The name Cyrus, *Kai-Kosrou* has about the same meaning.

Empire; thus all Asia and the greater part of Africa seemed to be united.

Europe began the hostilities. The Athenians passed into Asia, besieged the city of Sardis and burned it. The Persians, led into Europe almost within sight of Athens, were there defeated by Miltiades. Egypt profited by this event to throw off the yoke; but Xerxes,[1] after having brought again this kingdom under his rule, commenced his memorable expedition against Greece. His success is well known. The Will of Man triumphed over all that Destiny hurled against it, even the most formidable. More than a million soldiers, at first checked at Thermopylæ by three hundred Spartans, determined to conquer or die, were annihilated upon the fields of Platæa and Mycale, and the largest fleet which had ever floated upon the Mediterranean covered with its *débris* the shores of Salamis. Asia was vanquished.

If Greece had known how to profit by her advantages, she would then have carried away the sceptre of the world from Persia and have founded in Europe the Universal Empire. She needed only to listen to the voice of the Amphictyons and to believe in Providence, which by means of the Pythoness of Delphi designated Socrates as wisest of mortals. By becoming a united nation, by stifling all hatreds, all rivalries which separated the diverse members of the Amphictyonic confederation, by receiving from the mouth of Socrates the instructions which the genius of that divine man would have given her, Greece would have raised herself to destinies, the splendour and duration of which it would be impossible to determine. But no, this haughty Will, made proud by its victory, knew only how to obtain a passing and frivolous benefit; it sacrificed for a few moments of ostentatious enjoyment thousands of years of glory and of happiness; for I ought to say one thing here which has not been perceived, viz., that Greece died young and, so to

[1] *Shir-Shah*, the Valiant King or Lion-King.

speak, became extinguished in the flower of her youth. Vanity ruined her. Enamoured of a foolish liberty, she yielded to the storm of passions and did not bear the fruits which Orpheus and Pythagoras had brought to light and which Socrates and Plato were destined to mature.

Instead of strengthening herself by concentrating, she became divided, and, turning against herself her blind passions, broke with her own hands the wonderful instrument which Providence had given her for her preservation. The Athenians and the Spartans, scarcely having acquired the position of conquerors, quarrelled, and with their blood drenched the plains of Peloponnesus.[1] In a few years, Aristides, the most just of the Greeks, Themistocles and Cimon, the saviours of their native land, were banished. The city of Platæa was burned, and all its inhabitants were reduced to slavery. Athens, taken by the Spartans, was given over to the condemnation of the thirty tyrants; and, finally, Socrates, at first abandoned to the bitter sarcasms of Aristophanes, to the impious calumnies of Anytus, condemned by an insensate tribunal, drank the hemlock and expiated the crime of having been the greatest of the Athenians and the most virtuous of men.

From this moment, there was no more hope for Greece; her movements were only convulsions, sometimes caused by a mad joy, sometimes by a puerile fear. The Spartans, after having triumphed over the Athenians, were humiliated by the Persians, with whom Antalcidas concluded a shameful

---

[1] Notice that the name *Pelops*, from which this name is derived, signifies Black Land. It was the name of Greece while occupied by the Pelasges or Black People. The Heraclides who vanquished the Pelopidæ designate the Boreans called *Heruli*. All the different names which the Greeks have borne in different times explain the sects to which they belonged. By the name of *Hellenes* one should understand the Lunars, opposed to *Helices* or *Iliones* the Solars; by that of *Argives*, the Whites, opposed to the Phœnicians, the Reds; by those of the *Dorians* of *Achæans*, the Males or the Strong Ones, opposed to the Ionians, etc. As to the name of *Greeks*, which they gave themselves with difficulty, it came from the Celtic *Graia*, a crane, and proved that they were a part of the faction of the Salians against the Ripuarians.

peace. Defeated by the Thebans at Leuctra and at Mantinea they never recovered from this catastrophe. The women of Sparta then saw the smoke of the enemy's camp, and lost even the memory of their savage virtues. The Thebans, reputed the hardiest of the Greeks, seized the dominion in order to put it within reach of the King of Macedonia, and to let him take it most easily. Greece had still great men, but she was no longer a great nation, and could not pretend to be. She had great men only to ignore them, to persecute them, to sell them as vile animals in the marketplace, to give them up to death.

At this epoch, the Council of the Amphictyons had lost all of its authority, and the sanctuary of Delphi all its influence. This sacred place, pillaged by the Phocians and profaned by the Crisseans, gave pretext for a war in which Philip of Macedon found means of entering in his capacity as member of the Amphictyonic Council. It was in vain that Greece, frightened to behold so dangerous a confederate arriving in her midst, tried to put him out of the way. The philippics, with which Demosthenes made the tribune resound, excited only useless effervescence. In Athens there was agitation, in Sparta an insolent laconism was affected; Thebes was given over to secret intrigues; but nowhere did real strength exist. Philip pursued his plans; he triumphed over Olynthus, subjugated the Phocians, terminated the sacred war, paid honour to the Temple of Delphi, and, taking possession of the Council of the Amphictyons which these confederate imbeciles had always neglected, had himself named commander-in-chief of all the troops of Greece. The restrained Will uttered a cry of despair; abandoned by Providence, about to be crushed by Destiny, it sought means of saving itself, and, finding only crime, embraced it; Philip was assassinated; but this cowardly outrage, far from turning aside the peril which menaced it, on the contrary precipitated it. Such is the Eternal law that all crime draws with it its own chastisement.

Alexander, who succeeded his father, although still very young, displayed even greater powers. At the age of twenty he entered Greece, overthrew Thebes, subdued the Athenians, and, soon at the head of an army which his courage alone rendered formidable, landed in Asia and began the conquest of Persia.

It is quite useless, I think, that I should stop at the details of the expedition of Alexander. All the world knows how this young hero, vanquisher at the Granicus, fought Darius at the battle of Issus; cut the Gordian knot in passing through Gordium, so as to fulfil the oracle which promised the Empire of Asia to the one who should untie it; took possession of Tyre, after a siege of seven months; conquered Egypt, where he founded Alexandria; took Gaza; subjugated all of Syria; and finally made his triumphant entrance into Babylon, after having defeated entirely the army of Darius at Arbela.

After this, Greece no longer existed, and the future of Europe was once more compromised; for Alexander, yielding to Destiny which had taken possession of him, consented to establish his empire in Asia, and to adopt the habits and customs of the peoples whom he had conquered. It is a pity that this hero, susceptible of feeling all that which was great, should not have seen that it was only in order to effect a change of dynasty on the throne of Persia that he had been called out of Macedonia. Why did he not remember that his father had owed the force which he had bequeathed to him only to the course which he had taken in the sacred war in rendering to the Temple of Delphi its influence and to the assembly of the Amphictyons its dignity? Why did he not dream of keeping up the priesthood on the holy mountain? Why did he not see that he ought to establish the capital of his empire in Athens or at least in Byzantium? Blind pride! It alone told him what he owed to Providence and he believed that his star had led him to the conquest of the world. Content to be called the son of Jupiter, he did not concern himself about meriting this signal honour, and he delivered himself to Destiny which ruined him. His expedition into India was but a vain demonstration, and his death, which occurred at the age of thirty-two years, whether it was due to poison, or was the consequence of an orgy, was none the less the result of his mistakes.

CHAPTER III

GREECE LOSES HER POLITICAL EXISTENCE—REFLECTIONS ON
THE RELATIVE DURATION OF THE DIVERSE GOVERNMENTS

IT is known that, after the division of the Empire of Alexander among his generals, a certain Polysperchon proclaimed in the name of the new sovereigns the liberty of all the cities of Greece; but it was a mockery. Greece no longer had political existence, and all the liberty left to these cities was confined to that of corrupting their great men, when they had any, or of suppressing the philosophers, as Athens tried to do with Phocion and Theophrastus. But Athens, the most free, or rather the most turbulent of the Greek cities, fell successively in a few years under the power of Antipater, of Demetrius of Phaleron, of Demetrius Poliorcetes, of Antigonus Gonatas, etc. Whereas Sparta, after having massacred her Ephors, had tyrants whose very names do not deserve to be mentioned.

Thus, in going back in the political existence of Greece to the establishment of the tribunal of Amphictyons, about 1500 B.C. one can give to this existence a duration of only a dozen centuries at the most, of which five or six centuries were under the republican régime, and this is not comparable to anything that we have seen either in theocracy or even in royalty. This very agitated and very limited existence has, however, been praised to excess, perhaps on account of its very agitation and its brevity; for what men value above all in his-

tory is rapidity and movement. But does the happiness of the
peoples depend on that? I doubt it. When I see three or
four thousand years occupying hardly a few pages, have I
not the right to think that the most perfect calm has reigned
during this interval and that the rarity of events announces
the absence of wars and evils, crimes and other scourges?
There is nothing so soon depicted as felicity; it is the aspect
of a still lake which reflects a sky without clouds. But the
tempest which announces danger, the calamities which
rouse peoples, all this varies the scene in a thousand ways,
and furnishes material for an infinity of tableaux. Doubtless one loves to read those pompous descriptions, where
contrasts awaken attention, where oppositions of light and
darkness, of virtue and vice, stir the heart, where interest
is excited by the shock of passions; but is it only to amuse
posterity that peoples have a history? Who is the man who
would sacrifice the welfare of his whole life to the foolish
vanity of furnishing the material for a romance?

Nevertheless, this is an observation upon which I strongly
advise the reader to meditate. All ancient chronologies
which have come down to us from the Hindus, Egyptians,
Chinese, Iranians, or Chaldeans, and where the duration of
dynasties and of reigns are calculated equally, declare
generally the relative duration of the reigns from thirty to
forty years. It is not unusual to see monarchs remaining
on the throne for sixty, eighty, or a hundred years: Arrian
and Pliny agree in saying that from Rama, whom they call
Dionysus, to Alexander, 153 reigns were completed in India, a
space of 6402 years, and, on the other hand, Herodotus relates that the Egyptian priests showed him in a great hall the
statues of 345 pontiffs, and this would raise the general
duration of the priesthoods to 11,340 years. I myself have
observed, in glancing through the history of ancient
dynasties, that, during all the time that the theocracy of
Rama preserved its force, there had never been the slightest
revolution against the throne. Kings, succeeding each other,

according to the law of nature, fulfilled their long career and made the people happy, without having ever to fear either the passions of the multitude or the ambitions of the great. Protected by Providence, whose agent they recognized, they maintained in a just equilibrium, the fatality of Destiny and the free Will of Man. Neither daggers nor poison could approach them. It was not until a long time after the schism of the Phœnicians, the Parsees and the Chinese, and when the extinction of the Solar and Lunar Dynasties had taken place, that revolutions commenced. The insensate monarchs who succeeded them, moved by a calamitous pride, did not see that, by throwing off the authority of the sovereign pontiffs, they thus turned aside the hand of Providence which protected them, and opened to their rivals and their subjects the way of crime and rebellion.

It was about twenty centuries before our era that this fatal thought fell into the minds of kings. Belochus at Babylon, Pradyota among the Hindus, commenced the movement which was felt from the banks of the Hoang-ho River to the Nile. The evil went so far in Egypt, Herodotus assures us, that for more than a century, during the disastrous reigns of Cheops and Chephron, the temples of the gods were closed. On and after this epoch, royalty was subjected to storms which, up to that time had been unknown. The crown, ever stained with blood, passed to guilty heads, and parricidal hands bore the sceptre. Then the reigns were shortened more and more and kings multiplied in a frightful progression.[1]

But to return to my first purpose, I said that the political existence of the Greeks under the republican administration could be estimated at five or six centuries. Experience

---

[1] If we consider, for example, the dynasty of Cyrus, we will see that in the space of 228 years, that is to say, after the epoch when Cyrus took the crown of Persia, 559 B.C. until the death of Darius, dethroned by Alexander in 331 B.C., fourteen kings succeeded to the throne, nearly all of whom were assassinated or were assassins; this would give about sixteen years to each reign.

shows that that is about the limit of duration of the strongest republics.   That of Sparta, Carthage, and even Rome have not lasted longer.

The downfall of Greece brought to Ionia, that is to say, to all who shared in the Phœnician schism, an almost mortal blow.   This schism had covered so many countries, there remained only those over which Carthage and Rome extended their dominion; for already Tyre and Sidon no longer existed.   Some years after the conflagration of the Temple of Ephesus, the inhabitants of Sidon, besieged by the Persians, killed each other after having delivered their city to flames and after Tyre had become the prey of the successors of Alexander.   It was then, in Carthage and in Rome that the remnant of this ancient power was concentrated and that the Will of Man exercised its force.

CHAPTER IV

COMMENCEMENT OF ROME—HER WARS—HER STRUGGLE WITH
CARTHAGE—HER TRIUMPHS

BEFORE the Romans had established a republic, they
were dependent upon the Etruscans, called *Tusces*,
Tosques, and *Toscans*, who governed them at first by means
of viceroys. These viceroys, called *Tarquins*,[1] ended by
making themselves almost independent of the Etruscan
Lars, when the people, tired of their pride and avarice,
threw off their authority and declared themselves free under
the leadership of Brutus and Valerius. A senate was established, presided over by two consuls who were removable.

Etruria, which in earlier times did not differ from Thrace,
was, as I have said, only a Phœnician colony planted upon
that of the Hindus—a mixture of Atlanteans and of Celts.
Rome, destined to be so celebrated, was in the first place
only a sort of stronghold built upon the banks of the Tiber

---

[1] The word *Tarquin* is composed of two Phœnician words, *Tôr-Kîn*, the one
who regulates the possession or the conquest. As to the names that many of
these Tarquins appear to have had, they are rather epithets which designate
their works. Thus the name of *Romulus* indicates the founder of Rome, and
Quirinus the Genius of the city, *Numa*, the legislator, theocrat, etc. It is
certain that the latter was a powerful legislator among the Etruscans, whose
name was afterwards given as an honour to those who imitated him. We know
moreover that the first historian of Rome, Fabius Pictor, wrote only from the
time of the second Punic war about five hundred and forty years after the
epoch where the foundation of this city is placed, and that he was able to
consult only the most uncertain traditions.

to protect navigation. Its name, Etruscan or Phœnician, which became afterwards its secret and sacred name, was then *Valentia*, that is to say, the *rendezvous* of the force. It was not until after it was delivered from the Tarquins that it took the name of Rome, from an ancient Greek word which signified set at liberty.[1] This city, which remained a very long time in great obscurity, was not known to the Greeks until the epoch when it was taken by the Gauls. The historian Theopompus mentions this event, agreeing with Pliny, but without attaching very great importance to it. It appears, however, that about this time, the Romans had already sent magistrates to Athens to learn the laws of Solon.

Carthage was then well known by its military expeditions. This commercial republic had many settlements in Spain, on the occidental and meridional shores of Gaul, and as far as Sicily, and had already made herself formidable. Rome, too savage at first to love the arts, a refuge for a crowd of vagabonds without learning and without desire to acquire it, had fallen into a state of ignorance; whereas Greece possessed the Metonic Cycle and each year placed a nail at the door of the temple of Jupiter to preserve the chronology. The first sun-dial to be used in Rome was placed more than two centuries after the establishment of the consuls upon the temple of Romulus Quirinus. The Romans were, in their origin, only a sort of filibusters whom the lure of plunder united; courageous brigands, whose single virtue, adorned by the pompous name of patriotism, consisted for several centuries only in bringing to the common mass what they had pillaged from neighbouring nations. When these warriors went abroad, they bore as ensign a handful of hay, called *manipuli*. The crane, which

---

[1] *Valentia* is formed from the words *Whal-aûthô*. As to the name of Rome, it may come from Poμαι. But I know that the Brahmans cite several pages from the Pouranas which claim it is derived from *Rama*. They say that Rome was one of his colonies.

they received from the Salian priests and which they transformed into an eagle, did not appear upon their flags until much later. It is even possible that this emblem was taken by them only during the first Punic war, and then in order to compete with the Carthaginians, who carried the head of a horse. As the head of a horse was consecrated to Moloch, likewise to Saturn, so the Roman eagle was consecrated to Jupiter. Be that as it may, it was within the walls of Rome that the Will of Man, restrained in Greece and about to be crushed by Destiny, took refuge. It was there that it concentrated all its strength. Carthage, which could not offer it as sure a shelter, was sacrificed.

If one loves movement in history, if one is pleased with tumultuous events, rapid and violent; if the savage virtues of a certain kind, a heroism rough and without courtesy, can interest in the midst of scenes of carnage and devastation, one ought to read with delight the annals of Rome. Never did city, never did people furnish such examples. In a few centuries, the universe saw this struggling Etrurian village, still bruised by the chains which she had borne, hardly free from the hands of Porsenna who had humiliated her and from those of Brennus who was bought off and the Capitol saved, try her strength, extend herself, raise herself, and, from the depths of the dust, attain the height of grandeur. In the war with the Samnites, she came out from her obscurity; she challenged Pyrrhus in the siege of Tarentum, and, at first, frightened by the sight of his elephants fell back before him; but soon reassured, she attacked, beat, and forced him to retire to Epirus. Obliged to dispute the empire of the sea with the Carthaginians, she had need of a marine force; she soon created one and her first sea-fight was a triumph. In the interval between the first and second Punic wars, she took possession of Sardinia and Corsica, subjugated the pirates of Illyria, carried her arms even beyond Italy, and passed the Po for the first time.

Nevertheless, sinister signs occurred to intimidate these

warriors, who, superstitious as well as ignorant, believed that they could appease the gods by human sacrifice. Two Greeks and two Gauls, man and woman, were seized by order of the consuls and were buried alive in the market place at Rome. This abominable sacrifice did not prevent Hannibal, at the opening of the second Punic War, after having destroyed Saguntum in Spain, from crossing the Alps and from covering the fields of Trasimenus and Cannæ with Roman corpses. Fear was upon Rome, and, notwithstanding the vain boasting of several senators, it has always appeared certain that if the Carthaginian general had besieged her, he would have taken her. Why did he not profit by his advantages? It was because the same Will which had moved the two republics, being unable to preserve but one, preserved that one in which it had the most influence, the one which belonged to Europe, where the centre of its activity was, and, as I have already said, sacrificed the other. This is what appeared evident in this circumstance, where not only the particular will of Hannibal bent without knowing why, but where the citizens of Carthage, being divided among themselves upon the most frivolous pretexts, delivered their city to the destruction which awaited it. The battle of Zama, won by Scipio, decided its fate. It was in vain that Hannibal believed he could retard the march of Rome by invoking the power of Destiny against her. The war which he kindled between Antiochus and the Romans served but to augment their power, by enriching them with the spoils of this monarch, by enabling them to conquer Macedonia, and by rendering them arbitrators of Egypt.

Carthage, having been destroyed, nothing more could resist this colossal republic, which, extending its enormous arms, now in Asia, now in Africa, now in Europe, made its laws recognized from the Tagus to the Tanaïs, and from the Atlas to the Caucasus mountains.

CHAPTER V

THE Will of Man triumphed with the Roman power. Destiny, forced to draw back on all sides, maintained itself only in the south of Asia, where the blow already threatened to strike it. It needed for this only the overthrow of the Empire of the Parthians, which served as a barrier.[1] This would undoubtedly have happened if this victorious Will had not been divided; but that was impossible unless Providence intervened; for as I have often repeated, and as it seems to me that the history which I have unfolded to the eyes of the reader has sufficiently proved by its principal events, nothing durable can exist unless Providence consolidates it. Whether Destiny or the Will of Man act in concert or alone, they will never produce but transient things, forms, more or less brilliant, which will crush one another and will vanish into space. Now Providence was no more recognized in Rome than it had been in Athens. The public cult deprived of essential principle,

---

[1] This Empire had been founded by Arsaces about 250 B.C., upon the dismemberment of that of Seleucus. It included particularly ancient Persia. The dynasty of this Arsaces is known by the Persians under the name of *Ashkanide.*

consisted only of vain ceremonies, of atrocious or ridiculous superstitions, of allegorical formulas which were no longer understood. The mass of the people, indeed, still believed in a crude mixture of Phœnician, Etruscan, and Greek mythologies, and gave themselves over to vague beliefs; but the brains of the nation did not accept any of these ideas as true, considering them only as useful and of service politically. The augurs and haruspices despised each other, and, according to the remark of Cicero, could not look at each other without laughing. As early as the first Punic War, two hundred and fifty years before the beginning of our era, Claudius Pulcher, all ready to engage with the Carthaginians in a naval combat, seeing that the sacred chickens would not eat, had them thrown into the sea, saying jestingly that he would make them drink. The sovereign pontiff, maintained solely for form, as king of sacrifices, enjoyed but few barren honours without real authority. This office was canvassed for in Rome as that of ædile; and no difference was made in the choice between the moral instruction of the man who directed the religious ceremonies and that of the man who presided at the games of the amphitheatre. In general, as much in Europe as in Asia, under the dominion of Destiny as under that of the Will, religion was regarded only as a political institution, a sort of curb or bridle wisely conceived to check the multitude when it was aroused and to direct it at the pleasure of the government.

The conquest of Africa and Asia had introduced into Rome luxury and the love of wealth which is the consequence. That of Greece had brought the taste for arts and letters and that instinct for subtle philosophy natural to the Greeks. A mass of systems which were raised from the débris of one another invaded the schools. Nearly all opposed the dominating polytheism, but, without positively putting anything in place of it, lost themselves in equivocal reasoning which, sometimes supporting the *pro* and *con* of all things, led to scepticism. Many of these systems even, corrupted by ignorant sophistry, flattered the tastes of the voluptuous and perverted, in setting them free from any remorse for weakness or for crime, and in representing the gods as occupying themselves not in the least with what might be passing on earth. The system of Epicurus, thus disfigured, was opposed to that of Zeno the Stoic, establishing upon the order of the Universe the necessity of an intelligent primal Cause and founding the welfare of man upon the accomplishment of his duties; but this system, carried too far, as that of Epicurus, had lost its vigour through excessive praise, in the same manner as the other had become corrupt through transgressing its limits. So that Roman society was composed, either of men who too easily followed all impulses, or of men too inflexible to yield to any. This division of which I have shown the principle caused the ruin of the republic and prevented the consolidation of the Empire which followed it, even when force of things was not absolutely opposed to it,—for on the one side, too much indolence lent itself to too many forms, and, on the other, too much rigidity broke them all. There was in all this neither life nor truth.

Julius Cæsar conquered Gaul; although he experienced many great difficulties in this expedition, they were slight in comparison with those which he would have encountered had Gaul been formed of one single nation. But it was divided into numberless peoples, often jealous of one another, and a common bond no longer united them. It had been a long time since any Celts, properly speaking, had existed; the ancient name had been preserved but the nation had disappeared. Neither the Gauls, nor the Teutons, nor the Polabians existed any more; these names remained only as historic monuments. One would have searched in vain the nations which they had originally designated. One found in Gaul the Rhœtians, the Bibracte, the Ruteni, the Senones, the Allobroges, the Alvernes, the Carnutes, the Bituriges, the Hennetes and a host of other unimportant peoples which would be wearisome as well as useless to name. Germany which had taken the place of Teutoland, and Russia and Poland that of Sarmatia, were similarly divided among numberless like tribes. The irruptions which had succeeded each other a hundred times from the North to the South, and from the West to the East; the African and Asiatic colonies, which supplanted each other turn by turn during so long a space of time, had changed in a thousand ways the physiognomy of Europe. The variations which had taken place in the peoples had also taken place in the dialects, in the customs, in the laws, and in the cults; so that the confusion had become such that it was impossible to go back even in thought to any sort of unity. One would have believed, in comparing a Greek with a Breton and a Roman with a Sarmatian, that it was impossible that such men should have sprung from the same origin.

The Gauls then, whom Cæsar vanquished, were not precisely Gauls and still less Celts; they were a mixture of a hundred little peoples who often did not understand each other. They defended themselves with an obstinate valour, and yielded only to the superiority which the discipline, authority, and talents of their general gave to the Romans. During these long and bloody contests, a large part of the inhabitants of Gaul perished on the battlefields, and even greater numbers submitted to slavery, the rest, incapable of making a longer resistance, gave way to the victors.

Before this event, however, symptoms of dissolution manifested themselves at Rome. The republic, so extolled by men more passionate than wise, scarcely four centuries old, inclined towards its downfall and having no more people whose blood they might spill, prepared to drown themselves in torrents of their own.

Already Marius and Sulla, as divided in character as in ambition, had kindled a civil war whose bitter fruits had been the proscription of a great number of citizens. Catiline, ambitious, more obscure, trying to attain by conspiracy to the authority which could be obtained at that time only by military successes, had been easily overthrown by Cicero, who had not the same good fortune as had Cæsar and whom Antony had the cowardice to banish, as Antipater three centuries before had banished Demosthenes; when Pompey, whose glory had preceded that of Cæsar, unable to endure a rival who effaced him, whether he still believed in the possibility of a republic, or pretended to believe in it, drew to his party the majority of the senate and all those whom Rome still counted citizens, rigid observers of the ancient laws. Cato, Brutus, and Cassius declared themselves for him. But Cæsar, quicker to understand the mind of the Romans, and more prompt to profit by circumstances, concentrated his army when the senate ordered him on his return from Gaul to disband it, and with it, crossing the Rubicon, the limit of his government, entered Italy.   A new civil war was declared, whose events by their rapidity were astonishing.

At the first conflict, Pompey, besieged in Brundisium, escaped without daring to sustain the siege.   Cæsar wishing to prevent the reunion of his force hastened to Spain, and put to rout his lieutenants.   Retracing his steps, he besieged and took Marseilles, and, from there, passing rapidly into Macedonia, gave battle to Pompey in the plains of Pharsalus and defeated him utterly.   Pompey made his escape to Egypt, where he was assassinated by the order of Ptolemy. Cæsar who was upon his tracks, entered Egypt, made himself master of Alexandria, and, carrying the war into Africa, won the battle of Thapsus.   Cato killed himself, and with him expired what the Will of Man regarded as the noblest and grandest.   Brutus and all those of his party, irritated and exasperated by the event, plotted crime in order to escape from the evil.

Cæsar could have escaped the blow which awaited him; he had only to listen to the voice of Providence which warned him in all ways, to give to it the credit of his good fortune; but, having reached almost the same point as Alexander, he committed the same mistake as this conqueror; he attributed whatever great deed he had accomplished to his star, and, even more audacious, stretched out his hand to the tiara and declared himself sovereign pontiff. He was assassinated.

Before the outbreak of the civil war, a sort of pact was concluded among Pompey, Cæsar, and Crassus, and this unusual pact, which bore the name of *Triumvirate*, had had a most calamitous end. After the death of Cæsar, a new triumvirate, no less heterogeneous than the first, was formed among Octavianus, adopted son of Cæsar, Antony his lieutenant, and Lepidus an insignificant personage. The proscriptions recommenced; Rome was again inundated with blood and Brutus and Cassius, beaten by Antony, killed themselves. Pompey's son was slaughtered. Nearly all the assassins of Cæsar perished by the sword. At last, Octavianus and Antony having fallen out, their quarrel was decided by the naval battle of Actium, which gave the Roman Republic unconditionally to the victor; this victor, as astonished by his victory as overwhelmed by the crown which descended upon his head, dared neither refuse the Empire nor seize it with a hand honest and resolute. The bloody image of Cæsar, falling pierced with stabs in the senate, was constantly before his eyes. Octavianus was born without political courage; he had valour only on the day of battle; the title of *Augustus*, which was given him did not change his character[1]; he believed himself fortunate without believing himself worthy, and, although he was vested with the dignity of sovereign pontiff and that of Emperor, he had never either the providential influence of the one, nor the legitimate authority of the other; he was obeyed because he had the power that gave force, but not because he had the power which gave ascendancy, hence his conduct

---

[1] The Latin word *Augustus* comes from the word *Augur*, which signifies properly the action of raising the eyes to heaven to implore its aid or receive its inspirations.

with regard to the senate was a long deceit, and his equivocal reign, where names opposed to the policy of the Republic and the Emperor increased unceasingly, influenced so much the reign of his successors, that they all received a false colour which degraded them.   Tiberius would not have been led to rule by terror, neither would have Caligula nor Nero committed so many useless cruelties, had it not been for the false and ridiculous position in which the insidious and pusillanimous politics of Octavianus had placed them.

CHAPTER VI

MISSION OF JESUS: ITS OBJECT—MISSION OF ODIN AND OF
APOLLONIUS OF TYANA; TO WHAT END

ROME, subjected to Destiny, did not recover from the blow which had destroyed her. Not daring to declare that she was no longer free, she strove to force herself by vain formulas; but this miserable recourse to vanity turned to her disadvantage. Her citizens, basely servile or insolently independent, annoyed their masters equally by their adulation or their resistance. By turn humiliated or broken, they knew not how to adopt the golden mean of a legitimate submission. Disciples of Epicurus or of Zeno, imbued with principles of a philosophy too lax or too strained, had passed alternately from a systematic indolence to an ostentatious austerity; when suddenly there appeared among them a society of new men, ignorant and rude for the most part, but full of extraordinary enthusiasm. These men, driven ahead by an almost irresistible calling, strangers to all known systems, attacked the errors of polytheism, unmasked the deceits of the priests, the ruses of the philosophers, and, simple in their morals, irreproachable in their manners, died rather than deny the truths which they were entrusted to proclaim.

These men, who were at first confused with a Jewish sect called *Nazarenes*, gave themselves the name of *Christ-*

ians on account of their Master, surnamed *Christ*.[1] Their dogmas were little known; they were believed in general to be sad and mournful; their priests, who adopted the black colour, all spoke of the end of the world as very near at hand, they announced the coming of a Great Judge, they exhorted to repentance and promised expiation of sins through the waters of baptism, and the resurrection of the dead. As they assembled in secret in the most secluded places, in caverns and in catacombs, to celebrate there a mystery which was considered terrible and which they called nevertheless by a very harmonious name, *Eucharist*,[2] the Jews, their decided enemies, took every occasion to calumniate them and announced that in their nocturnal fêtes, they killed a child and afterwards ate it.

What chiefly impressed the leaders of the state in these new men who were called Christians, was their intolerance; accustomed as they were to consider religions only as human institutions, they had fallen into a profound indifference regarding the substance as well as the form, and did not conceive how anyone could attach so great a value to such or such dogma, or to such or such rite, to prefer them to all others even at the risk of their lives. The Roman magistrates would have admitted the cult of Christ into Rome, as they had admitted that of Serapis and Mithras, if its followers could have endured the fusion; but it was precisely this that they could not do without ceasing to be themselves. The Christians, persuaded that they alone recognized the true God, that they alone rendered to Him a perfect worship instituted by Himself, regarded all other religions, not only with contempt but even with horror; they shunned ceremonies as execrable abominations, and, transported by a holy zeal, charged with madness and rebellion, disturbed the

---

[1] From the Greek Χριστός, *Christus*. This word comes from the verb Χρίειν, which means to *anoint*, to *consecrate by unction*. It is the exact translation of the Hebrew word *Meshïah*.

[2] From the Greek Εὐχαριστία, thankfulness, gratitude.

mysteries and often maltreated the ministers. These magistrates, persuaded that any religion which accused the others of rendering to God an impious and sacrilegious worship tended to disturb the peace of the state, regarded, in their turn, that religion as dangerous, and promulgated against the Christians severe laws which were rigorously executed. They imagined that a few seasonable attacks would suffice to restrain these fanatics; but, to their astonishment, they saw that it was precisely the contrary and that the Christians, far from shrinking, eagerly offered themselves in crowds for death, braved torment, and, keen to obtain the palm of martyr, offered to the rage of their executioners a serenity which froze the latter with fear.

It had been a long time since one had seen on earth men subject to a Providential action which raised them above the fatality of Destiny and which subdued the Will; then one could see and judge their powers. Providence, which had wished for such men, deemed them indispensable. The earth, which for a long time had been the prey to all sorts of scourges, inclined, as I have shown, towards a perceptible degeneration; all was born corrupt and withered before its time. The Roman Empire founded under grievous conditions, a shapeless mixture of republicanism and despotism, could enjoy but an ephemeral *éclat;* this *éclat*, or rather this gleam which appeared under the reign of the Antonines from Vespasian to Marcus Aurelius, served only to render more painful the darkness which ensued. This Empire, though scarcely formed, collapsed, and whereas the one which it had the pretension of succeeding had itself existed for more than six thousand years, two or three centuries sufficed to dismember this one, and four to overthrow it completely.[1]

---

[1] If one wishes to apply here the rule which I have already applied to the Empire of Cyrus, one will see that in the space of about three hundred and sixty years from Augustus to Constantine, more than forty-five emperors occupied the throne; which gives only about nine years to a reign. The Roman Empire was then dismembered; that which was called the *Empire of the Occident* from Constantine to Augustulus, was nothing but chaos.

The darkness which from the moment of its birth had become thicker and thicker, covered at that time all the Occident and for a long time held it plunged in a profound night.

It was necessary that a new cult whose dogmas, inaccessible to reason and with inflexible forms, should submit likewise to Destiny. It was an immense effort on the part of Providence. The man whom it summoned to fulfil this terrible mission would without doubt be more than man, for an ordinary man would have been crushed beneath the overwhelming burden which was given him to bear. This divine man was called *Jesus*, that is to say *Saviour*.[1] He was born among these same Hebrews, to whom the keeping of the Sepher of Moses had been confided fifteen centuries before, and among those men of steadfast character, in the sect of the Nazarenes, the most rigid of all.[2]

There had been nothing up to that time comparable with the mental force of Jesus, His intellectual exaltation, His animistic virtue. He was not learned according to man, since it has been doubted whether He even knew how to write; but the knowledge of the world was not necessary to Him for His work. It would, on the contrary, have harmed Him; faith only was necessary for Him; no one, either before or since, made such a perfect surrender of the will. He began His mission when thirty years old and finished it at thirty-three. Three years sufficed for him to change the face of the world. But His life, however long it had been, with whatever miracles He had filled it, would not have sufficed. It was necessary that He should wish to die, and that He should have the power to rise from the dead. Wonderful effort of human nature aided by Providence! Jesus

---

[1] The name of *Jesus* is derived from the same root as those of Joshua and Moses.

[2] The Nazarenes, as their name expresses, formed a congregation separated from the other Jews, they distinguished themselves by parting their hair on the top of the head, and, sometimes, by making a tonsure which has been imitated by the Christian priests.

willed it, and found in it the means of delivering Himself to death, to endure its tortures, and to subdue it with indomitable power. This king of terrors did not terrify him.   I pause. The ignorant or fanatical enthusiasts by their own exaggerations have simply helped to destroy the most beautiful act which the universe has ever witnessed.[1] But even before Jesus had been called to subdue the assent of Man and dominate his reason, Providence had raised up two men, of a rank inferior to His, but equally strong in their way to take possession of the animistic and instinctive faculties. The first called *Frighe* son of Fridulphe, surnamed *Wodan* by the Scandinavians, is known to us under the name of *Odin;* the other, *Apollonius*, is designated by the name of *Apollonius of Tyana*, on account of the small city of Cappadocia in which he was born. These two men had different success but both served by dividing the Will, to prepare it to submit to the yoke which Jesus would give to it.

Frighe was of Celt or Scythian origin, as the name sufficiently indicates.[2] An ancient historian of Norway states that he commanded the Asa-folk, a people of Celtic origin whose native land was situated between the Euxine and the Caspian Sea.[3] It appears that in his youth he was attached to the fortunes of Mithridates and commanded his armies

---

[1] It is especially this that Klopstock has accomplished in his poem, as I have mentioned in my *Discours sur l'Essence et la forme de la Poésie*, p. 172.

[2] The word *Frighe* is derived from Celtic root which develops the idea, to set at liberty. It is remarkable that the name of the Franks is derived from the same source. The name of *Fridulphe*, father of Odin, signifies the sustainer of the peace.

[3] Pliny, who speaks of the Asa-folk, places them in the environs of Mount Taurus. Strabo cites a city named *Asbourg*, which appears to have been the capital of the Asa-folk. This city is called *Asgard* in the Edda. The word *As* signifies a prince and even a god in the primitive language of the Celts. One finds it with the same signification of prince or of principle among the Scandinavians, the Etruscans, and the Basques. The Romans used the word *As* to express a unit of weights and measures. The French apply it today to the first number on dice or on cards. It is from this very ancient word that the name given to Asia is derived. In all the Atlantean dialects it expresses the basis of things.

up to the time when this monarch, forced to yield to the ascendancy of the Romans, killed himself. All the countries which depended upon the kingdom of the Empire having been usurped, Frighe, not wishing to submit to the yoke of the victor, retired towards the north of Europe accompanied by those who shared his sentiments.

The Scandinavians, who bore at that time the name of *Cimbrians*, implacable enemies of the Romans, received them as allies. They opened their ranks to them and facilitated the accomplishment of the design which Providence had upon them. Circumstances likewise singularly favoured it. These peoples, who had started out to make an incursion into Italy, had experienced a considerable check there. A small number, escaped from destruction, nourished in the depths of their hearts a violent desire for vengeance. At sight of these fierce warriors who were already united by a strong bond with them, the prince of the Asa-folk realized that here was a condition of which he could take advantage.

Frighe was a follower of Zoroaster, he knew, moreover, all the traditions of the Chaldeans and the Greeks, as many of the institutions which he has left in Scandinavia conclusively prove. He was initiated into the mysteries of Mithras. His genius was heroic, and the elevation of his soul rendered him susceptible to inspirations. The principal virtues of the Cimbrians, in the midst of whom he found himself, was warlike valour. The Celtic nation, I repeat, had not existed for a long time. A continuous movement of peoples flowing from north to south had almost effaced any trace of it. The Romans occupied the most beautiful part of Europe. Their cult had penetrated nearly everywhere. The Druids preserved but a shadow of their ancient grandeur. The voice of Voluspa had been long silent. None of these fortunate conditions which could favour him escaped the disciple of Zoroaster; he saw at a glance that immense region which extended from the Volga on the confines of Asia, to the shores of Armorica or Bretagne, to the extremities of Europė, promised to his gods and to his arms. And in truth, these beautiful and vast countries which we know to-day under the names of Russia, Poland, Germany, Prussia, Sweden, Denmark, France, England belonged to him or became the conquests of his descendants; so that one can say that there exists not a throne and not a royal family in these nations that does not originate from him.

Frighe, in order not to alarm the peoples whom he wished to conquer, halted with his companions in a place favourable for his plans, and obtained permission to build there a city which he called Asgard, after the name of his ancient native land. There, skilfully displaying a new luxury, a religious and warlike pomp, he attracted to him the surrounding peoples, impressed with the magnificence and the *éclat* of his ceremonies. Monarch and sovereign pontiff, he showed himself at the head of his soldiers and at the foot of the altars; he dictated his laws to the king and announced his dogmas like a divine apostle. He acted then exactly as Mohammed did about six centuries after him.

The changes which he made in the ancient religion of the Celts were not great. The greatest was in substituting for Teutad the great Ancestor of the Celts, a supreme God called *Wôd* or *Goth*, from whom the whole Gothic nation afterwards received its name.[1] It was the same that Zoroaster called *Time without limit*, the *Great Eternity*, *the Buddha* of the Hindus, that Rama had found recognized in all Asia.

---

[1] I have often spoken of this name. We must observe that it is applied in India to the planet Mercury and to Mercredi, exactly as in the north of Europe; but here it has been continued further as designating the Supreme Being; whereas in Hindustan it is applied more particularly to the divine Messengers and to the Prophets. This same name written and pronounced *God* or *Goth* has remained that of *God* in the greater part of the septentrional dialects, notwithstanding the change of cult and the establishment of Christianity. It is confused with the word *Gut* which signifies good; but these two words are not derived from the same root. The name of *God* or *Goth* comes from the Atlantean *Whôd*, eternity, and the word *gut* or good comes from the Celtic *gut*, the throat, whence *gust*, the taste.

It is from the name of this supreme God *Wôd*, called also the *Universal Father*, the *living God*, the *Creator of the World*, that Frighe received the name of *Wodan*, from which we have made Odin, that is to say, the Divine.

The legislator of the Scandinavians united then, with great force and sagacity, the doctrine of Zoroaster to that of the ancient Celts. He introduced into his mythology an Evil Genius called *Loki*[1] whose name was the exact translation of that of Ahriman; he gave to mankind the ancient Bor as ancestor and continued to found all virtues upon warlike valour. He taught positively, and this was the principal dogma of his cult, that heroes alone enjoyed all celestial felicities in *Valhalla*, the great hall of valour.[2]

[1] That is to say the enclosed, the compressed, the gloomy. Observe that the Scandinavians, in attributing to *Loki*, Saturday, have assimilated the Genius, of Evil, with Saturn.

[2] In this manner Odin expressed himself regarding the lot which awaited heroes on leaving this life, thus conforming to the ideas and customs of his people: "Valhalla," he said, "that celestial abode of valour is vast enough to contain all heroes whom glory brings there. Forty doors open to give entrance to this magnificent place. Eight heroes can pass through each, followed by a multitude of spectators, going out to combat. For every day the bird of dawning with the shining crested head makes the dwelling of the gods resound with his song; the heroes awakened, hasten to their arms and range themselves about the Father of Battles. They enter the lists and with inexpressible transports of courage and joy cut each other in pieces."

"It is their noble pastime. But as soon as the hour of repast approaches they cease from fighting, forget their wounds and return to feast in the palace of Wodan. The number of these warriors can never be so great that the flesh of the wild boar Schrimnir cannot suffice to nourish them. Every morning it is cooked and every night it becomes whole again. As for their drink it flows from an equally immortal source. The vessels destined to contain it are never empty. The Valkyries fill without ceasing the cups which they present smilingly to these heroes."

One sees that in the Valhalla of Odin, the *Valkyries*, that is to say, those who search for the valiant, take the place of the Houris of the Paradise of Mohammed. Both have imitated the *houranis* of Zoroaster. Observe as a very singular thing and which supports what I have said, that the root of the word *houri*, used by the Persians and the Arabs, is purely Celtic. One says today in Gallic, *hora*, *whore* in English, *hure* in all the Teutonic dialects, etc. It is true that the sense has become very base and that it expresses less than a courtesan; but it is in fact from a change of customs. Formerly free love was not condemned by the cult, quite the contrary. One sees that the Sanscrit *devadasi* which the Celtic word translates *hora*, signifies only a young woman consecrated to the gods. The Greek Ἔρως, *love*, comes from the same source, or rather it is the root of the Celtic *hora* and the Arabic *houri*. This root develops the idea of a creative Principle according to the Ionic or Phœnician system.

CHAPTER VII

CONQUESTS OF ODIN: HIS DOCTRINE AND THAT OF APOLLONIUS
—FOUNDATION OF CHRISTIANITY

IN the meantime, Odin, setting out from the banks of the
Tanaïs had advanced to the heart of Vandalia, today
Pomerania, subjecting to his laws all the peoples who happened on his way, either by the brilliancy of his bearing or
by the force of his arms. His renown and power increased
at each step, by the number of his proselytes and by that of
his subjects. Already Russia had submitted to his laws
and had received Suarlami, the oldest of his sons, to govern
it. Westphalia and western Saxony had been given by him
to Baldeg and to Sigdeg, two other sons of his. He had
added Franconia to his conquests, and had left it as an inheritance to his fourth son Sighe. From there, taking the
Scandinavian route through Cimbrian Chersonesus, he
passed into Finland, of which he took possession. This
country pleased him, and he built there the city of Odense
which still preserves in its name the memory of its founder.
The name of this city proves that at this epoch the name of
Wodan the Divine was already given to the prince of the
Asa-folk by the enthusiasm of its followers. Denmark
which submitted wholly to his arms, received as king,
Sciold the fifth son. This country, if one can believe the
Icelandic Annals, had not yet had a king, and it com-
menced thenceforth to be counted among the septentrional

249

powers.[1] The successors of Sciold took the name of *Scioldungiens* and reigned a considerable length of time.

At last Odin marched towards Sweden for the purpose of conquering it, when Gylfe, king of that country, struck with astonishment at the tales which he heard from all sides, resolved to look into these rumours himself and to find out whether he ought to attribute the success of the prophet-conqueror to his prestige or to some divine inspiration. Having conceived this plan he disguised his rank, and, under the name of the old *Gangler*, came to the place where the prince of the Asa-folk held his court. The author of the *Edda* who relates this journey, said that Gylfe, after having questioned the three ministers of Odin about the principles of things, the nature of the gods, and the destiny of the universe, was so struck by the wonderful things which he heard, that being assured that Odin was a messenger sent by Providence he descended from the throne to give it to him. This event crowned the glory of the Theocrat. Ynghe, his sixth son, having taken the crown of Sweden, transmitted it to his descendants who took the name of *yngleingiens*. Soon Norway imitated the example of Sweden and submitted to the last son of Odin, called Soemunghe.

Meanwhile the Scandinavian legislator neglected nothing to make his new states flourish and to found his cult there upon a solid basis. He established at *Sigtuna*, the city of Victory, today Stockholm, a supreme council composed of twelve pontiffs whom he charged to look after the public safety, to render justice to the people, and to preserve faithfully the archives of religious knowledge.

The historical débris which has come down to us represents Odin as the most persuasive of men. Nothing, say the Icelandic chronicles, could resist the force of his address, in which he often inserted verses composed extemporane-

---

[1] The septentrional chronologists place this event sixty years before Christ; now, the defeat of Mithridates by Pompey dates from the year 67, which coincides sufficiently.

ously. Eloquent in the temples, where his venerable mien
won for him all hearts, he was the most impetuous and the
most intrepid of warriors in battle. His valour, praised by
the bards his disciples, has been transformed by them into a
supernatural virtue. They have, in the course of time, enclosed in his particular history all that which appertained
to the general history of the Borean Race, because of Bor,
who was their ancestor. Not content with confusing it with
Wôd, the supreme God whom he had announced, they confused him again with the ancient Teutad and have attributed to him all the chants of Voluspa. The Icelandic
poems which still exist represent him as a god, master of the
elements, disposing at his pleasure of the winds and storms,
traversing the Universe in the twinkling of an eye, taking
all forms, raising the dead, and predicting the future. He
knew, according to these same legends, how to sing airs so
melodious, so tender, that the valleys were covered with
new flowers, the hills trembled with joy, and the shadows
drawn by the sweetness of his harmony emerged from the
depths and remained immobile about him.

These exaggerations were inevitable: one finds them expressed in the same manner for Rama, Orpheus, and Odin,
in the Ramayana of the Hindus, in the Greek mythology, and
in the Edda.

But, to re-enter the domain of positive history, this is
what is related as a certainty regarding the death of Odin.
This Theocrat, crowned with happiness and glory, would
not await in his bed a death slow and devoid of éclat. As
he had always declared, in order to strengthen the courage of
his warriors that those alone who died a violent death would
be worthy of celestial pleasures, he resolved to terminate
his life with the sword. Having then assembled his friends
and his most illustrious companions, he made nine wounds
in the form of a circle with the point of a lance, declaring
that he was going into Valhalla to take his place with the
other gods at the eternal feast.

Odin wishing, in accordance with the design of Providence, to form a valiant and audacious people and to found an animistic cult, eminently impassioned, could die only as he did die; his death was the masterpiece of his legislation. Without being as heroic as that of Jesus, it was more so than that of Apollonius of Tyana, and likewise put the seal upon his doctrine.

Thus while a cult entirely intellectual, destined to dominate reason was preparing itself in Judea, an animistic doctrine, violent in its precepts, was established in Scandinavia, solely to prepare the way for this cult and to favour its propagation, and, in the meantime, a man powerfully instinctive, capable of great will power, passed through the Roman Empire teaching that life is only a chastisement, a painful medium between two states, indifferent in themselves, birth and death.   This man, called *Apollonius*, followed in the doctrine of Pythagoras what that doctrine held most positive.   His favourite axiom was that nothing perished; that there were only appearances which were born and which passed, whereas the essence always remained the same, and, according to him, this primary Essence, both active and passive, which is all in all, is nothing else than the eternal God, who loses his name in our tongues through the multitude and variety of things connoted.   Man, he said, going out from his state of essence to enter that of nature, is born, and if on the contrary, he leaves that of nature to enter that of essence, he dies; but indeed he neither is born nor dies; he passes from one state to another, that is all; he changes the mode without ever changing the nature or the essence: for nothing comes from nothing and ends in nothing.

In spreading this doctrine, Apollonius weakened necessarily the power of the Will.   This power, thrown thus into void, saw no longer an aim for its efforts, if indeed, as was taught by Apollonius, it acted only upon appearances and if the Universe were in reality only a divine automaton indifferent to all forms.

Apollonius led a most austere life. He performed many miracles either of restoring the sick to health or in foretelling future things. He had many disciples, and his success was at first more striking than that of Jesus; but his doctrine, not having the same basis, could not have the same duration. After an existence of more than a century, he disappeared as had Moses; and even Damis, the most cherished of his disciples, could not say what had become of him. This theosophist taught nothing new, properly speaking; but he gave to the instinctive sphere an impulse which restored the inner sight of man to the very elements of things. This impulse was singularly favourable to the progress of Christianity, furnishing to its followers the opportunity of settling many difficulties which embarrassed the minds of philosophers.

At this epoch, a number of men whose most cherished interest the elevation of the Roman Empire had injured, indulged in introspection and turned upon themselves the activity which they could no longer exert upon political subjects. These men sought after the origin of the world, and above all that of Matter, the cause of evils, the nature and destination of Man. Now the Christians answered this without the least hesitation. Their replies, it is true, were brusque, but they were announced with that profound and intense persuasion which penetrates and persuades. They said that the World had been created by God Himself; that Matter from which this World had been created, taken from nothingness had been made of nothing; that the cause of evils was owing to the mistakes of the first man, who, created free and in the image of God, had transgressed his commandments. And as to the nature and the destination of Man, they were no more concerned than to say, that Man was the creature of God, destined to be eternally happy in heaven or eternally unhappy in the infernal regions, according as he followed the way of virtue or that of vice.

Such decisive solutions, which, coldly offered, would

have disheartened indifferent minds, struck with astonishment ardent ones who saw death recoil before the enthusiasm of their encouragers. The miracles performed by
Jesus, and above all His resurrection, affirmed by a multitude of witnesses who had sealed their testimony with their
blood, were arguments difficult to destroy when one could
not deny their existence. [1]

At the point where these things happened, in consequence
of the deviation of the Will of Man, it was nevertheless difficult to prevent their entire dissolution, and Jesus, called
to this great work, would not have succeeded in arresting
it, even after the immense victory which He had won over
Destiny in triumphing over death its most terrible weapon,
if Providence had not again accorded the means by appearing to the eyes of Saul and by changing the particular Will
of this man to the point of rendering him the most zealous
protector of its doctrine, whereas before this event, he was
the most desperate persecutor. Saul who afterwards
changed his name to that of Paul [2] was the real founder of
Christianity. Without him nothing would have been
effected. The twelve apostles whom Jesus left had not
the requisite force to fulfil their apostleship. Christianity
therefore owed to St. Paul its moral and dogmatic form and
its spiritual doctrine. Later it received its sacred forms and
rites from a theosophist of the school of Alexandria named
Ammonius.

[1] We know well that in our day there are men so injudicious as to deny
the physical existence of Jesus. These men must have been very much perplexed by His Providential existence, to reach this height of absurdity.

[2] The name of *Saul* comes from a root which reveals the idea of pride;
that of *Paul*, on the contrary, from a root expressing humility.

CHAPTER VIII

TWELFTH REVOLUTION IN THE SOCIAL STATE—CONSTANTINE
IS FORCED TO EMBRACE CHRISTIANITY AND TO ABANDON
ROME—INVASION OF THE GOTHS—DOWNFALL OF THE
ROMAN EMPIRE

BUT whilst all these things had come to pass, the disorganizing movement which menaced the Roman Empire commenced to manifest itself. It seemed that one might already hear the dull cracking which announced the downfall of this badly constructed edifice. In the North, the Bretons had revolted and had massacred the Roman legions. In the South, the Jews, still covered with the blood of a divine Messenger, but ever sustained by the hope of a liberator to come, had tried many times to throw off the yoke. Vanquished on all sides and dispersed among all the nations of the earth, they carried their hatred with them. The Parthians in Asia, the Goths in Europe, had already menaced the frontiers. The germs of revolt which the genius of Emperor Severus had restrained, developed with furor under Caracalla. All passions which produce revolutions and which upset states fermented from one end of the Empire to the other. One saw more than twenty emperors in the third century, nearly all raised to the throne by sedition or by the murder of their predecessors. Scarcely had one emperor been murdered and the crown seized by his assassin, when three or four competitors, each at the head of an army, disputed with him for it.   The Roman senate, miserable instrument of the vilest passions, placed among the number of the gods the most execrable tyrants.   It did not blush to award divine honours to Caracalla, the murderer of his father and of his brother, the scourge of Rome and horror of mankind.   Polytheism, debased, could no longer raise a barrier to these disorders.

It was in the midst of this trouble, while fire from heaven encompassed the Capitol and plague destroyed the people of the Orient, that the followers of Odin, after disturbances on the frontiers, finally crossed them.   At first, known under the general name of Goths, they were soon distinguished by the surnames which they gave themselves.   The Franks and the Sicambrians were the first known.[1]   These peoples inflamed with a religious and warlike enthusiasm, not content with attacking the Roman Empire in Europe, invaded even her possessions in Asia and soon in Africa.   At first, they were destroyed in great numbers; but no defeat could cool their daring.   They seemed reborn under the iron which mutilated them as mythology relates concerning the Hydra of Lerna.   Vainly Claudius II. had massacred three hundred thousand Goths, properly speaking,[2] and Aurelian as many Alemanni; these two victories did not prevent the Romans a few years after from being obliged to cede to them Dacia and Thrace.   The Burgundians, Vandals, and Franks succeeded each other and carried desolation everywhere.

Constantine, justly alarmed at the situation of the Empire, seeing its moral part wholly corrupt and its physical existence evidently compromised in the Orient, determined to embrace the cult of the Christians to consolidate the

---

[1] The name of Sicambrians (*Sig-Kimbres*) signifies the victorious Cimbrians.

[2] I repeat that one should understand by the Goths, the followers of Odin in general.   The Sicambrians, Franks, Vandals, Alemanni, etc., are surnames given to these same Goths, relative to their career or their customs, as those of the Ostrogoths or Visigoths are relative to their geographical position. The Goths, Gothans, or Gothins were with regard to Odin as were the Christians with regard to Christ.

religious revolution which the force of things had brought
about and to transfer the imperial throne to the shores of the
Bosphorus. This double movement had become indispensable. It was necessary to abandon a worn-out cult
which no longer offered any protection, and, in the midst of
the storm which was rising, to concentrate upon a point
bordering on Asia or on Europe, a part of the enlightenment
which Rome was no longer in a condition to preserve. This
audacious city, whose arrogance nothing could humble,
was given over to destruction. Whatever judgment posterity may have concerning the private character of Constantine, it remains none the less true that he was a man of
genius who judged his century and who performed with
intelligence and force what circumstances required of him.

Thus the Christian cult triumphed, and from the very
depths of the dust where it was born it was raised suddenly
to the throne. It presented to the flood of barbarians, by
whom the Empire was inundated, a moral obstacle against
which all their efforts broke. Whereas nothing physical
could resist the violence of their impulse, this cult seized
them by spiritual bonds where the rage of their passions was
subdued. The darkness of ignorance advancing with them
had covered Europe and held it long plunged in a gloomy
atmosphere. An appropriate cult was necessary for this
painful condition, and Providence, having foreseen it, had
prepared everything that this cult might be established.
It had been placed by the intellectual force of its Founder
above the fatality of Destiny and the arbitrary power of
the Will, likewise vanquished by the voluntary sacrifice of
His life and by the victory which He had gained over death.

It is quite useless for me to pause at this awful epoch of
modern history. It is well known that the terrible Alaric,
the first who had the honour of taking and sacking Rome,
had been general of the army under Theodosius I., Emperor
of the East. One knows that Theodosius, who had employed
Alaric and his Goths to defeat his competitor Eugenius,

gave them a reward which was changed to tribute during the reign of the weak Arcadius. However, Alaric discontented with this tribute, and claiming more noble trophies, left his tributary there to attack Honorius, Emperor of the West. Stilicho, general of the armies of Honorius, who alone was able to resist this formidable enemy, was afterwards put to death by Honorius. Rome was taken, and the Empire of the West destroyed. The followers of Odin, seeing it unprotected, assembled there on all sides. Alaric had made the breach; all the other barbarians hastened there and wished to take part in the pillage. The Vandals seized Spain; the Burgundians and Franks invaded Gaul; the Visigoths took possession of Oscitania; the Lombards inundated Italy. The Romans, forced to evacuate Great Britain, met on all sides only reverses. During this time, the Huns, led by the fierce Attila, menaced at the same time the vanquished and the victors, pillaged and massacred whatever they found before them, without distinguishing either cult or name, and added to the general confusion. Finally, Odoacer, at the head of his Heruli, arrived in the midst of the disorder, entered Rome, and dethroned Augustulus in 476 A.D. Some years after, Clovis, King of the Franks achieved the conquest of Gaul, begun by Merovæus and Childeric, and founded there the kingdom of France. It is well known how Clotilda, his wife, daughter of Childeric, King of the Burgundians, persuaded him to embrace Christianity. This event was of the highest importance; in submitting the cult of Odin to that of Jesus, it consolidated the designs of Providence and saved European society from the assured ruin into which the fatality of Destiny had dragged it.

It must not be forgotten that the Goths, by whose hands the Roman Empire was overthrown, under whatever names they present themselves in modern history, were the followers of Odin formed of a conglomeration of Asiatic and European tribes descended from the North. They had the characteristics, manners, laws, and almost the same cult as the primitive Celts. As their sole virtue was their warlike valour, they were ignorant of all accomplishments, all the sciences of pure speculation, and they gloried in ignoring them. The hatred which they nourished for the Roman name and which their legislator had inculcated in them some five or six centuries before had rendered odious to them everything that was attached to it; this name was for them the expression of everything base and cowardly, vicious and avaricious, that one could imagine. They held in horror the sciences and the arts cultivated by the Romans and attributed to these the state of degradation into which this people had fallen.[1]

Thus, wherever the Goths turned their steps, their tracks were stained with blood and their presence bespoke devastation; the most fertile provinces were converted into deserts, cities were destroyed, fields were burned, the inhabitants killed or dragged into slavery, and soon famine and pestilence added to the horrors of war and crowned the desolation of the peoples. Not for two thousand years had the universe been the prey of so many scourges at once. The contemporaneous writers who had had the misfortune to be witnesses of these scenes of devastation and carnage had difficulty in finding expressions strong enough to depict all the horrors.[2]

[1] They included in this proscription even the art of writing. So that it is only to the Greek or Latin historians that we owe the few conceptions that we have regarding them. When, having recovered from their prejudices, they began to write their annals, the memory of their origin was wholly lost. Jornandès, Paul Warnefride, Grégoire de Tours, although the most ancient and most accredited of their historians, give only confused and unsatisfactory information concerning their origin, manners, and laws.

[2] Procopius said that it was through a sentiment of humanity that the details of the cruelties practised by the Goths were not transmitted to posterity in order not to terrify it by these monuments of barbarism. Idace, an eye witness of the desolation which followed the invasion of the Vandals in Spain, said that when these barbarians had ravaged all with the utmost ferocity, pestilence came to add its horrors to this calamity. The famine, he said, was so general, that the living were obliged to feed upon corpses. St. Augustine confirmed the tale of these evils. The shores of Africa were as ill-treated

Europe, laid waste, was covered imperceptibly with uncultivated lands and fetid marshes; civilization was succeeded by the most frightful barbarism.

Italy herself, the centre of luxury and of art, this country where agriculture was pursued with an extreme care, was so put to confusion by the barbarians, that still in the ninth century it was covered with forests which served as haunts for savage beasts.

When this violent storm had somewhat calmed, when the victors, fatigued with murders and devastations, rested upon the débris which they had accumulated, the vast political body called the *Roman Empire*, miserably rent, was divided into many small states between which all communication was interrupted. Commerce was abandoned; the most useful arts found artisans no longer; agriculture likewise was neglected; pirates alone traversed the seas; inhabitants of distant parts of the same kingdom could hold no intercourse.[1] The least journey was a perilous undertaking; chained by a thousand obstacles to the place where fate had caused them to be born, most men were ignorant of the names of other countries, and having fallen into adversity they retained no idea of their ancient prosperity.

---

as those of Europe. It is stated that in the single war of the Vandals more than five million men perished.

[1] Communication was so difficult, there was so little commerce among men, that even towards the end of the tenth century an abbot of Cluny in Burgundy, having been solicited to come and direct the monks in a monastery near Paris, excused himself saying that he did not wish to risk his life journeying in a strange and unknown region. More than a century later at the beginning of the twelfth the monks of Ferrières, in the diocese of Sens, did not know that there existed in Flanders a city called *Tournai* and the monks of St. Martin de Tournai were likewise ignorant of the whereabouts of the convent of Ferrières. An affair which concerned the two convents obliged them to have some communication; they sought each other with great trouble, and found each other finally only by mere chance. Geography was so little understood that the respective places of the three divisions of the world were not even known. On maps fabricated in these times of ignorance, Jerusalem was placed in the middle of the earth and Asia, Africa, and Europe so scattered around that Alexandria was as near to the holy city as Nazareth.

CHAPTER IX

THUS the European population found itself, after many
vicissitudes, more or less painfully in the same state
whence it had issued several thousand years before. There
was, however, this advantage for it, that it had the experience of the past, and that a providential cult, raising around
it protecting barriers, defended it against its own ignorance
and against its own madness. The Will, violently restrained
by these last events, submitted one part to the yoke of
Destiny and the other to that of Providence. It was a
question of seeing whether, coming out from the state of
oppression, it would freely recognize either one or the other
of these two powers, allying itself to one in particular or
serving them as a common bond. On the one side was the
civil and military authority; on the other, the spiritual and
priestly authority. At first these two authorities hardly
recognized each other; still agitated by the reiterated blows
which the political body had just experienced, being badly
established, badly arranged, sometimes too much confused,
and sometimes too much separated, they ignored their
reciprocal limits and their true functions. For about two
centuries, during the invasion, it was impossible to distinguish anything through the thick gloom which the barbarians brought with them; one scarcely suspected whether

there was a sovereign pontiff and this sovereign pontiff
knew not in the midst of the storm whether monarchs still
existed. But, at last, when reappearing calm permitted
the state of things to be examined, it was seen with astonishment, not only that these two authorities had no knowledge
of each other, but the diverse members, of whom they were
composed, recognized each other still less; so that under the
appearance of a sacerdotal and royal rule there were in truth
only two anarchies whose efforts tended to dominate each
other.

Notwithstanding the blows which had just fallen upon
it, this indomitable European Will persisted in its movement.
Incapable of throwing off two yokes as rigorous as those of
Jesus and of Odin, which it carried together, it sought to
destroy them by dividing them; and this it attained. Already Christianity, attacked at its very foundations, had
been disturbed by a number of bold innovators called *Arch-
Heretics*, owing to the peculiar opinions which they professed.
Whereas some regarded Jesus as even God, descended from
heaven to enlighten men, others wished to see in Him only a
celestial genius, a divine prophet, and even a man inspired
as Moses, Orpheus, or Socrates. If, on one side, men attached to orthodoxy, such as Berylle and Paul de Samosata
tried to establish the mysteries of the Trinity and that of
the Incarnation; on the other, Arius and Macedonus attacked them with violence. Artemon and Theodoret found
the dogmas of Christianity too obscure and its morals too
severe and suddenly Montanus and his eucharists arose, who
pretended to be called there, to bring still more obscurity
and rigour. The discipline of the Church, the worship of
the Virgin had also a host of followers. There were philosophical or systematic Christians who sought in good faith
to make the mysteries of Christianity conformable to the
ideas which reason furnished them, striving to explain by
the doctrine of Pythagoras or of Plato, by the system of the
Emanations of the Chaldeans, by the belief in the principles

of Zoroaster; Valentine, Basil, Saturnin, Carpocrates, Marcien, Bardesanes, and above all Manes, made themselves noticeable in this way.

In the midst of this tumult, the sovereign pontiffs, called *Patriarchs* or *Popes*, who should have been invested with sufficient force to establish the orthodoxy of the Church, maintaining its rights and suppressing the innovators, saw with consternation that they were stripped of real authority; that their decisions were not respected on any side and that, forced to adhere to the movements of the multitude, they had to sanction alternately the *pro* or the *con*, according as the *pro* or the *con* was adopted by the majority of certain assemblies called *Councils*, to which general opinion wished that they should be submitted. To cap the evil, these sovereign pontiffs, despoiled thus of all sovereignty, and finding at that time no weapon in their hand sufficiently strong to arrest the progress of the heresies, —since the heretics would submit neither to their decisions nor their anathemas,—irritated at the resistance, and yielding to the passions which never fail the heart of a man of utmost integrity when he believes the Divinity interested in his own cause; these pontiffs, I say, accustomed to consider as criminals men who were only dissenters, denounced them to the civil authority of the monarchs. The latter, flattered at taking this advantage over the priesthood, and without perceiving the terrible disadvantage that it would entail in consequence, gave their support, and converted into affairs of state, religious quarrels which ought to have been confined and extinguished within the precincts of the Church. Banishment, exile, loss of property, and death were decreed against these opinions. The Christians, at first persecuted, became persecutors; blood flowed and the parties alternately victors saw no other evil in the state than that of not entirely exterminating the opposed party.

Thus, then, the Christian priesthood allowing itself to be usurped by republican forms—submitting, contrary to all reason, its supreme chief to the will of an assembly, ignoring this chief, disputing with him his rank, title, and authority—delivered itself to anarchy and surrendered to nullity or despotism. It authorized the monarchs not to recognize that which it did not recognize and provoked that scandalous contest which during more than a thousand years afflicted Europe. The importance which it gave to heresies multiplied them; the appeal which it made to civil power rendered it dependent upon this body, and, when in the thirteenth century, it was divided and destroyed, it could attribute its division and destruction only to these same republican forms, which a foolish pride, an undisciplined will had caused it to adopt.

These unusual forms by which the monarchs had at first skilfully profited to diminish the influence of the sovereign pontiffs and to escape from their supervision were, moreover, a two-edged sword whose blows they soon felt; for since they considered it right for the authority to be divided on the one side and submitted to the sanction of the sacerdotal body, they could not find it wrong on the other, that it was so and that the feudal body dominated them. This reaction was all the more inevitable, as it was more natural for the barons to regard themselves as independent of the kings, as it was for the priests to consider themselves as freed from obedience towards their supreme chief. The hordes of Goths, who, under different names, invaded the Roman Empire, were by no means composed of mercenary soldiers subject to a despot, but savage men led by a chief, their equal and conquerors for themselves.[1]   Before under-

---

[1] It appears certain that, at about this epoch, some sort of revolution had placed upon the head of the mayor the crown of khan and that in consequence, the hereditary civil power existed no more.   The chiefs of the barbarians who inundated the Roman Empire, were not then *kings*, properly speaking, but *mayors*, whose power, purely military, was elective.   They did not take the title of king until later, when the conquest, and particularly the change of cult, had consolidated their authority.   They distinguished themselves once more from the mayors, so as to sanction heredity in their house; but they were

taking any affair, they deliberated in common and decided with the majority. The authority of the chief was limited to executing the general will. After the conquest, each warrior regarded the portion of land which fell to his lot, with the several families which were dependent on it, as a recompense for his valour. He revived in these countries nearly all the customs, nearly all the laws which had existed formerly, of which I spoke at the beginning of this work; but with this notable difference, that finding no unity in the new cult which he adopted, he did not concern himself about putting it in the royal government; each baron considered himself as absolute master of himself, and recognized no other obligation than that of following the king to war; and, constituting himself his own judge and his own avenger, he depended only upon God and his sword. At that time, Europe was broken up into an infinity of little sovereignties whose extent was often limited to the donjon where the sovereign resided.

Such was the end of the Universal Empire, and such had been its commencement. This Empire after having reached its highest degree of elevation descended to the lowest degree of abasement. It remained in this condition for a considerable time according to circumstances and according as the action of the three great Powers of the Universe would again be united to accomplish its reconstruction.

---

not long in submitting to the influence of the military power which finally usurped the civil power and claimed all its rights. It was in the person of Pepin, King of France, that the definite union of royalty with the mayoralty was effected. Pepin did not, however, give his name to his race, because he was not judged legitimate king; this honour was left to his son Charles.

CHAPTER X

CURSORY VIEW OF THE STATE OF ASIA—MISSION OF MOHAM-
MED AND ITS RESULTS—THIRTEENTH REVOLUTION

IT is necessary to remark that at the time when darkness
spread more and more over Europe and covered the
western part of the hemisphere, the east and the south of
Asia recommenced to enjoy some light.   The violent storms
which had agitated China after the reign of the famous
Tsin-che-hoang[1] had subsided and this Empire had afterwards enjoyed a considerable splendour.   Many men of
genius had appeared in her midst.   There was seen for the
first time a Chinese embassy crossing its frontiers, traversing
Upper Asia, Persia, a part of Europe and India to draw new
knowledge from their sciences and arts.   The Japanese
had been subjected to a tribute and Korea had been conquered.   The Great Wall, undertaken formerly for the purpose of preventing the invasions of the Tartars, but which
fell in ruins after several centuries, had been raised again,
and covered an extent of more than five hundred leagues.
At last, one of the most wonderful inventions which has
honoured the human mind, that of paper, advanced the
progress of science.[2]

  [1] The one who wished to annihilate all the literary monuments prior to
his reign, and who united all the empire under him after having destroyed
the seven kingdoms which had formerly composed it—221 B.C.
  [2] This wonderful invention dates from 105 B.C.

India was likewise flourishing; the reign of the celebrated King Vikramaditya had reproduced all that had formerly been remarkable in this country; poetry had especially been cultivated with great success. It seemed that these peoples, already old, but still vigorous and healthy, took upon them a new life after the violent malady which had menaced their existence.

A new dynasty, that of the Sassanians, sprang up in Persia, and this kingdom, embellished and better governed, had conquered Arabia.[1]

Nor had Africa remained idle and without its portion of glory; the Abyssinians had even penetrated several times into Yemen, and had tried to introduce Christianity there.

In general, the fifth and sixth centuries, which were for Europe an epoch of desolation and of barbarism, were for Eastern Asia, and particularly for China, centuries of luxury and of magnificence. Some distinguished theosophists, such as Sotoctaïs of Japan and a new Buddha among the Siamese, had even made this epoch illustrious; when Providence, judging the miserable state into which the Will of Man, always refractory to its laws, had brought Europe, seeing the royal power without force and the priesthood without virtue (both given over to endless divisions which had reduced them to the most absolute nullity) contemplating Rome and Constantinople after they had become the centre of interminable quarrels, schisms, and heresies as ridiculous in substance as in form, without hope of bringing back for a long time to sacerdotal and royal unity, minds so divided by their own interests and their particular passions; Providence, I say, wished at least to arrest this flood which, threatening to invade entire Asia, could take away the remnant of the grandeur which was manifested there. Already, as I have said, the Abyssinians, imbued with the heterodox

[1] The commencement of the dynasty of the Sassanians was from 155 B.C., and the conquest of Arabia from 240 A.D.

opinions of some Greek monks, had tried to introduce them
into Arabia. Asia Minor, corrupted by the opposed doctrines of a host of arch-heretics, had almost involved Persia
in exciting the ambition of a young prince, son of King Nour-
shirvan.[1] It was evident that there was not a moment
to lose, a very strong barrier was necessary to separate
Asia from Europe and it was Mohammed who was commis-
sioned to raise it.[2]

Mohammed was, like Odin, a man powerfully animistic,
capable of a passionate enthusiasm, and was like Jesus
endowed with a will of extraordinary force. He was not
learned, but he himself recognized his ignorance, and he
knew how to take advantage of it and how to make the most
wonderful part of his inspiration felt. He is the only prophet
who has said of himself that he could not penetrate the
future, and that he was not sent to perform miracles, but
only to govern men and to teach them the truth.[3] Mohammed, left to himself and acting by his own faculties, was an
ordinary man, very loving, of a gentle, modest disposition,
a friend of peace, and taciturn; but when he yielded to the
divine spirit which took possession of his soul, nothing
could resist the impetuous outbursts of his eloquence; the
fire of his glance consumed souls, by his voice he exerted a
supernatural authority; one had to follow him or shun him.
When at the age of fifty-two, an iniquitous persecution for

[1] He is the same whom our historians named Chosroes or Cyrus the Great.
His son, blinded by the zeal of some Christian priests, took arms against him
after having embraced their cult. But the monarch, having discovered and
punished the crime of the prince, conceived such a hatred against the religion
to which he attributed it, that, after having proscribed it in his states, he
attacked it on all sides wherever he could reach it.

[2] Mohammed was born about 569 or 570 A.D. He began his apostolate
at the age of forty-two years, 612 A.D., and was banished to Mecca in 622. It
is from this epoch that the glory of Mohammed dates and the era of the Mussulmans called *Hegira*, because their Prophet was obliged to flee to Medina.

[3] The miracles which have since been attributed to him are either allegories
wrongly interpreted or ridiculous impostures with which his fanatical friends
or rather his enemies have charged his memory.

which he was unprepared, forced him to flee his native land and resort to arms, he displayed an intrepidity and military ability which none of his enemies had suspected. The warlike enthusiasm with which he imbued his disciples is beyond all expression; Odin himself could not have inspired a greater.

It is to be observed here, that if Jesus had wished to follow the road of conquests which was opened before Him, when the people of Galilee offered Him the crown, and if He had put Himself at the head of the Jews who awaited a conquering Messiah, He would inevitably have conquered Asia; but Europe would have resisted Him, and, as it was in Europe that He was to exercise His influence principally, He had to choose a victory much less brilliant at first, but much greater indeed in the future, and He had to resolve to overcome the fatality of Destiny rather than to make use of it.

Jesus had inherited the inspiration of Moses, Mohammed inherited the inspiration of Moses and that of Jesus, which he recognized as equally divine; but he alleged that the followers of Moses had deviated from his doctrine and that the disciples of Jesus had misunderstood that of their Master.[1] He restored in consequence the absolute Unity of God, such as the Hebrews had received from the Atlantean tradition, and all his religion was contained in these few words: *There is no God but GOD and Mohammed is His prophet.* Moreover, he established with the greatest force the immortality of the Soul and the dogma of chastisements and of future recompenses, according to the vices and the virtues of men; but, wishing to impress the animistic imagination of the multitude, he, like Odin carefully conformed to the

[1] It is worthy of comment, that this was the same reproach as the oracles of polytheism constantly addressed to the Christians. These oracles, consulted about the new religion and the unusual intolerance of its followers, replied that one must not accuse Jesus of these excesses, but His disciples only, who had corrupted His doctrine; Jesus being a divine man, the most wonderful of all those who had appeared upon earth.

ideas of his people, in the picture which he presented to them of the delights which awaited his elect. In the Valhalla of Odin, the warlike Scandinavians fought each other and drank; in the paradise of Mohammed, the voluptuous Asiatics enjoyed an enchanting repose and all the delights of love.

One should not forget that the Atlantean tradition concerning the absolute Unity of God had been principally preserved by the Bodohnes Celts, who after becoming mixed with the Atlanteans of Africa had constituted the Arab people and afterwards the Hebrew people, by refusing to submit to the Phœnician yoke; so that this tradition, having been brought back without alteration to its source, acquired in the mouth of Mohammed an authority all the greater, as he cleverly detached any foreign element that might have been inserted among the Hebrews by the frequenting of the Chaldeans, who had become disciples of Zoroaster and Krishna; that is to say, the Duality of the cosmogonic principles and the Trinity of the divine faculties. He maintained with great force the dominance of the masculine faculty over the feminine, and did not forget that Moses, in attributing to woman the first sin, had made her subject to man. Accordingly, he instituted the dogma of polygamy which was claimed by the custom of his people and the immemorial custom of Asia. He neglected thus the influence of women which had helped so much and which would help so much again in the establishment of Christianity in Europe.[1] But the success brilliant as rapid, obtained by the doctrine of Islamism, proved that it was not needed.

Mohammed was already master of Mecca and of a great

---

[1] I have said that it was Clotilda who persuaded Clovis to embrace Christianity. A sister of the Emperors Basil and Constantine, married to a grand duke of Russia, named Volodimer, induced her husband to be baptized. About the same time, Miscislas, Duke of Poland, was converted by his wife, sister of the Duke of Bohemia. The Bulgarians received the cult in the same manner. Giselle, sister of Emperor Henry, made her husband, King of Hungary, a Christian. The same thing happened in England.

part of Arabia when he died; his death, which he had fore-told and announced in his Koran, far from diminishing the enthusiasm of his followers, appeared to increase it further. It was worthy of his life. He did not take it, as did Odin, but he accepted it,[1] and perhaps it testified to a greater soul. In a few years, his successors, who took the title of *Caliphs*, vanquished the Persians at that time dominating Asia, seized all their possessions, entered Jerusalem in triumph, conquered Egypt, and, already masters of an immense empire, in less than a century were established in Spain and from there threatened frightened Europe.

After having seized Aquitania and all the coast of Provence as far as Avignon, the Saracens, for it was thus they were called,[2] had advanced to the very heart of France, when Charles Martel, coming upon them in the plains of Poitiers, gained over them the famous battle which put to an end for a long time their progress in Europe. This victory has been much lauded and no doubt with reason, since the one who was chosen to effect it had all the necessary qualities for this; but it was inevitable. Europe would not have been entirely vanquished without the face of the world being changed and the influence of Mohammed did not reach so far. The particular results which this victory brought about for France was the extinction of the race of Clovis, the elevation of that of Charles Martel, the coronation of Pepin, and the prophetic reign of Charlemagne, of which I will speak later on.

Mohammed, besides, committed a grave mistake which shortened much the duration of the Caliphate. He did not think of separating the sword from the censer, and, as he

---

[1] Mohammed, after having been to the temple to give his last sermon and his last prayer, returned to his palace and lay down. His daughter, Fatima, was at his bedside with several of his disciples. Taking his daughter's hand he said: "Behold Death at the door, asking permission to enter" . . . and after a moment of contemplation, having embraced his daughter for the last time, he turned towards the door and added: "Let him enter!" and he expired.

[2] That is to say the rulers of Asia.

had united both in his hand, he transmitted them thus to his successors; but should this mighty theocrat have expected that there would always be a hand firm enough to hold them together? This was not the case. After the glorious reign of Haroun-al-Raschid, the Caliphate fell into decadence, and already towards the beginning of the twelfth century, the Caliph Radhi reigned in Bagdad only under the guardianship of the Emir, chief of his guard. This Emir, becoming more and more powerful, no longer had any consideration. After having made sure of a body of Tartars called *Turks*, which he had under his command, he made himself master of the very person of the Caliph Kaiem, prostrating himself before him and conducting him to the palace which was to serve him as a prison; while holding the bridle of his mule under the appearance of outward respect he stripped him of all temporal power.[1]

From this time the priesthood was distinguished from royalty in the Moslem cult; but as this distinction was accomplished by force, a veritable union never existed between them. Nevertheless, as the dogma of Destiny had been admitted by Mohammed, the priesthood submitted promptly enough and did not abandon themselves to a contest as stubborn as in Europe.

Although the duration of the Caliphate was not so long as it might have been, it was, however, sufficient to fulfil the aim of its institution. Europe was restrained. The gloom which had covered it was tempered by its *éclat;* the sciences and arts cultivated in Spain by the care of the Arabs could spread and be propagated there more easily when the auspicious moment had arrived for this.

[1] This usurper was called *Ortogrul-beg.* The Ottoman race, which descends from him, dates its power from this event, which happened in 1050 A.D.

CHAPTER XI

REIGN OF CHARLEMAGNE—FOURTEENTH REVOLUTION—THE
CRUSADES—TAKING OF JERUSALEM BY THE CHRISTIANS
—TAKING OF CONSTANTINOPLE BY THE MUSSULMANS—
CAUSES AND RESULTS OF THESE THREE GREAT EVENTS

FROM the epoch of the invasion of the Goths, the downfall of the Roman Empire, and the extinction of learning in the West, till the time when learning commenced to
revive after a space of a thousand years, that is to say, from
the fifth to the fifteenth century, several remarkable events
occurred in Europe, among which three are especially distinguished: the reign of Charlemagne, the taking of Jerusalem by the Crusaders, and that of Constantinople by the
Mussulmans. The first and the last of these events were
the work of Destiny. The middle one depended only upon
the Will of Man which awoke in the eleventh century as
from a long stupor. My intention being to return many
times to these major events and even to examine somewhat
in detail the interval of time which separates them, I shall
be content to sketch the most salient features.

Charlemagne was the first monarch of modern times,
whose genius having risen to high conceptions, dared to form
the project of re-establishing the Roman Empire destroyed
more than three centuries before, and to build upon its
débris the foundations of a new universal empire. This
extraordinary man, especially so for the time when he lived,

a giant raised above a people of pygmies, succeeded at first in his enterprise. Fortunate conqueror and able politician, he covered Europe with his trophies and seized in Rome the imperial crown which was offered to him by Pope Leo. The Empire which he possessed surpassed even that of the Romans in the West.[1] But this unexpected splendour which had not been looked for was for France a sort of aurora borealis which, appearing suddenly out of the gloom, dissipated it for a moment only, in order that all the depths might be perceived.

This effort of Destiny could not last. To consolidate the astonishing effects, it would have been necessary for Charlemagne to consider making Providence intervene; but his intelligence was not open on this side. Forgetting that his father Pepin was only a mayor, elevated to the throne in place of a legitimate king whose doubtful and wavering authority was sustained by the assent of the sovereign pontiff, he depended solely upon the force of his genius and his arms. He disdained to found the edifice of his grandeur upon the solid basis of religion. He embraced the cult for policy and propagated it for ambition and rendered to the pope only an illusory homage; although he feigned to receive the imperial crown from his hands, he took care not to recognize openly his authority, and, being vexed by some condescending acts, some frivolous presents, he indicated haughtily that he did not pretend dependence upon the priesthood, from the time when at Aix-la-Chapelle he commanded his son Louis, whom he had associated with him in the Empire, to take the crown himself from the altar, not wishing him to receive it from a pontiff. This insolent pride, which has been imitated sometimes, has always succeeded badly. This crown for which Charlemagne disdained to be indebted to Providence did not remain long

---

[1] It comprised Italy to Calabria, Spain to the Ebro, all of Gaul, Istria, Dalmatia, Hungary, Transylvania, Moldavia, Poland to the Vistula, and all of Germany.

in his line. After having been the pretext of many misfortunes, it fell from the head of Louis le Débonnaire to that of the Count of Franconia, as I will relate further on.

I have said that the reign of Charlemagne was the work of Destiny, and that the event which followed—the taking of Jerusalem, the principal object of the Crusades—was that of the Will of Man. One will ask, perhaps, how these two events could be placed in the same class and what is the means of recognizing this classification. If any one should ask this question, I should be more than content, as it would furnish me the occasion of settling many like questions regarding which I have not paused because, too full of my subject and considering the thing too obvious according to the previously given principles, I have neglected to do so. Besides, in a work of this kind, one can neither say all at once nor explain all at the same time; the mind of the writer must speak of things as they suggest themselves, and it would be unjust for an impatient reader to accuse him of obscurity before having finished reading the whole work. It is only by the whole that one can judge the details. This is why a second reading is indispensable to those who would grasp any system, no matter how it may be unfolded.

The reign of Charlemagne was the work of Destiny, because it depended upon the position of this monarch and his particular genius, and upon all the previous events which had brought about the coronation of Pepin, his father. No one but himself wished the end toward which he inclined; often no one saw it. His ascendancy alone brought about all things which would have stopped, if he had stopped, and which, indeed, ceased to go on as soon as he ceased to be. Nothing around him moved unless he moved. His prophetic impulse was so necessary that, as soon as it no longer existed, all the machinery of his government was out of order. The edifice, which he had raised with a thousand hardships, collapsed as soon as it was no longer sustained by him, because the wills which had seconded him in its es-

tablishment were all passive; his alone was active in his own
destiny. If Charlemagne had interested Providence in his
work, his work would have continued exactly in proportion
to the providential action which he would have evoked. Do
you wish to know how? I shall tell you and unfold a great
mystery. His work would have continued, because Providence would have continued to conduct it. In relying
on his destiny, he entrusted himself to a transitory effect,
which could not stretch itself beyond its cause, and, as it
reserved nothing beyond this life, his death was the limit
of his labours.

Now, let us turn to the Crusades. The movement
which produced them was inherent in the moving mass.
All the exterior wills appeared to unite in one interior will
which was fixed upon the same object: to rescue Jerusalem
from the Infidels. The commonest rascal did not differ
on this point of sentiment from the monarch, and the destiny
of the one, as the destiny of the other, was likewise forced to
follow the given impulse, which came neither from the former
nor from the latter; no one knew whence it came. It was a
whirlwind which was very difficult to avoid, and one could not
escape from it after one had once entered it. The intensity of
its movement was increased in proportion to its mass, and its
mass in proportion to its movement. In a whirlwind of this
nature, which one may call a volitive whirlwind, the centre
is everywhere; it fails in effect until it settles, and this can
be accomplished only by Destiny or by Providence. In a
prophetic whirlwind, as that of Charlemagne, for example,
the centre is only at one single point; if this point fails, all
fails, unless the Will of Providence assists it. The Will
was nothing and Providence was no longer invoked in the
time of Charlemagne. During the Crusades, there was no
destiny capable of regulating the movement and of calling
Providence to it. Thus this immense whirlwind had only
very mediocre results, where they were specially anticipated.

If one can believe the testimony of contemporaneous

authorities, six million men took the cross. Entire Europe, according to a Greek princess writing the history of her father, seemed torn from its foundations and ready to precipitate itself with all its might upon Asia. A powerful leader was needed, a man capable of conceiving a great thought and of executing it, but there was none, and torrents of blood flowed to no purpose.

The ostensible reason assigned for this extraordinary movement was the rumours which suddenly spread in Europe that the end of the world was coming. Consternation was general. Many men, as credulous as pious, assembled in great haste at Jerusalem, where they imagined that Jesus Christ would soon reappear to judge men. The Turks, who had been masters of Palestine since they had divested the Caliphs of their authority, did not welcome this influx of Christians and maltreated many of them. One of these maltreated pilgrims, known under the name of Peter the Hermit, returned to Europe, related his troubles, and excited the Christians to vengeance. The Christian Church was stirred. The Council of Piacenza at which more than thirty thousand persons were present decided war against the Infidels, and that of Clermont, still more numerous, confirmed this decision.

It was, as I have said, an immense movement of the Will which manifested itself. If there had been found a providential or prophetic man, that is to say, a man of genius who could have attached either Providence or Destiny to this movement, it is impossible to say what tremendous consequences might have resulted. But Charlemagne had been dead some time. Pope Gregory VII. had just died, and Charles the Fifth was not yet born. More than forty-five thousand men, ignorant and fanatical, led by Peter the Hermit, merely stained their route with blood and covered it with their dead bodies. They did not even reach Palestine. Many other Crusaders, who followed a German preacher named *Gotescalc*, were massacred in Hungary. Godfrey

de Bouillon had a more fortunate experience, since he succeeded in taking possession of Jerusalem and founding there
a transient kingdom.   But this conquest was still a thing
of small moment in comparison to the means which he
employed.   It needed only forty thousand men at Alexandria to subjugate Asia, and when Mohammed began his
career, he had but three hundred men under his command.

In general, the Crusaders obtained but poor military
success, and it was always in connection with the particular
destiny of the one who obtained it.   The taking of Jerusalem
was the most important of these successes, and no doubt
Godfrey de Bouillon was the most illustrious of the Crusader
heroes, since he attained in some way the great aim of the
Crusades; but if Godfrey had been a man of genius, he
would have felt that it was not to make him King of Jerusalem that all Christendom had been stirred.   It was a
miserable idea and well worthy of its insignificant glory and
duration to wish to confine there such a violent movement.
He should have considered all the greatness and magnificence
of this success, and should have known how to make the
Will itself proud of its own triumph.   He should have declared Jerusalem the capital of the Christian world, a holy
and sacred city; he should have installed the Pope there,
vested with a universal authority; and, in following the
course of events which could not fail to arise, and which
indeed did arise, he should have taken possession of Constantinople and have destroyed the Greek schism there,
making of it an imperial city, as it was under Constantine.
Nothing of this sort was done.   Thus, for the same reason
that the prophetic Empire of Charlemagne collapsed, for
want of a strong will which might sustain it, so the volitive
movement of the Crusades became extinguished, since it
lacked a sufficiently strong destiny which might centralize
it.   In less than two centuries, the Christians, having been
driven from all their possessions in Asia, had preserved none
of their conquests there.   Nevertheless, the volitive action

of six million men could not be entirely lost. These distant expeditions, although without apparent results, had, however, salutary effects upon the form of the social state and upon its customs. The Crusaders, marching towards the Holy Land, saw flourishing countries and magnificent cities; they found in Asia a luxury of which they had no idea. The utility of sciences and of arts struck them, their prejudices were weakened, their mental horizon was expanded, new ideas sprang up in their minds; they felt the difference between them and other peoples. Many religions and warlike associations which were formed, and especially the order of the Templars, acquired theosophical knowledge which they brought into Europe. It was a fusion of learning. Those who came from the Orient mingled with those from Spain and were mutually beneficial.

I shall return further on to the greater part of these things which demand a more profound examination.

But this violent movement which had just taken place alarmed Asia. This terrible European Will, always ready to rise in rebellion, had need to be restrained. The enthusiasm was contagious and had become so great that the widow of a king of Hungary took up the cross and placed herself at the head of a band of women; several thousands of children passed into Palestine, led by fanatical pedagogues. A contrary movement broke out.

The chief of a Tartar horde, named *Temugin*, believed himself called by Destiny to make the conquest of the world.[1] He assembled the principal khans of the Tartars in a sort of Diet called *Cour-Ilté*, revealed to them his mission, and persuaded them to follow him. A great number of these khans having consented, he took the name of *Genghis Khan*, the great king, and marched to fulfil his destiny. His successes surpassed even his hopes. In less than twenty years he had already conquered more than eight hundred leagues from East to West and more than a thousand from

[1] In 1206.

South to North. His successors extended his conquests still more, and pushed them from the eastern frontiers of China to the very centre of Europe, Hungary, and Bohemia. The Christians, driven back on every side, caused the religious conflagration which they had kindled to consume themselves. No longer being able to undertake Crusades against those whom they had named *Infidels*, they attacked and mutilated each other. They took up the cross against those to whom they had given the name of *Heretics*, without concerning themselves what heresy really was. It is well known how the ambitious fanatic, Simon de Montfort, at the head of more than five hundred thousand soldiers of the Cross, under pretext of subduing the Albigenses, ravaged the south of France, which was then the centre of letters and arts, and stifled in their cradle the Oscitanic muses. [1]

The storm which had shaken Asia during the reign of Genghis and his descendants had hardly calmed down, when the Christian princes tried to renew their religious and political expeditions against the Mussulmans; but the volitive movement had ceased. These princes, overcome by their own destinies, were everywhere repulsed, and, to make matters worse, a cruel malady attacked their army. Saint Louis, one of the best kings of France, unfortunately drawn on by the infatuation of his century, was seized in Africa with a deadly miasma, and died as pious as he was courageous. [2]

These new aggressions in Europe called forth new reactions on the part of Asia. The Ottoman Empire, founded

---

[1] More than sixty thousand persons were killed at the siege of the city of Béziers. Before mounting to the assault, the Crusaders, upon their entrance into the city, asked of the legates how to distinguish Catholics from Heretics. "Kill them all," replied Izarn, "God will recognize those who belong to Him." The consequence of this abominable Crusade, which shattered the hope of France and retarded for several centuries its destiny, was the establishment of the Tribunal of the Inquisition, the terror of humanity and the shame of the Christian cult.

[2] His death occurred in Tunis, August 25, 1270.

in Bithynia at the close of the thirteenth century, had grown
in silence, and had acquired formidable strength. Suddenly
it appears upon the scene of the world and enters upon a
career of conquests. In a moment it invades all Syria, and
soon it menaces Europe. The Christians, alarmed, proclaim in vain a new Crusade. The time for it had passed.
Amurath crosses the strait and takes possession of Adria-
nople. His son, Bajazet, gains the famous battle of Nico-
polis against Sigismund, King of Hungary, in which perishes
the flower of the French nobility commanded by Count de
Nevers. Under the successors of these princes, the Greek
Empire is parcelled out, restricted more and more, and reduced to the sole city of Constantinople, which, towards the
middle of the fifteenth century, comes at last into the possession of Mohammed II. The taking of this city put an
end to the Empire of the East, and delivered to the Turks
the most beautiful and one of the strongest positions in
Europe. Here, the most formidable Islamism and the most
vigorous Destiny established its seat to watch over this
indomitable country and to restrain the impetuosity of its
movements. The keys of Asia and the new Gordian Knot
are in Constantinople, and this makes her the all-powerful
mistress. There is no universal monarchy outside the enclosure of its walls. It is there that Memphis and Mecca,
Rome and Jerusalem have united the force of their destinies. The conquerors, who have pretended to a universal
empire and who have not known what I here disclose,
properly speaking, have not known the history of the
world; they have entirely ignored the progress of the three
great Powers which rule the Universe and have attributed
to hazard or to their star that which did not pertain to
them.

As soon as this formidable point of support was established, Spain was abandoned. Destiny, to which it was
no longer necessary, withdrew, and King Ferdinand was
able to cover himself with an immortal glory in gaining

an easy victory over the Moors. The Saracens, forced to recross the seas, spread over Africa, and the Jews, banished a short time after, took away a great part of the population and wealth of this kingdom.

CHAPTER XII

RECAPITULATION

MORE than two thousand years have passed between the commencement of this book and its end. This long space of time has offered us hardly more than the history of the struggle between the Will and Destiny, Liberty, and Necessity. We have seen Europe and Asia struggling with all their might, triumphing alternately. In the midst of these bloody contests, Providence, always impartial, always ready to succour the weakest side, has constantly prevented the entire ruin of one or the other power and, at the moment of its greatest danger, has given to it tutelary protection. The reader will no doubt have observed this admirable action. He will indeed have seen that the mission of Kong-tzée, of Zoroaster, of Pythagoras had, for aim, the preserving of intellectual lights in the midst of the material gloom which had been brought about by the universal degeneration of the cults; he will indeed have judged that if Odin was destined to overthrow the Roman colossus which threatened to annihilate Asia, Jesus, on the other hand, had to arrest the impetuosity of his movements and prevent the entire dissolution of the social state of Europe; dissolution inevitable without Him. In examining the situation of the world at the time when Jesus appeared in Judea, the reader must have seen that it was necessary to prepare the minds for the great change which was about to be effected, and

283

that Apollonius of Tyana was completely fitted to fulfil
this purpose. But if Europe was to be saved, Asia must not
perish, and her downfall was assured if Europe, freed from
her lethargy, should be furiously aroused and full of religious
enthusiasm should precipitate herself upon her, as it happened at the time of the Crusades. Providence, which
foresaw this movement, as it had foreseen all others, anticipated it by the mission of Mohammed. This powerful
theocrat, supposing that he had not been strong enough,
was sustained by Sotoctaïs and the last of the Buddhas;
by Genghis Khan and Tamerlane, who were their heirs.

Providence, in submitting to the laws of Liberty and
Necessity, which the Will and Destiny develop, has not
pretended that either one of these two powers should ever
remain absolute master of the other. This is why their
greatest efforts are in vain when they aim at absolutism.
Always after their most decided triumphs some unexpected
obstacle is found which paralyses them. This obstacle is
the work of Providence.

The struggle which unfortunately has begun between
Liberty and Necessity has lasted a long time. It will last
until these two powers agree to recognize Providence and
bend to its august authority and permit it to unite them.
Then, the trouble, which has existed for nearly five thousand
years, will give place to a calm, and the Social State will
assume a more regular form and one more favourable to
prosperity and the welfare of Mankind.

FIFTH BOOK

Having come to the most important point of modern history, I shall pause a moment, in order to recall to mind the principal events which have been presented, adding some new reflections following contemporaneous events and attaining at last the aim which I proposed at the commencement of this work: that of acquiring less confused ideas concerning the Social State of Man than those which have been given us up to this time.

CHAPTER I

DIGRESSION UPON THE KINGDOM OF MAN—ITS INTIMATE NA-
TURE, ITS COMPOSITION, THE SOLIDARITY OF ITS MEM-
BERS, AND THE MEANS OF ELABORATION CONTAINED
WITHIN IT

I FLATTER myself that a reader, even moderately attentive, if he does not accept all my ideas, will understand them at least, and will allow me to reason regarding
them. He must know now that I do not consider man as
an individual, but as an universal species, which I have
called the *Kingdom of Man*. This kingdom always presents
itself to me as a unique being, delighting in an intelligible
existence, which becomes sentient by individualization.
When philosophers have said that nature makes only individuals, they have said the truth when they apply this axiom
to physical nature; but they have uttered an absurdity
when they extend it to intellectual nature; this superior
nature, on the contrary, creates only the kingdom modified
by inferior nature first into species, afterwards into races,
and finally into individuals. In the Kingdom of Man, the
species is the race distinguished by colour, physiognomical
forms, and the natal place; races are the nations or peoples
diversified by language, cult, laws, and customs; individuals
are men particularized by their respective position in these
nations or races and with their own faculties and their individual will. All men who compose a people, compose a

rational being of which they are the sentient members; this rational being, called *Body Politic, People,* or *Nation,* possesses a double existence, moral and physical, and can be considered, as well as individual man, under the triple relation of body, soul, or mind, as a being corporal and instinctive, animistic and impassioned, spiritual and intelligent. This double existence is not always in harmonious proportions; for often the one is strong when the other is weak, one living when the other is dead. The same inequality which exists among men exists also among peoples; with some the passions are more developed than with others; there are the purely instinctive as well as the purely intellectual.

Men in nations and nations in races are as different colours spread over the painter's palette. The Kingdom of Man places them at first according to their most glaring tints, to mix them afterwards into softened tints with which he will compose his painting. This kingdom, as I have said, is one of the three great powers which rule the universe; it constitutes in particular what I have called the *Will of Man;* but this Will is not simple, as I have just made clear; it acts with three modifications, without which it could not manifest itself; these modifications, which are particular in the individual man, are universal in the universal man, that is, in the Kingdom of Man. The proper place of the Will in this kingdom is the universal soul. It is by the universal Instinct of Man that it is bound to Destiny, and by its universal Intelligence that it communicates with Providence; Providence is for the individual man only this universal Intelligence, and Destiny only this universal Instinct; therefore the Kingdom of Man contains in itself all the Universe. There is absolutely outside of it only the divine Law which constitutes it and the primal Cause whence this Law emanates. This primal Cause is called *GOD,* and this divine Law bears the name of *Nature. GOD* is *ONE;* but as Nature seems at first to offer a second principle different from God and that itself contains a triple movement—whence appear to result three different natures, the providential, the volitive, and the prophetic—it follows that the individual man can grasp nothing which is not double in its principles or triple in its faculties. When by a great effort of his intelligence he arrives at the true idea of *GOD*, then he attains the famous quaternary of Pythagoras, beyond which there is nothing.

I have said just now that the Kingdom of Man, the result of this divine Law called *Nature*, constituted one of the three great powers by which the Universe is ruled—the Will—and this must be conceived thus, although it contains also the two others, which are Providence and Destiny; because it is the Will which causes it to be what it is and which inclining it towards Providence or towards Destiny leads it to one of the two ends of nature, which are unity or divisibility, spiritualization or materialization.

The essence of the Will is liberty. Necessity exists equally in Destiny as in Providence; but this Necessity, whose form appears the same, differs singularly in substance. Providential Necessity acts by assent; prophetic Necessity, by sensation. The sentiment which depends upon the Will adheres freely to one or the other of these two necessities, or repulses them alike in order to remain in its centre. The Will can remain in its animistic centre as long as it is not divided.

What happens to Universal Man, to the Kingdom of Man, happens also to individual man. The Will which moves this kingdom, free in its essence, remains equally free in the least of human individuals that physical nature manifests. Note this with care. These individuals, although free, are not isolated; they are part of a Whole upon which they act, and which reacts upon them. This continual action and reaction, which renders them dependent one upon the other, forms a sort of bond which is called *solidarity*. Individuals are, then, jointly answerable in peoples; peoples in nations; nations in races; races in the Kingdom of Man. Universal solidarity unites, then, the whole to the least of its parts, and the least of its parts to its whole. Nothing can be destroyed, but everything can be elaborated. It is by the elaboration of the individual that that of the masses is effected and by that of the masses that that of the whole is operated.

Now, there exist two great means of elaboration which, although employed under diverse forms and designated by different names, issue none the less from a same cause in order to arrive at a same result. These two means are unity and divisibility, attraction and repulsion, formation and dissolution, life and death. In the political sphere I shall consider only these two means, under the names of *formation* and *dissolution*. Life and death act in individuals; attraction and repulsion in elements; unity or divisibility in principles. It is by means of formation that the Kingdom of Man tends to unite individuals which compose it from the most absolute particularization, that is to say, from that state of individual isolation whence man, recognizing only himself, has not even the idea of conjugal ties—the first of all to social universalization, where the same cult, the same laws, the same tongue, unite all men. It is by means of dissolution that the contrary movement takes place and that the Kingdom of Man, after having gathered the fruits of social universalization, falls back into absolute particularization, in repassing through all political phases from the Universal Empire to the narrowest individualization of savage man.

We have seen this double movement act and develop in one of the principal races of the kingdom, the Borean Race to which we belong, and we have been able to follow it in its principal phases of formation and dissolution. Beginning with the first elements of the social state we have been raised to the Universal Empire, but without attaining, however, to the perfection of this Empire, as I have observed; this fact would make us conjecture that it was for us only a

first elaboration followed by a second. Indeed, the movement of dissolution has not brought us to the lowest step of
the social ladder as might have happened, but only to one
of the middle steps where civilization, although interrupted,
is not destroyed. We owe this favour to Providence, which
wished that the destructive cult, given by Odin to the Gothic
nations, should be redeemed by the conservative cult instituted by Jesus. I have indicated forcibly enough the causes
and the consequences of these two cults. Let us retrace
our steps a moment in order to continue our historical
exploration.

CHAPTER II

UTILITY OF FEUDALISM AND OF CHRISTIANITY—MODIFICATION
OF THESE TWO RÉGIMES BY EACH OTHER—CHIVALRY
AND ITS CONSEQUENCES—REFORMATION OF THE SOCIAL
STATE IN EUROPE

IT was no doubt a spectacle as wonderful as unexpected
to see these savage peoples, for whom ravage and destruction were a necessity, armed with fire and sword, carrying death and incendiarism everywhere, stopping suddenly
in the midst of their victories and receiving from the very
ones whose sciences and arts they held in horror a religion
which chained their furor and thwarted all their inclinations. It is necessary, in order to judge the astonishing
contrast of their character with their position, to glance
through the terrible annals from the middle of the fifth
century to the commencement of the eleventh. I do not
believe that anything more remarkable has been shown on
earth. One sees on all sides a decided tendency towards
absolute dissolution and the incredible efforts to precipitate themselves there always arrested by the impossibility
of attainment. One of the most extraordinary men who
appeared at this time in Europe was Charlemagne; he did
not in any way realize the Universal Empire to which he
aspired, for the reasons which I have given; but he rendered
a notable service to the social state by tightening the knot
which prevented dissolution. Writers, whose intentions

were sincere but who possessed little learning beyond exterior forms of things, have greatly blamed this prince for his expedition against the Saxons. They have accused him of fanaticism because he forced these peoples to embrace the Christian cult; but they have not reflected that it was the only means of arresting their destructive passion, which if he had not done it, Europe, exposed some years later to the invasions of the Scandinavians called Normans, would have been unable to resist them and would have inevitably perished, if the Saxons had united their efforts to those of these barbarians.

Two extremely strong institutions, one political, the other religious, saved European civilization then from absolute dissolution; these were the feudal system and Christianity. Some systematic philosophers have ranted much against these two institutions, and this was assuredly very easy if one considers them isolated and outside the time where they were applied. Wild bulls and untamed horses do not greatly love the yoke which makes them captive nor the bit which hurts them; but man who understands the utility of these two things applies them when this is necessary, regardless of their feelings; Providence does likewise regarding man when he abuses his liberty and turns against himself strength which has been given him for other use.

But, at last, these two terrible institutions, equally rigid, equally severe, feudalism and Christianity, imperceptibly yielded as customs became gentler and as passions less destructive, and ceased to push the social state towards its utter dissolution. This relaxation began to manifest itself in the feudal régime, upon which the spirit of Christianity acted strongly at the time of the Crusades. This régime towards the close of the eleventh century attained its highest degree of greatness; it could only decline in proportion as its utility diminished and as its practices repulsed by customs, becoming more and more intolerable, injured equally masters and subjects. The kings, justly irritated at the haughti-

ness of their barons, and the barons themselves weary of
their authority, demanded a change. The latter grasped
with avidity the hope which was held out to them, and the
greater part sold for almost nothing their feudal domains
in order to seek conditions more analogous to their tastes.
The sovereigns, enriched by these partial acquisitions,
progressively augmented their power, and made themselves
agreeable to a great number of communes to which they
gave political liberty, and found in commerce considerable
resources to strengthen their authority. Having become
more and more respectable, according as they became more
powerful, they stopped quarrels and private hostilities,
which up to that time had banished peace from their states.
In order to render justice in their name, they founded regular
tribunals from which judiciary combats, lists of appeals,
and judgments of God were by degrees removed.[1]

[1] The judiciary combats in use among the Gothic nations dated back to
great antiquity. They had been in use among the primitive Celts, as well as
the other trials called *judgments of God*. There are found among all the
nations of the globe traces of this Celtic jurisprudence, which authorized the
accused to prove their innocence by submitting to certain tests called *Ordeals*,
such as grasping a mass of red-hot metal, plunging the arm into boiling water
or oil without burning oneself, swallowing a poisoned beverage without experiencing any fatal symptoms, etc. These extraordinary practices, having
spread over the earth, give a new proof of what I stated regarding the dominion
which the Celts enjoyed in earlier times, due to the conquests of Rama and
the establishment of his Universal Empire. The Gothic nations, in renewing
these practices, added to them the touch of barbarism which was characteristic
of them. After their conquests, and when the feudal government was solidly
established, the grand vassals, being assured of the hereditary property of
their lands and of their dignity, still claimed the power of administering justice,
the right to coin money, and the privilege of waging war in their own name on
their particular enemies; all these privileges passed imperceptibly from the
most powerful princes to the least barons; so that each country of Europe,
given over to continual ravages, became an arena of a thousand petty sovereigns
who destroyed each other. Feudal strongholds were everywhere; all was
divided; everyone was at natural enmity. The king, adorned with an empty
title, remained without authority; the people, a plaything of passions, rivalries,
hatreds of masters, fell into most miserable brutishness. There was not a
barony which was not the prey of some internal war kindled by ambition
or a spirit of vengeance. The kings had tried in vain to oppose this blood-

The feudal government having, however, been attacked by Christianity, and having been considerably ameliorated in the space of less than a century, reacted in its turn upon this religion, and constrained it to modify considerably the rigidity of its precepts and the obscurity of its teaching. This reaction which had birth in the heart of the Crusades, and issued only in consequence of the principles admitted by the two institutions—the feudal and religious—depended entirely upon the foundation of the order of Knighthood; a foundation which many writers have treated in a bizarre fashion through not having examined its aim, and not having been instructed in this great political truth: that no radical institution either in cult or in form of government ever modifies or changes itself, except by interior means furnished by itself—exterior means which one employs sometimes through ignorance or through necessity are always dangerous and almost never arrive at the desired end.

The order of Knighthood, founded towards the commencement of the twelfth century, was the result of the peculiar circumstances in which European society was found. The same spirit which had inspired so many of the gentry to

---

thirsty custom. Charlemagne, alone, had had sufficient force to stop these disorders; but his feeble successors, incapable of maintaining his institutions, had let the devastating torrent take its course. The evil finally became so much worse and the peril became so urgent that Providence was obliged to make its voice heard. About the year 1032 A.D., a bishop of the province of Aquitania announced that an angel had appeared to him, ordering him to proclaim to all men, that they should cease their private hostilities and be reconciled; such being the will of God. This announcement had its effect. It resulted in the seven years' truce. It was resolved that no one should attack or trouble his adversary during the time set apart to celebrate the great festivals of the Church, from the evening of Thursday of each week until the Monday of the following week. This regulation which was at first only a private convention of a kingdom became a general law throughout all Christendom. It was confirmed by the Pope and ratified by several councils. It was called the *Peace of God*. This peace dictated by heaven would still have been insufficient to restrain the spirit of violence which agitated these unfortunate centuries, if the event of the Crusades, giving a new direction to the ideas, had not furnished to the kings the necessary means of making them observed.

take arms for the defence of the oppressed pilgrims in Palestine excited others to declare themselves the protectors of the weak and the avengers of oppressed innocence in Europe. Humanity, love, justice, honour were the distinctive qualities of knights; qualities which religion had to recognize and sanction. It recognized and sanctioned them perhaps without foreseeing all the consequences; but these inevitable consequences becoming developed had roots in its very midst, and drawing from there an enthusiasm which, exalting them more and more, made them bear fruit which it was obliged to let ripen.

Humanity at first mitigated slavery, and, notwithstanding the protestations of interest and of fear, aimed to abolish it and did abolish it. Love polished customs, carrying with it graces long since unknown, and caused a number of pleasing virtues to spring up which gave birth to fine arts. Justice worked upon characters, moderated the passions, and succeeded in repressing to a certain point their fire. Honour illuminated valour and gave to glory its real reward. War was waged with less ferocity; violence and oppression diminished. Respect for truth, devotion to his duties, exactness in keeping his word, formed the character of a gentleman. A man of honour was a new man, a man peculiar to this epoch of the social state, a man whose model one would have searched for in vain either among the Greeks or among the Romans or among any other nation on earth.

This creation was necessary, was even indispensable. The feudal government, excellent in arresting the dissolution of society, was worthless in following the developments in a new formation; its abuses would then have been manifested with too much impunity and one would have seen too often useful men, weak and unarmed, exposed to the insolence of turbulent armed men. The Christian religion, admirable for arresting the impetuosity of the ferocious passions of ignorant and barbarous peoples whom it had to muzzle, could not preserve any longer its austerity in the midst of the new nations which were formed under the influence of chivalry and literature. It had to forget that it had made gallantry a crime, and that the fine arts, and even the human sciences, had been represented by its first followers as pernicious inventions, suggestions of the infernal genius, snares set for men in order to lead them from the paths of sanctity. The knights wished for love, they wished for honour, these must be granted them; and they wished to transform into virtues that which but lately had been considered weakness and even vice. The poets desired illusions, they desired fables; they sought charms of eloquence outside the Gospels and the Vulgate; it was necessary to permit them to read Ovid and Vergil, which had been anathematized, and to allow them to renew the remembrance of a hostile mythology which was regarded as a tissue of impieties.

Thus things reacted. The love of knights excited the poetic fancy of troubadours; the fancy of troubadours inflamed the imagination of artists; the imagination of artists developed the philosophical mind of scholars. Glory being shown elsewhere than upon the crest of helmets and each being able to grasp it from the lyre of the poet, the palette of the painter, the desk of the writer, they threw themselves into the career which honour, justice, and humanity had opened to all. This veritable equality, whose aurora was seen shining, filled the minds with an unheard-of enthusiasm before which the severity of the cult was obliged to yield. Honour required that all work should receive its reward, that all talent should have its recompense, that all distinguished men should rise to their place; it was necessary to yield to honour.

The movement given to exploratory minds carried them at first towards the metaphysical. Scholastic theology alone occupied them for a long while and enveloped them as in a network of subtle distinctions. The first men who called themselves philosophers in these centuries, scarcely

lightened by a faint dawn, exhausted the force of their genius
in researches or in speculations as difficult as trifling; but,
at last, some were found fortunate enough or bold enough
to disentangle, in the obscurity of the labyrinth where they
were engaged, the thread which could aid them to escape;
they seized it, and encountered Aristotle; Aristotle conducted them to Plato. Then a new light struck them. And
when their dazzled eyes were sufficiently strengthened to
gaze upon the torch which they held in their hands, they
directed the light upon the objects which surrounded them;
and they were greatly surprised to find them very different
from what they had imagined them to be. Some, too eager
to speak, were punished for their intemperate loquacity;
others, having become wise by these examples, kept silent
and awaited a more propitious time to express their opinions,
or, indeed, retracted them after having uttered them.[1]

Meanwhile, the universities and colleges opened on all
sides; everyone was eager to enter upon a new career, which
rivalled that of the army, and, like it, led to glory and distinction. Ordinarily the foundation of the first university
has been attributed to Charlemagne; but this idea seems
most unlikely when we recall the terrible troubles which
followed his reign. Public instruction scarcely received
genuine encouragement until the pontificate of Gregory VII.[2]

---

[1] Among these last is Bérenger who was the first to deny the real Presence
and to see only the Impanation in the Eucharist, as Luther did three centuries
later.

[2] Ignorance was still so profound in the ninth century that the art of writing had become extremely rare. By the favour of the clergy a robber who
knew how to read was not hanged. The ecclesiastics were scarcely more
learned on this point than the most simple laymen. We see by the acts of
the Councils that many of them appointed to dignities could not sign their
names. Our word *signature* and our verb *to sign* are a proof of this state of
barbarism; they used a sort of sign which everyone adopted in place of his
name. It was ordinarily the sign of the cross. Alfred the Great complained
that in his time there was not a single priest in his kingdom who understood
the liturgy.

To this ignorance of the most simple elements of letters was added that

This sovereign pontiff, endowed with audacity and an extraordinary force, was alone capable of conceiving a grand idea and executing it. Public instruction, however, took a regular and certain form only towards the beginning of the thirteenth century, when the degrees of the University of Paris were definitely fixed.[1] It was also the period when science and jurisprudence increased greatly. It was scarcely less than a century since a copy of the *Pandects* of Justinian had been found in Italy. Such a work must have struck the minds with admiration. It was studied, commented upon, and, a few years after its discovery, throughout the principal states of Europe, professors of civil rights were appointed to give public lessons. Gentlemen trained to arms generally abandoned this study to men whose ancestors fortune had favoured either in agriculture, the fine arts, or commerce, and left thus a new course open for their emulation. This condescension soon gave them formidable rivals; for it was quite obvious that men who held in their hands the life and honour of others should enjoy soon a great consideration and acquire a great fortune. This was what happened. Men of the robe and men of the sword, gentlemen and judges, knights and artists were equally esteemed and, as the judicious Robertson has very well observed, the arts and virtues of peace began to be put in their place and receive the recompenses which were their due.

---

of all the arts. They no longer knew any comforts of life. The luxury of the Romans had disappeared to make place for grossest necessities. Scarcely any feeble traces of past events were preserved in the monasteries. The mass of the nation knew nothing beyond the actual moment. The human mind languished without culture, without emulation, without memories, without hope.

[1] About 1230 A.D. At this time the fact that ten thousand persons had voice in deciding a question agitated in the University of Paris presupposes a very large number of scholars, since only graduates had a right to vote. In 1262, there were ten thousand scholars at the University of Bologna and some time after thirty thousand at Oxford.

Such were the first efforts that the Will of Man made to throw off the yoke of Destiny which had overwhelmed him and which would have annihilated him, if Providence had not opposed it. These efforts were good; if they had been managed with care, they would have been able to lead to noble results; but exaggeration, so ready to mingle with animistic passions, did not delay to push them beyond limits that they should have kept.

CHAPTER III

HISTORICAL AND POLITICAL VIEW OF THE PRINCIPAL NATIONS
OF EUROPE—SPAIN

THUS after several centuries of profound ignorance and misery, European civilization, arrested at the edge of the abyss by two powerful institutions,—those of feudal government and of the Christian cult,—was awakened from its lethargy and commenced its ascending movement. It had from the eleventh to the fifteenth century taken such rapid steps and had displayed such formidable strength that Asia, alarmed, had been obliged to take precautions against her: I refer to what was effected by the invasion of Spain, and later by the taking and occupation of Constantinople.

It was a question of seeing which side the Will of Man would take in this state of things and whether it would at last recognize the power of Providence or that of Destiny. Already, thanks to the weakness of the feudal system, many great kingdoms were formed whose peoples, rivals in power as in glory, were eager to assume control. All had more or less titles; all were more or less urged on by their position. Spain was then in the first rank; after her came France and England, Italy and Germany. Neither Poland nor the powers of the North, Sweden and Denmark, were in any condition to rank with them and Russia was unknown.

Let us glance rapidly at each of these states and see what their hopes could be.

Spain, invaded by the Goths, submitted to the lot common to all the parts of the Roman Empire and fell beneath the iron arms of these barbarians, who spared them no more than all the rest; happily their yoke did not weigh upon them such a long time.   The Saracens of Africa, invited by Count Julian, made the conquest at the commencement of the eighth century and brought there with the sciences and arts of the Arabs much useful knowledge.   This kingdom then enjoyed a more fortunate destiny than the other states; and when it succeeded in recovering its independence, it could, with just reason, place itself at the head of European civilization; but this situation, favourable on the one side, drew from the other some grave disadvantages.   The change was not made abruptly; the conquests over the Moors had taken place, on the contrary, in different times and under different chiefs.   At first, King Pelagius, quartered in the mountains of Asturias, had assembled about him some courageous Christians who, refusing to submit to the Mussulmans, had formed under his command a small state which was maintained chiefly by the roughness and poverty of the country in which it was hidden.   This state, profiting by favourable conditions, grew imperceptibly.   The quarrels which had occurred among the Moors had encouraged several cities to throw off their yoke; so that at the end of the eleventh century, at the time when the ascending movement recommenced in Europe, there were in Spain twenty kings, as many Christians as Mussulmans, independent of each other, not counting a considerable number of knights, who also considered themselves sovereigns, riding on horseback, fully equipped and attended by their squires, offering their services to any one who was disposed to give them the best pay.[1]

---

[1] Knighthood, founded at this time, and received throughout all the Christian world, flourished chiefly in Spain.   It was there especially that the knights-errant, aptly called, appeared.   The most celebrated among them was Rodrigo, surnamed the Cid,—or rather the *Sid*, that is to say, Lord,—even

As it had not been possible to conquer the Saracens without the co-operation of the Spanish people, who had often driven these strangers to surrender to Christian princes, it was found that the feudal system had taken on a peculiar character in Spain, participating in some way with democracy. Everywhere the royal prerogative was restrained to the narrowest limits; everywhere the nobles affected great haughtiness and the citizens of the towns great independence; it was in Spain that one saw for the first time people sanctioning insurrection as a legitimate right and even as a duty, revoking their oath of obedience, deposing their kings, and even prosecuting them. This terrible abuse of popular power by the common people was called the *privilege of the Union*, and was a part of the legal customs of the kingdom of Aragon. In this kingdom, the kings, long since elective, enjoyed but an empty title: the real exercise of sovereignty devolved upon the Cortes, a sort of parliamentary assemblage without whose permission the monarch could neither impose taxes, declare war, make peace, nor coin money. But, as if such barriers had not been sufficient to stop his usurpations, it was deemed quite fitting to establish a sort of guardian over him, whose function had some resemblance to that of the Ephors or the Tribunes of the people; he was an Interpreter of laws, a Grand Judiciary, called *Justiza*, authorized to exact accounts from all the magistrates and from the king himself, all of whose acts he controlled.[1]

It was difficult to limit any further the royal power, and it would have been just as well not to have had any kings;

---

by the Saracens, who were astounded at his courage. His wealth was considerable. Few kings were as powerful and more respected than he. His exploits and his marriage with Ximene, whose father he had killed, have furnished the subject for a multitude of romances which are still told in Spain.

[1] It was through this *Justiza* that the barons of Aragon said to their kings the very day of their coronation these words so often cited: "We who are as important as you and who together are more powerful than you; we promise to obey your government, if you maintain our rights and privileges; and if not, no."

for how could one expect a prince with any force of character to submit to such restrictions? He who supported them was incapable of reigning and the state suffered from his incapacity; he who felt the virtues of a monarch sought to break them and the state was a prey to revolutions.[1] It was in Spain chiefly that the Will of Man had exaggerated its efforts; it would have even aimed to establish there the centre of unlimited liberty, if Providence, in determining the mission of Mohammed, had not furnished to Destiny arms sufficiently strong to oppose it.

The kingdoms of Castile, Valencia, and Catalonia, although adopting in their constitutions forms somewhat less democratic than that of Aragon were hardly more favourable to royalty; they had also the legislature of the Cortes with all its prerogatives. The nobles who possessed the greater part of the lands were very proud of the privilege of their caste. The peoples, conscious of their strength, which the continuous wars sustained against the Moors had displayed, manifested a spirit of insubordination, impatient of all rule. In general, Spain lacked unity, and, even after the complete expulsion of the Moors and the reunion of all its kingdoms by the marriage of Ferdinand and Isabella, its different parties, badly joined, did not form a regular whole. It is to this want of harmony that must be attributed the slight advantage which this nation drew from the learning it had received from the Arabs, and the precocious knowledge, which, far from leading to the end which it had expected, only inspired a sterile pride which destroyed it.

Several kings of Castile and Aragon had vainly tried to extend the royal prerogative at the expense of the privileges of the nobles and the liberties of the communes; but Ferdinand alone found the means of attempting it to good purpose when, having united the two sceptres in his hand, he saw himself invested with a power great enough not to

[1] This is what often happened and principally during the thirteenth and fourteenth centuries, under the reigns of Alphonso III. and of Peter IV.

fear any competitors among his vassals and with a glory sufficiently striking to draw the respect of his peoples. His decisive victories over the Moors gave him both. At the head of a victorious army, he skilfully turned his forces against a feudal aristocracy which had annoyed him and striking it in its most solid foundations—knighthood and the Cortes—he restrained to such an extent the influence of the feudal body, that, deprived of power and of consideration, it finally disappeared entirely.

Thus was the Spanish aristocracy demolished; but the monarch in avoiding one danger fell into another: he espoused the cause of democracy which, at first obedient, did not fail to claim all its liberties, even that of rising in rebellion on the slightest occasion and as soon as it found a prince weak enough to fear it. Ferdinand saw it well and seeking a means of evading such a difficulty had the misfortune to attach himself to the worst of all, the religious terror. Ferdinand was not really pious; indeed, how could he have been while Borgia, under the name of Alexander VI., occupied the pontifical chair? He regarded religions only as political institutions, to which governments could help themselves according to their positions and their interests. Providence was to him Destiny, and Destiny the force or the ability of men. The crusade against the Albigenses had created the calamitous tribunal of the Inquisition; the Spanish monarch saw in this tribunal a sort of check which was necessary to him, and he took it without concerning himself regarding the strange abuse for which he was culpable. The Aragons, at first frightened at the sight of this phantom, hastened to arms, opposed the establishment of the inquisitors with all their strength, and even had the chief killed; but the military force, then all powerful in the hands of Ferdinand, had soon repressed these rebels, who, fighting in the name of heaven, had finally submitted. One can never struggle with advantage against consequences avowed by a principle which one is obliged to respect. Ferdinand, after the victory,

20

received from Pope Alexander VI. the surname of *Catholic*. He would better have deserved that of *Despot*.   Providence, outraged, withdrew then from Spain, and the Will of Man, violently restrained by Destiny, tried to break forth in the manner which I shall relate further on.

CHAPTER IV

FRANCE, ENGLAND, ITALY

FRANCE was, after Spain, the most flourishing of the European states of the fifteenth century; monarchical government had advanced towards unity across a multitude of obstacles, several of which had been fortunately overcome. The feudal rule, established from the beginning of the first race, had begun to give way under the second, and in the hands of Charlemagne had received some important modifications, which tended to give it imperial forms; but under the feeble successors of this prince, everything that he tried to unite was divided, and, in the contrary movement which followed, greatly surpassed its natural limits; so that it was principally in France and in Germany, where this reaction was most felt, that feudalism offered the smallest divisions and inclined the most towards aristocratic anarchy.[1]

This was an inevitable effect of the reign of Charlemagne; this reign, entirely prophetic, having exaggerated the power

[1] At this unfortunate time, safety was nowhere. All was brigandage and confusion. England differed not in this respect from France, and Germany was still more infested with disorders. The ideas of justice and equity were so perverted there, that, at the beginning of the thirteenth century, several German Margraves still counted among their rights those of exacting ransom from travellers passing through their territories, and of debasing coin. Emperor Frederick III. had great difficulty making them listen to reason in this regard, and was obliged to constrain them at the Diet of Egra to take oath to abandon these rights.

of Destiny, without giving it any other support, either in the Will or in Providence, had necessarily been drawn along to its dissolution; for it seems to me that I have sufficiently repeated that the consolidation of things is given to Providence alone. That which comes from the Will alone is divided by exaltation; that which comes from Destiny alone is dissolved by corruption.

In the course of the ninth century, no more authority existed in France; the people there were in slavery. The feudal system, fallen into dissolution, was without force, and the royal power, debased, was nothing more than a vain counterfeit without consideration. The kings, stripped of army, of domains, of even subjects, languished without honour, until at last Hugh Capet, chief of the third race, was called to the throne by the assent of the grandees of the realm. This event decided the fate of France in giving to royalty a real force, which, increasing, soon surpassed that of the barons. The successors of Hugh, nearly all distinguished in their time, skilfully profited by circumstances quietly to take possession of the States of the nation, which, under the name of the Field of Mars (or of May), had represented the feudal body from the time of the first race. These States finding no longer in this body either common bond, general interest, or principle of union which they could grasp, allowed themselves to be dominated by princes capable of acting opportunely with the motive of interest or of fear, and consented to surrender the legislative power to them. The first step taken, the kings of France, Louis the Fat and Philip the Fair, successively affirmed it, giving liberty to the communes, opening to the deputies entrance to these same States, which thenceforth took the name of *States-General*. All the rest was dependent upon it.

The monarchs became legislators, assuming the title and all its functions, even to claiming the right to impose taxes and arbitrarily raise armies. Gradually they set aside the convocation of the States-General, of which they had no further need, and they even replaced them by judges of their court, of whom they formed a political body, called by the name of "*Parlement*," to which they attributed, outside of the judiciary functions, those of verifying and registering their edicts and their other legislative acts. At this time, France was inclined towards absolute monarchy, and, during this crisis, it was necessary that royalty should be all or nothing; and this depended always on the genius of the reigning prince, whose Destiny made that of his kingdom. If this genius was powerful, France was powerful and well governed; if, on the contrary, it was weak, France fell into a state of weakness and confusion. This singular situation had its advantages and its disadvantages. I shall shortly point out why, when ready to ascend to the highest rank of the powers of Europe, France did not ascend. It was neither the States-General, the nobility, nor the "*parlements*" which prevented her, as some superficial writers have advanced; it was the blindness of Charles the VII. and his ingratitude towards Providence.

England, long-time rival of France, and often a fortunate rival, had experienced the same vicissitudes. Overrun by the fierce disciples of Odin, as all the other parts of the Roman Empire, she had resisted even less than the continent. Successively invaded by the Angles, the Saxons, the Danes, and the Normans, she had bent beneath their yoke, changing masters as well as laws, language as well as customs. At first she had been divided among a number of petty sovereigns, almost always at war, who, by dint of destroying themselves, were at last reduced to seven and had formed the Saxon heptarchy, to which a king of Wessex, named Egbert, had, however, put an end, when he united the seven kingdoms into a single one, and called it the Kingdom of England. This reunion had this in its favour, that it produced the reign of Alfred, justly called *the Great,* an extraordinary man for his time, and a prince worthy of commendation in all respects.[1]

This reign was for England what that of Charlemagne had been for France. At the death of Alfred, all was confusion again. The Danes inundated England anew; the Normans followed, and brought with them the scions of the ancient Franks who usurped the crown. At this time, the English barons profited by the weakness of many of their kings to turn to account their ancient privileges, which the successive conquests of the Danes and Normans had caused to disappear, and as they could not do this without the support of the common people, it developed in the course of a certain period that the concessions, which they had extorted from the monarchs, turned more to the profit of the commons than to the advantage of the nobles. The people, trained by this spirit of turbulence which had agitated the barons, turned it against the barons themselves, so that the feudal system yielded to the multitude and could preserve itself only by favouring democracy, which was embraced.

Thus, in England it was upon democracy that feudalism supported itself; in Spain, royalty triumphed over feudalism, by relying upon religion considered as a coercive means; in France, royalty believed that upon itself alone it could be established, flattering itself to restrain by the force of arms and the illusion of the sceptre alone, the pretensions of feudalism and the encroachments of the commons. There was more of Will than of Destiny in England and more of Destiny than of Will in France and in Spain; but France

[1] Fortunate warrior and able politician, Alfred conquered exterior and interior enemies; he gave a code of laws to his people, in which he introduced for the first time the institution of a Jury. He favoured commerce, and caused a considerable number of vessels to be built. It is said that he laid the foundations of the University of Oxford, and that he used all his power to make arts and sciences flourish in his states. He was himself a man of letters and some of his writings are still preserved. Alfred died in 900 A.D. after having reigned about thirty years.

had this advantage over Spain, that, at least, it did not profane the power of Providence in taking advantage of its name to prop up its authority, and, the bases of its government being more true, they were consequently stronger.

If the fate of Italy differed in some respects from that of other countries of Europe after the invasion of the barbarians, it was because it was more terrible, as much on account of the great abundance of wealth which constantly attracted them there, as on account of the keen hatred which they felt towards the Romans. The Goths who remained there after having ravaged it were called *Lombards.* The reign of Charlemagne arrested for a while the general disorder, and shed some rays of hope upon Italy; but this calm did not last long. The edifice which this monarch had raised was immense; no one after him could support the burden. His empire, divided at first by his son Louis, called *le Débonnaire,* was subdivided at the death of Lothair, son of Louis, and soon came to an end. The crown of Germany was forever separated from that of France and the descendants of Charlemagne, more and more unable to preserve them, let them both fall; the first fell to a Count of Franconia called *Conrad,* and the second to a vassal called *Hugh Capet.*[1] But, before these two events, all the energies of the government were exhausted; unity of action had disappeared; so that the feudal members of this great corps, from the greatest to the least, had all become sovereigns in their domains.

Now, among the extraordinary things which came to pass, we must carefully observe this one: that the domains, particularly the cities, at the time of the change of which I have just spoken, were without either military chiefs or barons who could, at this point, seize the authority; but bishops or abbots, judges, municipal magistrates, seeing themselves masters, consolidated their power without any one having the force to oppose them or dreaming of

[1] In 912, and in 987 A.D.

doing so in this frightful chaos; so that the feudal system, thus parcelled, comprised a considerable number of petty theocracies and petty republics, whose unusual existence was one of the great singularities of this gloomy time. Assuredly, there was no true theocracy, and still less true republicanism: all was limited to forms; the substance did not issue from feudal anarchy.

Spain, France, and England either did not receive these forms at all, on account of opposing circumstances, or if they did receive them, did not keep them long; but it was not thus in Italy and in Germany, where the absence of harmony in the government made it felt the more. These two countries were crammed with small ecclesiastical and municipal sovereignties, which at first were entitled *imperials* and feigned to be dependent upon the Empire, but which finally became independent. Germany had the greatest number of ecclesiastical sovereignties; Italy the greatest number of municipal. This last country was surcharged with a number of these would-be republics, which devoured each other in turn, and which, leaving the hands of an aristocratic council to fall into those of an ephemeral usurper, caused only a change of tyranny. Factions, jealousies, plots, conspiracies, and deceits were everywhere; there was no fighting because there were no armies, but assassinations took place and the greatest victories were obtained by poison.[1]

In the midst of this anarchical chaos, there were, however, some cities which were distinguished from others, thanks to commerce which furnished them the means. Venice, Genoa, Pisa, Florence were of this number; Venice especially which had opened a profitable commerce with Alexandria.[2] One might say that it was principally in Italy

---

[1] See, in Machiavelli's history of Castracani, tyrant of Lucca and Pistoja, what this writer says of Cæsar Borgia. Such plots, fortunate or unfortunate, are the history of all Italy.

[2] These cities found in the Crusades an opportunity for increasing their wealth and power by furnishing the Crusaders with means of transportation

that the feudal system yielded to the mercantile spirit from which it received the volitive movement. The government which was here established was not republican, as injudicious historians have described it; it was emporocratic.[1] Emporocracy dominated this country everywhere; it produced distinguished men, who gave to Italy the few beautiful days that she had in the sixteenth century. This sort of government, which passed from Italy into Flanders, became naturalized a little later in Holland. It was still entitled there *republican*, although it was really only municipal and emporocratic. A genuine republican government can exist only where the people assemble *en masse* and appoint their magistrates as they did in Athens and in Rome. Whenever the government becomes representative, it turns to emporocracy. Rousseau was perfectly right on this point. He saw clearly that the popular Will, essential principle of every republic, could not be represented. The idea of representatives is modern, as he said, or rather it is renovated from the ancient government of the Celts, and modified according to the feudal system of the Goths.

Before the Hollanders, the Swiss in escaping from the yoke of Austria had had the pretension of constituting a republic; but it was simply a municipal association which they had constituted. Since the downfall of the Roman Empire, there did not exist in Europe a single government[2]

---

and by making for them a station for ammunition and food; by establishing their independence by legal acts, which forced the Emperors to ratify their privileges. Frederick Barbarossa tried in vain to establish imperial jurisdiction over them; he could not attain this end and signed at Constance in 1183 a treaty of peace by which he abandoned all his rights.

[1] A new word to express a new idea.   It is taken from the Greek ἔμπορος, a merchant, and κράτος, force.

[2] It is in vain that some writers have regarded the government of Venice as a perfect aristocracy. It was rather a municipal tyranny. There was nothing noble in this government but the title which it gave itself. All were severe and cruel because all were timid; all were restless and partial because all were jealous. The people, always trembling and disarmed, were fitted

which could qualify as homogeneous and as perfect in its kind. They have all drawn along with them a mixture of most opposed elements.

---

neither for attack nor for defence; thus they were the victims of the first vigorous undertaking which was formed against them. The League of Cambrai dealt it a mortal blow. Commerce, in which Venice could still place any hope, was taken from her a short time after by the Portuguese. In considering Venice as a strict aristocracy, Florence might have been regarded as a temperate democracy; but the real truth is that there was neither aristocracy nor democracy in all this; there was municipal usurpation, vigorous on one side and weak on the other. The people in Florence were more fortunate but also more exposed to revolutions. The Doge of Venice was an alderman, sometimes tyrannical and sometimes tyrannized. When Florence had a chief, it was under the name of *Gonfalonier*, a mere legal alderman, somewhat as the Doge of Genoa, a sort of mayor, despotic without violence and absolute without severity. One of them named Cosmo de' Medici, loved by the people because he knew how to form their taste in feigning to flatter them, gave his name to his century in divining the opinion of the centuries following. History deals at length with the city of Milan, only on account of the bloody wars which its possession excited between Germany and France. There was nothing remarkable in her form of government. Of Naples I shall speak later.

CHAPTER V

IF I have not spoken of Rome in the preceding chapter,
it is because it is very difficult to fix one's thought regarding her, and to know whether she should be considered
as a sacred, an imperial, or a free city. She has pretended
according to circumstances to each title, and they have been
given to her according to the parties which have ruled; but
she has not entirely merited any of them. Providence,
Destiny, and the Will of Man have appeared there alternately
and have displayed in turn considerable strength, without
ever being able either to be united or separated, recognized
or mutually subjugated. Rome has been the scene of an
eternal combat among these three powers. She has been
the theatre of numberless revolutions, and has presented,
according to the epochs, a picture of the general situation
of Europe.

It is evident that if the Christian religion has to have a
sovereign pontiff, and that, if this sovereign pontiff has been
in the essence of its cult, he necessarily has to live somewhere,
and to possess a seat inviolable and sacred; for, after all,
this first person of the sacerdotal hierarchy cannot be left
to the mercy of civil power, whatever it may be. It is
neither with his arms nor with those of his priests that a

sovereign pontiff can defend himself if attacked. He must
have a place of refuge so revered that no one can enter
without his consent, unless he incur immediate anathema
and be reputed impious. It is an irrefutable maxim and
every just mind must feel it, that a sovereign pontiff must
be, in the place where he resides, all or nothing. Providence,
which he represents and whose organ he is, cannot endure
division; supposing that he really represents it and that he
possesses the right to speak, which is irresistible if he is
admitted as sovereign pontiff. Every time that a real
sovereign pontiff has existed, this pontiff has resided in a
sacred, inviolable place beyond the reach of civil power.
The moment that he has mingled with citizens and has resided within the same walls as the sovereign, whatever may
have been the nature of this sovereign, he has been under
the iron hand of Destiny and has enjoyed no liberty.   Then,
one could do with him whatever one wished: to name Hildebrand as well as Borgia; as did Frederick I., kissing the feet
of Adrian IV., leading him in triumph through Venice; or
as Philip the Fair, sending hired assassins to Boniface VIII.
in Agnone to deal him blows.

But is it the essence of the Christian cult to have a sovereign pontiff? It does not belong to me to decide this question; neither do I decide it as a theologian; I solve it only as
a politician, and I say in general that royalty can no more
exist without a king than can priesthood without a sacerdotal priest. However, one might say that a king is not so
necessary to the government of men that one cannot do
without him; for example, in republics. I admit it. But I
reply that then it is not a monarchy, and that the peoples
who give the laws give them according to their will, make
and unmake them at their pleasure; and I add that if these
peoples have a cult, they have it as they wish it, adding
here or retrenching there, according to their caprice, and
naming for sovereign pontiff Anytus as well as Cæsar.   I
know that this state of affairs is expedient to certain minds,

but as it is equally permissible for me to have an opinion on
this subject, mine is: that in supposing the peoples able to
give laws unto themselves, which I doubt, it is not true that
they can ever give themselves a cult; because all cult implies
an inspiration or a divine revelation of which, considered
en masse, they are absolutely incapable.

Besides, the difficulty in Europe has always been to know
if there was not only a sovereign pontiff there but also an
emperor; if this pontiff would be the Patriarch of Constantinople or that of Rome; and the Emperor, that of the East
or of the West. We must not forget that after the invasion
of the barbarians and their establishment in the West, the
Empire of the East aspired to the dominion and that its
Patriarch at first claimed all the rights of supreme priesthood. The Greek Church treated with contempt the Latin
Church; ancient Rome was regarded at Constantinople as
annihilated and new Rome as ignorant and savage. Even
at the time of the Crusades, the Greeks saw the Franks arrive
among them with terror. Anne de Comnène never spoke
of these peoples but with the most profound disdain; she
was loath to tarnish with this barbarous name the majesty
and elegance of history. From the commencement a
struggle was established between the two churches; a struggle
which, always rankling on account of the two Patriarchs
who would not consent to recognize each other, ended in a
rupture and brought forth a schism for which Photius
furnished the first pretext.[1]

The Patriarch of Rome remained then sole sovereign
pontiff of the Latin Church, under the name of *Pope*, and
enjoyed at first a brilliant existence due to the munificence
of Pepin, whom Etienne II. had crowned. Charlemagne, as

---

[1] This schism, which still lasts, is based upon the claim of the Greek Church
that the Holy Spirit emanates from the Father alone, whereas the Latin
Church considers it as emanating from the Father and Son. This schism,
which began about the middle of the ninth century, was consummated in
1053 by the Patriarch Cerularius.

magnanimous as generous, confirmed all the gifts of Pepin and, to put an end to the attempts which the Lombards constantly made to gain possession of Rome, overthrew their kingdom and confined their last king in a monastery. Everything went very well up to this point; Charlemagne, as I have said, preferred to be obedient to the grandeur of his character than to the illumination of his intelligence. At his death, all that he had built collapsed. In none of his descendants was seen any of the qualities which had made him illustrious; instead of cherishing harmony, by mutual consent, between altar and throne, they were divided into factions, and this ruined them. One would have said that the more the blood of Charlemagne receded from its source, the more it degenerated. At last, the imperial crown passed from the Franks to the Germans, and fell almost immediately to the lot of those same Saxons whom this monarch had so cruelly persecuted to make them embrace Christianity. One feels that still bruised from the tortures which they had experienced, they had not much love for the pontiffs, who had stirred up the Franks against them; thus they seized with avidity the slightest pretext to persecute them. Henry-the-Fowler and the three Othos were important enough as princes for the times in which they reigned; but they held too much to the cult of Odin, making their valour fierce and their politics sanguinary.

The pontifical seat, little respected by them—and perhaps it had become unworthy of respect—was a prey to horrors of all kinds: the memory of Pope Formosa was outraged by his successor and the body of this pontiff was exhumed and thrown into the Tiber. Etienne VI., who dared to permit this indignity, was justly punished and was hanged in his prison. Etienne VIII., pursued by the Roman populace, had his face so cruelly scarred that he dared not appear in public. At this time, Rome no longer belonged to the priesthood; two artful women held the principal authority there; Marozia and Theodora directed by their intrigues the elections of the sovereign pontiffs; Pope John X., whom Theodora had chosen, displeasing Marozia by the austerity of his manners, had been strangled by order of this lewd woman and was replaced soon after by a son whom she had had by Pope Sergius. This son, extolled under the name of John XI., had died miserably in prison with his mother, and John XII., accused of adultery, had been solemnly deposed by order of Otho I. and had been put to death a short time after.

There was no more dignity attached to the tiara, no respect accorded to the sacerdotal character; the holy throne was bought, sold, and blood-stained in turn. Italy, entirely conquered by the Germans, struggled beneath their yoke. The subjugated Romans freed themselves as soon as they could. Otho II., justly called the *Bloody*, irritated by the opposition which he encountered in the Roman senate, finding no other means of reducing them to obedience, ordered the principal senators massacred; execrable means, which dishonoured his reign, without giving him the tranquillity which he sought, since there was seen, a few years after, a consul named *Crescentius* proclaiming the independence of this city and attempting to recall the age of Brutus. It is said that Otho III. having had the rebel seized, had him hanged by the feet, notwithstanding his promise to spare his life. Pope John XXII., suspected of having fomented the rebellion, experienced a most cruel fate: the Emperor caused his hands and ears to be cut off and his eyes torn out. To palliate this crime he proclaimed that this John was an anti-pope.

But how could one imagine that such horrors would remain unpunished? It would be very unsophisticated to believe that spiritual power would allow itself to be thus degraded and that such cowardly actions would not bring their own punishment. The German, or rather the Saxon emperors wished then, that sovereign pontiffs of the Christian cult, called to exercise so great an influence over their minds, should be absolutely denuded of their civil power, that they should have no refuge, no place to lay their head; that they should be at their discretion and that they could be outraged with impunity and even killed if that was agreeable to the monarchs.

But finally this was impossible. In considering them only as bishops of Rome, had they not as many rights over Rome as those of Mayence, Cologne, and Treves had over those cities? Did it occur to anyone to object to the abbots of Fulda, Saint Gall, Kempten assuming the regalia of office? Did anyone ask these prelates for the qualifications on which they founded their authority? Since the bishop of Mayence was a sovereign, why should not the bishop of Rome be one? Was it because he was pope, patriarch, or sovereign pontiff that he should be without patrimony, without *éclat*, without surety for his person or his dignity? What folly! One would make of a spiritual chief whose power was becoming more and more formidable a pastor of the primitive church, a mendicant priest awaiting in humility and abjection his sustenance of tithes and voluntary alms from the people. Miserable contradiction which showed well to what degree the Will of Man had let itself be abused by the most base and obscure passions; even the shadow of Providential power revolted his pride, irritated his desire; it liked better to submit to the iron yoke of Destiny and console itself with its evils, saying: it is force, it is necessity.

Force and necessity were placed accordingly above the pontifical throne. The monarchs, who had not wished to recognize the pastoral staff, were obliged to bow beneath a rod of iron. A man endowed with a great character, intrepid, audacious, inflexible as severe, was chosen pope under the name of Gregory VII. He was formerly called Hildebrand. His father was only a poor artisan in a small town of Tuscany. Hardly had he seized the censer, when, having resolved to strike a violent blow at the civil authority, he declared all those excommunicated who had received from a layman the investiture of any sacerdotal office and those who gave them, and threatened at the same time to anathematize the Emperor of Germany, Henry IV., and Philip the I., King of France, who were guilty of this abuse. At these tidings the German monarch assembled a council at Worms and deposed Gregory; but the latter was not a John XII. or XXII., that could be intimidated, outraged, or injured with impunity. He convoked another council more regular than the first, since it was legitimate, and declared Henry excommunicated and deposed. This unexpected blow amazed Europe; the prince, stripped of all his moral force, was overwhelmed and nonplussed by it. The principal sovereigns of Germany, ecclesiastics as well as temporals, rose up and took arms against him. His wife and children were seen even breaking all bonds of nature and of duty, offering themselves as his accusers and joining his enemies. He was forced to bow before the terrible power which was shown for the first time.

Let us turn our attention for a moment to this monarch, invincible up to this time; he appears as a suppliant before the gate of the château of Canossa where the Pope was, he remains there three days, bareheaded, his body covered with hair cloth, in the middle of winter, exposed to a most rigorous fast to implore a pardon which he obtained at last only with great difficulty and under the most humiliating conditions. And do not think that Henry was a weak man; he was a courageous prince, indomitable in war. In the course of his life he had fought in person more than sixty battles, had subjugated the Saxons, had triumphed over two formidable competitors, and had even fought his own children who had risen against him. At the time of his humiliation, he was the terror of Europe and was advancing rapidly to the universal monarchy. This is what the greatness of Gregory did; he stopped him by a single word, in the middle of his career, without the need of any physical force. It was in vain that the humbled monarch, after having recovered from the first shock which had caused his downfall, believed himself strong enough to violate his oaths. All that he could do with his passionate outbursts and his intrigues was to increase the trouble which already existed, and to give rise to two opposed factions, which, for three centuries, agitated Italy and Germany without relaxation. The factions of the Guelphs defended the sacerdotal authority and that of the Ghibellines sustained the pretensions of the emperors. In the midst of these open or secret wars which were brought about by these two factions, the imperial power became weakened more and more by murders, poisonings, crimes of all sorts with which the throne was sullied, and vanished completely during the long interregnum which followed the death of William of Holland. Rudolph of Hapsburg, founder of the house of Austria, was at last chosen emperor in 1273, not because anyone believed him capable of raising or extending the imperial power, but, on the contrary, as Robertson has very well observed, because his domains and his credit did not appear sufficient to excite the jealousy of any of his rivals. Thus, the two chiefs of this Gothic feudalism which was called an empire, the pope and the emperor, were destroyed, as neither wished to respect the other and as they had alternately tried to be everything, they finished by being nothing. Notwithstanding his genius, Gregory VII. did not succeed in obtaining the universal power to which he aspired, because the very essence of his cult opposed it.[1] He could indeed humble the imperial majesty, and, in bequeathing to his successors the formidable weapon of anathema, make them the terror of kings and the arbitrators of nations; but notwithstanding the three crowns with which their tiara was encircled and the three crosses which surmounted their sceptre, he could neither make

---

[1] It was impossible that reigning monarchs should adore a priest preaching humility, comparing the slave to the king; and that bishops, his equals, should obey orders of one who, taking only the title of servant of servants, should recognize and consecrate this maxim: "that the first shall be last," etc.

the sacerdotal body wish to recognize them as infallible sovereigns nor the councils not claim supreme authority over them. This lack of unity was inherent in the Christian cult. The Church was invested from its birth with republican forms which it had found in the Roman Empire, and this Empire, in reconstructing itself after a fashion three or four centuries after its downfall, had again added to these incoherent forms all the abuse of Gothic feudalism.

The same difficulties which existed in the Church existed also in the Empire and their effect, still more grave, disturbed the harmony on all sides. Although the German Emperors regarded all the princes of Europe and even the doges of Venice and Genoa as their vassals, and although they believed they had the right to summon them to their tribunals and put them under the ban of the Empire, there was not one of these princes who would submit to their orders. Even those who had elected them, accorded them empty honours without any shadow of authority. On certain occasions, it is true, the greatest princes accompanied and served them with the title of officer of their household; the day of their coronation they served them drink on horseback; in their charters, they gave them the name *Cæsar*, and the title *Master of the World;* but they left these Masters of the World, these *Augmentateurs de l'Empire*, as they were called, without treasure and without power. Always suspicious of each other, one saw, on one side, the vassals unceasingly occupied with arresting the aspirations of their chief, and, on the other, the chief unceasingly seeking to encroach upon the privileges of his vassals. What dignity could the whole appearance have? At Rome they wished a mendicant for sovereign pontiff, always occupied with saying *amen* and who could be employed as a political machine. In Germany—for the emperor did not possess officially a single city, a single château, that I might name—they wished a shadow of a king, one merely for parade, who could be put aside when the parade was terminated.

Such was the general situation of the principal cities of Europe and the point to which the development of their individual Will had conducted them, when the Turks, drawn into Europe by the fatality of Destiny, came and in taking possession of Constantinople, raised a protecting barrier for Asia and presented to the usurpation of the Will an insurmountable obstacle.

CHAPTER VI

EACH of the European nations of which I have spoken, although imbued with the same sentiment of ambition which inclined it to dominate over the others and to seize universal monarchy, could not conceal the fact that each was too weak for this. It was necessary then that, by force or by ruse, one of them should seize the other in order to unite its means to theirs and proceed afterwards to the conquest of the rest. The union of France and Germany, attempted several times, had always been a failure. The imperial dignity placed in this latter country, seemed to give it an advantage over the other; but this advantage, purely nominal, influenced in no way the mind of the kings of France, which the memory of Clovis and of Charlemagne filled with a just pride. After some attempts on the part of the Germans, the famous battle of Bouvines, gained by Philip Augustus, decided forever that France would never be their subject. The Germans then turned towards Italy, but the hatred which the popes nourished against them, the dissensions fomented by the Guelphs and Ghibellines, the rivalries which they encountered on the part of the French and the Spaniards, all this prevented them from making permanent conquests. Besides, if one considers the time which had rolled by from the accession of Rudolph of Hapsburg to the reign of Maximilian, immediate predecessor of Charles the Fifth, one will see that Germany, a prey to all the calamities which a government without unity and without energy involves, could not form any regular plan and follow it. It was only during the reign of this prince that the empire enjoyed any tranquillity, due to the institutions which he founded there or to which he gave a better form.[1]

Spain, after shaking off the yoke of the Saracens and after being united under a single monarch, as I have said, having turned her attention to the situation of things, saw that the best thing for her to do, was to seize the power in Italy, in order afterwards to take possession of France, crossing both the Alps and the Pyrenees. She neglected for the moment Portugal, which was first formed from the conquests which Alphonso I. had made over the Moors[2]; judging with reason that there would be time enough to make herself master of it once the rest of Europe should be subjected. Already the princes of Aragon had made great efforts to take the kingdom of Naples and at last succeeded in spite of the vigorous contest which first the Germans and then the French had sustained.[3] They awaited only

[1] The most important of these was the one which bore the name of the Imperial Chamber—a sort of federal tribunal, authorized to arbitrate on all the differences between the members of the Germanic corps; this tribunal, which bore some resemblance to the Amphictyonic Council, would have led Europe to its aim, if anything could have been able to lead it.

[2] This Alphonso, founder of the kingdom of Portugal, was son of Henri de Bourgogne of the House of France. He was crowned in 1139, after having defeated five Moorish kings at the battle of Ourique.

[3] It was about the year 1019 that some Norman knights, having disembarked in Italy, formed there settlements from which the kingdoms of Sicily and Naples originated. The sovereigns of these kingdoms had long disputed with the popes who claimed authority there. Instead of realizing the great advantage of living on good terms with these pontiffs and even of recognizing themselves their vassals, in order to protect them, they, on the contrary, persecuted them, made war upon them desperately and treated them often with the utmost indignity, so that their states became prey to the greatest calamities. There is no country in Europe whose history offers a series of crimes more

a favourable moment to rush forth from there, and this opportunity was afforded them.

As for France and England, which diverse vicissitudes had, so to speak, mixed and rendered successively dependent one upon the other, they mutually felt that it was important for one of them to conquer her rival. Several unfortunate events had given great advantage to England. After the cruel battles of Crécy and Poitiers, the taking of Calais, the captivity of King John, and the ravages caused by the mob of rebel peasants known by the name of *Jacquerie*, after the stormy minority of Charles VI., the madness of this prince, the perfidious reign of his wife Isabella of Bavaria, the bloody factions of the Burgundians and the Armagnacs, and finally the famous battle of Agincourt, it was difficult to foresee how France could survive so many disasters.

However, in glancing over the annals of the different states raised upon the débris of the Roman Empire, one must concede that France, among all the others, has been more often favoured by extraordinary and remarkable events. Was it not in her midst that Clovis appeared, the founder of the first regular monarchy after the invasion of the barbarians? Charles Martel, who arrested the progress of the Saracens and prevented Europe from becoming again a dependency of Asia? Charlemagne, who refounded the Empire of the West? William the Conqueror, who made himself King of England? Godfrey de Bouillon, whose name is attached to the only triumph of the Crusades? and a host of other heroes whom it would take too long to name: Hugh Capet, Philip Augustus, Saint Louis, etc.? If one considers the succession of kings upon the different thrones of Europe, from the middle of the tenth century to the close

---

odious, of revolutions more rapid, more numerous, and more cruel. One cannot read without horror the bloody annals. It is well known how all the French who were found in Sicily were massaced there in 1282. The name of the *Sicilian Vespers*, given to this massacre, indicates the time and depicts the profound impiety of the assassins.

of the fifteenth, it will be seen that there was a great advantage of force, grandeur, talent, even legitimacy among the
kings of France, and this proves what I have advanced:
that Destiny, upon which these kings relied, favoured them.

How could one imagine then that this state was about to
perish; that her language, the most beautiful and the most
virile of all those which sprang from the débris of the Latin
and Celt, heritage of the *langue d'Oc*, so unfortunately
drenched in the blood of the Albigenses,[1] this tongue destined
to enlighten Europe, was about to give place to the Saxon
or at least receive a bizarre mixture from it? This seemed,
however, inevitable, had it not been for a providential event,
for at the moment Destiny was evidently too weak and the
Will was divided or impotent.

Who could describe the situation in which France was?
Charles VI. had lost his mind. The French, a prey to internal factions, were hated and persecuted by enemies. The
massacre at Genoa had just been ordered. The Duke of
Burgundy, all powerful in Paris, after having caused the
assassination of the Duke of Orleans, sent to the gallows
or condemned to exile all those of the party of Armagnacs
who offended him. The English, conquerors at Agincourt,
inundated and ravaged the provinces. Isabella of Bavaria,
ambitious queen, adulterous spouse, and unnatural mother,
favoured the enemy, oppressed her husband, and persecuted
her son. This young prince, too much irritated perhaps
by so many outrages, had seen the Duke of Burgundy struck
down at his feet from the blow of a hatchet, by one of his
servants eager to avenge him. Accused of this murder he
had been summoned by the *parlement* of Paris, condemned
for contumacy, and declared incapable of reigning. His
sister Catherine had been given as wife to the King of Eng-

---

[1] It was in the *langue d'Oc* that the first attempts of poetry have been made
by the troubadours; it is this tongue which has preceded and polished the
Castilian and Italian and which has given grammatical forms to them as well
as to the French.

land, and without respect for the laws of the kingdom which excluded daughters from the throne, the crown had been bestowed upon her as dowry. The Destiny of England prevailed, France was about to succumb.

Nevertheless, Providence, which wished her welfare, arranged from afar the extraordinary event which would save her. Three women, too celebrated unfortunately, had been the prophetic instruments of as many calamities: Eleanor of Guienne, wife of Louis-le-Jeune; Isabelle of France, sister of Charles the Fair; and that Isabella of Bavaria, wife of the mad Charles VI. of whom I have just spoken. The first had stripped France of her most fertile provinces, to carry them as dowry to the King of England, Henry of Anjou, whom she had married after having been divorced by Louis-le-Jeune, because of her love-intrigues in Palestine; the second, murderess of her husband, had given her claim to the crown of France to her son Edward III. and kindled the first war between the two kingdoms; the third had consented to disinherit her son, in order to call her son-in-law, Henry V., to the throne. All three were dishonoured by their intrigues, their cruelties, or their vices.[1] Providence,

---

[1] It is said that Eleanor, becoming enamoured in Palestine of a young Turk of rare beauty named *Sala-Heddin*, had forgotten for him her duty to her husband, her country, and her religion. The king, who should have punished her misconduct by shutting her up in a cloister, contented himself with divorcing her and giving her all her inheritance, with which she enriched her second husband. The King of England, as the result of this marriage, united the dukedoms of Normandy and Aquitaine, the earldoms of Anjou, Poitiers, of Touraine and Maine, and became thus one of the most formidable vassals of the crown of France. Some years after, John, brother of Richard Cœur-de-Lion, having stabbed his nephew Arthur who was the legitimate heir of Richard, in order to reign in his stead, being summoned to the tribunal of Philip-Augustus, King of France, was judged by his peers and declared guilty of felony. All the lands which he possessed in France were confiscated, which resulted in his being surnamed *Jean-sans-Terres*. It was this assassin-prince who signed the *Great Charter* and thus gave place to a new parliamentary organization in England.

Isabelle of France married Edward II. and lived unhappily with her husband. She profited by the troubles in the kingdom to arm herself against

having resolved to overthrow by the arm of a pure and
saintly woman the edifice of shame and scandal raised by
these three dishonourable women, determined upon an
extraordinary movement, and its all-powerful action, dominating both the fatality of Destiny and the strength of Will,
struck, in a humble village, the heart of a young girl, of
whom it made a new Voluspa. Joan of Arc was her name.
She was called *la Pucelle* because of her chastity. Let us
give honour to her memory and may France, whom she
saved from an odious yoke, rejoice to have given her birth.

This maid, the honour of her sex, was born in poverty;
but from the most tender age had manifested a quiet inclination for religious ideas of a certain form. She believed
in fairies, whose names and mysterious fables had echoed
around her cradle, and when she was old enough to lead the
sheep to pasture, she wandered often in the woods, thinking
of those deities of the groves, whom her ancestors, the Gauls,
had worshipped. She did not give any account of her senti-

---

him and declare war. She pursued him and his favourite, Spenser, with an
incredible obstinacy. After having taken possession of Bristol, she had the
father of Spenser, aged ninety years, hanged, and soon, seizing the favourite
himself, subjected him, before her own eyes, to unspeakable atrocities. This
implacable and jealous woman, having afterwards convoked a parliament,
caused the judicial deposition of the unfortunate Edward, who a short time
after suffered a most cruel death. Edward III. who succeeded his father,
avenged him by having Mortimer, the lover of the queen, hanged, and by
shutting the queen herself up for the rest of her days; but that did not prevent
him from taking advantage of the pretended rights which she had given him
to the throne of France, to kindle a violent war against Philip de Valois,
successor of Charles the Fair, which put France within an inch of her downfall.

Isabella of Bavaria, mother of Charles VII., was angry with her son, chiefly
because this young prince, having discovered in a certain church some money
she had hidden there to satisfy her passions, had used it to assist the needs of
the State. It is said that her husband, in a lucid moment, having surprised
her with one of her paramours, had him sewed in a sack and thrown into the
Seine. She was imprisoned in a stronghold, but she found the means of calling
to her succour the Duke of Burgundy and to interest him in her rescue. He
rescued her and formed with her a league in which the King of England was
concerned. Such were the three women without honour and without virtue,
upon whose rights the English based their claims to France.

ments. Her meagre instruction did not enable her to distinguish its nature from the more modern ideas which were imparted to her. The Virgin Mary, with whose devotion she was inspired, was for her only a fairy more sympathetic and more powerful than the others; she had often invoked her, in the ruins of an old chapel, hidden in the woods, and asked her to make her virtuous and strong.

This habit of Joan of Arc, which had taken root in her childhood, remained with her when, to help her parents, she was forced to go into service in a hostelry in Vaucouleurs. She went as often as she could to visit her cherished chapel, placing flowers there and offering her prayer. Her position at the hostelry permitted her to see and hear many of the travellers; she heard their narratives regarding the misfortunes of France and the deplorable condition into which King Charles VII. was reduced, at that time banished and a fugitive, wandering over the ruins of his own kingdom, which a foreign regent possessed, in the name of an infant of nine months; for in the space of a few years the King of England had died as well as the unfortunate Charles VI. These tales, often accompanied with sighs, imprecations, or tears, electrified the young heroine; she felt her heart beat with indignation and her brow redden with anger; she asked why it was that no man was found strong enough to fight these insolent foreigners and replace the legitimate king upon the throne. She was answered that a great many brave ones had died in the battles of Agincourt, Cravant, and Verneuil, and that the others, besieged in Orleans, the last resource of the French, might be considered prisoners. If this city were taken, she was told, there would be no more hope, and it would be taken unless there were a miracle. "This miracle will take place!" she cried with an inspired voice. They looked at her with astonishment; but how dare to hope for a miracle?

In the meanwhile she carried the flowers to her solitary chapel and prayed there with a fervour so earnest that, one day, drawn on by the impulse of her devotion, she swooned without losing consciousness, and seemed to feel the air agitated and driven back against her by the movement of a celestial being lowering himself majestically on two extended wings: "Joan," he said, "thou asketh who can save France and her king; it will be thou. Go, don the cuirass and seize the sword; thou wilt triumph in the name of God who sent me; the siege of Orleans will be raised and thou wilt crown thy king at Rheims." At these words, it seemed to her that the divine messenger directed towards her an undulating flame which attached itself to her heart and burned her with an ardour heretofore unknown. All disappeared.

The young Voluspa arose from her ecstasy, transported with joy and full of a prophetic hope; she told to whom would listen, the vision which she had had, and declared without any mystery, as though inspired by heaven, that she would change the destiny of France. The firmness of her voice, the divine fire which shone in her eyes showed neither deceit nor madness; the force of truth made itself felt. She was taken to a venerable priest, who, having heard her, did not hesitate to present her to Seigneur de Beaudricourt, then governor of Vaucouleurs. This seigneur, after having questioned her many times, decided to have her conducted to the king. At the moment when she appeared before the monarch, he had just received news that the city of Orleans, although defended by the brave Count de Dunois, was on the point of surrendering; he was already planning his retreat into Dauphiny; the words of the heroine, the firm and modest manner with which she explains her mission, impress and reassure him; he feels in her presence a hope which he believed lost, reborn; he commands that arms be given her and that her orders should be obeyed. She hastens to victory. In a few days, she is beneath the walls of Orleans; she forces the English to raise the siege, attacks their General Talbot at Patai, puts him to rout, hastens back to the king, and conducts him in triumph into Rheims, carrying herself the oriflamme, and has him crowned in the midst of the acclamations of his army; thus was the oracle of Vaucouleurs accomplished.[1]

Joan, who saw her mission happily fulfilled, wished to retire. Timid outside of battle, modest at the height of glory, without letting herself become dazzled by the adorations of a people drunk with joy, who came in crowds before her, censer in hand, she asked only to return to her humble hermitage. Charles opposed it. In yielding to the wishes of the king, she gave herself to another destiny than hers: could she expect to be deceived? No, without doubt; the king, who abandoned her, was abandoned by Providence. France was saved because it had to be; but the ungrateful monarch, who disregarded the hand which had protected him, did not enjoy his triumph; he perished miserably and after a little time his line became extinct.[2]

---

[1] When Joan of Arc was presented to the king, this prince, undecided as to what he should do, thought it fitting to have this inspired maid examined by the *parlement* of Poitiers. At first she was asked to perform miracles to confirm her mission. "I have not come," she replied, "to perform miracles; but lead me to Orleans and I will give you positive signs of my mission."—"But," they replied, "if God wishes to save France, what is the need of armies and battles?"—"The men of arms," she added, "will fight for my God and the Lord will give the victory."

When she returned from Poitiers the king received her with the greatest honours. He had a complete suit of armour made for her, except the sword, for which she sent to Sainte-Catherine de Fier-Bois, in the tomb of an old knight, where it was found as she had described it without ever having seen it. In appearing before Orleans to raise the siege, she had this remarkable letter written to the English, which she herself threw into their entrenchments on the tip of an arrow: "Listen to the message of God and *la Pucelle*, English, who have no right to the kingdom of France, God orders you by me *Jeanne la Pucelle* to evacuate our forts and retire."

[2] After the coronation of Charles VII. at Rheims, Joan asked earnestly permission to go. "Henceforth," she said, "I shall not regret to die." And when asked if she had some revelation concerning death, replied: "No; God commanded me only to raise the siege of Orleans and to conduct the king to Rheims. . . . The king will give me pleasure in restoring me to my parents and to my former condition." The king detained her only to abandon her

Never perhaps had Providence manifested its power in a less equivocal manner; one might say that the arm which it extended over France was shown without disguise. The laws of necessity and liberty which she had imposed upon herself had been suspended; this was evident and France did not feel it. France saw her wonderful heroine given over by a calamitous destiny to the Duke of Luxembourg, sold by this wretch to the English, dragged to Rouen before an iniquitous tribunal, to perish in flames like an infamous sorceress inspired by the infernal Spirit.[1] France saw it and

---

afterwards in a cowardly manner. It is well known how, tormented by continual terrors, this prince let himself die of hunger at the age of fifty-eight, for fear of being poisoned by his son Louis XI., in 1461. His line ended in 1498 in the person of Charles VIII.

[1] Joan of Arc was wounded and taken prisoner while defending Compiègne. Her place was no longer there. Her warlike mission had been fulfilled at Rheims, as she herself said. It appears certain that the University of Paris presented a petition against her, accusing her of heresy and magic, because she believed in fairies. This divine heroine was judged at Rouen, by a bishop of Beauvais, named Cauchon, five other French bishops, a single English bishop, assisted by a Dominican monk, vicar of the Inquisition, and by the doctors of the University. Thus it was the Franks, Burgundians or Normans, who were the most guilty, since they sold to the English innocent blood. The duke of Bedford said to these iniquitous judges: "The King of England has paid dearly for her and he wishes that she be burned." The English who acted openly in this affair as implacable and obstinate enemies, were cruel, but not traitors and vile as the judges whom they influenced.

The divine heroine could not at first, however, be condemned to the stake; she was simply to fast on bread and water in a perpetual prison, as a *superstitious person*, a *diviner of the devil*, a *blasphemer of God* and *His saints*, erring many times in her faith in Christ. But soon accused of having again resumed her male clothes, that had been left to tempt her, her execrable judges delivered her to the secular arm to be burned alive May 30, 1431. She had raised the siege of Orleans May 8, 1429, and crowned the king at Rheims July 17, the same year. The manuscript procedure of Joan of Arc still exists in the original. One notices in it that the responses of the heroine are always equally prudent, truthful, and firm. She said several times to her judges: "Good Fathers, consider now the burden you are imposing upon yourself." Questioned as to why she had dared to assist at the coronation of Charles with her standard, she replied: "It is just, that the one who has taken part in a labour should have the honour." When asked by what sorcery she had inspired the soldiers, replied: "'Look,'" I said, "'enter bravely among the English,' and I

could allow it! Charles did not make a movement, did not risk a hair of his head, did not cover the fields of Rouen with dead bodies to save her! And France still dared to complain of the evils which she endured, which she still endures because of this horrible outrage! But Providence is just; the pest which ravaged Athens avenged the death of Socrates; the Jews, dispersed over the face of the earth for eighteen centuries, still expiate their cowardly deicide; France, retarded in her career, delivered to endless evils, has been obliged to be absolved of the death of Joan of Arc. The fellowship of peoples is not a chimera. It is not with impunity that nations can kill their great men or with their hands blindly break the instruments of Providence. The reaction is in that case always equal to the action and the chastisement equal to the forfeit. It is in vain that one says that individuals are, for the most part, innocent; this is not true: there are no innocents other than those who are opposed to crime; those who allow it, share it.

---

myself entered first." Accused of having profaned the names of Jesus and Mary, she replied ingenuously: "It is from your clergymen that I have learned to make use of them, not only for my standard, but even for the letters which I have written." As for her visions, she did not once contradict them: "Whether they be good or evil spirits, it is true," she said, "that they have appeared to me."

CHAPTER VII

CAUSES OF A DOUBLE MOVEMENT OF THE WILL IN THE POLITI-
CAL SYSTEM AND IN THE CULT—FIFTEENTH REVOLUTION
—DISCOVERY OF THE NEW WORLD

PROVIDENCE had wished France to be saved; she was
saved; but the French, guilty of horrible ingratitude
towards it, had to suffer and did suffer. All that pertained
to the feudal system was particularly encumbered with
evils. The sanguinary reign of Louis XI. gave her a mortal
blow from which she never recovered. This terrible reign
left in the minds of all a profound impression, which could
not be effaced by the brilliant but useless reigns of Charles
VIII., Louis XII., and Francis I. At this time an immense
movement took place in Europe. If Providence could have
been recognized in it, the dawn of grandeur and of felicity
would have opened for her. But as we have seen, France
eminently favoured, voluntarily closed her eyes to its light
and her victorious monarch, attributing all his success to
his star, abandoning the wonderful instrument which had
procured it for him, occupied himself only with prophetic
or volitive objects. After having established a corps of
permanent troops, after having founded by his own will
the levying of taxes, he dominated by means of both the
barons and the peoples and annihilated the sacerdotal
supremacy by the promulgation of a schismatic act
called *Pragmatic Sanction*. All these means which he

bequeathed to his successors were so many weapons which they abused.

Whereas the Will of Man received thus the laws of Destiny in France, they were also received in Italy. The pontifical throne dishonoured by Alexander VI. had become, under Julius II., a purely monarchical throne. This pope had been only an audacious warrior and able politician. Leo X., who succeeded him, was a splendid monarch, a generous king, protector of letters and of arts; but he was not a sovereign pontiff. Although he possessed virtues which placed him far above Borgia, the real truth must be stated: he had no more faith in the dogmas of his cult than the other. In general, the popes having become temporal sovereigns, unable as sovereign pontiffs to place themselves above the councils, they had done so as monarchs from the time of Eugene IV. and were accustomed, as other kings, to regard religion in general and that which they professed in particular, only as a necessary bridle, a political instrument, of which, by their position, they were declared trustees and governors. All the rigour which the greater part of them displayed against heretics and innovators, no longer had its source as formerly, in religious fanaticism, in holy zeal, respectable though blind, but only in the necessity of preserving the forms of a useful cult whose foundation they did not judge susceptible of examination. In ecclesiastical affairs all their maxims were fixed and invariable, because they had no aim except to preserve that which was, without seeking in the least to go deeply into it, and in this respect each new pontiff adopted, as far as the spiritual was concerned, the plan of his predecessor; but as to the temporal, on the contrary, each one had to yield to conditions, to trace a particular course, and often resort to ruse in order to supply the force which he lacked. Thus the court of the popes was regarded as the cradle of that modern policy which consists in finesse of negotiations and in astuteness of behaviour. There was almost nothing that this court did not attempt in this respect and if it did not ostensibly ally itself with the Mussulmans of Constantinople, there exist only too many proofs that it listened more than once to their propositions.

But what the court of Rome dared not do, at least openly, that of France did. This court, having lost sight of the real interests of Europe, thinking only of her own, united with the Turks and with the same pen with which she had made her alliance with the Swiss, signed her treaty with the Grand Sultan. Thus as I have already said, she united the fatality of Destiny to the force of Will and believed herself sufficiently skilful to maintain both and to master them equally. This boldness, which emptied upon France a deluge of evils under the reigns which followed that of Francis I., procured for her nevertheless a moment of splendour under that of Louis XIV., a splendour too soon dimmed even during the lifetime of this monarch and too dearly paid for by the humiliations which afflicted that of Louis XV. and the horrible misfortunes which terminated that of Louis XVI.

If we reflect a moment upon the situation of Europe, after, on one side, the Turks established in Constantinople had raised there an insurmountable barrier on the Asiatic side and, on the other, France, having annihilated the feudal system, had united in one single man, under Louis XI., only to form a monarchy almost despotic; one will feel that the Will of Man, whose essence is liberty, menaced on all sides with an absolute compression, must find ways to burst forth. Everywhere despotism tried to establish itself and with it, the necessity of Destiny. This inflexible Will just missed in France the most excellent occasion of becoming united with Providence; but Providence and Destiny displeased it equally. It rejected any sort of yoke and sought to submit all to its free will. In its constantly increasing distress, it considered a double movement whose means were chosen with an admirable art. On the one side, it roused the mercantile industry of the Italians and the Portuguese, which had been hindered by the conquests of the Turks in the East, and drove them to new discoveries in the West; on the other, it exalted the systematic pride of the English and German monks, offended by the arrogance of the ultra-popish, and excited them to submit to the examination of the reason of the dogmas which the popes had resolved to sustain. By the first means, it extended its domain and prepared places of refuge in case of defeat; by the second it engaged with the only weapons left to it, in a combat whose chances offered it advantages.

At the beginning of the fourteenth century, an inhabitant of the town of Amalfi in the kingdom of Naples, named *Flavio Giola*, had invented or rather renewed the use of the compass, and by means of this instrument as simple as sure, had made navigators able to undertake long voyages. Already the Portuguese had profited by it in crossing the Atlantic Ocean, on the bosom of which they discovered the island of Madeira and the Azores. They had crossed the equinoctial line and seen a new sky roll over their heads, whose constellations were unknown to them, when a Genoese named *Christopher Columbus*, hearing of their enterprises towards the South, imagined that sailing westward, following the course of the sun, he would undoubtedly find another continent. Genoa, his native country and the court of France, of whom it is claimed that he asked for ships to accomplish his hazardous scheme, rejected his proposition. Spain accepted it. He set sail August 3, 1492, and on Christmas day of the same year arrived at Haiti, today San Domingo. Soon the rumour of his discovery spread abroad and when, after having returned to Europe, Columbus undertook his second and third voyages, a crowd of adventurers of all nations followed him. Americus Vespucius, whose name was given to the New World which he did not discover[1]; Alvarez Cabral, who was the first to land on the

---

[1] This Americus Vespucius, who gave his name to America, passed into

shores of Brazil; Fernando Cortez and Pizarro, conquerors
of Mexico and Peru, were the most famous. Fortune did
not follow their success, in which Providence had not taken
part and they had not even the glory of it. Nearly all
perished miserably, and Columbus himself, persecuted by a
base intriguer named *Bobadilla*, sent back from Haiti as a
criminal, arrived in Spain loaded with chains. King Ferdinand set him at liberty, but without doing him justice,
which so angered Columbus that, when dying in sorrow a
short time after, he ordered that the chains with which he
had been burdened should be buried with him in his coffin.

---

that part of the world as an adventurer with a certain Ojeda, who, without
his consent, followed directly in the footsteps of Columbus. Americus was
a Florentine. He wrote an account of his voyage, and it was this account
written with elegance which gave him his reputation. Columbus, with all
his rights, failed before this skilful writer. Unjust posterity has not called
Columbia, as it ought, the fourth part of the world, which Columbus had discovered, but *America*. All that the impartial historian can do at present is,
in speaking of the entire hemisphere, to call it the *Columbian Hemisphere*,
as I have done.

CHAPTER VIII

THE new hemisphere which Columbus did not discover himself but rather caused to be discovered, was a new world relatively to the old, younger, more recently sprung from the depth of the waters, producing in the three kingdoms substances or beings upon which nature impressed visibly all the traits of youth. The general and geological forms disclosed a remarkable magnificence, but the vital principle little developed was still languishing. Mountains were higher than in the other hemisphere, rivers greater, lakes more numerous and more vast, and yet the vegetable kingdom lacked sap and vigour. There were no animals which could compare with those of the Old World. Even the lions and the tigers, or rather the pumas and the jaguars called by these names, had neither the intrepidity of those of Africa, nor their voracity. The climate was in no way like that of the other hemisphere. It was colder and more humid. Pliant and latescent vegetables, venomous reptiles, troublesome insects propagated there in abundance and with astonishing rapidity.

The soil but little productive and as though struck with a native impotence supported only a small number of inhabitants. At the time when Europeans first stepped foot

in this immense region, there were only two nations entirely
formed: that of Mexico and that of Peru. All the rest of
the continent was peopled with small independent tribes,
often at enormous distances from each other, destitute of
laws, art, and industry and, what is very remarkable, deprived
of the assistance of domestic animals. The two nations,
which had begun their career of civilization, had as yet
taken only the first steps. They had scarcely the first
features of the social state. They were infant peoples,
who, left to themselves, protected by Providence which
they were beginning to recognize, submitted to a Destiny
by no means rigorous, would have developed gradually
and would have succeeded in astonishing us perhaps by their
grandeur, if, too soon exposed to the fatal movement of the
European Will, they had not been crushed in their flower
and indeed long before they could have reached their zenith.

Can this cruel event be explained? Without doubt.
Up to this point I have not hesitated to give explanations,
and this one here cannot escape any more than the other
from the principles which I have laid down. I have often
said that the Will of Man, good or bad, is irrefragable and
that Providence cannot arrest its action without infringing
upon its own laws. But Destiny, which draws with it an
irresistible necessity, by its very essence opposes this action
and combats it. On whatever side the victory remains,
the result is always favourable to the end which Providence
has proposed; for it never can have anything but loss of
time or change of form. Besides, note this: whether Destiny
triumphs or the Will, neither of these two powers can triumph
without causing its opposite to be created instantly, that is,
without the victory of Will throwing a germ of a prophetic
event which will develop, or without the victory of Destiny
provoking a volitive cause which will have its effect.

Now, the Will, strongly restrained in Europe by Destiny,
escapes, and takes a course towards America which it cannot do without using instruments among men of volition,

in whose breast more or less violent passions were fermenting. If these men had been enlightened and moderate, they would have readily felt that their glory as well as their interest recommended them to care for the mild, timid people whom fate exposed to their arms; they would have seen that they could subdue them without destroying them and conquer America without ravaging it; but unfortunately it all happened otherwise. The Spaniards, whom the impressed movement hurled from one hemisphere to the other, were ignorant men, greedy and savage, who, long bent beneath the chains which adroit politics had given them, avenged themselves by falling with furor upon an infant people incapable of resisting them. Like wolves, after a long tormenting hunger, they precipitated themselves upon these weak sheep to devour them. They acted in a body as a single brigand acts when encountering a traveller in the depth of a wood: he kills him for his money. Providence cannot prevent this voluntary crime, when the Destiny of the traveller does not prevent it, unless through a miracle, which is repugnant to its laws; but it avenges it by attaching the punishment to the crime, as effect to cause. Thus the Spaniards in massacring the Americans committed a national crime, for which all the Spanish nation became responsible and had to expiate it. Remember here what I said in the beginning of this book, regarding the solidarity of the peoples. This solidarity extends throughout all generations and binds the children as well as the fathers, because in these cases the fathers do not differ from the children.

But perhaps an attentive reader and profound thinker will stop me at this point to say to me that, supposing the national crime be punished as the individual crime, he does not see what reparation, what good this chastisement procures, either to the people destroyed by savage conquerors or to the traveller killed by a brigand. To this I reply that I should have taken care not to write upon matters so arduous, if I had thought that a man in losing his life lost all, and that a people could be destroyed. I do not think this at all. I believe that individual or national existence is suspended by death or by destruction, but not destroyed. There is only, as I have recently said, loss of time or change of forms. What is but interrupted will begin again. I beg the reader to recall a comparison which I have already made.[1] I see an acorn which sprouts and which, if nothing stops its destiny, will produce an oak. My Will is opposed to this effect; I crush the acorn; the oak is interrupted. But have I destroyed, annihilated the principle which acted in the acorn? This is absurd; a new Destiny begins again for it. It becomes decomposed, enters into the elements and, insinuating itself again into the roots of the tree, mounts with the sap and reproduces an acorn similar to the first and stronger. What did I accomplish by my destructive action? Nothing at all with regard to the acorn; but much perhaps with regard to myself; especially if I did it with malice, envy, impatience, or with any other bad sentiment; for while I believed I was operating on the acorn, it was upon myself that I operated. This comparison, well understood, can solve many difficulties.

Let us return to the Americans. When the Spaniards encountered them they were still in the infancy of the social state; none of their faculties was wholly developed; they were weak physically as well as morally; it could be distinctly seen that they belonged to a race different from the White and the Black.[2] They belonged to the Red race but were

---

[1] In the Introductory Dissertation.

[2] At the time I am writing, America for more than three centuries has been known and frequented by Europeans who have worked great changes there, as much by the mingling of their own blood with that of the natives, as by that of the black people whom they have imported. They have also influenced much the two inferior kingdoms, the vegetable and animal, by cultivation and the cross-breeding of animals. So it is not in America itself that one can know what this country was before its discovery, but in the descriptions which were made of it at this time. The natives of the Columbian hemisphere had,

not pure. They were the result of a primal mixture at a very remote epoch when the White race did not yet exist and of a second mixture much less ancient when this race had existed for some time. These indigenous peoples had lost the trace of their origin; only a vague tradition survived amongst them which declared their ancestors descended from the highest mountains of that hemisphere. The Mexicans claimed that their first legislators came from a country situated at the north-east of their empire. If attention is given here, the two principal epochs of which I have spoken will be found in these two traditions; the first dates back to the disaster of Atlantis, whose memory is perpetuated among all nations; the second belongs to an emigration of the Borean Race which was effected from Iceland to Greenland and from Greenland to Labrador, as far as Mexico, traversing the countries which today bear the name of *Canada* and *Louisiana*. This second epoch is separated from the other by several thousand years.

The most authentic narrative which we have of the dis-

---

in general, a red-brown complexion inclining to copper. They were beardless, and with no other hair than their long black hair, coarse and thin. Their constitution was weak and without virile force. There were men who had milk in their breasts like women and who could in case of necessity have nursed their children. They ate little, endured fatigue with difficulty, and rarely attained old age. Their short and monotonous life was not exposed to any excess of violent passions. Ambition and love had but little value in their mind. Their virtues and their vices were likewise undeveloped. Their intellectual faculties had hardly attained a first development. In several tribes were individuals so destitute of foresight that they took no care for the morrow. The women were not very prolific, not much esteemed, and enjoyed no rights. In certain places their servitude was intolerable. With the exception of the two nations whose civilization was roughly sketched, the other tribes were in still the most savage condition, strangers to industry, and having only confused ideas of property. Among these tribes, those who lived by fishing were the most stupid; afterwards came the hunters whose instincts were more developed, but who were lazy and poisoned their arrows to hunt with more facility. Wherever farmers were, there civilization began. The entire hemisphere did not possess a herdsman. They had no domestic animals.

aster of Atlantis has been preserved by Plato, who attributes it, in his dialogue of *Timæus*, to an Egyptian priest discoursing at Saïs with Solon. This priest dates back the catastrophe of which he speaks to more than nine thousand years; which gives us an antiquity of about eleven thousand four hundred years.

The island of Atlantis was, according to him, greater than Africa and Asia together; it was situated in the Atlantic Ocean, facing the Pillars of Hercules. There were kings celebrated for their power who, not only reigned over this magnificent country, over all the adjacent islands, but even over a great part of Africa as far as Egypt and over all western Europe as far as Tyrrhene. They sought to enslave the rest of the Eastern hemisphere, when there came unexpectedly terrible earthquakes followed by a frightful deluge; the people opposite were all swallowed up in the abyss and in the space of a day Atlantis disappeared.

It is difficult not to recognize, in the description given by the priest at Saïs of this island greater than Africa and Asia, the Columbian hemisphere, situated exactly as he says, on the bosom of the sea, which we still name, from this famous island, *Atlantic Ocean*, and opposite the Pillars of Hercules; thus it is certain that the new continent called today *America* is no other than this island of which antiquity has related so many wonders; only it was not represented then as we see it in our day; it was spread out much more towards the Austral pole, to which it perhaps inclined, and less towards the Boreal pole. The Austral Race had dominated here as the Borean Race dominates our hemisphere today. The race was red; it had civilized the Black Race and as the Egyptian priest said, it supported numerous colonies in Europe and Asia which belonged to them almost entirely. At this epoch, that is to say, about twelve thousand years ago, the terrestrial globe was not in the position where we see it; the Boreal pole instead of being about twenty-three degrees higher, was, on the contrary, lower in the same proportion and allowed the Austral pole to dominate; so that the mass of waters that weigh today upon this pole weighed upon the opposite pole, and covered chiefly the northern part of the Columbian hemisphere, perhaps to the fiftieth degree. It is equally presumable that upon the Eastern hemisphere the waters extended to the sixtieth and covered all the northern part of the ancient continent from Norway to Kamchatka.

At the most flourishing moment of the Atlantic Empire and when this Empire was about to achieve the conquest of the world, a horrible catastrophe took place. Length of time has been able to conceal the causes, but has not hindered the rumour from being handed down to us. There exists almost no nation which has not perpetuated the gloomy memory in lugubrious ceremonies; it is narrated in all the sacred books; and the very traces which have remained, imprinted on the surface of the globe and even in its interior, announce everywhere a frightful upheaval which proves sufficiently in the eyes of thoughtful men that these tales are not illusions.

Philosophers and naturalists of all centuries searching the physical causes which could have brought about these crises of nature called *deluges* or *cataclysms* have found them either inadequate or visibly erroneous. Theosophists have all agreed on the metaphysical cause; they have said that it was the absolute perversion of the peoples and their entire abandonment of Providence that brought it to pass. Moses, who speaks of it as a calamitous possibility, is precise on this point. Pythagoras and Plato do not differ from Kong-tzée or from Meng-tzée, and Krishna agrees with Odin. But although the metaphysical primordial cause may be admitted, there remains none the less, great difficulties respecting the secondary and physical causes.

However, I must say here an important thing, of which I shall speak elsewhere at length; it is, that there are two kinds of deluges which must not be confused: the universal

Deluge, the one of which Moses speaks under the name of *Maboul;* the one which the Brahmans know under the name of *Dinapralayam* is a crisis of nature which puts an end to its action; it is a renewal by absolute dissolution of created beings. The description of this deluge, the knowledge of its causes and of its effects, belong to cosmogony[1]; this is not the place to speak of it, since it does not influence alone the Social State of Man by interrupting it but by destroying it altogether. The deluges of the second kind are those which occasion only an interruption in the general course of things by partial inundations more or less considerable. Among these cataclysms the one that destroyed Atlantis is the most terrible, since it submerged an entire hemisphere and caused a devastating flood to pass over the other, which laid it waste. The savants, who have occupied themselves searching for the cause, have not found it, as I have said, because they had not the requisite data for this and, furthermore, they were so prejudiced that they regarded it from a viewpoint either too remote or too near; as when they contented themselves with the eruption of a volcano, an earthquake, the overflowing of a lake, an inland sea, or indeed when they accused the tail of a comet of this catastrophe. I am drawn on to unveil entirely this natural cause, of which I have just allowed a glimpse in speaking of the earlier condition of the globe. I could not give now the geological proofs because they would lead me into details too foreign to this work; but if the geologists wish to examine attentively the configuration of the sides of the two hemispheres and the movement which the currents of the sea still preserve, they will feel that I have spoken the truth.

The frightful cataclysm that submerged Atlantis was caused by a sudden movement of the terrestrial globe, which, suddenly raising the Boreal pole, which had become lowered, caused it to take a contrary position to what it had formerly.

[1] I shall speak of this in the *Commentaire* which I am planning on the *Sepher* of Moses and principally on the ten chapters of the *Bereshith.*

In this movement, which perhaps had many oscillations, the mass of waters, which had been upon this pole, rolled with violence towards the Austral pole, returned to the Boreal pole, and back again many times towards the opposite pole, where it finally became fixed, overpowered with its weight. The earthwork gave way in many places, particularly where it covered caverns and deep anfractuosities and, in falling, opened immense abysses where the waves rushed furiously, engulfing the débris which they had drawn after them and the multitude of victims whom they had deprived of life. The Eastern Hemisphere resisted longer and was only washed, so to speak, by the waves which crossed over it without stopping; but the other was everywhere sunk and covered with stagnant waters which remained there a long time. All the Austral lands, where Atlantis properly so-called was, disappeared. At the opposite pole, the Borean lands emerged from the depths of the waters and became the cradle of the White or Borean Race, whence we issued. Thus it was to the disaster of Atlantis that we owe in a way our existence. The Black Race, that I have named *Sudeen*, of African origin, being born, as I have said, in the neighbourhood of the equinoctial line, suffered much from this catastrophe, but infinitely less than the Red or Austral Race which perished almost entirely. Only a few men, whom a fortunate destiny found upon the Appalachian Mountains, the Cordillera, or the Tapayas were able to escape from the destruction. The Mexicans, Peruvians, and Brazilians had a special veneration for these mountains. They had a vague memory that they had been a refuge for their ancestors· It is said that still in our day the savages of Florida make a pilgrimage four times a year to Mount Olaymi, one of the highest of the Appalachians, to offer a sacrifice to the sun, in memory of this event.

CHAPTER IX

CONQUESTS OF THE SPANIARDS AND THEIR CRIMES IN AMERICA —SETTLEMENT OF THE PORTUGUESE IN ASIA— GENERAL RESULTS

BACON believed, as I do, that America had been part of the ancient Atlantis. He makes it clearly understood in his *Atlantida Nova*. He said that the inhabitants of this part of the world were once very powerful and that they tried to subjugate the ancient continent. After the submersion of their empire a few scattered men saved themselves upon the summits of the mountains. These men, he adds, rapidly degenerating, forgot all the arts and became savages. They lived for a long time isolated and without laws and were only united when the plains were uncovered and they were able to inhabit them. Boulanger, who has made great researches in this regard, thinks with just reason that after the loss of Atlantis the people of this hemisphere who survived fell into a stupor and wandered for a long time without daring to found a settlement; he believes that the savage life was the result of the terror imprinted by this event and was the fruit of isolation and ignorance. Many of the savants have since expanded and commented upon these ideas which are only a renewing of those that Plato had received directly from the Egyptians and which he admirably described in his *Book of Laws*. The men, said this philosopher, who escaped from the universal desolation were for the most part herdsmen, inhabiting the mountains, deprived of education, where all the discoveries in art, politics, and sciences were unknown; they were lost and not the slightest vestige remained of them. The most flourishing cities situated in the plains and on the borders of the sea had been carried away with their inhabitants. Everywhere was a picture of vast solitude. The immense country was without inhabitants. When two men encountered each other upon these gloomy ruins, they wept with emotion and with joy.

The Sudeen Race was, as I have observed, the one which remained the strongest on the Eastern Hemisphere. It propagated there the first and seized the dominion after having passed through all the phases of the Social State and having revived in its entirety the mass of human attainments. I have told how it encountered the Borean Race, still in the childhood of civilization, and I have clearly shown the reasons which prevented it from destroying the Boreans. I have even touched, incidentally, upon some of the opposed reasons which later caused the ruin of the Austral Race, when the European encountered on the Columbian hemisphere the débris which was beginning to take shape again. The principal of these reasons was that the great societies were already fixed and had constituted considerable empires, before having acquired the strength and necessary attainments for preserving them in case of attack. I am sure that if these empires, thus constituted, could have raised themselves to the highest degree of perfection, they would have offered to the world a spectacle as novel as it would have been interesting; but it was necessary for them to remain for many centuries unknown to Europeans. Providence, which had furnished the principle of these brilliant associations which were formed in Mexico and Peru, and Destiny, which had protected them in silence, had not opposed it; but the Will of Man, driven to seek outside of the old hemisphere a refuge against the absolute servitude by which it was menaced, dreamed of a New World and discovered it. At first it could only put ahead men of an audacious and passionate character, of whom the greater part, deprived of learning and of true morals, showed themselves as ferocious as greedy, and changed into base profit the noblest motives which guided them and which they did not comprehend.

It is impossible to read the details of the cruelties practised in America by the first Europeans who penetrated into this country without experiencing a feeling of horror. From their entrance into Haiti, and even under Columbus, the Spaniards conducted themselves like tyrants. In their fury they dared to use dogs trained to fight and to devour the unfortunate natives and regulate the grades of these animals according to the amount of ferocity which they could detect in them. Undoubtedly they believed, in advance, what some writers, fanatics or liars, said afterwards to excuse them, that the Americans were not men and that they could be massacred with impunity. When Columbus discovered Haiti it had a million inhabitants; fifteen years after only sixty thousand, and this number reduced to fifteen thousand disappeared utterly after some years.[1] To remedy this depopulation they deceived forty thousand unfortunates of the Lucayos Islands that they transported

---

[1] The Spaniards joined to force the most atrocious perfidy to repress the revolts which their extortion brought about. The unfortunate Anacoana who ruled over the western part of Haiti was seized during a festival which his blind bounty had prepared for these tigers and, conducted to the town of San Domingo, was hanged there. A man named *Ovando* was the scoundrel in charge of this cowardice. It is good that his name has passed to posterity branded with the hot iron of reprobation. Acting from the same motive I shall name the infamous Velasquez who, having made prisoner the Cacique Hatuey in the island of Cuba, condemned him to be burned alive. A fanatic monk approaching the unfortunate cacique, whilst he was tied to the stake, counselled him to embrace the Christian religion so as to enter paradise: "Are there any Spaniards there?" asked Hatuey. "Yes, good ones are there." "That is enough," added the cacique, "I do not wish to go to a place where I shall meet a single one of these brigands."

to Haiti to suffer the same mortality. Las Casas, witness
of these atrocities, after having made some vain efforts to
oppose them, misled by his humanity, counselled buying the
Blacks in Africa to furnish the Spanish Colonies in America.
This idea was adopted and the fatal commerce established
by an edict of Charles V.

It should be observed that the Genoese, then constituted
in a sort of emporocratic republic, were the first to be entrusted with this odious monopoly. Thus there was not
enough oppression in one entire hemisphere; the other also
had to furnish slaves and a decrepit people had to come to
share the adversity of an infant people; but in the movements
which things had taken in America this was indispensable.
Since the Will meditated an establishment there, and
dragged with it the spirit of emporocracy, which is only a
degenerate republicanism, it was necessary for slavery to be
introduced so as to evade absolute misery for a part of the
people; for this is true that every emporocratic republic,
where slavery is not established, will have.to found its grandeur upon the absolute misery of a part of the population.
It is only by means of slavery that liberty can be sustained.
Republics are oppressive by nature. When oppression,
that is to say, slavery or misery, is not manifested in its
midst, as happened in Holland, it is manifested at a distance;
and this amounts to the same thing. Slaves are always
necessary to a republic, especially if emporocracy dominates
there; whether the slaves are in their midst or beyond their
precincts, it matters not; slavery always has been and with
it all the harm that it entails.

After the Spaniards had ravaged the islands which surrounded the Columb an hemisphere towards the east,
they turned their efforts to the continent itself, discovered
the two sole empires which existed there, and took possession
of them. The conquests of Mexico and of Peru seemed pro-
digies of audacity when one considers the Mexicans and
Peruvians as already established peoples, capable of the

same resistance; but this was not so; they were infant peoples of whom one could easily become master with some force and much perfidy.

The beginning of the Empire of Mexico does not go back beyond six centuries before the arrival of the Spaniards. One cannot doubt, after examining their laws and their cult, that they had received their religious and civil legislation from the north of Europe. When, it is impossible to say. All the documents upon which a chronology might have been founded have been destroyed.[1] It appears probable that this was the time when the Scandinavians, under the name of *Normans*, sailed over all the seas; that one of their vessels coming from Iceland was driven by a tempest and touched upon the shores of Canada or Florida. Be that as it may, according to tradition at this time there appeared a man, favoured by heaven, who engaged several wandering tribes to settle in the country of Anabac, the most fertile and most pleasant in the land and there to establish themselves under a regular government. This state, at first somewhat limited, extended gradually by the agglomeration of several tribes who became united and formed finally a flourishing empire, of which Montezuma, dethroned by Fernando Cortez, was the ninth emperor. The city of Mexico, which became the centre of this empire, was founded about the thirteenth century. This city was quite large and thickly populated, but the structures, even the greatest, such as temples and palaces, were badly built and indicated an architecture still in its infancy. The religion, gloomy and ferocious as that of the ancient Celts, permitted human sacrifices. Forms of the feudal system were found in the government. The emperor had under his dominion thirty nobles of highest rank each of whom had in his own territory about one hundred thousand citizens, among whom

---

[1] It was *Jean de Zumaraga*, a French monk, first bishop of Mexico, who ordered that all the archives of the Mexicans, consisting of hieroglyphic pictures, should be thrown into the flames.

were three hundred nobles of an inferior class. The caste of the *Mayeques* or Mayas was similar to that of our ancient serfs. In the cities as in the country the ranks were distinguished, and each was set apart according to his profession.

The Mexicans had only a crude knowledge of nearly all the arts without perfecting any. Their writing consisted only of hieroglyphic pictures. They had nevertheless a sort of post by means of which the orders of the Emperor or important news was sent forward from the centre to the extremities of the Empire. Their year was divided into eighteen months of twenty days each, to which they added five complementary days, which indicates some astronomical knowledge. Their agriculture, however, was imperfect. As they did not understand money, the taxes were paid in kind. Each thing, according to its kind was arranged in storehouses, from which they were drawn for the service of the state. The right of territorial property was known in Mexico; every free man possessed there a certain extent of land; but the social ties, still uncertain, showed as I have said, a social state at its dawn.

The Empire of Peru, equally in its infancy, offered, however, more agreeable forms than that of Mexico. The more gentle religion, the more brilliant cult, gave more charm and *éclat* to the government. The Peruvians worshipped the sun and the moon and paid certain homage to their ancestors which indicated that their legislator was of Asiatic origin. According to the Peruvian traditions, this legislator, named *Manco-Capac*, appeared with his wife *Mama-Ocollo* upon the shores of Lake Titicaca and announced himself as the son of the Sun. He assembled the wandering tribes and persuaded them to study agriculture which he taught them. After this first step, the most difficult of all, he initiated them into useful arts, gave them laws, and had himself recognized as their theocratic sovereign. It was on religion that he founded every social edifice. The Peruvian Inca was not only legislator and monarch, he was revered as son of the Sun. His person and his family were sacred. The princes of the theocratic family espoused their own sisters to avoid mixture with any other blood, as the Egyptian monarchs had done in former times.

When the Spaniards arrived, the twelfth monarch after Manco-Capac was upon the throne. He was named *Huana-Capac ;* he died and left a son named *Ata-hualpa,* to whom he wished to give only the half of his empire, the kingdom of Quito, declaring his brother Huascar, whom he loved dearly, heir of the kingdom of Cuzco. This unprecedented division caused a general discontent and kindled a civil war, of which the perfidious Pizarro took advantage to offer aid to Ata-hualpa, to approach him and carry him off from the midst of his subjects, which was done in such an odious manner that one cannot recall it without indignation. A priest, named *Valverde,* loaned his services for this execrable act and dared even to confirm the sentence of death which was pronounced by the ferocious Spaniard against this unfortunate monarch. Ata-hualpa was strangled in Peru by special grace instead of being burned alive as the sentence ordered. In Mexico, Fernando Cortez, after having forced Montezuma's own subjects to massacre him, had his successor Guatimozin placed upon live coals to force him to disclose the place where his treasures were hidden. [1]

The empires of Mexico and Peru were thus conquered and subjected to the Crown of Spain, but conquests bought with such crimes could bring with them neither glory nor happiness.

The Portuguese as cruel as the Spaniards were not more fortunate. Their immense discoveries in Asia gave them only a moment of splendour and of force to make them feel a little later their weakness and their obscurity. Conquests whose sole motive is greed for riches produce no glory. I

---

[1] It was in this cruel position that Guatimozin said to his minister, who suffered the same torment and from whom the pain drew forth groans, these words which show a great soul: "And I, am I on a bed of roses?"

have mentioned how the Portuguese had been driven to seek a new route to the Indies; the one which Venice formerly followed was entirely obstructed by the successes of the Ottomans. After having passed the equinoctial line and observed the stars of the Austral pole,[1] they cleared at last the Cape of Storms which they named *Cape of Good Hope.* Commanded by Vasco de Gama and by Alphonse d'Albuquerque they fought successively the kings of Calcutta, Ormus, Siam, and defeated the fleet of the Soudan of Egypt. They captured the city of Goa and soon after took possession of Malacca, Aden, and Ormus. They established themselves all along the shores of the island of Ceylon, pushed their colonies into Bengal, trafficked in all the Indian archipelago, and founded the city of Macao on the frontiers of China. In less than fifty years they discovered more than five thousand leagues of coast, were the masters of commerce from the Atlantic Ocean to the Ethiopian Sea, and traded in everything useful, rare, pleasing, and brilliant which terrestrial nature produces. They overthrew the fortunes of Venice by spreading throughout Europe at much cheaper cost all necessary or precious objects and eclipsed the glory of that emporocratic aristocracy, whose power was annihilated forever. The route from the Tagus to the Ganges became frequented, and the discovery of Japan seemed to be the climax of the grandeur of Portugal. All this occurred in the first half of the sixteenth century.

These discoveries, these conquests made in both hemispheres, the immense riches which they procured, far from enriching the Spaniards and the Portuguese, finally impoverished them; for in exploiting at a distance mines of

[1] It is a remarkable thing that the famous Italian poet, Dante, had spoken more than a century before of these stars which rule over this pole: "I turned to the right," he said in the First Canto of his *Purgatory*, "and observing the other pole, I saw four stars, which have been known only in the first ages of the world." That is to say, at the epoch when the Austral pole dominated the horizon, before the disaster of Atlantis.

gold and silver, going in search of diamonds and pearls, they neglected the real mines and the real treasures of industry which are agriculture and the work of the manufacturer. The colonies of Asia, those of Mexico, Peru, and Brazil had depopulated the Spanish; so that after the death of Sebastian and that of the old cardinal—who had succeeded to the throne of Portugal when this kingdom fell into the hands of Philip II., King of Spain, at the close of the sixteenth century, making the monarch apparently the most powerful of the globe, since he dominated the two hemispheres and as the sun, according to his haughty expression, never set upon his states—one can see that this grandeur was illusory and had never been raised for him; this is what I wish to have clearly understood. It was by no means the grandeur of Spain that the Will of Man had in view in the movement which it had aroused there. This became, I think, quite obvious when in the coincident movement in morals, operated in Germany by means of Luther, one saw several miserable revolted provinces resisting this formidable colossus and consolidating their revolt by an emporocratic confederation which braved all his efforts. Holland, thus constituted, took possession of all the conquests of the Portuguese with a remarkable facility. England, a short time after having entered the same movement, dominated Spain after having resisted her, and threw into septentrional America a germ of emporocracy destined to invade the whole hemisphere, reacting sharply upon her mother country and menacing Europe with a complete upheaval. Thus the Will of Man, succeeding in the depths of his designs, escaped from Destiny which thought to have crushed it and always indomitable prepared itself for new combats.

CHAPTER X

SCHISM OF LUTHER—HOW CHARLES V. WAS ABLE TO ARREST IT

A LL those who have written the history of modern
nations have been struck by the grand spectacle
which Europe presented at the beginning of the sixteenth
century, but no one has thought to explain why this great
spectacle ended everywhere in catastrophes. The new
world, it is true, was discovered and conquered, but it was
devastated. The old continent saw extraordinary men
born in nearly all the races, but these men disturbed it
instead of strengthening it and inflamed it instead of enlightening it. Italy gloried in Leo X., and this sovereign
pontiff saw a formidable schism created under his pontificate, which rent the Christian Church. Charles V. and
Francis I. were great princes; they brought only misfortune
to the states which they had governed. Luther and Calvin
were men of genius; their genius produced only calamitous
divisions, wars, massacres, and persecutions. Whence came
this contradiction? From the constant struggles between
Will and Destiny, Liberty and Necessity, in the absence of
Providence which neither of the two would recognize.

Before Columbus had discovered the New World, the
possibility of its discovery was not believed; the existence
of this New World was denied; those who admitted it were
anathematized. Before Luther had drawn half of Europe
into his schism, such a revolution seemed so improbable

359

that his predictions were mocked; he was not even considered
worthy of the stake where Savanarola, John Huss, Jerome
of Prague, Arnold of Brescia, and many others, had perished.
Pope Leo X., who had just been raised to the pontificate at
the age of thirty-six, promised a magnificent reign to Europe;
a descendant of the Medicis of Florence, he had all their
virtues and all their faults; he protected artists and savants;
he was a generous, noble, sincere friend; he could be an
accomplished prince; but he did not believe in the dogmas
of his cult and therefore was a bad pontiff.   His magnificence
was the pretext rather than the cause of the schism; he
wished to finish the Basilica of St. Peter commenced by
Julius II. and not having enough money for this expense,
he imagined that he could put a tax upon the consciences and
sell indulgences throughout Christendom as had been done
already.   He could have done much better no doubt had
he taken a more honest course and said openly to the Christians that their sovereign pontiff, being in need of a certain
sum to raise a magnificent palace to the Prince of the Apostles,
asked of each one a slight contribution; but this course
would have been contrary to the spirit of a cult which
preached humility.   One might say, What is the use of raising a palace to Cephas the poor fisherman?   It was necessary to find an expedient and adopt a ruse according to the
method of the Court of Rome forced by her position to be
always in contradiction to herself.   This ruse, which at any
other time would not even have been perceived, or having
been, would have passed as a mere trifle, was considered
an enormous crime and treated with unparalleled severity.

It is true that John Huss and particularly Wyclif had
prepared the minds for this insult; the Hussites in Bohemia
and the Lollards in England were heard declaiming against
the authority of the popes, declaring that neither patriarchs,
nor archbishops, nor bishops should have after the Evangel-
ist any pre-eminence over other priests or any different power;
that the riches which they possessed were usurpations of

which justice wished that they should be deprived; that kings owed nothing to the holy seat and that the holy seat could exercise no jurisdiction over them or their kingdoms; as to the dogmas, that it was certain that the substance of the bread and wine remained after the consecration and that the body of Jesus Christ is in this substance only as the fire is in the red-hot iron; both exist together without any transubstantiation from the iron by the fire.

Luther then in preaching this doctrine said nothing new. In attacking the authority of the popes, the forms of worship, the monastic vows, the integrity of the dogmas, he only repeated what others had said before him, but he repeated it under very different conditions. It was not he who created the movement, it was the movement which created him. Note well this decisive point, judicious reader, and you will realize for the first time, perhaps, that which happens so often, when a very ordinary man succeeds where superior men lose. Luther was assuredly not worth as much as John Huss or Jerome of Prague. He had neither the austere virtue of the former nor the remarkable talents of the latter.[1] He was a man of passionate character, ardent, of a genius somewhat elevated, but without dignity; speaking with enthusiasm, but writing without method and without talent, and this shows that he felt keenly and thought with difficulty. He caused strong emotion, but minds were already stirred. He himself was astonished at the effects he produced. How many times, thinking he had gone too far, would he not have liked to stop! But once launched on the career, there was no time to reflect upon the consequences. All the fruit which he drew from his internal combats was great mental fatigue, which he attributed afterwards to the infernal spirit.

As early as the year 1516 and before the publication of

---

[1] It is said that Jerome of Prague displayed before the Council of Constance, where he was condemned with his friend John Huss, an eloquence unknown at that time. He spoke like Socrates and died with the same firmness.

the indulgences in Germany, Luther had announced his opinions as conforming with those of John Huss; this publication only served him as a pretext to spread them with more *éclat*. In the meantime Leo X., indifferent to the attacks of this obscure monk whom he regarded as an ignorant and harmless fanatic, scorned his predictions, continued his works, and turned away his eyes from the too manifest scandal which the sacerdotal body caused by the luxury which it displayed and the indolence into which it was fallen. Only a violent revolution could give him back a little of his energy. Luther provokes this revolution. Supported by the protection of Frederick, Elector of Saxony,[1] he goes ahead; he makes the crimes of Alexander Borgia and the fits of passion of Julius II. fall upon the prodigalities and pleasures of Leo de' Medici. The Pope condemns him and summons him to the next council; the Pope anathematizes him; he retaliates by publicly burning the bull of excommunication at Wittenberg. From that time Luther becomes a powerful and formidable man; his maxims spread. Zwingli, curé of Zurich in Switzerland, adopts them and deduces from them new results. He changes entirely the forms of worship, abolishes the offering of Mass, and no longer sees in the sacrament of the Eucharist anything but a commemorative ceremony. The Senate of Zurich assembles and declares itself for reform. Berne does the same. Soon the majority of Switzerland is influenced and joins Saxony, Wittenberg, and other parts of Germany, already schismatical.

Emperor Charles V. summons Luther to come to give account of his conduct, in his presence, at the Imperial Diet of Worms. Luther dares to expose himself to the fate of John Huss; he obeys; provided with a similar safe-conduct but more valid, because Charles V. had not the pusillanimity of Sigismund and besides the diet was not a council; it could

[1] This prince in competition with Charles V. and Francis I. had been elected Emperor and had refused this dignity.

only judge arch-heretics under purely political relations. Luther, condemned under these relations, continues none the less his movement. Docile to the Will which guides him, he adheres, notwithstanding the Emperor and the Diet, to the ideas of Zwingli regarding the inutility of the Mass; he abolishes it, as well as exorcism; denies the existence of purgatory and the necessity of confession, absolution, and indulgences; opens the cloisters; releases the monks and nuns from their vows, and himself sets the example of marriage of priests, by marrying a nun. What greater triumph could the Will of Man have gained over Destiny!

In the midst of all this the Pope dies. The circumstance was admirable for Charles. It was said that his predecessor Maximilian had had the intention of joining the tiara to the imperial crown; this was not a good thing, even if it had succeeded, for nothing could prevent the changing of the forms of papacy. A man whose genius had not been mediocre would have felt it easily. He would have seen in the state of things that there was no other means of annihilating the schism which was staining with blood and destroying the Church than in sanctioning it. He should have called Luther to the supreme priesthood. The stroke would have been bold; the only one that could have saved Europe from the peril that menaced her. Luther becoming Pope would have been capable of submitting the Will of Man to the yoke of Providence and I am sure that he would have done it. Up to that point he would only have been led, then his inspiration would have commenced. Charles in recognizing him would have been recognized by it and the Universal Empire would have dated from his reign. The Turk; scarcely entered Europe, would have been driven out; Jerusalem would have been conquered and the Old as well as the New World would have seen in this city a holy city towards which all the people of the universe would have turned themselves in prayer.

Charles felt nothing of all this. Yielding to his petty

interests, he raised to the pontifical throne his preceptor, under the name of Adrian VI., an upright man, but weak, incapable of sustaining a burden such as that which fell upon his head. This Adrian was followed by Clement VII., Julius de' Medici who, possessing all the faults of his family, without any of its virtues, succeeded through a misplaced pride and an ill-timed obstinacy in exasperating the schism and delivering Europe to the dissensions which awaited it.

CHAPTER XI

L UTHER considered as a reformer of the cult by the
incapacity of Charles V. who neither knew how to
generalize its form nor to arrest it; an audacious innovator
because he could not be anything more, and apostle of the
Will when he was not permitted to be that of Providence;
Luther knew at least his position and profited by the circumstances as an able man. He gave three terrible blows to
Destiny, which have not been sufficiently noticed because
historians, though exact enough in relating effects, almost
never go back to causes. Christian monk, he released
himself from his vows and publicly married a nun; he approved of the divorce of Henry VIII., King of England, from
Catherine of Aragon, and permitted polygamy to the Landgrave of Hesse. It was breaking boldly the most austere
part of the Christian cult and was submitting without re-
striction Necessity to Liberty. The divorce of Henry VIII.,
opposed by Pope Clement VII., who recognized neither men
nor times, brought about several very grave consequences;
the first was to render all alliance between Spain and England impossible, which made France secure for a long time,
prevented her usurpation by Philip II. at the time of the
League, and permitted Henry IV. to ascend the throne;
the second produced the reign of Elizabeth, who came after

the disastrous reign of Mary, giving to England an extraordinary impetus which might have led this kingdom to the
highest destinies, if a fatal event had not disturbed its
course. This event which I am going to indicate, although
it may invert a little the order of time, was the legal murder
of Mary Stuart. This murder, which stained the life of
Elizabeth, brought about an effect wholly contrary to that
which that princess, blinded by jealousy and pride, intended.
Instead of strengthening the royal authority, as she believed
it would, it shook it in its most sacred foundations and gave
to the Will of Man all that of which she thought she was
depriving it, by her fleeting despotism. England learned,
by the forms which were followed in that execrable regicide,
that crowned heads could fall by the sword of justice and
that the people had a right to this sword. The murder of
Anne Boleyn and that of the other wives of Henry VIII.
must not be confused with that of Mary Stuart. These
crimes, although similar in their results, do not at all resemble each other in principle. Henry was a savage tyrant
who assassinated his wives if they were innocent, or who
punished them in an atrocious manner if they were guilty.
The crime weighed upon him alone; but Elizabeth had no
right over Mary, a queen her equal and queen of another
kingdom. It was not she who put her to death; she caused
her to be put to death by her own people, to whom she gave
this unhappy princess, recognizing in this people a right com-
petent to judge her. Now, if the English people, according
to Elizabeth, had the right to judge a queen of Scotland and
to condemn her to death, all the more right should they
have to judge a king or queen of England and to send either
to the scaffold. They would have been able to execute
this fatal right upon Elizabeth herself, if the conditions
had permitted them to do it. They were not long in making
use of it when, about sixty years after, the unfortunate
Charles I., delivered to the mercy of a fanatical and sedi-
tious populace, was sacrificed to the ambition of Cromwell

by a regicide parliament. It was to the crime of Elizabeth that this monarch owed his death, and this crime, which was the work of royalty, could only have a like result; for, in order that royalty might be legitimately subjected to the sentence of the people, it was necessary for royalty to wish it, otherwise this would have been impossible.

To return from this digression: look at the principal consequences which the divorce of Henry VIII. brought about; they were, on the one hand, the security of the grandeur of France under the reigns of Henry IV. and Louis XIV., and, on the other, the glory and sovereignty of the English people and the evils of which this sovereignty was the source— evils which should be imputed chiefly to the character of Elizabeth, as I have said.

As to the consequences which followed the permission accorded by Luther to the Landgrave of Hesse to take two wives, they were likewise important. The princes of the North, but little attached to the pontifical power of Rome whose rigour seemed to grow in proportion as it became distant from the centre, saw with pleasure an occasion arise for throwing off the yoke. They and their people, notwithstanding their conversion to Christianity, retained in the depths of their hearts a secret leaven of the cult of Odin.[1] The concessions of Luther and the spirit of liberty which were the basis of his doctrine pleased them singularly. They found therein something of their ancient ideas and they united willingly. They protested therefore against the decisions of the different diets which had condemned Luther and his adherents[2] and formed at Smalcald that

---

[1] The cult of Odin existed for a long time in the North and was not entirely extinguished until the death of Sweyn, the last King of Denmark who professed it, at the beginning of the eleventh century.

[2] It is on account of this protestation that the followers of Luther have been named *Protestants*. The name of Huguenots came to them from the corruption of the German word *Eingenossen*, which signifies the *United*. This name was given them on account of their reunion at Smalcald. Charles V. having convoked a new Diet at Augsburg received there from the confederate

famous league which consolidated the schism and made a political body of the different members of which it was composed. It was not until after this league and in proportion as they entered it that the powers of the North commenced to have weight in the political system of Europe. Even Sweden, separated from Denmark by the valour of Gustavus Vasa, showed herself formidable sometime after, dominated the Empire of Germany during the reign of Gustavus Adolphus, and during that of Charles XII. balanced the power of the Czars of Russia. It is well known how the Swedish monarch, notwithstanding the genius of his rival Peter I., called in question one time whether the Russian Empire would be founded. Denmark after having escaped from the tyranny of Christian II. formed a reputable state. Saxony, Hesse, Hanover, Brandenburg, raised to the rank of kingdom with Prussia, exercised in turn a remarkable influence. Holland, after having thrown off the yoke of the Spaniards, dominated the seas, obtained possession of the power of the Portuguese in Asia, and gained the commerce of the world. England given over at first to violent convulsions, being victorious, seized the preponderance which her position and her relative force had necessarily given to her, and dominating the two hemispheres made them equally tributary to her vast marine. Switzerland even did not remain without some *éclat*, on account of Geneva, which made herself one of the mother cities of reform.

Finally, such having been the success of the doctrine of Luther, that before the death of this arch-heretic, in 1546, and in less than thirty years, more than half of Europe previously Catholic submitted to it. The other half, beginning to give way, would infallibly have followed in the same course, and thenceforth the Will of Man triumphant over that part of the world would have brought about a

---

princes a profession of faith, drawn up by Melanchthon, disciple of Luther; this profession of faith, called the *Confession of Augsburg*, contained the principal points of their doctrine.

moment of absolute liberty; that political phantom after which it ran unceasingly without ever attaining it. But it is the essence of this Will to become divided at the moment when Providence unappreciated abandons it. If this were not so, that is, if it could preserve its unity of movement, in using itself as a point of support, it would triumph always; for it is irrefragable in its nature and nothing in the universe can resist its action. Now if this action is perverse, ought it to endanger the universe? No; the Divine Decree which has endowed this Will with this irresistible action has willed it to exist only in its unity and its unity to subsist only in the good, or what is the same thing, in providential harmony. As soon as this harmony is broken, unity is destroyed, the action is divided, and the Will of Man, opposed to itself, combats and devours itself.

Luther could have been a providential man, but in order to be that he should have recognized himself as the instrument of Providence, so that Providence might be recognized in him; but if he considered himself only as a reformer of the cult, and one was accustomed to consider his reform and not him, and in his reform, that which conformed more or less to the prevailing ideas, so that in adopting the reform of Luther it was not Luther that one adopted as chief or regulator of this reform, but only as primal cause of a movement of which each one appropriated himself the centre, reserving for himself the power of spreading or limiting the circumference according to his particular inspiration; in agreeing, nevertheless, about certain bases, of which the principal was, that one ought to recognize only the Holy Scriptures as the rule of faith: thus there would be, properly speaking, in the new cult no chief invested with any spiritual power. Everyone with the Bible or the Gospel in hand could dogmatize at his will.

In the states which embraced this cult, the temporal sovereigns were declared chiefs; and without any apostolic mission, without any right to the sovereign pontificate, acted as sovereign pontiffs in all that which had relation to the discipline of the Church. Europe saw with astonishment, particularly in England, women exercising the rights of the papacy and presumptuously assuming a calamitous influence upon the priesthood[1]; which was assuredly most contrary to the spirit of Christianity.

This lack of unity, which was noticeable from the birth of the reform, would presage that the consequences would be stormy; they were, indeed, more than one could ever imagine. Hardly had Luther begun his predictions, when Zwingli appeared in Switzerland and drew new consequences from his doctrine; war was kindled among the cantons; it continued with different success. Zwingli was killed there. The cantons, justly fatigued with their dissensions, put down their arms, and each agreed to keep the doctrine which suited them and to tolerate each other. Before this time two men named Carlstadt and Münzer, ignorant and fanatical enthusiasts, trained in the teachings of Luther and outdoing the ideas of this reformer, declared themselves inspired to finish what had been only roughly outlined. It was necessary according to them to renew the edifice of Christianity from its foundations and to rebaptize all children. Under the name of Anabaptists, they committed frightful ravages; they filled the minds with a sort of religious intoxication which roused them to delirium; each of their followers believed himself to be inspired by the Holy Spirit and took for certain knowledge, for sacred orders, dreams of their bewildered imagination. One who believed that he was ordered to kill his brother came from remote parts of Germany to Paris or Rome and murdered him. Another understood the Spirit to tell him to hang himself and he did so. A lover killed his mistress; a friend sacrificed his friend. Allegorical histories were received as affirmed

---

[1] Bodin said amusingly on this subject on returning from England that he had seen in this country a most extraordinary thing. When asked what, he replied: "I have seen a chief of the Reformed Church dancing."

facts; one spoke only of imitating Abraham who sacrificed his son; Jephtha who sacrificed his daughter; Judith who beheaded Holophernes. Germany fell into a frightful confusion. People were obliged to combat these madmen and surround them as ferocious beasts. They were shut up in Münster, where one of the most audacious, Jean de Leyde, had himself recognized as king. Blood flowed in torrents. Wherever they were found, they were exterminated. Münzer perished on the scaffold at Mülhausen with his disciple Pfeiffer. Jean de Leyde, seized in Münster, was torn with red-hot pincers. They returned fury for fury.

During this time Calvin appeared; Calvin, of hard and austere character, of melancholy disposition, without recognizing either Luther, Münzer, Zwingli, Melanchthon, or Æcolampade, or any of their adherents, traced a new course in the midst of the reform. He renounced the vague and loose system of Luther, blamed his concessions to the sovereigns, his attachment to things temporal, and, withdrawing also from the frenzy of the Anabaptists, who standing up as their own masters wished neither priests nor magistrates, announced openly his intention of attaching the evangelical doctrine to the republican forms. Geneva, which had at first rejected his propositions, finally accepted them.

Geneva had been at first an imperial city in which the bishop had usurped the authority as in Cologne, Mayence, Lyons, Rheims, etc. This bishop had afterwards yielded a part of his authority to the Duke of Savoy. The Genevans attacked the validity of this transfer and revolted against the Savoyards, drove out their Catholic bishop, and named Calvin their legislator. Calvin lacked neither force nor talent; he wrote better than Luther, although he spoke with less facility. His legislation bore the impress of his character: it had firmness without grandeur and regularity without any sort of elegance. Its customs were wise but melancholy; the laws just but hard. The fine arts were banished. For more than a century not a single musical instrument was heard in Geneva. Games, plays, all the pleasant arts were regarded as impious and sciences even as corruptible. Mercantile industry on the one hand, religious quibble on the other usurped all the faculties. This was an emporocratic theocracy. Geneva was, properly speaking, a convent of merchants, as Sparta had been a convent of warriors. Lycurgus and Calvin were not wanting in traits of resemblance; but Lycurgus, weapon in hand, delivered no one to the edge of the sword, and Calvin, leaning over the Gospel, declared heretic by the Catholic Church with which he had broken, caused his friend Servetus whom he himself accused of heresy to be lawfully burned, according to confidential letters which the latter had written to him. What more terrible abuse of the Will momentarily united to Destiny!

This was the remarkable school whence came a man endowed with a rare sensibility, a decided inclination towards fine arts, musician, novelist, writer of the greatest distinction who, imbued from the cradle with ideas entirely opposed to his inclination, was placed by his strange paradoxes in a perpetual contradiction with himself, anathematized arts and sciences, proclaimed the sovereignty of the people, cosmopolitan by spirit, and Genevan by instinct, believed he was making everything harmonious by generalizing Geneva in the universe. That this man should have believed what he said to be good is only very natural; but that the greater part of Europe should have believed it, this requires attention. To reach that point Rousseau had to be the interpreter of a power which made him move without his knowledge and which will become more and more evident in what I still have to say.

CHAPTER XII

I HAVE advanced slowly in this last book and I have lingered over details more than in any other. This was necessary. My work can be considered as a vast picture which I unroll before my readers, while explaining the subject and distinguishing the effects and groups. I began first with vapoury bases and heights almost lost in the shadows. The features were but dimly traced at that time, the forms uncertain, and the daylight and darkness equally faint; but as we passed from one plane to another, the colours acquired more strength and the personages became more striking; more space was necessary to contain less, because we saw them nearer and the perspective did not permit representing them further *en masse*. We have now arrived at the first draft. I shall be obliged to suppress many details in order not to prolong my discourse and not to overstep the limits which I have prescribed for myself.

SIXTH BOOK

In the last book we have examined anew many subjects which we had already seen, so as to appreciate better their relations with those which were to follow. It was important to consider with attention the double movement which operated afterwards and the two great events which resulted from it: the discovery of America and the schism of Luther. We will continue now our historical inquiry to arrive at last at the application of the principles which we have received.

CHAPTER I

INVENTION OF GUNPOWDER AND THE ART OF PRINTING—
CAUSES AND EFFECTS OF THESE TWO INVENTIONS—FINE
ARTS—USEFUL ARTS—COMMODITIES OF LIFE

A T the time when the two great movements were operating, the principal circumstances of which I have related
many important things co-operated in giving to the Will
which had provoked them the necessary means of drawing
all the advantages which were promised from them. Among
these means are two especially, which having exercised a
great influence upon the human mind and upon the destinies
of the world, merit particular attention: these are the invention of gunpowder and that of printing. These two inventions which preceded a little the discovery of America and
the schism of Luther were destined to second these two
movements, which without them would have experienced
many greater difficulties. They acted strongly upon the
constitution and upon the morals of society and changed
in a short time all the military and civil habits.[1]

[1] The invention of gunpowder is attributed to a monk named Berthold
Schwartz, native of Freiburg in Germany, who, it is said, found this fulminating
composition by mixing together sulphur, saltpetre, and mercury, while searching for the golden powder of Hermes. The art of printing was invented shortly
after this time, at Mayence, by Gutenberg, Fust, and Schoeffer, a clerk or
servant of Fust who accomplished it by designing movable letters and ink
suitable for printing. They tried to stop the effect of these two inventions
by considering them as the work of the Devil and by denouncing their inven-
tors as sorcerers. Schwartz was put in prison; Fust and Schoeffer were cruelly
persecuted; but fortunately the accusation of magic against them had no result.

By means of gunpowder, firearms were easily invented; the invention of artillery and musketry made all men equal in combat by depriving the ancient knights of defensive armour. Infantry hitherto scorned became formidable, and the cavalry could no longer massacre them with impunity.[1] Knighthood, rendered useless by this invention, gradually lost its importance and soon disappeared entirely, at least in substance, for as to form it existed as it exists still as an honorary institution. The feudal system already shaken found in the new weapons and in the military tactics which they called forth, an obstacle insurmountable for its consolidation. These weapons, terrible in the hands of all men, effaced the differences of individual strength and of armour and gave an irresistible ascendancy to the talent of the general and to the real valour of the soldier. Thus was the Will armed.

The art of printing in multiplying the copies of intellectual works spread instruction throughout all classes of society and gave to thought an impetus which it had never before known. Intellectual knowledge was rapidly propagated. Men found themselves in a sort of spiritual communion, due to this wonderful invention which permitted them to share one another's ideas. Political affairs and events which, in particular or in general, might interest society were more easily divulged. The real condition of things could be much less imposed upon. Ignorance was

---

[1] The battle of Bouvines, won by Philip Augustus in 1215, furnished proof that knights fully armed were invulnerable. It is related that the King of France having been thrown from his horse was for a long time surrounded by enemies and received blows from all kinds of weapons without losing a drop of blood. While lying on the ground, a German soldier tried to thrust a doubled-barbed javelin into him but did not succeed. Not a knight perished in the battle, except Guillaume de Longschamp, who unfortunately died from a blow in the eye, directed at the visor of his helmet. Emperor Otho lost the battle. It is said that thirty thousand Germans died in it; they were without doubt the infantry, whose armour was neither as complete nor as finely tempered as that of the knights.

no longer a forced state. Public opinion was formed and this opinion became one of the most powerful resources of public life. Thus was the Will enlightened.

Firearms contributed powerfully to the success of the Portuguese in Asia and of the Spaniards in America. It was only with terror that the weak Americans could face these men, whom they saw possessors of lightning, hurling death from enormous distances. Printing gave to the followers of Luther a power which they never would have obtained without it; it made clear their real intentions, destroyed the calumnies which might be fabricated against them, and reaching the masses at great distance, showed from its beginning what a powerful lever this wonderful invention furnished to move them. Its action was the stronger at this time, as people possessed few books and were not surrounded as in our day by a mass of ephemeral pages which absorb the attention and encumber one with a heap of useless rubbish.

These two means were not the work of chance, as superficial writers would have it understood; they were, on the contrary, the fruit of a reflecting Will. This must not be forgotten. Never, perhaps, had the human mind made so great an effort. It was neither Destiny nor Providence which brought them about; it was the Will of Man alone to serve his passions. At the time when these things were happening, the genius of Arts was awakened in Italy and in Spain.[1] The Umbrian troubadours, driven from their native

---

[1] Already since the thirteenth century the Venetians had found the secret of crystal mirrors. Pottery had been invented in a town of Italy called Faenza. A man called Alexander Spina had discovered the use of spectacles. In general it was in Italy that industry made the greatest efforts. There were seen the first windmills and the first clocks with wheels. The clock of Bologna was already famous in the thirteenth century. Flanders was next to Italy the most industrious country of Europe. Bruges was the mart of all the merchandise which passed by sea from the Mediterranean into the Baltic. It was Edward III., King of England, who thought first to naturalize commerce in this kingdom by bringing Flemish workmen there in 1326. The countries of Europe where emporocracy has ruled have been successively Italy, the Netherlands, and England.

land by the bloody Crusade of Simon de Montfort against the Albigenses, were separated; and while one part crossed the Alps, the other part crossed the Pyrenees. It was there they had carried the knowledge of prosodic verses which they improvised while singing and naturalized the rhymes which they had learned from the Arabs. These poets had also composed comedies which the Spaniards and Italians have imitated. The English had a theatre some time after, as well as the French, who inferior at first to the other nations finally surpassed all.

Painting, sculpture, architecture, and music received a very great impetus, especially in Italy.[1] The sixteenth century saw many talents come to light. This was in general the century of fine arts. The seventeenth was that of erudition. In this century, copies of Greek and Latin works were multiplied; they were studied, criticized, and imitated as models, especially in France where *poésie rimée* attained its highest degree of perfection under Louis XIV.

The Spaniards who had given the tone to Europe during the sixteenth century gave nothing more in the seventeenth. It was the turn of the French who succeeded them, as they themselves had succeeded the Italians. It was in this century where delicacy and taste united with luxury to embellish life and joined utility to magnificence. Until that time only a luxury of ostentation devoid of comfort had been

---

[1] Painting was reinvented in the thirteenth century by Cimabue, a Florentine. He acquired such a great reputation that Charles I., King of Naples, made him a visit. Giotto followed him. Some frescoes of Cimabue remain which prove his genius and some pleasing paintings of Giotto. This Giotto was a young herdsman whom Cimabue encountered in the fields guarding his sheep and sketching them upon a brick while watching them graze. The renovator of Greek architecture in these modern times was Brunelleschi who built the dome of the cathedral of Florence in 1294. He was the first who abandoned the Gothic style. The invention of paper made with crushed linen dates from the beginning of the fourteenth century. A certain Pax is said to have established a factory at Padua.

known.[1] During the reign of Francis I., the father of arts in France, one was destitute of the simplest commodities of life. While this prince at Ardres received Henry VIII., King of England, under a tent of cloth of gold, he did not have a coach for travelling as a shelter from the rain. The only two coaches which he had then at Paris were for the Queen and for Diane de Poitiers. A century later the court of Henry IV. was scarcely better furnished. The greatest nobles in these times travelled on horseback and when they took their wives to the country, they took them on the crupper, and they wore a cape of oilcloth if the season was rainy. This condition of destitution increased as one advanced towards the north. In Russia, for example, it was very rare to find a bed in the middle of the seventeenth century. Everybody, even the greatest boyars themselves, slept on boards; other things were in proportion.

In general, the efforts of the human mind, after those which it had to make for the preservation of its existence and that of the social state, equally compromised after the invasion of the barbarians, had been directed towards the *ensemble* of things. Before thinking of living well, one had to think of living. It was not until the whole was assured that they concerned themselves about details. The Italians were occupied with the magnificence of the arts; the Spaniards with the ostentation of luxury; the French dreamed of the pleasures of life and perhaps of the enjoyments of vanity. The century of Louis XIV. was a century eminently vain-

[1] The luxury of these times consisted chiefly in one's retinue; bishops never went out unless attended by a prodigious number of servants and horses. This custom dated back to the ancient Celts. Even in the middle of the fourteenth century nearly all the houses in the cities of France, Germany, and England were thatched. The use of chimneys was not yet known. A common hearth was raised in the middle of the principal chamber and the roof was pierced. Wine was rare even in Italy. Meat was only eaten in the largest cities three times a week. The taper was unknown and the candle was a great luxury. Light was made with the aid of pieces of dried wood. Private houses were constructed from rough timber covered with a sort of mortar called *clay*. The doors were low and the windows small, almost without light.

glorious. If the letters of Madame de Sévigné have been so much prized, it is because these letters offer a perfect picture. The French of that time loved everything as Madame de Sévigné loved her daughter.

CHAPTER II

INSTITUTION OF THE JESUITS: FOR WHAT END—WHO IGNATIUS
LOYOLA WAS—NEW REFLECTIONS UPON THE CONDUCT
OF CHARLES VII.; UPON THAT OF FRANCIS I.; PHILIP II.,
KING OF SPAIN; AND HENRY IV., KING OF FRANCE—
ASSASSINATION OF THIS MONARCH

DURING these centuries, religion experienced diverse
vicissitudes. At first, it was divided, as I have said,
by the schism of Luther, and this schism which no one had
the force to consolidate was subdivided almost directly
from its birth. The Will of Man which had brought it to
light could not prevent the division, since this division resulted from its essence which was liberty. But Destiny, as
if frightened by the peril to which it had just been exposed,
raised in orthodoxy a man of extraordinary force, inflexible
character, and capable of great devotion; this man was called
Ignatius Loyola. The Christian cult has not produced one
more devoted to its interests. As he was to be opposed to
Luther he was in every way his counterpart. Luther was
a German monk who broke his vows, who emerged from
the solitude of the cloister to enter the career of dissensions
and arms. Ignatius was a Spanish soldier who threw away
the sword to put on haircloth and left the guard-house to
enter the sanctuary. The former trained in the sciences
from his youth was eloquent and erudite. The latter, who
hardly knew how to read, who spoke badly, entered college

at the age of thirty-three, submitted to the duties like a child, wished to receive corrections, and triumphing over an unpromising nature made all his classes, took all his degrees, and was finally received as Master of Arts of the University of Paris about ten or twelve years after.[1] Having attained this point he realized the project which he had conceived of founding a Society of Savants devoted to the instruction of youth, and continually occupying themselves with the care of enlightening infidels and fighting heretics. Ignatius added a fourth vow to those already in use: that of obedience to the Pope. He renounced by the rule which he established all ecclesiastical titles. Pope Paul III., to whom he submitted his project, was exceedingly impressed[2]; he promulgated the bull of the institution with the express condition that the members of this society, which was called *Society of Jesus*, should never exceed sixty in number. But it would have been in vain for the Pope to have tried to restrain the zeal which brought to Ignatius a crowd of followers, anticipating at a distance what importance this new religious order which he had established could have in the future. At the time of his death he had more than a thousand Jesuits as his followers and without the least political idea, without the least personal ambition, founded the most political and most ambitious order which has ever existed in Christianity. It had to be thus; the Spanish soldier was only an instrument of Destiny, as the German monk was of the Will. The one drew his force from necessity and the other from liberty.

The reform of Luther not being generalized on account of the mistake of Charles V., and the order of the Jesuits having had time to gain strength, Europe was given over to interminable dissensions; for the two parties had from that time chiefs incapable of submitting to each other. During

---

[1] In 1533.

[2] It is related that after having read the project, he lifted up his hands and cried with enthusiasm: *Spiritus Domini est hic !* " This is the spirit of God."

the bloody debates which these dissensions produced, and of which France was principally the theatre on account of the two parties in her midst, it was seen that Catholicism had obtained the upper hand over the Reformation, which came chiefly from the force of concentration which it opposed, thanks to the Jesuits, to the sole enthusiasm of some sectarians deprived of a sacerdotal chief, which tended always to division. The conduct of Francis I. in the very beginning of the schism appeared ridiculous and contradictory; it could not be different, however, considering his false position. All the evil came from a greater distance. It had its source in the blind folly and ingratitude of Charles VII. If this monarch had wished to recognize in the person of Joan of Arc, Providence which revealed itself to save France, things might have happened entirely different; he would have driven the English from the continent. If he had not succumbed to the terror which an unnatural son inspired in him, he would not have died of hunger at the age of fifty-eight, through fear of being poisoned; if his life had been prolonged only fifteen or twenty years he would have saved France from the calamitous reign of Louis XI.; the Flemish people irritated by the tyranny of Louis would not in their turn have tyrannized their young princess, Marie de Bourgogne, to make her marry against all reason and all decency Maximilian of Austria[1]; the quarrels between France and Austria which this union caused would not have taken place. Charles VIII., strong in his alliance with Marie, might have easily kept his conquests in Italy; Louis XII., less pressed by circumstances, would not have been forced to approve of the horrible perfidies of Cæsar Borgia and bend before the

---

[1] It was principally the inhabitants of Ghent who formed this alliance. These insolent citizens caused the chancellor and the chamberlain of Marie, who had negotiated for France, to be beheaded. Later they had the audacity to put Maximilian, husband of their princess, in prison for having violated their privileges in 1488. This people, imitating the Venetians, inclined already to emporocracy, which Holland attained finally by sustaining the schism of Luther.

imperious genius of Julius II.; he would have been able with all freedom to exercise the characteristics of kindness which were befitting him for the good of France. Francis I., coming to the throne under the most fortunate auspices, would not have vainly competed with Charles of Austria for the imperial crown; he would have obtained it at the outset and France would thus have entered into all the rights of Charlemagne. Mistress of the Netherlands and of entire Italy nothing would have resisted her movements. Francis I. might have displayed at ease that noble and magnificent genius with which he was endowed. He would have seen what ought to be done when Luther appeared and he would have done it. The Christian cult would have been reformed without shock, and Providence, seated upon the throne of Saint Peter, would have led France to the Empire of the World.[1]

But nothing of all this was done; the time which should have been employed to bring forth wonders was not only lost but was used to produce a thousand calamities. In this state of affairs, Francis I. could not admit the reform of Luther into his realm without losing it. He could not dispose of the papacy as Charles V. could have done at the death of Leo X., nor regulate a movement which in his hands would have remained what it was, that is, schismatic. Forced to persist in the Catholic communion, he was therefore obliged to let the Protestants be persecuted at home to prevent them from submitting to the influence of England, while he protected them outside so as to oppose the ambition of his rival. When it was fully decided that the emperor would not embrace the Reformation, Francis favoured it still more. It was he who gave to Geneva the necessary facilities to free herself and who let this city, bordering on his states, become the capital of a sect which he needed. Without this political stroke he was lost. Charles V. and Henry VIII., King of England, being united notwithstand-

[1] Consider, in support of all this, that the papal schism which existed then favoured this event.

ing the diversity of opinions, entered France. Already Charles was at Soissons and Henry had taken Boulogne. One trembled for Paris. The situation of Francis saved him. The Protestant princes, whom he had protected, united against the Emperor to force him to abandon his conquests; the Catholic party all-powerful in France furnished the King with necessary means to send off the English by procuring for him the money that he needed.

Francis I., being dead, Charles V. still kept up the struggle in which he had been engaged for ten years; but at last weary of so many shocks, deceived in all his hopes, grown old before his time, he let the helm, which he could no longer hold, fall from his hands and abdicated the throne.[1] His brother Ferdinand I. became Emperor and his son Philip II. King of Spain.

After this no one approached the grandeur of Charles V., except Henry IV., Louis XIV., Charles XII. and Peter the Great. It seemed that Spain, by the extent of her states and the wealth of the New World, should have dominated Europe. She did not even dominate Holland which escaped her and which finally despoiled her of almost everything that she possessed in the Indies. Philip II., having married Mary, Queen of England, wished to seize the crown after the death of that princess; he had prepared against this kingdom an armada which was called the *Invincible*. He desired his daughter Eugénie to be recognized as Queen of France and he himself to assume the title of protector; he held Italy in his hand; he anticipated invading Germany. From his cabinet he caused all the sovereigns of the world to tremble. His fleet, joined to that of the Pope and the Venetians, commanded by Don John of Austria natural son of Charles V., had won the famous battle of Lepanto over the Ottomans; he seemed at the height of his power; but this was not so. The Invincible Armada which he sent against England was beaten by the storms and

[1] In 1558; he was then only fifty-eight years old.

broken upon the rocks.   The English ravaged his possessions in America and, after having burned his galleons, threw terror into the city of Cadiz.   France whom he had disturbed for half a century during the weak or calamitous reigns of the descendants of Francis I. came off victorious from all the crises into which he had thrown her.   The factions which he excited in his midst, vying tore each other to pieces; he caused a Thanksgiving to be offered at Madrid for the execrable massacre which had taken place on St. Bartholomew's day; he armed the hands of a king against his people and turned the arms of the people against their king; he secretly sustained the ambition of the Guises, fomented the League, and for a long time persecuted the King of Navarre, heir presumptive to the crown of France.   Yet what result did he obtain from so many efforts?   Not any.   His power was eclipsed by the genius of Henry IV. who, by going to Mass, made him lose in a half-hour the reward of nearly forty years of labour.

One has often wondered if Henry IV. could have excused himself for abandoning the Reformation which he had sustained up to that time?   No, he could not.   If he could have done so, Francis I. would have been able more justly to embrace it.   But to accomplish such a movement in France, it was necessary to possess Italy and to have the power to create a pope there.   Henry IV. was not in this position.   This prince, poor and without arms, was banished by the *parlements*, anathematized not only by the Sorbonne but also by the priesthood, and rejected by the majority of the nation.   Political arms and those of superstition were used against him.   Besides, the Reformers supported him badly, their zeal commenced to weaken.   Henry IV. had to abandon a weak and tottering will to enter the prophetic career which opened before him.[1]   If this monarch

---

[1] Paris opened her gates to him in 1594; he strengthened his power in 1598, by the peace of Vervins, forcing Philip II. to recognize him and to restore all his cities which he still retained.

is compared with all the contemporaneous princes, it will be seen that he was the greatest; but the conditions were beyond him. More than fifty attempts were made upon his life. Ravaillac, who accomplished the aim of his cruel undertaking, was an arch-fanatic without direct accomplices, but inspired by a jealous faction, which, doubting always the genius of this prince, had resolved upon his death.

Could Henry IV. have evaded it? Yes; his genius had warned him of his danger; but the suspended blow would not have remained less menacing. It was only in triumphing over Italy that he might have assured his welfare, if indeed he could have triumphed. He had in Sully an able administrator, but who would have guided his armies under his orders? The Catholics opposed his plans and the Reformers not only lacked force, but were not, in general, inclined to serve him. At his death, in 1610, the European Will lost all the hope that it had. This prince had been its last resource to make France enter the religious movement which it had agitated in Europe. Germany too divided, and besides being respected by Austria, supported by Italy and by Spain, and England too much isolated from the continent, did not offer it a sufficient guarantee. Its attention was turned towards America, whose discovery it had planned and it resolved to pass there through England, concentrating at this point so as to be able to react upon Europe when the time should come.

CHAPTER III

ALREADY the idea of transporting the Reformation to America had been conceived by Admiral Coligny, who, during the reign of Henry II., had made the attempt in Brazil, where the Chevalier de Villegagnon had been sent. Calvin himself was interested in the enterprise; but the ministers whom he sent prevented it from succeeding. They divided by their controversies and their ambition the growing colony which was destroyed by the Portuguese. Coligny did not lose courage and as if he had foreseen the calamitous fate which awaited the Reformers some years later, he made a fresh effort towards Florida; but the colony which he sent there in 1564 was exterminated by the Spaniards. France had not the impulse necessary for these expeditions. Besides it was not the followers of Calvin that were needed there. Predestination which the head of these Reformers adopted and the rigid forms of his legislation submitted them too much to Destiny. It was among the most vehement and most enthusiastic disciples of Luther and among the Anabaptists that the European Will chose the

390

germ of liberty which it wished to propagate in the New World. It is true that these Anabaptists, who at first behaved like madmen and were massacred everywhere they were encountered, suddenly giving up their frenzies and yielding to a new spirit, had become the most pacific of men. It is from them that came not only the Herrnhuters or Moravian Brothers, but also the Quakers or United Brethren. The latter had their principal centre in England, but they urged their people to settle in the old and new continents.

The English were already established in North America, and had formed several colonies there, when James I. succeeded Queen Elizabeth and brought to the throne the spirit of controversy with which he was filled. An unfortunate event, the Gunpowder Plot, incensed him violently against the Catholic party; this party was accused of having conceived the culpable plot of blowing up the House of Parliament with all the members of its assembly and the king himself. This angry prince began persecutions which displeased the Protestants more than the Catholics themselves, by the arbitrary way in which he carried them out. The prerogatives with which he wished to strengthen the royal power and the concessions which he forced from Parliament dissatisfied this body and caused two new opposed factions to spring up in the nation—the *Tories* and the *Whigs*—the former attached to the interests of the king and the latter to those of the people. In the midst of these dissensions, excited minds were ready to embrace the most exaggerated ideas. It was at this moment that the Anabaptists exerted their influence. They first appeared under the name of *Puritans* and concealed their republican ideas under a sort of religious austerity. James died with the reputation of an adroit controversialist and a weak monarch. His son, Charles I., who succeeded him, appeared to ascend the throne under favourable conditions, whereas, on the contrary, it was under eminently difficult conditions. The

parties formed by his father were keenly opposed and only
awaited the occasion to burst into open antagonism. This
occasion was offered in the person of Strafford, viceroy of
Ireland, who displeased the Whigs and whose death the
House of Commons demanded. His only crime was in
having served his master too well. Charles, instead of supporting his minister and dissolving the factious assembly
which tried to dictate to him, thought he was yielding to a
cruel necessity; he had the weakness to sign the death warrant of a zealous servant who had aided him with his own
fortune; but it was to a rebellious will that he yielded and
this death warrant was the forerunner of his own. Puri-
tanism had made progress in Ireland and already some
Quakers appeared there. Whether the manners of these
Reformers, still more unusual than those of all the others,
displeased the Catholics more or whether the spirit of the
party had exasperated them more there than elsewhere,
the Catholics, unable to arm themselves openly against their
antagonists, meditated an atrocious crime and assassinated
them. It is estimated that about forty thousand of them
were massacred. The news of this horrible outrage roused
England. Charles was accused of having provoked these
murders, and the indignant nation armed itself against him.
This prince was no doubt innocent, but the people incapable
of reflecting were influenced by a blind delirium. Parliament having become the instrument of an irresistible Will
forced the king to leave London. He had recourse to force
and force betrayed him. A man endowed with extraordinary talents and as politic as warlike, enthusiastic and cold,
prudent and capable of any undertaking, Cromwell rose
from the ranks of the humblest citizens and mounted in an
instant to the highest rank in the State. He appealed to
the imagination of the people, took possession of the army,
and commanded both. The troops of the king were beaten
and his followers were powerless. The English Parliament
encouraged by success showed no further moderation; it

allied itself to that of Scotland by a solemn act which proclaimed all the principles of the republic. The unfortunate Charles who had believed to find a refuge in Scotland was seized there and delivered to the English parliamentarians. His misfortune seemed to touch them for a moment. The sombre and savage austerity of these Puritans was about to yield to the illusion of royalty, which all the furies of the civil war had not yet dissipated. Cromwell saw it; he broke up Parliament, too little submissive to his orders, and summoned another in which the parliamentary army dominated. Master then of the three kingdoms, he seized the monarch and brought him before Parliament which prosecuted him. The fatal example given by Elizabeth was followed and the blood of the unfortunate Stuart family for the second time flowed upon the scaffold.[1]

The fatal blow which caused the head of a king to fall beneath the edge of the popular axe resounded throughout Europe and did not strike it with horror; the monarchs were absorbed in petty intrigues of the cabinet and petty wars. Did they even see in what such an event could end? No, they did not see it. They only saw in the blood-stained tomb of the King of England an assassinated prince; they did not see that royalty, sacrificed to the sovereignty of the people, was buried there with him.

I make here the same reflection that I made with regard to Elizabeth. If Cromwell himself had sacrificed his sovereign, the crime would have been his; it would have been an individual outrage which would not have attacked the universality of things and which above all would not have delivered one power to another; but Cromwell did not assassinate the king any more than Elizabeth assassinated Mary. The crime was committed for them but not by them. The consequences were indeed different and much more terrible.

[1] The House of Stuart reigned over Scotland from 1370. Never has a race been more unfortunate. Nearly all the scions died a violent death.

But, after all, Cromwell, all-powerful as he appeared to be, all-protector of the whole kingdom as he was called, was only an instrument determined by an invisible power to serve a movement which it imparted. The real head of this movement was a shoemaker of Drayton called George Fox, a simple, ignorant man, but endowed with a great force of exaltation and tenacity in his ideas. Scarcely was royalty destroyed in England and the republic proclaimed when he emerged from his shop and poured forth his opinions. Cromwell while listening felt that he had a master; he had him arrested and forbade his followers to hold any meetings; but all his power failed. That terrible hand which had shaken England and precipitated her prince to the tomb could do nothing against a shoemaker. His weak protectorate which had not been the aim of the movement expired with him, and his son Richard preserved hardly a few months the shadow of the power which he had left him. The son of Charles I. was recalled; monarchy was re-established in England; and nevertheless the shoemaker Fox leaving his prison, easily took possession of the mind of an infinite number of discontented ones to whom he gave his doctrine and formed a considerable party. Among his disciples was a man of distinguished genius, profoundly meditative and capable of becoming a legislator. This man called William Penn has been celebrated. Having adopted in their company the ideas of Fox regarding the liberty and equality of all men, based upon the qualifications which they all had of being their own pontiff and their own magistrate without owing to each other any deference or any mark of respect, he formed the project of establishing this doctrine in America. He travelled with Fox through all England, Holland, and Germany making proselytes. When he had a sufficient number, he obtained from Charles II., in 1681, for him and for his successors, that province of North America which from his name and the forest which surrounded it has been called Pennsylvania; he sent there several colonies of Quakers and founded the city of Philadelphia to which he gave his laws.[1]

Thus after the most violent shocks the designs of the Will were accomplished. The germs of liberty and equality which it had transplanted in America developed in silence, multiplied, and acquired a force great enough to invade the world when the time came. All the English and Dutch colonies were penetrated by it and became emporocracies of a certain form, where all political and religious ideas fell into absolute indifference, one only excepted which had been dominant in the creative head of Fox and in that of his disciple, the legislator Penn—the idea of equality and independence.

[1] In 1699; about twenty years after, more than thirty thousand German families migrated there; so that in a short time the number of other Europeans surpassed that of the English.

CHAPTER IV

ESTABLISHMENT OF THE JESUITS IN PARAGUAY—GLANCE AT
ASIA—REVOLUTION IN CHINA AND JAPAN—ANCIENT HIS-
TORY OF JAPAN—MISSION OF SIN-MOU: HIS DOCTRINE
AND FORM OF GOVERNMENT—MISSION OF SOCTOTAÏS,
FOLLOWER OF FO-HI—DOCTRINE OF DISCIPLES OF
KONG-TZÉE—MISTAKES COMMITTED BY THE CHRISTIAN
MISSIONARIES

IN the meantime the spirit of liberty could not act without
that of necessity acting also and always in an opposed
manner. The movement which the disciples of Luther
made in America was imitated instantly by those of Loyola.
Whereas Fox and Penn gave in septentrional America a
shelter for the Will, the Spanish Jesuits gave one to Destiny in
the meridional; they founded among the savages of Paraguay
what they called the Country of the Missions, an extraordinary establishment, the laws of which, exactly opposite
to those of Pennsylvania, were destined to balance the disadvantages. It is inevitable that the powers of the North
and the South of the Columbian hemisphere will one day
clash. It is then that Luther and Loyola will measure their
forces and overcome each other, or mingle together; they
will necessarily mingle if Europe takes, by means of Providence which never ceases to offer itself, the dominion which
is due her over the universe and which if she loses, she will
only lose by her fault.

Asia is not at all in condition to dispute with Europe this pre-eminence if Europe ever starts on the career, consenting to submit her Will to Providence, which she has never quite wished to do since the origin of the Borean Race which dominated it. Nor has Africa any right there, and America will enjoy it only in proportion to Europe's unworthiness.

After the conquests of Genghis Khan and those of his children Oktai and Kublai Khan, Asia had offered only a picture of an agitated sea whose waves contrary winds caused to rise and fall; nothing there was stable; everything changed its form every instant according as Destiny ordained it; her peoples, grown old without a will of their own, obeyed her inconsistent laws in modifying them, nevertheless, by a residue of the providential influence which they had formerly possessed. Among the descendants of Genghis, Batukhan, son of Toushi, to whom had fallen Turkestan, Bactria, the kingdom of Astrakhan, and the country of the Usbeks, invaded Europe and ravaged, in the course of the thirteenth century, all the eastern part of that country as far as Hungary. On the other hand, Houla-Kou, son of Tuli, who had inherited Persia, had crossed the Euphrates at the same time and put an end to the caliphate of Bagdad; while a son of Genghis named *Zagatai* had possessed Transoxiana, Kandahar, northern India, and Tibet. All these conquests lasted but a short time. It is the essence of things subject to Destiny alone or to the Will to vary forms and to change masters often; only the substance remains because of the providential principle which is in it. The principal error of the Will is believing itself able to take the place of this principle by dominating Destiny.

China, in passing under the dominion of the descendants of Genghis, only changed the dynasty. Such is the force of the institutions of this ancient empire that no revolution has ever been able to injure her. This depends chiefly upon what these institutions, all reposing upon the mass of the people, keep steadfast in the midst of the storm which agitates only the surface. The army there being only a guard to the throne and not her sole support, its destruction does not bring about, as in the purely military government, the downfall of the edifice, but only its usurpation; the monarch places himself at the head of the State and forms anew the army about him, and the nation which often has not experienced the least disturbance does not perceive that it has another master; this master, whoever he may be, can only support himself as long as he possesses enough genius to impose upon his rivals. The people, who feel by instinct that their numbers protect them from all danger, are only roused with much difficulty at the rumour of a danger which cannot reach them. The descendants of Genghis neglected their army too much; so an audacious adventurer was sufficient to overthrow them. This adventurer had been, it was said, a valet in a convent of bonzes; he became emperor towards the middle of the fourteenth century. China preserved, as was her custom, her laws, her cult, and her manners. She did this again at the commencement of the seventeenth, when the Manchurian Tartars, becoming masters there, founded one of the noblest dynasties that she has had. This dynasty produced the celebrated Kang-hi who during a glorious reign of more than sixty years was patron of the arts and sciences in this Empire. [1]

This prince protected the settlement of the Christian missionaries in his vast states on account of the physical sciences and mathematics which they taught there and he permitted the exercise of their cult. This cult made, in a short time, rapid progress there and without doubt would have finally held a very high rank among the different cults which were practised in China, if the monks who had been

[1] One can judge of the promptness with which the fusion of the vanquishing people with the vanquished was effected by the difficulty that the Emperor Kang-hi experienced only fifty years after his victory in setting up a vocabulary of the Manchurian tongue which was fast becoming extinct.

sent there had been willing to give up their intolerance and bend more to the pacific spirit of the government; but the dissensions which arose from their disputes, their arrogance, and their foolish pretensions, obliged Yon-tchin, successor of Kang-hi, to send them away; Kien-long banished them entirely and forbade them ever to enter his empire.

These missionaries, who were dismissed from China with the most polite forms and consideration of which the Chinese alone are capable, did not experience so much gentleness in Japan. It is true that they conducted themselves in this country in a manner still less endurable. Hardly had they obtained influence there when they engaged their neophytes to burn the statues of the Ancestors of the Nation and to overthrow their temples. These acts, as unseasonable as impolitic, had roused against them a part of the people. Before the arrival of the Christians in Japan, other sects, a dozen in number, existed as sisters who, mutually jealous, watch over without excluding each other; who seek to rule in the paternal household without driving each other away and above all without dreaming of killing each other. But such is the character of the sacerdotal Christian that he cannot live in peace with any other priest. Wherever he is received he must dominate and overthrow all that is opposed to him, or, persecuted in his turn, he must be buried beneath the débris of the altars which he has wished to destroy.

When the Portuguese discovered Japan in the middle of the sixteenth century, this country enjoyed a perfect tranquillity. It preserved in its government all the forms of ancient, theocratic, and royal government. The Daïri, who occupied the pontifical throne, resided in the sacred city of Meaco, and the Cubo-sama who held the royal sceptre had established his residence in the city of Jesso. Through the obscurity of the Japanese annals it was seen that this form of government dated back to most remote times and was attached not only to the Universal Empire of Rama, but perhaps even to that of the Atlanteans. [1]

The Japanese call themselves autochthonous, and give themselves, as first legislators and first sovereigns, gods to the number of seven, who during a long sequence of centuries had governed them. They said that the last of these gods had for a son a demi-god, named *Tensio-Daï-Dsin*, who was the father of men, as his name expresses it in the Japanese language. After many centuries had rolled by in prosperity and peace, there came great dissensions upon the earth and long wars which occasioned great changes there. Japan as all the rest of the world was the prey of a thousand calamities. At last the wrath of heaven was appeased, a divine man was born. This man, whom the Japanese annals call Sin-mou, appeared about the year 600 before our era. War, famine, and pestilence had just ravaged his native land. These terrible scourges vividly disturbing the imagination of the Japanese had in a manner prepared the way to legislation and reform. A people is always more docile when having escaped from shipwreck they recall the evils which they have suffered and feel the need of a courageous pilot and of a protecting divinity.

Sin-mou, attributing the dissensions which had shaken the world to the separation of the two powers, sacerdotal and royal, conceived the bold project of uniting in the same hand the sceptre and the censer; this project succeeded for him. During eighteen centuries this institution was maintained in Japan without the least change in the family of this great man. This example is perhaps unique; for as I have said in speaking of Mohammed, it is very rare to find a line of men capable of sustaining both the tiara and the sceptre, daring to take upon themselves such a burden.

---

[1] The memory of the disaster of Atlantis had survived in Japan and was preserved in a solemn fête which was celebrated with much pomp. It was the fête of lamps or lanterns which is still celebrated in China and in India, such as was celebrated formerly in Egypt.

The Japanese, favoured by their geographical situation which isolates them in the midst of the seas, born with a vivid imagination, an upright mind, a great and strong heart, and filled chiefly with the sentiment of their own dignity and of their high calling—the Japanese were alone fitted to receive and preserve this form of government for such a long time.

Before Sin-mou, there existed no other cult in Japan than that of the Ancestors, which had survived the wreck of all others. This theocrat added to the celestial region where they were placed, a suite of similar regions inhabited by superior spirits, whose essence increased continually their purity, unto the point of being absorbed in the universal Principle, whose infinite elevation did not permit either the name or the attributes to be known. These superior spirits were named *Kamis*. Spread in companies throughout all parts of the universe, they inhabited according to their perfections the ethereal heavens, the sun, the moon, the luminous stars, the earth, and the other elements. Each, free to address his vows to one of these spiritual hierarchies, chose the one that appeared the most analogous to his taste, to his character; tried to imitate its virtues and prepare himself beforehand for the Elysium which pleased him most.

The Japanese theocrat had established as a fundamental dogma the immortality of the soul and its future state of happiness or sorrow, according to its virtues or its vices; but in accordance with a doctrine which was found only in his cult, he left to each the faculty of creating for himself, by his virtues, the sort of happiness which pleased him the best. Sin-mou knew the peculiar spirit of his people and conformed his teachings to it. The wicked, according to him, had to wander in the emptiness of space repulsed by the celestial spirits of all regions, to suffer there a thousand torments until the expiation of their crimes. Without telling them positively that these perverse souls would be called at the end of their sufferings to recommence another life and

animate earthly bodies, he inspired them with a great horror of noxious animals and forbade them to kill and eat the
domestic species and those which rendered daily services
to man.

To these simple, clear dogmas, Sin-mou added several
legal ceremonies, certain solemn fêtes, to keep up the purity
and health of the body, which, uniting the citizens, caused
inequality of rank to disappear and strengthened the social
ties, and finally an indispensable pilgrimage to the cabin of
Isje, sacred and respected monument, where the venerable
Tensio-Daï-Dsin had given the laws to the first inhabitants
of Japan.

The temples dedicated to the *Kamis* or immortal spirits
were of the greatest simplicity, consisting only of a sanctuary
without decoration and more often without any image.
The garlands and ribbons of white suspended from the roof
indicated the purity of the place and a great mirror placed
upon a sort of altar was there to show the worshippers of
the immortal spirits that as they saw distinctly in this glass
the picture of the beauties or the defects of the body, thus the
Divinity could see imprinted in their soul the picture
of their virtues or their vices.[1]   These temples were called
Mia.   Since the introduction of the cult of Fo-Hi in their
island, the Japanese have much more magnificent temples,
called *Tira*, into which they have admitted the divinities
of foreign nations, principally those of the Chinese and the
Indians.   The interior of these temples often contains more
than a thousand statues placed about the principal statue
raised upon a superb throne.   The magnificence of the
marble and gold rival each other.   The mighty theosophist
who built the first Tira was called *Soctotaïs*; he appeared
towards the end of the sixteenth century of our era and
understood perfectly that after the revolutions occurred in

---

[1] It is worthy of notice that the most ancient Egyptians admitted the same
symbol in their temple which leads one to believe that this usage goes back
to the primitive Atlanteans.

India and in China the simplicity of the cult of Sin-mou no longer satisfied the Japanese and offered to the vivacity of their imagination only a worn-out bridle which must be reinforced. His disciples in great numbers did not fail to surround his cradle with many wonders. According to their accounts, he appeared to his mother before his birth and announced to her that he would be holy.[1] From the age of four he already possessed all the science of Fo-Hi. It was said that being upon a high mountain, he received a divine inspiration which was communicated to him in a dream by an old Indian prophet called *Darma*. The conversations he had with Darma concerning the cult of Fo-Hi were put in verse and as soon as published found enthusiasts and violent adversaries. Soctotaïs triumphed over all obstacles and was at last recognized by Daïri Jo-Mei, whose son, aged only seven, explained the new doctrine in the temples. This cult reanimated the spirit of a people naturally inclined to virtue and enthusiasm. Japan then ceased to be tributary to China; she exchanged her industries for the riches of neighbouring nations.

Besides the ancient cult of Sin-mou, called *Shinto*, and that of Soctotaïs, called *Budsdo*, on account of Buddha, one of the surnames of Fo-Hi,[2] the Japanese some time after received a third, from a disciple of Kong-tzée, which they called *Siuto*, the Path of the Sages. The followers of this last doctrine, raising themselves above all popular prejudices, place perfection and supreme good in a tranquil and virtuous life. They recognize no other reward or punishment than the necessary consequences of virtue and of vice; that is, the satisfaction which one enjoys in doing good and the remorse which accompanies evil actions. They believe the souls emanated from the universal Spirit, Soul of the

---

[1] While the mother of Soctotaïs had this vision in Japan, Amina, mother of Mohammed, had a similar one in Arabia.

[2] Fo-Hi is called in Japan *Amida* and in China *O-mi-to*. This Sanscrit name signifies the *Immense*.

world, supreme, immortal Being; they think that they will become united to their principle when they are no more held by bonds of the body. According to them, there is no other divinity than *Tien* or heaven. Nature, which they personify, governs the world without having created it and she herself has been produced by *In* and *Jo*,[1] two powers, the one active, the other passive; the one the principle of generation, the other of death. All that exists in the world proceeds from them and the world is eternal. The only exterior acts of religion permitted by the Shintoists, who differ but little from the Chinese literati, are reduced to a few ceremonies in honour of their ancestors.

The three principal sects were again subdivided and raised to twelve, when the Christian missionaries arriving in Japan, the thirteenth place was offered them. They could have taken it without causing any trouble and perhaps attained, insensibly, dominion over the others. But this is not what they did. Hardly installed, their bishop without any regard for the Daïri, whom all the other sects recognized, proclaimed the sovereignty of the pope, pretended to depend only upon him, and wished to take precedence of the kings. These extravagant pretensions roused the Japanese, more proud than indulgent, and the bishop was driven out; the missionaries intrigued and were banished; their proselytes, already numerous, armed themselves; they were opposed and vanquished; they conspired; the conspiracy was discovered and a frightful civil war ensued in which the Christians were all exterminated. Finally in 1637 there appeared a formal edict forbidding any Christian of whatever nation, rank, and condition to appear in Japan under penalty of death.

The Dutch profited a little while by these disasters by making public abjuration of Christianity and by trampling under foot the symbols of this cult; but their triumph was fleeting and had very disagreeable consequences. All doors

---

[1] *Yn* and *Yang* in Chinese.

were closed to them and they were banished to an unhealthy
island where they remained prisoners as long as their commerce lasted.

The revolution which separated the royal power from
the theocratic occurred in 1118 of our era, upon the death
of Daïri Takacura. This revolution, prepared in advance,
was carried out with the greatest tranquillity. The Seogon,
a sort of military officer, for a long time entrusted with all
the jurisdiction of the civil administration, made himself
independent under the title of *Cubo-sama*. He seized the
royal crown which he detached without effort from the
tiara; but he vowed none the less to the Daïri an unlimited
religious respect. He realized indeed that he would be
nothing unless he recognized a supreme chief. He recognized
him and the latter having sanctioned a usurpation which
was now indispensable, there were seen in Japan two distinct
monarchs, one sacerdotal, exercising the functions of supreme
pontiff, and the other royal, fulfilling those of civil magistrate
and head of the armies. The respective duties of these two
monarchs are easily distinct and the few troubles occasioned
by their opposed pretensions are promptly suppressed.
Cubo-sama possesses, it is true, an imposing material force;
he is feared and obeyed; but the Daïri enjoys a veneration
and respect so profound that this force is always found as
nothing when it is a question of turning it against him.
There was in Japan more possibility of the Daïri obtaining
possession of the royal power than of Cubo-sama seizing
the religious and this has depended upon the opinion of the
people and upon the influence which religion in general,
although divided in many sects, has not ceased to exercise
over him. It has not happened thus in other countries,
and above all in Syria, where the Turks have despoiled
without effort the Caliphs of Mohammed; but these Caliphs,
for reasons which can easily be deduced from all that I
have said, no longer believed in their apostleship and consequently had no force. A maxim which I cannot refrain

from repeating is this: Every sovereign pontiff who doubts himself must not hope that others will believe. In point of cult, politics counts nothing: Truth alone is the basis of Truth.

CHAPTER V

CONTINUATION OF OUTLOOK UPON ASIA—POWER OF THE OT-
TOMANS—CONDITION OF THEIR EMPIRE AND ITS
DECLINE—RAPID GLANCE AT PERSIA AND INDIA

SINCE the Empire of Rama had lost its unity, divisions
and subdivisions succeeded each other with an increasing rapidity; Asia had become the theatre of a multitude of
continual revolutions which rolling one upon another had
left only confused traces, difficult to distinguish and ever
disappearing beneath those more recent. The Tartars,
principal motive of these revolutions, had become the instruments of Destiny; whatever name they bore, whatever
cult they followed, they could always be regarded as urged
on by a blind necessity. It was not in vain that the doctrine
of Mohammed, destined for them, had made a dogma of
fatality; they were in this wholly opposed to the Goths although perhaps equally barbarous. The Goths had received
from Odin the arbitrary movement; this movement is
obliged constantly to offend the other or be offended by it,
until the moment when Providence will blend them.

Towards the middle of the fourteenth century, the Kingdom of Kashmir, then the most ancient of all India and the
sole fragment of the Indian Empire which had remained
until then intact, came to an end. It had lasted since 3100
B.C. and had had one hundred and fifty-three kings. A
Mussulman prince named *Shems-heddin* made this important
conquest. About the same time, the Turks, of whom I have

spoken several times, having advanced to the shores of the Strait of the Dardanelles, after having torn the civil power from the Caliph of Bagdad, had crossed this strait and established themselves in Europe.

The Genoese, then possessors of the faubourg of Galatea, are said to have favoured this passage by furnishing the necessary vessels for a few gold marks. Thus the emporocratic spirit, indifferent regarding all things except those which restrained its independence or which touched its interests of the moment, furnished the means of placing between Europe and Asia this barrier which nearly annihilated it and which would have annihilated it if the Cape of Good Hope had not been doubled. The expedition of Tamerlane at the beginning of the fifteenth century and the victories which this famous conqueror gained over the Ottomans retarded somewhat this event, but did not prevent it. Tamerlane, or Tamer-the-lame, was a Tartar prince endowed with great audacity and more civilized than those of this nation ordinarily were. It is said that among the European nations he particularly esteemed the French; and that he even sent an embassy to King Charles VI. He extended his conquests over entire Persia, subjected the greater part of India, broke open the great wall of China, and ruled over Asia Minor and Egypt; to one of his successors, named *Ulugh-Bey*, is due the first Academy of Sciences, founded at Samarkand towards the commencement of the fifteenth century. This monarch had the earth measured and had a share in the composition of the astronomical tables which bear his name. He merited children more worthy of him: one of them eager to reign had him assassinated.

The Turks after having overthrown the Empire of the Orient, as I have said, and placed that strong barrier destined to restrain Europe from the coast of Asia, pursued their conquests. Profiting by the dissensions which arose among the descendants of Tamerlane, they again took possession of Syria and Mesopotamia and subjugated Egypt. Salim

I., Suleiman, and Salim II., who succeeded each other in the sixteenth century, were the greatest monarchs of the Ottomans; they took away the island of Rhodes from the Knights of St. John of Jerusalem, regarded as the bulwark of Christianity,[1] invaded Moldavia, Wallachia, a part of Hungary, and laid siege to Vienna. Western and Southern Europe were menaced; the island of Cyprus had just been conquered when Pope Pius V., believing rightly that the time for the Crusades had passed and that he must act by himself, had the courage to make war; he formed a league with the Venetians and King Philip II. of Spain and co-operated at the famous battle of Lepanto in 1571. This was the first time the standard of the two keys had been seen unfurled against the crescent. The papal standard triumphed and it had to be thus, because it was not the destiny of Mohammed to surmount that of Christianity, but only to arrest its invasions into Asia. Whenever Rome has been menaced by the Mussulmans it has been in vain. It was from this very date when the two destinies clashed that the Ottoman power commenced to decline.

This power was no longer so necessary, since the European Will had opened two routes to the West: so it was seen degenerating rapidly in the seventeenth century and becoming only a shadow of itself in the eighteenth. Its last remarkable exploit was the siege of Candia. The Vizier Achmet-Cuproli took possession of this place after one of the most stubborn sieges which history mentions.[2] The barrier continued to exist but it was only guarded. Those who had placed it could not extend further their ravages.

The majority of *politiques systématiques* have considered the government of the Turks as despotic; but they are mistaken in some respects. This government is not despotic as to its essence, only as to form. It is the corruption of a the-

---

[1] Charles V. some time after in 1525 gave the island of Malta to these knights.

[2] This siege lasted twenty years, and only terminated in 1669.

ocracy and its usurpation by military force. This government is the most prophetic of all, that is, the one where the necessity of Destiny makes itself felt with greater force. The power of the sultan appears unlimited and nothing is more constrained than this power, at every instant pressed between the religion which restrains this prince and the military force which urges him. The tiara which he has usurped hinders him in his movements, and the sword which is in his hands a two-edged weapon, wounds him when he uses it unskilfully and strikes him down when he is weak enough to fear it. The body of the Janissaries is that in which lies this redoutable force. Under a prince whose talents and courage render him worthy to command, the Janissaries[1] are docile instruments animated with military enthusiasm, intoxicated with love of glory, and a feeling of their superiority; but under weak or unfortunate sultans, these instruments having become rebels, refuse the hand which attempts to seize them, and make themselves masters of the crown, which they take or give at their pleasure.

The sultan, considered as the delegate of God Himself, is venerated while he is fortunate and his person is sacred, because he is believed to be favoured by heaven. He can then do many things. But if fortune abandons him, the illusion is dissipated and, being regarded as reprobate, his downfall is hastened instead of retarded. Destiny, his force, crushes him as soon as he no longer sustains it.

During the course of the fifteenth and sixteenth centuries, this Destiny favourable to the Ottomans was very powerful. The writers of this time, celebrated for their intelligence and their impartiality, recognized the Turks as greatly superior to the Christians in the knowledge and practice of military art. Guichardin goes even to the point of saying that it is from them that the Italians have learned the art of fortifying places. But this superiority did not exist in the centuries

[1] The real name of the Janissaries is *Yengi-Cheri*, that is to say, new warriors; these are the young Christian slaves instructed and disciplined from childhood.

following and their power diminished greatly when Destiny
having achieved its movement stimulated them no further
in this manner.

Since the conquest of Persia by the Arabs, this country,
twice invaded by the Tartars under Genghis-Khan and
Tamerlane, at last drew breath under the very mild laws of
the Sufis, whose race, issued from Armenia, had brought
with it the manners of this country, the taste for arts and
magnificence.   It is very curious that from the time when
Luther scattered over Europe the first germs of the schism
which divided the West, a Persian, of a character equally
bold, founded the sect which today divides the Persians and
the Turks.   This man, called *Haidar* and surnamed *Sufi-
the-Sage*, made himself so powerful by dogmatizing in favour
of the followers of Ali against those of Omar, that Shah-
Rustan, still insecure upon the throne which he had just
usurped, had him assassinated.   Ismayl-Sufi, son of Haidar,
was endowed with sufficient courage to sustain, weapon in
hand, the opinions of his father and continue to propagate
his doctrine.[1]   His disciples became his soldiers.   He conquered and converted Armenia, whose forces gave him the
means of subjugating entire Persia and as far as the Tartars
of Samarkand.   The crown of Persia, which he left to his
son Tahmasp, passed to his descendants who kept it for
several generations.   Their kingdom became at the close
of the sixteenth century, during the reign of the great Shah-
Abbas, great-grandson of Ismayl, one of the most flourishing
and fortunate countries of the world.   This monarch successfully fought the Turks and his conquests were great enough
to weaken their power and to hasten the decline towards
which they were tending.   He recaptured from the Portuguese the island and city of Ormuz and diminished consider-

[1] The followers of Omar are called *Sunnites* and those of Ali, *Shiites*.
The difference which exists between these two sects is that the latter regard
Omar and the four Caliphs who supplanted Ali as usurpers, making almost no
difference between Ali and the Prophet.   The Turks are Sunnites; the Persians, Shiites; these two sects hate and curse each other.

ably their influence in Asia. He built several cities, embellished greatly Ispahan, which he chose for the capital of his states,[1] and made useful institutions everywhere. After his death, which occurred in 1629, his son Shah-Sufi who came to the throne did not have the talents of his father. He was indolent and left the government of the state to vile favourites who caused its ruin. The weakness of Shah Hussein lost everything. The factions of the black and white eunuchs disturbed so much the empire, throwing it into such confusion, that a handful of adventurers known under the name of *Afghans* or *Agwans* were sufficient to overthrow it.[2] These Afghans easily destroyed an enervated power which would have destroyed itself even if it had not been exposed to their attacks. Mahmud, successor of Mir Waiz, the first chief of these barbarians, besieged Ispahan and received the keys of this immense capital from the very hands of the weak Hussein, who, not having the power to defend himself, acknowledged him as his master and was only too glad to give him his daughter.

[1] It is said that Ispahan before having been ravaged by the Afghans at the beginning of the eighteenth century was one of the most beautiful cities of the world. The number of inhabitants is said to have exceeded a million before the siege which it sustained in 1722. It had a great number of magnificent palaces, among which towered that of the Sufi, which was more than a league in circumference, one hundred and sixty beautiful mosques, eighteen hundred caravansaries, two hundred and sixty public baths, a great many cafés, bazaars, colleges, promenades, etc.

[2] There exists among the Afghans a curious tradition. It is asserted that this tribe whose unique *métier* was war and pillage is a remnant of the ten tribes of Israel scattered throughout Asia by the Assyrians. They consider themselves descended from the Jews and claim Saul as their ancestor. At the appearance of Mohammed they became attached to Islamism and valiantly fought to make it triumph. At first they enrolled under the flag of Mahmoud of Ghazvanid who ascended the throne of Hindustan in 387 of the hegira (993 A.D.), and afterwards under that of Sultan Khebal Al-Dyn Gaury under whose orders they took possession of the city of Delhi.

The Afghans made, on their own account, the conquest of the mountain of Solomon, *Kuh Solyman*, and there formed a regular sort of settlement. The Grand Mogul Akbar built for them the city of Peshawar, situated on the route from Astok to Kabul. These people enjoyed a high reputation for bravery, but they are accused of mingling much ferocity and barbarism with it.

In the meantime a son of this Hussein named *Tahmasp* having survived the disaster of his family was saved by the son of a herdsman named *Nadir*, who afterwards assumed his protection. This Nadir, having become in time a formidable warrior, was placed upon the throne of Persia under the name of *Tahmasp Kuli-Khan* and conquered India, where he overthrew the Empire of the Moguls in 1739. Since that time India has not had a moment free of agitations. Many ephemeral sovereigns almost all Tartars have succeeded each other in the interior; and her coasts were at first exposed to the ravages and quarrels of the Portuguese and Dutch, and later to similar enterprises of the French and English. The latter, having remained sole masters, have displayed there all the arrogance of their exclusive emporocracy and have made the rights of their monopoly recognized from the Cape of Good Hope to the waters of Japan. In the midst of these repeated revolutions one must not believe the Asiatic people have been unfortunate to the same degree as Europeans placed in the same circumstances would have been, or that they have experienced the same pangs and suffered the same griefs. Subject to Destiny, which holds them captive, they do not rebel against it; they bend beneath the blast of the tempest and are exempt from the moral pains which a ruffled Will and wounded *amour-propre* give. The revolutions which change the form of governments there do not reach the mass of people who remain indifferent to the success of their masters, nearly all foreign. The wealth which has been brought them from all the countries of the earth impresses them little. They let it be seized by avaricious merchants, who are obliged to yield the greater part of it to nabobs still more avaricious than they. The extreme fertility of the land and the heat of the climate leave little to desire for their needs. Nourishment and clothing they acquire with such facility that there is never any perplexity about obtaining them. Uneasiness concerning the future which devours European peoples is hardly known by the Indians. They live upon so little that nowhere is the labour of man cheaper than in India. The workman who fishes for pearls in the sea of Bengal, or who searches for diamonds in the mines of Golconda, earns ten times less than the one who clears the streets of mud in London or Paris.

CHAPTER VI

IT was at the moment when the power of the Ottomans began to decline that a formidable power which had scarcely been observed until then was seen rising over the eastern limits of Europe towards the north. This power to which is given the name of *Russia*, because of the part of Europe which she inhabits, anciently called *Russland*, is composed of diverse peoples of whom the principal ones are the Slavs, the Finns, and the Varangians. It has been but a few centuries since the Russians were known only under the name of *Muscovites* on account of their capital city called *Moscow*.

Before the Czar, Peter the First, whose reign commenced in 1689, Russia had remained almost entirely unknown to the nations of Western and Southern Europe. One does not know what became of this country after the legislation of Odin. The Finns who inhabited it alone, encroached upon by the Slavs coming from the border of the Orient, were forced to cede the territory to them. The city of Slavensk built upon the shores of the Volkoff a short distance from Lake Imen, was the first capital of these conquerors. A pestilence having depopulated it, Novgorod was built at a short distance. The new city was beginning to prosper, when pirates, designated only by the name of *Varangians*, that is, the Occidentals, came under the leadership of their chief Ruric[1] to establish themselves in the environs. They profited by some troubles in Novgorod, then a republic, to offer their services to one of the parties which, having accepted them, was conqueror only on condition of becoming tributary. Nevertheless the three peoples finally became mingled and united by means of the Christian religion which they received at the end of the tenth century.[2]

From the eleventh century the Russian Knès were tributaries of the Tartar Tsars of Kazan. Ivan Basilowitz succeeded in throwing off completely this shameful yoke and began the foundations of the Russian Empire towards the middle of the sixteenth century. He made the conquest of Kazan and Astrakhan, and changed his title of *Knès*, which signified prince, into that of *Tsar*, which meant Sovereign Autocrat. This word, which has since been written *Czar* is confused with the name of *Cæsar*, which the feudal sovereigns of Germany took and has been more justly translated by that of Emperor; for at least the Czar of Russia was vested with a real power and ruled over an immense empire, the most extensive which had existed since that of Rama. It is true that this extent comprised as yet, chiefly in Asia, only deserts deprived of cultivation and inhabitants; but the savage tribes which scourged the north and east were able to settle in time and be taught agriculture and the arts and multiply them by means of good legislation. A popu-

---

[1] I suppose it should be written Rolrich; this name, equivalent to that of Roland or Raoul, signifies Regulator of the Empire and indicates a Scandinavian origin. The Varangians were a division of Scandinavians who advanced to the Orient, while the others moved towards the Occident or the Midi. They received from the Slavs the name of Occidentals, for the same reason that we call them *Normans*.

[2] It is said that a princess named Olga, having been baptized at Constantinople, brought the Greek religion into Russia. Her grandson named Vladimir was the first Christian grand duke of Russia. For quite a while the Archbishop of Novgorod was dependent on the Patriarch of Constantinople; but he was finally consecrated patriarch in 1588 and took rank after the one in Jerusalem.

lation is never wanting where mild, protecting laws and a fertile land are united.

The Czar Peter, justly surnamed the *Great*, undertook to finish what Ivan Basilowitz had commenced, and succeeded by force of genius in overcoming the obstacles which things and men opposed to his efforts in placing Russia in the rank of the first powers of Europe. There was between this Ivan and Peter a fatal resemblance: each caused the death of his son. Ivan, suspecting his of plotting a conspiracy during the siege of Pleskov, killed him with the thrust of a pike; and Peter judging that his son Alexis was upsetting his work through incapacity had him condemned to death.

The ancestors of Peter had occupied the throne since 1613. They had been called there after most cruel revolutions by an assembly composed of the chief boyars who, needing a sovereign after the assassination of young Demetrius, last scion of the princes of Vladimir, elected Michael Romanoff, son of the Archbishop of Rostov and a nun and allied to the ancient czars. The young Romanoff, after having received the crown, ransomed his father who was prisoner among the Poles and created him patriarch. The conditions were extremely favourable for founding a regular theocratic and royal empire, but they failed. Alexis, son of Michael Romanoff, far from allowing the patriarch to continue supervision over the morality of his actions, as his father had done, was indignant at this humiliating subjection and wished to reduce the priesthood to the same nullity in which it was before the revolution that had placed his family upon the throne. The Patriarch Nicon, who was endowed with a haughty character, resisted; not only did he wish to preserve what they were trying to deprive him of, but also to acquire new prerogatives to which he had no right; the struggle between the two powers commenced, and the emperor profiting by the mistakes which his antagonist committed, turning against him the constitution of his own cult, having convoked a national synod, solemnly

27

deposed him and confined him in a cloister for the rest of his days.

From that time all theocratical power was annihilated; the Russian Government became very nearly like that of the Turks. The imperial guard—the Strelitz, strongly resembling the Janissaries—began to assume the same ascendancy and showed itself disposed to regard the emperors as its creatures and the empire as its patrimony. Peter on his accession to the throne was well aware of this as he nearly became a victim of it. After having happily escaped the snares of his enemies, thwarted the bloody intrigues of his sister Sophia, banished this artful woman to a convent, and seeing himself firm upon the throne, he conceived the indispensable but dangerous project of abolishing the imperial guard. But before dealing this decisive blow, without which the reform which he meditated in his empire could not have been effected, he wished to win the esteem of his subjects by his accomplishments and his victories.

He was instructed in all the arts and chiefly in that of navigation, for which nature had given him an almost invincible aversion; but he triumphed over his aversion and even vanquished nature by causing himself to be thrown into the water notwithstanding his horror of this element. He became by dint of study and labour the best mariner of his states. He wished also to understand military tactics in its smallest detail and fulfilled the duties of soldier from the grade of corporal to that of general in a regiment which he had created. Afterwards, having assured for a certain time the tranquillity of his empire and having given his confidence to an able foreigner named Le Fort, he travelled through the states of Europe, as a simple individual in the suite of his own ambassador. He saw everything important in this extraordinary journey and learned all that could be useful to him, and worked with his own hands in the ports of Holland on the construction of ships, in order to learn everything that he wished his subjects to learn. In the meanwhile, he had quieted down several seditions, fought with advantage the Tartars of the Crimea, made the Chinese respect his frontiers, assured his commerce over the Black Sea, and conquered the important place of Azov.

So much foresight and activity astonished Europe. His character struck her with terror. Peter while still at Vienna learned that a conspiracy had broken out in Moscow during his absence and that the Strelitz had formed the plan of replacing his sister Sophia on the throne; he hastened there and arrived in the midst of the tumult; he restrained the factionists and struck the blow which he had long since contemplated. The formidable guard was crushed. Two thousand of these unfortunate Strelitz convicted of having plotted in the conspiracy were hanged from the battlements; their chiefs, several officers, some priests, had their heads cut off; two women were burned alive and the rest sent to Siberia and the neighbouring countries. After this event, where the Czar displayed a mixture of grandeur and remarkable cruelty, nothing resisted him further in the interior of his empire. He could make at leisure all the changes that he wished and even suppress completely the dignity of patriarch which disturbed him. But an enemy or rather a formidable rival appeared outside his empire. This was the terrible King of Sweden, Charles XII.

Since the elevation of Gustavus Vasa to the throne of Sweden, and his adherence to the schism of Luther, this kingdom had acquired a great preponderance among the Northern powers. This preponderance still increased under the weak reign of the Emperor of Germany, Rudolph II., when a Protestant league being formed against a Catholic league plunged this country into a civil war of thirty years which reduced it to the most deplorable state. After divided successes, where the two parties, alternately victors or vanquished, had heaped ruin upon ruin, and poured blood upon blood, the Protestants, as much weakened by their victories as by their reverses, had yielded almost everywhere when Gustavus Adolphus, King of Sweden, changed the face of things and took from Emperor Ferdinand II. all the advantages which he had hoped to draw from these disasters, to increase his authority and perhaps annihilate the schism forever. This prince, everywhere victorious, became the arbitrator of Germany. France became an ally with him and furnished him with forces to weaken by this means the power of the House of Austria. Unfortunately the King of Sweden was killed at the battle of Lützen, but he left very able generals whom he had trained and who completed his work; while the emperor, having deprived himself of the only able man who might have opposed them, by having the famous Duke of Wallenstein, whose ambition and talents he feared, assassinated, found himself without support and obliged to renounce all his hopes. After the death of Gustavus Adolphus, his daughter Christina ascended the throne. The victories of her father and the genius of her chancellor Oxenstiern made Sweden the first power of Europe. She was not at all dazzled by so much grandeur. After having jointly with France pacified Germany by the peace of Westphalia, whose famous treaty forms still the basis of public right, this extraordinary woman astonished the world by a voluntary abdication of a throne which she had occupied with so much glory. At the age of twenty-seven, she left the court of which she was the ornament and renouncing the Reformation of Luther went to Rome to devote herself to the culture of sciences. It appears that this queen felt that in the singular situation in which Sweden was, this kingdom, enjoying a great military regard, with very weak power in all other ways, had need of a warrior monarch. Charles Gustavus, Duke des Deux-Ponts, whom she chose, was perfectly fitted for the occasion. He had the force necessary to sustain a crown upon which the European Will founded its hope. This Will, after having prepared everything in England to effect towards America the movement of which I have spoken, made again an effort in Germany by means of the schism of which Sweden was declared the head. If the monarchs who succeeded Charles Gustavus had felt their position as Christina felt hers; if, instead of turning the strength which the Will of Man had given them against this same will and aiming at despotism instead of at popular power, they might have favoured the movement which had raised them; it is difficult to say here what point Sweden might have reached. She might easily have acquired Poland, conquered Denmark, dominated the whole of Germany, and perhaps would have pushed back into Asia these very Russians who crushed her. But to do this it was necessary that circumstances should be favourable. Christina, who did not wish it, felt at least her insufficiency and retired not only from the schism but from the throne; whereas Charles XI., bringing there a spirit utterly opposed to that which he should have, lost all and prepared the downfall of his son. He wished to reign with despotism over provinces that yielded to him only in the hope of preserving their liberty, and he committed the great blunder of condemning to loss of honour and life the unfortunate Patkul, a Livonian gentleman, whose only crime was bringing to the foot of the throne the respectful and severe complaints of his country. This same Patkul who had had the good fortune to escape, having been seized some years after by Charles XII. and accused of having incited Augustus, King of Poland, to enter into possession of Livonia, was condemned to the most cruel torment by the implacable King of Sweden. But this dishonourable act checked this prince in the midst of his triumphs and made useless all the warlike and even civil virtues with which he had been favoured in the highest degree.

The victory of Narva, which had given in a moment to this young monarch the reputation of a hero and the strength of a conqueror, had only ephemeral consequences; it was a brilliant but fleeting light which vanished in the darkness. After having been for a moment the arbitrator of Germany, master of Poland and Saxony, victor in all places, he lost at Pultava the result of so much labour and appeared to have acquired so much glory only to decorate his rival with it. The fortunes of Peter surpassed his, precisely because the Czar of Russia was what he ought to have been, the instrument of Destiny, whereas he, who should have been that of the European Will, had wished to be as his father, only the instrument of his own will. Thrown after his defeat into the possession of the Turkish Sultan he had plenty of time to reflect upon the indiscretions of his conduct, which he did not do; he dreamed only of fomenting against Russia a war which indeed did burst forth between this power and the Sublime Porte, but which had finally no other result than that of showing Europe the genius of Peter the Great in all his splendour and of giving her some idea of what a new empire could become which, from the first moments of its foundation, had contested with so much advantage against an empire strengthened by victory and by time.

From this time, Sweden lost all her rights to supremacy; she was only what her own strength and extent of her territory permitted her to be. The Russian Empire constituted and civilized by Peter I. became consolidated and polished under the successive reigns of four women endowed with different qualities but all appropriate to the conditions; sometimes mild, sometimes severe, but always brilliant. This empire was the work of Destiny which, in bringing these four princesses to the throne, confirmed a thing whose example the history of the world offers everywhere; to wit: that it is through women that all civilization, all intellectual movement, of whatever nature it may be, commences; and that, more precocious than men, speaking generally or individually, they must appear where Destiny, Providence, or the Will of Man determines an early growth; now the Russian Empire is in the number of political creations extremely forward, which must be so in order to fulfil its object.

CHAPTER VII

ELEVATION OF PRUSSIA UNDER FREDERICK II.—MISTAKES
COMMITTED BY THIS PRINCE—DISMEMBERMENT OF
POLAND—GLANCE AT POLAND, DENMARK, AND OTHER
POWERS OF EUROPE — SOME REFLECTIONS ON THE
MINISTRY OF CARDINAL RICHELIEU

THUS, by the mistake of the Swedish monarchs Charles XI. and Charles XII., Sweden did not attain the end that she should have attained and the schism of Luther failed again as a basis. The European Will made a new effort and decided that the Elector of Brandenburg, Frederick I., should assume the title of King of Prussia in 1701. This new kingdom, by no means great at first, reached a remarkable ascendancy from the accession of Frederick II., surnamed the *Great;* it dominated Germany, and served it as a safeguard against the attacks of Russia. If Frederick had possessed as much sagacity as valour and *bel esprit*, he would have again seized the occasion which was presented to give his power a basis; and he would have taken care not to ally himself with his two natural enemies, Austria and Russia, to tear Poland in pieces and divide the shreds among them; for it was not with a few square leagues added to his states that he could hope that his successors would later resist a colossus such as Russia. It was necessary to conquer and not divide Poland, to change her form and not destroy her political existence; which would have been easy by gaining the affection of the people and meriting from her the title of king. Frederick was destined to this. The movement imparted by the Will urged it; and if he had wished it, all obstacles which appeared in opposition would have been levelled.   He preferred to follow another movement and unfortunately for him it was that of Russia.

Poland, which was thus dismembered by the three powers that I have just named, was the most extraordinary constituted state of Europe; she was neither a monarchy nor a republic, neither a feudal state, nor an aristocracy; she was all this together.   She was entitled a republic and had a king; she had a king and no one wished to obey him.   This king was almost always a foreigner.   The Palatinate, who took away the liberty of the people and who crushed their subjects or rather their slaves with the hardest and most injurious yoke, were occupied only in defending their liberty against the attempts of the king.   The state was always in tumult and the diets resembled less a senate than an arena of gladiators; the veto of a single nobleman sufficed to prevent the most important discussions.   They foolishly pretended to unite in this kingdom, without intermediary bond, Destiny to the Will and pretend to make the laws of necessity and liberty move together; thus the state was exposed to continual revolutions.   Nevertheless several distinguished kings are counted there and among others John Sobieski, who gained the famous battle of Kotzim over the Turks and forced them to raise the siege of Vienna.   The wisest was, perhaps, Cardinal Casimir, who followed the example of Christina and abdicated the throne in 1668, and died at Paris, Abbot of Saint-Germain-des-Près.   The kingdom of Poland in all these circumstances did much less than it was able to do; thus all that it lost at different times would have sufficed to constitute a flourishing state.   It was compelled in 1671 to become tributary to the Turks; and a century after it was dismembered and lost its political existence.

Denmark, since the infamous action of Christian II., who caused the Swedish Senate with a large number of the principal citizens to be killed at a solemn fête in 1520, has exercised no direct influence upon Europe. The absolute separation from Sweden has weakened her too much for the extraordinary conduct of the states of the kingdom in 1660 to have any results. These states bestowed upon King Frederick III. hereditary right and absolute sovereignty. Under any other condition a similar act would have ruined the Danes or made them formidable to their neighbours. It did nothing of this; which goes to prove that these peoples had neither the strength to consent to a like act when free, nor to refuse it when forced.

Hungary and Bohemia not only have not exercised the influence upon Europe that Denmark has, but these two kingdoms have certainly experienced greater misfortunes; Hungary particularly which appeared to enjoy a moment of *éclat* under the reigns of Carobert and of his son Louis. This Carobert had been chosen for the throne by Pope Boniface VIII., one of the most enterprising pontiffs that the holy seat has ever had. He was the son of a nephew of Saint Louis, called Charles Martel. He united to his kingdom Dalmatia, Servia, Transylvania, and Wallachia and made Hungary the most powerful state in Germany; but this power was only transitory. Two queens, adulteresses and regicides, were the cause of her downfall: Jeanne of Naples and Elisabeth of Bosnia.[1] Louis, son of Carobert,

[1] One of these queens, Jeanne of Naples, having married the unfortunate André of Hungary, had the cruelty to have him strangled before her eyes with a bow-string which she had woven herself. At the news of this outrage, Louis, King of Hungary, brother of this André, raised an army and hastened into Italy to avenge the death of his brother. He took possession of the kingdom of Naples and being able to keep it, left it to the pope, contenting himself with pursuing the queen. This act of clemency was too great. Providence did not approve it. Jeanne, surprised some time after by her adopted son, whom Pope Urban VI. had made King of Naples, was smothered between two mattresses.

The second of these queens was Elisabeth of Bosnia, wife of this same Louis, whom Providence made use of to punish the crime of Jeanne. At the death of this prince, in 1382, the States of Hungary elected first his daughter Marie who was not yet marriageable, and shortly after chose Charles Durazzo for king, a direct line descendant of a brother of Saint Louis. This being

was a great prince for the time in which he lived; he was cherished by his people, admired by foreigners, and chosen at the end of his life to be King of Poland. He was surnamed the *Great*. Unfortunately he left no male heir. His widow Elisabeth of Bosnia, having had Charles Durazzo, the elected King of the States of Hungary, assassinated so as to preserve the throne for her daughter Marie, drew the kingdom into bloody dissensions of which she was the first victim about the middle of the fourteenth century. From this time Hungary incessantly ravaged, now by the Turks, then by the Austrians who had wished to subject her and whose rule she would not permit, did not enjoy a moment of tranquillity. At the beginning of the sixteenth century her king, Louis II., was killed at the battle of Mohács against the Turks and his army was cut to pieces. Suleiman took away with him more than two hundred thousand captives. All was annihilated by fire and sword. Those who survived in Hungary were obliged to dig subterranean habitations to escape the rapacity of the victor.

I have said enough of Germany in connection with the imperial power and of Italy in respect to the pontifical power; it is useless to return to similar things where only the names would be changed. One must know that if, since Charles V., the emperors of Germany possessed any power, they owed it to their own states and not in the least to their titles. As

---

displeasing to Elisabeth, widow of Louis and mother of Marie, she had the unfortunate monarch assassinated before her. This execrable regicide revolted the Hungarians so, that a short time after, Elisabeth and Marie travelling in Lower Hungary were seized by a noble of Croatia who, believing himself authorized to avenge the death of the king, brought the two queens to trial. Elisabeth, having been recognized as guilty, was drowned. Marie was retained in prison and without difficulty given over to Emperor Sigismund, who had arranged to marry her so as to unite Hungary to his States. This noble believed he had done an act of justice; but the emperor, judging otherwise, had him arrested and condemned to death as regicide. This action having roused all the nobility caused a most stubborn civil war. The Turks, arriving unexpectedly in the midst of these discussions, beat the troops of Sigismund and, surprising him, confined him in prison.

sovereigns of Austria, Hungary, Bohemia, part of Flanders, or other countries, they held without doubt the highest rank in Germany and a very distinguished rank in Europe; but it was not, I repeat, as emperors, it was as monarchs. If the empire had existed a moment under Charlemagne, it was long since it had existed at all.

The pontifical power, which had existed scarcely more than the imperial, was entirely crushed at the beginning of the seventeenth century by the resistance of the Venetian Republic to Pope Paul V. This pope having put an interdict upon the Republic and excommunicated the Doge and the Senate, nowhere was the interdict published and the excommunication was scorned. The most extraordinary thing about this affair was that it was Henry IV. who acted as mediator between these two powers and set them to rights. It was seen on this occasion how the times were changed. The popes with no force of opinion and, reduced to vain ceremonies, became exactly what it was hoped they would become; but the emperors also enjoyed no power beyond that of their real strength as was seen several times and particularly in 1740 when Maria Theresa, Queen of Hungary and Bohemia by the will of her father, disputed the empire with Charles VII., stripped him of his duchy of Bavaria, and had the power to have her husband, Francis I., elected to reign under her name, as she reigned afterwards under the name of her son Joseph II. It was on this occasion where the imperial power was really extinct in the person of Charles VII. and where the election of the emperors of Germany was only a vain formality.

Thus, as I have said, Spain, having reached the highest point of grandeur in the sixteenth century, declined rapidly in the seventeenth and finally had no power in the eighteenth. The court of Philip III., like that of Louis XIII., was only a chaos of intrigues. The Duc de Lerme reigned in Spain under the name of his master, as Cardinal Richelieu did in France; but by no means with the same genius. The Duc d'Olivares who succeeded him under Philip IV. was the reason that Portugal separated once more from the Spanish monarchy and that all the possessions of the Portuguese in the Indies became the prey of the Dutch. The regency of Maria of Austria and the weak reign of Charles II. finished by losing all.

Owing to the genius of Henry IV., France began to take a firmer position in Europe and renounce the weak, evasive politics which she had been obliged to follow since Francis I., when this monarch was assassinated. It was seen then how one man can influence the fate of nations. All was in harmony under his administration; all was discord under the regency of his widow Marie de Médici. The drowsy factions awoke; the religious peace reinstated with so much trouble was disturbed anew; the people who lived in abundance fell again into misery. Civil war was rekindled, murders recommenced, the most hideous prejudices revived. The prime minister of the Regency, Concini, was assassinated and his body, dragged through the streets, was torn by brigands who devoured his heart; his wife Galigai was burned as a sorceress; Parliament, ridiculous instrument of most ridiculous opinions, forbade under penalty of death to teach anything contrary to the doctrine of Aristotle.

Louis XIII., drawn against his will into a fatal war, experienced only disasters; everything inclined towards his utter ruin when Cardinal Richelieu entering the council believed himself sufficiently strong to sustain the edifice ready to pass away. He was indeed. This man, of whom as much evil as good has been said and much of both, merited neither the excess of blame nor the excess of praise which has been lavished upon him. Sailing on a tempestuous sea and always about to be shipwrecked, his merit was never to have doubted himself. As yielding as violent, his friends were his instruments and his enemies his victims. He did not change the politics of France which were bad, but he put into them an order and a vigour which made it succeed. While he persecuted the Protestants in France and crushed forever their power, he allied himself with those of Holland and Germany and protected their pretensions; while in France he shamefully treated the mother and the guardian of his king, his queen, and his benefactress, he humiliated himself before the Queen of Sweden and offered to Europe the singular spectacle of a cardinal forming a compact with a Protestant queen. He strengthened royalty in France and left it shaken in England. He founded the French Academy and restrained the liberty of the press; he was a free thinker and had Urbain Grandier burned as a sorcerer. Finally, it was only by humiliating his king that he succeeded in making him powerful; and by tyrannizing France that he succeeded in making him respected. This extraordinary man died in 1642. The widow of Henry IV. had preceded him by five months and Louis XIII. followed him five months after. It is a question which of the three was the most unfortunate. If certain pleasures of pride and vengeance are effaced before the hatred which one inspires and the continual terror which one experiences, it is evidently Richelieu, whose fatal destiny never permitted him to attain general or particular good, except by dangerous or bloody routes.

CHAPTER VIII

THE reign of Louis XIII. was for France a time of conspiracies and torment. The minority of Louis XIV.
was one of trouble and anarchy. Cardinal Mazarin was
only the pale image of an original character whose traits
were firm and decided. He sailed, however, amid tempests;
but it was in yielding to contrary winds and in tacking
without cessation that he reached port. His principal merit
was understanding himself and understanding other men.
However, the French nation had become civilized in the
midst of the troubles and perplexities of its government;
it had grasped moral influence on all sides. The century
which has been called the *century of Louis XIV.* opened as
early as the ministry of Cardinal Richelieu with the tragedy
of the *Cid*, which Corneille brought out in 1636. Poetry
and all the fine arts in general had received a great impetus.
Commerce was doubtless far from rivalling that of the Dutch
or the English; France did not have numerous colonies
which could furnish her with gold and silver from America,
nor the precious products of Asia; but she possessed a fruitful soil, inexhaustible in an infinity of productions of fore-

most need and always ready to respond to the care of a
patient and laborious agriculturist.[1]

Before Louis XIV., France had no doubt displayed courage, but almost always a courage of circumstance which
appeared with the vehemence of lightning and disappeared
like it. French impetuosity has become a proverb. Louis
XIV. was the first to lay hold of this impetuosity to moderate it and give it steadiness and persistence, so as to transform it into real valour. This prince was the creator of
that national virtue of which France has given so many
proofs since. He was truly great in this respect. He disdained the insidious politics of Richelieu and Mazarin and
left the shadowy course where all his predecessors foundered.
He believed the French nation strong enough to be genuine,
and himself strong enough to rise above intrigue. All that
he did in the vigour of his age he did openly. As soon as
Madame de Maintenon had forced him to change his character in teaching him to dissimulate he was lost. Dissimu-
lation could not ally itself with the majesty of his genius. If
this monarch had had an aim, a plan, more extensive knowledge, or even a ministry strong enough to second him, he
might have changed the face of the world; but all this he
lacked. He made war from choice and conquests for glory.
He had ministers, sycophants or weak in conception. Lou-
vois and Colbert who have been cited were not on a level with
their master. At the most they could have served as secre-
tary to a prime minister if there had been one. His generals

---

[1] It has been remarked for some time in France, that agriculture is the
basis of national prosperity and furnishes to the manufacturers their principal
elements and to commerce its principal activity. This state differs in this
from others and chiefly from England where commerce gives, on the contrary,
the impulse to agriculture and furnishes to the manufacturers the greater part
of their raw materials which is sought from afar. This observation, which
I make here only in passing, will become later of the highest importance when
it will be a question of that sort of government which I have called *Emporocratic*—a government in which commerce dominates not only as integral part,
but as political power disposing of a large army and possessing abroad, subject
peoples and slaves.

only were great because he inspired them. When he no longer inspired them, when a cold ambitious woman had deadened his soul, had covered with a veil of hypocrisy the elegant manners of a voluptuous and proud court, everything was changed. Falsehood took the place of truth and all became petty where all had been great.

France was indeed close to her ruin. The King, in allying himself with this profoundly artificial woman, spoiled the beautiful character that nature had given him; he followed no longer his own inspirations but the inspirations of a false and egotistical mind which he believed substantial and prudent. The revocation of the Edict of Nantes which this mind suggested to him was the most impolitic and most ill-timed measure. His life was divided into two parts—the one fortunate and brilliant, the other gloomy and miserable. It was in vain that Pope Innocent XI. had the *Te Deum* chanted with joy at Rome; the Pope had no longer the force to have the slightest share in this event, even if he had been just and wise; but how far he was from being so!

When Francis I. and the kings his successors, persecuted the Protestants they did not persecute them so much as followers of Luther or Calvin, but as subjects rebellious to their laws. These laws had been promulgated against them and they exposed themselves, in infringing them, to the penalties which they inflicted. These monarchs acted thus in their functions, and did not abandon the rights of their crown. But when a civil war had broken out, as the two parties were legally recognized, they fought each other, at first with equal arms and afterwards in stipulating conditions of peace; these conditions, freely accepted on both sides, bound the kings as much as the subjects and it was no longer permitted either of them to break them without committing a perjury. This is the reason, so little known, which puts a great difference between actions which appear the same. Writers, otherwise estimable, not having observed it, have not conceived for the massacre of St. Bartholomew all the horror that it should have inspired. They have seen it with the same eye as they have seen the massacres of which Francis I. was guilty, but the position was not the same. Francis had promised nothing; on the contrary, he had threatened, while Charles IX., having recognized the Protestant party in signing with it a treaty of peace, became a perjurer in violating it as he did. So the massacre of St. Bartholomew was not a royal act, purely criminal, a *coup d'état;* it was an execrable assassination. And in the same way, the Edict of Nantes, being the effect of a treaty of peace concluded in 1576, and renewed in 1598, its revocation did not depend on Louis XIV. unless this prince wished to declare war upon his subjects and consequently authorize their rebellion. These two acts, which I cannot compare, although I show their illegality, had consequences analogous to their criminality. The one annihilated the House of Valois; the other obscured the glory of Louis XIV. and greatly influenced the prosperity of his family which was dimmed by it.

This monarch, notwithstanding the adversities which overwhelmed the end of his reign, almost all of which had their origin from the fatal source which I have just indicated, had, however, the force to place his grandson on the throne of Spain; but this event which under other conditions would have been very great, especially if France had not again missed the place which was her due, at the head of European civilization, was confined to nothing much and became sometimes disadvantageous on account of a certain family pact which frequently made Spain more embarrassing as an ally than she would have been as an enemy.

After the death of Louis XIV., all the *ressorts* of the government, which the mind of Madame de Maintenon had restrained to excess, were relaxed into a contrary excess; the veil of hypocrisy in which this woman had forced the court and the city to be enveloped was torn with violence and all was invaded by an audacious license which soon knew no bounds. The Duke of Orleans, Regent of France, during the minority of Louis XV., deceived by the counsels of Cardinal Dubois whom he had made his prime minister, relied upon all the errors of a disordered imagination. Pressed by the heads of finance he adopted Law's system regarding paper money and did not confine himself within the limits which alone could secure its success. The people, confident and credulous, took up this system with an incredible blindness. Bank-notes multiplied beyond all imagination. A fatal struggle was established between the adroit man who had nothing and the ignorant but avaricious man who, having something, risked it to run after a fictitious fortune where all the chances were against him. A treacherous speculation took place by which morals, already shaken, received a fresh shock. Fortunes abruptly changing hands brought about a general confusion. The lowest part of the nation, finding itself suddenly on top, gave opinion a new movement which bewildered it.

At this time began the philosophism of the eighteenth century, an incoherent mixture of wit and pure reason; a distinctive instrument able to destroy everything, incapable of constructing anything, friend of the ruins over which it soared with pride. Its appearance was the work and the triumph of the Will. Frightened Destiny sought in vain arms against it. The reign of Madame de Maintenon and that of the Regent had left nothing intact. The *Unigenitus* bull and Jansenism, the unseasonable pretensions of the Council of Embrun, the madness of the fanatics, only increased the phantom by giving it occasion to display its accustomed weapons, sarcasm and ridicule, and to gain, over its weak adversaries easy triumphs. Destiny gave way.

Meanwhile Louis XV., still a child, left to the ignorance of his counsellors, was bewildered from his first step. All the measures which he was made to take were in contradiction with circumstances and clashed equally with men and things. In the midst of an incredulous and depraved court he issued a severe edict against the Protestants and directed new persecutions against them. Astonished Europe asked in vain where was the principle of this excess of zeal. Sweden and Prussia profited by this mistake and gained the best French manufacturers. The alliance of Spain for which Louis XIV. had lavished so much treasure and so much blood was abandoned; the Infanta whose marriage with the king was stopped was unceremoniously sent home and this prince was given as wife the daughter of a dethroned king. This impolitic alliance drew France into a disastrous war which disturbed Europe to no end. The second war in which Louis XV. entered as ally of the Duke of Bavaria against Maria Theresa was equally calamitous. Its result increased the influence of the Will and diminished that of Destiny. France was eclipsed. Prussia seized the rule. The Will triumphed. Philosophism which it had brought forth sat upon the throne with Frederick II.

Then, among the multitude of men who rushed into the whirlwind of the Will to take part in this triumph, two were chiefly observed. One, a universal wit, decided sceptic, man of the world, and adroit courtier, substituting for the depth which he lacked the extent and *éclat* of superficialities, declared himself against Providence whose power, only suspected, afflicted his pride, and led against it a crowd of athletes more or less strong who followed his colours. The other, profound reasoner, brilliant writer, eloquent to enthusiasm, endowed with a genius, vigorous as independent, threw himself with lowered head against Destiny which had replaced him in the world, and drew after him all those who could kindle the same spirit of paradox and the same love of liberty. Voltaire and Rousseau, although naturally enemies and opposed on all other points, agreed, however, in this one: that the Will of Man is everything. The first declared as imposture and falsehood everything which emanated directly or indirectly from Providence; the second as usurpation and tyranny everything which came from Destiny. The one overthrew the altar, denied the pontiffs their sacerdotal authority, and only wished for all religion a divine phantom seated upon liberty unlimited by conscience; the other shook the throne, refused legislative power to the kings, and proclaimed loudly the sovereignty of the people on whom he established the whole social edifice. Fontenelle had preceded Voltaire, and Montesquieu had written before Rousseau. But the two pupils far surpassed their masters, assuming that they recognized them as such, for philosophism did not recognize them.

These two men usurped all the voices of renown. The power of the Will of which they were the promoters carried them on likewise. It did not appear that one could be anything outside of the activity of their vortex. Such was their influence that although they declared quite formally that they needed neither priests, nor kings, nor priesthood, nor nobility, a great number of priests, nobles, magistrates, and kings were among their disciples. Frederick had given the lead; he dominated over the highest opinion. How could he help being what he was? All the Protestant princes were philosophers; Emperor Joseph II. was a philosopher, Catherine II. herself, and, what is still more astonishing, even Pope Clement XIV., were philosophers. Everything was philosophy from one end of Europe to the other except the Turk, however, who was always there to arrest the too-petulant impetus of the volitive principle whence this philosophism emanated.

CHAPTER IX

CONSEQUENCES OF THE REVOLUTION IN ENGLAND—MOVE-
MENT OF THE WILL IN AMERICA—ITS PROPAGATION
IN FRANCE

WHILST these things were happening, the revolution
in England, which appeared arrested by the recall
of Charles II., was resumed by the expulsion of King James
and the nomination of the Prince of Orange, his son-in-law,
under the name of William III. This William died without
children; his sister-in-law, Anne Stuart, second daughter of
James, succeeded him without the least difficulty and without paternal respect having the slightest power to prevent
her usurpation, which is a most peremptory proof of the
triumph of the Will over Destiny. After the death of this
queen whom the intrigues of her favourites urged now to
war and then to peace, according to their interests and by
the most petty means,[1] the English Parliament, considering
itself able to express the wish of the English nation, called
the Elector of Hanover to ascend the throne in 1714, under
the name of George I. Since this time England has been
a royal emporocracy whose king is the honorary sovereign
and Parliament the real master, or lacking it, the ministry
which subjugates or corrupts it. Holland, which had fore-
stalled her in this sort of government, has been eclipsed, and,

[1] It is said that the disgrace of the famous Marlborough who brought
about the peace with France and saved this kingdom depended on a pair of
gloves.

obliged to follow a movement stronger than hers, has been only a humble satellite of this maritime star whose splendour has covered the two hemispheres.

But, at last, after fifty or sixty years of this brilliant existence, this star has had to receive a check. The moment has arrived when the germ of liberty, settled in America by the care of Fox and Penn, after being nourished and developed in the shade, has had to manifest its strength and produce its fruits. This is what happened in 1774 when the English colonies of North America, under the pretext of some vexations on the part of the mother country, had suddenly resolved to withdraw from its domination, and a general congress being formed to this effect at Philadelphia the command of the insurgent armies was conferred upon Washington. This movement, at first judged of little importance, scarcely attracted the attention of Europe, which did not suspect the immense results that it would have when the act of union appeared, by which these colonies declared themselves independent and constituted themselves a republic under the name of the *United States*. It would no doubt be difficult to conceive, without all that I have said, what strange infatuation prevented the European powers from seeing the danger which was concealed for them in this act of union. They would have seen it, no doubt, if the same force which had provoked it had not also produced their blindness. But all had been prepared in advance to favour the effect which was about to take place. France, just emerging from a difficult reign where royal authority without energy could neither make herself respected abroad nor obeyed at home, delivered to the ministers of a king animated by the best intentions but young and inexperienced, —France was not in a condition to evade the snare which was set for her. She saw in the movement which was taking place in America only a means of weakening England and of diminishing the preponderance of this power in Europe. Louis XVI., to whom his counsel presented it under this point of view, could not look upon it otherwise; he determined to favour it and drew Spain and Holland into the same decision.

Thanks to this powerful diversion, and to the French troops which had gone to America, liberty triumphed in that part of the world. The English Parliament was constrained to recognize the independence of the United States, and this was done by an authentic bill in 1782. But the disturbance caused in America was felt in Europe; the energy of the insurgents, their bravery, their devotion to the country, their love of liberty had formed the subject of all conversations. Their manifestoes were read and admired, their speeches in Congress were similar to those which in former times resounded in Athens and in Rome and which reminded the greater part of literary men and statesmen of what had been their delight while in college. Soldiers having returned from America brought with them the seeds of insubordination and disputes which they sowed in the army; and the superior officers, instruments of an insurrectional will whose action they did not suspect, admirers of Washington or Franklin, were all disposed to imitate them if the occasion should present itself; which it did.

The land wherein the Will of Man scattered these seeds of revolution brought from America was marvellously prepared to receive them and make them fruitful. The sceptic philosophers at whose head were Voltaire, Mirabeau the father, Diderot, Helvetius, and all the Holbach set, so called on account of Baron Holbach at whose house they gathered, the political philosphers, among whom Rousseau, the Abbé de Mably, the Abbé Raynal, and some others had ruled by turn, had all together stirred the minds in diverse ways and had roused them to fermentation. Their opinions, in some way opposed, left, however, in the heads which received them, —and these heads were the foremost and strongest in Europe, —two clear and fixed ideas which were reduced to this: that the one could do without priests and kings in the government and that the altar and the throne were the inventions of fraud and tyranny, good for times of ignorance and weakness, but which could be broken without fear and relegated to the storeroom of fanaticism and despotism in times of wisdom and strength, where knowledge, having attained its highest degree, would no longer permit their continuance.

These two ideas, cultivated chiefly in France, passed into Prussia and from there were propagated throughout the rest of Germany. Weishaupt seized them and, as I have already announced at the beginning of this work, saw in their union the realization of the famous golden age described by the poets. Full of this fantastic dream he imagined a Utopia in which he claimed to make all men without exception their own sovereigns and their own pontiffs. His doctrine, which was decorated with the name of *Illuminism*, made rapid progress and, mingling with the lost mysteries of the Freemasons, entered France, where it threw a new source of agitation into the minds already in fermentation.

Financial embarrassments, court intrigues, mistakes of the ministry had aroused France, had disturbed *parlement*, and had obliged Louis XVI. to take vigorous measures which his character, too easily influenced, had carried out badly; but one cannot understand both things and men very clearly if one believes that such weak motives could cause such a violent and complete overthrow as that which took place, if this overthrow had not been the effect of a moral movement prepared long before. This movement depended entirely upon the free Will of Man, acting in the absence of Providence upon the necessity of Destiny which it surmounted, like an overflowing torrent which demolishes its dikes, destroys its banks, tears, breaks, and drags along all that resists it, and rolls at last, laden with débris, over devastated fields. This movement was in politics what the schism of Luther had been in the cult a little less than three centuries before; it had the same cause, as I have taken pains to state, and was one of the results of the combat long since established between liberty and necessity, the Will of Man and Destiny.

I shall not enter into the details of this horrible subversion which has been called by the more restricted name of *Revolution*. These details are too present, too well known to the greater part of my contemporaries, so that I dare to abridge them. The slightest events which happened have left too profound traces in the memory of those who have survived them, that one can omit one part and make choice of another. In a narrative like this one must tell all or nothing. There are several good works on this subject and that of Madame de Staël is assuredly not one of the least. This wonderful woman, endowed with an exquisite sensibility and a quite remarkable vigour of thought, has left little to desire in the picture of events; it is true she did not know the metaphysical causes which I unfold in general, but at the time when she wrote, her ignorance was forced.[1]

[1] I shall perhaps relate some day in another work what I have seen of the Revolution and what has been particularly connected with me; but here would be neither the place nor the time. During the whole course of the revolutionary tumult and for more than thirty years I have not left Paris. Unperceived in the midst of the parties, I have observed them quite closely, without ever coming into collision with them. Bonaparte alone has persecuted me for particular reasons which I shall expose later.

CHAPTER X

NOTE this singular coincidence. Just when the first symptoms of the Revolution manifested themselves in America and when the Will, ready to burst forth in Europe created vigorous defenders in the sceptical and political philosophers, Destiny lost its strongest supports there. The Jesuits were no more. This formidable institution preyed upon by the movement of the century collapsed almost without resistance. This is one of the greatest phenomena which has ever appeared on the religious and political horizon and it has been almost ignored. Who would have believed it! The *Parlement* of Paris declared itself against them. France, Spain, Portugal, the Pope! the Pope himself banished them. It seemed that the volitive action which was manifested would draw into its vortex even Destiny itself, forced to follow the magic impulse which it gave to everything. Perhaps never had this action been displayed with such energy. A veritable frenzy took possession of the minds. If religion still took refuge in some sacerdotal heads, they were taxed with weakness and blindness. The *parlements* would have been ashamed to show themselves royalists. It was good form for them to be opposed to the court in everything. The nobility itself mocked the prejudices which constituted it. The ministry filled with a puerile presumption, still believing to command opinion, when opinion commanded it, gloried foolishly over its successes in America, when these same successes were to ruin it. Finally, there existed almost nothing religious in religion, nor real royalist in royalty. When, recalled by reflection, the religious sentiment and royalism wished to reappear, it was no longer the time. The necessity of Destiny, vanquished by the force of the Will, had allowed events to march with such rapidity that the defenders of the altar and the throne, always behind the circumstances, presented themselves in the arena only to be crushed there.

Those who have been witnesses of these deplorable events and who remember the rapidity with which they succeeded each other must still shudder with terror. This was no ordinary time, be assured; the destiny of no one, whoever he might be, could resist the violent movement which involved all things. No position was strong enough, no inference irresistible enough, no prudence, no foresight extended enough. Everything gave way before the terrible power which was moving. Providence, absent, unrecognized, or veiled, acted only by laws too universal to be felt. Destiny was nothing. The Will was everything. Let us follow for a moment the unfolding.

Hardly had the States-General assembled at Versailles at the beginning of May, 1789, when in the month of June the deputies of the communes, then called the *Tiers-État*, assumed control over the nobility and the clergy. The royal authority which wished to oppose it only gave more impetus to the torrent and hastened the famous declaration of the Rights of Man, which, in imitation of that of the United States of America, sanctions insurrection. In the month of July the insurrection bursts forth. Paris rises in rebellion; the Bastille is demolished in a moment and its governor killed.[1] Many magistrates are massacred who

---

[1] The great Condé had uselessly besieged for three weeks this same fortress of which men without a chief and nearly without arms took possession in two hours.

endeavoured to oppose the tumult.   France imitates Paris. At the voice of Mirabeau the national guards arm themselves.   There are arms on all sides.   Three million soldiers appear to come out of the ground like the warriors of Cadmus and like them destined to destroy each other.   In the month of August the feeble barrier which still surrounds the throne is overthrown.   The nobility itself destroys its rights and treads upon them.   Vainly in the month of September the National Assembly, frightened at the precipice into which it feels itself thrown, wishes to retrace its steps by decreeing the inviolability of the person of the king.   This illusory inviolability is violated on the 6th of October.   A multitude of furious women rush into the palace of Versailles; some brigands who follow them kill the guards and with their blood-stained hands attack the monarch and his family.   He is hurried away to Paris; he is forced to sanction acts which debase the throne and overthrow the altar.   He has the weakness to agree.   Before the end of the year, the property of the clergy is declared the patrimony of the nation and the nation itself is covered with a mass of paper money, which soon increasing with frightful progression makes fortunes change hands and causes an upheaval like that which had already resulted from the system of Law, but more radical and more vast.

The year 1790 opens with the persecution of the priests who refuse to swear allegiance to the new constitution which the pope does not recognize, and with the institution of the famous club of Jacobins.   On one side the last resources of Destiny are taken away and on the other a limitless field is given to the arbitration of the Will.   This Will triumphs in the federation of the 14th of July.   More than four hundred thousand French, assembled at Paris from all points of France, bind themselves by the same oaths.   That day was great in its inconceivable nullity!   If Providence had been present, I do not believe that anything in the universe could have equalled the magnificence.   In 1791, the persecutions against the refractory priests become more intense; the nobility migrates; the foreign powers begin to look at France and appear to interest themselves in the consequences of the struggle which they see established there. These consequences are no longer doubtful. The National Assembly, all-powerful in opinion, declares that it alone has the right to renew itself and that the king has not the right to dissolve it. The king, from whom this act tears the crown, tries but too late to save himself by fleeing; he is arrested before his departure from the kingdom; he is brought back in triumph to Paris where he sees himself constrained to accept the shadow of power, which they indeed are willing to allow him in a constitution which its founders believed immortal and which did not live ten months.

The throne collapses the 10th of August, 1792; it collapses apparently under the blows of a handful of factionists, but in reality under the effort of the popular Will, which, provoked abroad by insulting manifestoes, becomes irritated, burns to avenge itself, proclaims war, and not finding anything to strike quickly enough, strikes everything that it supposes to be in accord with its enemies. From the palace of the kings, which it has just stained with blood, it drives the fatal instruments of its ravages to the prisons filled with unfortunate victims and orders their massacre. The National Convention succeeds the Legislative Assembly; it proclaims the Republic upon the heaps of ruins, while innocent blood still reeks around it. Everything which Providence holds holy and sacred, everything which Destiny holds august and imposing is trampled under foot. This Convention, political colossus, assemblage deformed by the most opposed elements, outrages the priesthood in its first steps by ignoring the sovereign pontiff,[1] and royalty, by

---

[1] Having written to the Pope regarding some persecutions which French artists had experienced in Rome, the government of the Republic gave him only the title of *Bishop of Rome*.

humiliating its monarch. Forgetting that the person of the king had been declared inviolable by a law not revoked, it dares to call to its bar the unfortunate Louis XVI. and submit him to a judicial interrogation. This indignant prince should have challenged this iniquitous tribunal, and, summoning it in turn, ask by what right rebellious subjects dared to become judges of their king. He had not the force to do it; he was condemned. If he had done it, if he had challenged his judges, the Convention might have been able to go further, perhaps, but the sentence would have been an assassination and the consequences would have been very different. The fatal compliance of Louis ruined him. This prince delivered Destiny into the power of the Will. In vain were all the sovereigns of Europe leagued against France. Nothing could stop the devastating torrent, which, having overthrown the last barriers, raised their menacing waves above all obstacles and rolled their enormous mass over all heads.

Force of arms could do nothing. When one of the three great powers of the Universe alone dominates the other two, there are no exterior means that can arrest its course. It reaches by its own movement the dominion of the world and from that of the world to that of the Universe, if it does not carry within itself a germ of destruction which arrests its progress. This germ is developed more or less late, but always irresistibly by a sequence of universal laws emanating from the Divine Wisdom. The exterior forces ordinarily employed are all broken; death even is without power; it can do nothing against the Will. Men die, the instruments change place, but the thought which moves them remains immortal and irrefutable. There are even cases where death is the most powerful of vehicles. If one had had only the force of arms to oppose the movement which was determined in France, the subversion which it drew after it would have been general; Europe and the entire earth inundated with blood, after having experienced for several centuries all the scourges which France experienced for several months, would have found, instead of the golden age which a blind Will had promised, the age of its utter destruction. But in order that this should happen, it was necessary that this Will should not be divided; which was impossible for the reasons which I have given. It was therefore divided, and so much the more quickly as its action was the more violent.

At first, the Convention being divided into two factions, that of the Girondists, and that of the Mountainists, clashes and is broken. The Girondists are sacrificed and their partisans die on the scaffold. Then begins the 31st of May, 1793, the formidable epoch which is called the Reign of Terror. Robespierre is its chief. Blood flows in torrents through the interior; the most frightful famine devours the inhabitants and Victory meanwhile pushes forward the Republican colossus. The war is general. Europe is ravaged by the most numerous armies that it has ever seen assembled. Those of France alone exceed eight hundred thousand men. Everything yields to their forces. France is covered with immense glory which unfortunately deprived of principle brings about no result. The Convention, already divided, divides itself again. The faction of the Mountainists, triumphant for fifteen months, is thrown into disorder in 1794. Robespierre and his adherents are crushed beneath the débris. After this memorable epoch of the 9th of July (Thermidor), the colossus is shaken in long convulsions. In May (Prairial) 1795, a new division brings about the abolition of the Jacobin Club and the suppression of the revolutionary tribunal. The violence of the movement is greatly diminished and many treaties of peace are concluded. The French Government without form up to this moment assumes one. It is the form of the Republic of Carthage which the Convention gives as a new invention, throwing aside, however, the only things in it which might have given it force: the statue of Moloch and the slavery

. of the Numidians. The popular legislators, still divided amongst themselves, divide the people. Paris takes sides against them. The forty-eight sections of this capital arouse themselves and throwing more than fifty thousand men against the Convention determined to destroy it. Then appears on the scene of the world a prophetic man endowed with a strong will and a rigid destiny. This man, called *Napoleon Bonaparte*, saves the Convention, lost without him, and begins, on the 13th day of September (Vendé-miaire), the first union of the Will and Destiny and effects the first submission of liberty to necessity.

The year 1796 is memorable for having seen the weaving of this formidable knot; it is famous too for the campaign of Bonaparte in Italy where the number and rapidity of his victories astonish Europe although accustomed to the triumphs of the French. Since 1797, peace has been concluded with all the potentates of the continent; England alone remains at war and this has to be thus; for henceforth she becomes the rival of France and her competitor and has in view the same end. The Directorate (as the republican government in France is called) is composed of five directors and a legislative body separated in two chambers; the Directorate having become the centre of a volitive movement begins to follow the fortunes of this movement, and, being always divided in opinion, strikes itself, is mutilated, and grows weaker until the 18th of August (Fructidor). Bonaparte, adroit in seconding this mistake profits, by it; and seeing that these ignorant politicians did not comprehend in the least their position, that they still took as the product of their strength what was only the product of his, resolves to withdraw and abandon them to their nullity; he goes with forty thousand men into Egypt, of which he makes a useless conquest,[1] and while he pursues the war in Africa and in Asia with a mixture of success and reverses, that which he

[1] I have already said and I repeat it that the destiny of Africa and of Asia is in Constantinople.

had foreseen in France happens. All is disorganized there and the acquired advantages lost; the frontiers are invaded and the legislative body, struggling against the Directorate, strikes and breaks it without knowing with what to replace it. Bonaparte abruptly abandons his army in Egypt, crosses the sea, reappears unexpectedly in France, and provokes a revolution which places him, with the title of First Consul, at the head of the French government. The two other consuls, which he gives himself as colleagues, and the senate, the so-called conservator, the debating tribunal, and the mute legislative body by which he is surrounded, are there only to support his growing power and to veil its progress.

Thus finishes with the eighteenth century the volitive movement whose principal cause, having come from America twenty years previous, had begun to manifest itself openly in 1789. Bonaparte, a prophetic man as I have said, endowed with an enormous force of centralization, believes himself powerful enough to become master by throwing himself into its vortex, and after having seized it, fortunate enough to attach to it his destiny. He laboured twelve years at this great work displaying in it an obstinacy of character and military and administrative talents of remarkable distinction. He did not repulse the crime of his political career but neither did he summon it. He was hard without being cruel, and crafty without being perfidious. Ready to dominate Europe, and, while his first wife, was still alive, having married the daughter of the Emperor of Germany, the successor of Charlemagne and of Augustus, he believed that he had reached the goal of his desires; but he was mistaken. He understood well enough his destiny and put into what he calls his *star* a boundless confidence; but he did not know either the nature of the movement of which he had taken possession or that of the knot which he had undertaken to form. Liberty and necessity which he wished to unite, are incompatible in their essence. They can never be united except in the interest of a third power which he must know how to seize where it is; now this third power, which is called *Providence*, Napoleon never knew and never sought to know.

CHAPTER XI

BONAPARTE was not capable of restoring peace to the world troubled for such a great number of centuries by the ever-increasing struggle between Necessity and Liberty, the Will of Man and Destiny. I repeat here, without any animosity entering my thought which the memory of his persecutions concerning me could arouse; I am at this moment an historian and I must forget all to speak the truth.[1] Napoleon was only the expression of military tyranny, his authority was only complete where his armies could move and where they had weight. Great spaces were necessary for him to display his strength. Wherever his soldiers could not penetrate, his power was weak and almost insignificant. He has sometimes been compared with Robespierre, but without reason; they were exactly the opposite. Robespierre a volitive man, without learning, having all his force in instinct, must be regarded as the expression of popular tyranny, whose action was reflected in the slightest revolutionary committee; there was no public opinion aside from it; those who had the misfortune to confide in

---

[1] What follows is in part a copy of another of my works entitled *Notions sur le sens de l'Ouïe*. The portrait which I made there of Napoleon is better placed here. This portrait is only sketched. To understand perfectly this extraordinary man one should read what Madame de Staël has said of him. No one knew him better than she did, or has depicted him with more force and truth.

it were lost. The more limited the space, the stronger he was. In great spaces he could do nothing. Thus this subaltern tyrant fell, as soon as, the circle of his authority being extended, he wished to move great masses. The contrary happened to Napoleon a prophetic man, dominated by the opinion that he himself created and that he knew how to inspire in others, very powerful in the animistic part of his being, weak in all the rest; whose head, half in light and half in darkness, astonished by the vivacity and *éclat* of certain faculties, while others ever plunged in a gloomy mist remained inert and by their pettiness and their immobility escaped notice. While victory followed his steps and success enlarged his horizon more and more, his moral being dilated in proportion; but when reverses came and according as the space narrowed around him he felt his strength diminish; this colossus breathed no more when the atmosphere of Europe failed him.

Having reached, in 1811 and 1812, the highest point of his prophetic grandeur he felt by an intuitive inspiration that all was not accomplished. It was in vain for courtiers and flatterers to say that his empire was built upon firm foundations and that he could, resting on his laurels, contemplate in all their superiority the immensity of his work; he did not believe it. He always saw an obstacle to surmount; and this obstacle, always uppermost in his thoughts obsessed him eternally. Fatigued by seeking it without ever seeing where it was, he ended by seeing it where it was not. He persuaded himself that Russia was this terrible obstacle which was troubling his repose and that he would find, as he announced it, the keys of London in the Kremlin of Moscow. For this purpose, he shook entire Europe, and at the head of an immense army attempted against this empire the expedition that ruined him. Everything on this occasion was limited to this; his destiny, with lowered head, rushed against a destiny more stalwart which shattered it. What he did afterwards was futile, even his famous departure from the island of Elba. The violent movement which he roused at this time was an act of despair. He himself felt perfectly sure during his reign of a hundred days that he was displaced, that his star no longer ruled France, that his destiny was worn out, and that if he had succeeded in awakening that terrible Will of 1793 which he had dulled, instead of drawing it into his vortex, he would have been drawn into its vortex.

This moment of exaltation served only to make him fall lower. In 1814, he had been vanquished by the conspired elements in favour of Russia; in 1815, it was by the English sustained by the Prussians. Sovereign in the island of Elba, he became prisoner on that of Saint Helena. Treasons were mentioned under the walls of Paris as well as in the field of Waterloo; there were no treasons; it was inferiority of destiny. All that had been favourable to him till then became contrary to him; his wisest precaution failed in effect and his slightest faults were enormous follies.

However, this same Destiny which abandoned Napoleon favoured France by bringing back the family of her kings, the descendants of Saint Louis and Henry IV. the legitimate possessors of the crown of Hugh Capet. Everything appeared to return to the ancient order of things and yet it was difficult for all to return, because for twenty-five years time had gone on and the Will of Man, having been drawn into an irresistible movement, had razed to their foundations institutions whose rebuilding was impossible. Louis XVIII. felt it with a just sagacity and thought it fitting to give to France a representative monarchical government in which an inviolable monarch, assisted by a responsible ministry, proposes the laws to a legislative body composed of a chamber of hereditary peers and a chamber of deputies of the departments elected by an electoral college. This form of government, sanctioned by a charter solemnly granted to the nation, rules France today.

Submissive as all Frenchmen are to their law and ready

to obey religiously her slightest injunctions, my intention is
not to examine in particular this constitution of my country,
to point out either its defects if it contains any, or the advantages which can be found there. I wish, since this is
permissible, to rise to the highest and most general considerations, and after having traced with a sure hand the principal
events which, relating to the Social State of Man, have taken
place in the world during the space of more than twelve
thousand years, after having linked them to the simultaneous
action of the three great powers which rule the Universe,—
Providence, the Will of Man, and Destiny,—and after having
mentioned the causes and results, as far as possible; I wish,
I say, to show to which of these three powers the different
peoples of the earth attach most particularly the diverse
forms of government which they have adopted, are adopting,
or will adopt; and what relations these constitutional political forms of the social body have with the constitutional
metaphysical forms of Man.   I hope that the reader, after
having followed through a multitude of centuries the diverse
phases of the Social State, and having progressed from causes
to effects with a chain of physical and metaphysical proofs
which no doubt have not escaped his sagacity, will follow
with attention the corollary which I am going to present for
his meditation, so as to draw from it for the future, useful
inductions and luminous conclusions regarding what may
or may not be.

CHAPTER XII

RECAPITULATION

IN this book we have just seen the last results of the struggle engaged between Liberty and Necessity, the force of the Will and the fatality of Destiny. The history of the earth offers no example of an explosion so violent, of a subversion so complete as that of which France has been the theatre and of which Europe and the entire world have felt the effects. After a victory which one has believed absolute, this superb Will which has figured already as having attained the culmination of its desires, being seized in a snare as adroitly as vigorously set, is seen drawn into a prophetic whirlpool, which it has at first confused with its own, and which has drawn it beneath the yoke of Destiny, which it has broken with violence. In order to flatter its disappointed pride, it has been told that this day was its own and it has feigned to believe it to manage the right of disposing of it. Let no one be mistaken; the struggle is not finished; Providence alone can terminate it. All that men can do, whether they consecrate themselves to Destiny or whether they follow the impulses of the Will, is limited to this; making repose longer and combats more rigorous. The intentions of nearly all men are pure; they all wish the same end although with opposed means. General welfare, in which particular welfare is necessarily found, is the object of their desires. Some can see it only in the exercise of a free will, and others only in the stability of an established order. Some seek a midway state equally mixed with volitive movement and prophetic repose, progression and stability, liberty and necessity. It is the great work of politics. Although I am quite convinced that this great work is impossible independent of Providence which gives it, nevertheless I shall not cease, after having spoken of simple governments, from examining the manner by which these governments can be modified by mingling with each other; and I shall try to show what is the presumable hope, good or bad, that can be conceived from their diverse modification. I shall not fear in this examination to approach the difficult question of which I have spoken: that of knowing if monarchical and republican governments can be allied in the absence of Theocracy; and if they are, what is the political jurisdiction that could be applied to them in a constitutional monarchy. Volitive and prophetic men, named today *Liberals* and *Royalists* occupied in seeking this jurisdiction, will know my thought in this regard and will judge of it.

SEVENTH BOOK

I have said in advance in my last chapter of the preceding book what I am about to accomplish in this one.   It only remains for me to develop my thoughts.

CHAPTER I

POLITICAL INFLUENCE OF THE THREE GREAT POWERS OF THE
UNIVERSE UPON MEN AND GOVERNMENTS

A T the present time, man has arrived at one of the most
important epochs of the Social State where, according
to the part that he takes, a long sequence of prosperity or
of misfortune will be decided for him. None of his steps
is indifferent. He is at present too old, so to speak, in
civilization, not to be responsible for his errors. Experience
should have taught him; and after the violent shocks which
he has experienced, even since eight centuries, it is no longer
permitted him to say that he is absolutely ignorant of the
essence of things and that he cannot distinguish good from
evil. One pities a child who burns his finger in the flame of
a candle, who wounds himself trying to put his arm through
a pane of glass; but a youth would be laughed at who would
do such things. There is an age where the child wears
a tumbling cap, where he is led by leading-strings, where
little wire guards are placed before the windows and fire-
places; but when he is grown up, he no longer needs such
safeguards which would be not only ridiculous but annoying
and harmful.

Men, be no longer children; know the extent of your
strength and the nature of things; and, having ceased to fall
into puerile digressions, do not reach out your hand to grasp
the moon, and cease troubling yourselves with idle tales. I
have just unveiled your annals before you. Be assured

that it is not without reason I have done it. I know well that you will doubt most of the things I have related; but examine their connecting links and do not hasten to decide. You are called to high and noble destinies, why do you fear to fulfil them? The Empire of Rama of which I have spoken to you seems like a vision. You cannot imagine that there has existed a time when the entire earth and all the men who inhabited it formed one and the same nation, speaking the same language, having the same laws, the same customs, and whose peoples, submitted to the same sacerdotal and royal government, adored the same God, and respected the same prince. This is, however, true. If it were not so, how would you explain the existence of a primitive language whose débris, diffused through a thousand diverse dialects, has struck with admiration all the philological savants? How would you understand the astonishing relations of decimal numeration, of duodecimal mensuration, of classification of the stars by asterisms? Come, leave your gothic caves, for it is thus that Bacon calls the prejudiced, and see that there is nothing impossible in what I have said, but that there is even nothing so natural. Why should men live forever isolated and penned in, always mistrusting, always at war with each other? Is there not in the depths of their hearts a universal sentiment of goodwill which draws them together? Do not doubt it; man is a universal being, cosmopolitan in his nature. He is isolated only when degrading himself. The love of a hut is no doubt far from that of the Universe; but the sentiment is the same. The difference is only in extent. It is by transporting this sentiment from a hut to a hamlet and from a hamlet to a city and from a city to a state and from a state to an empire and from an empire to the Universe, that man, at first centred in himself, expands, grows, and becomes universalized.

Rousseau has assumed that the sentiment thus extended lost its intensity. Rousseau is mistaken in this as in many other things. He has confused the love of birthplace with love of country. The birthplace rests on one point; the country is wherever the soul can exercise all its activity. There is between the effects of these two sentiments the same difference which exists between homesickness and national enthusiasm. National enthusiasm acquires as much more activity as the nation is greater; homesickness becomes more profound as the country is smaller. A certain Greek philosopher, being reproached for not loving his country sufficiently, looking at the sky replied: "You are mistaken, I love it infinitely." This philosopher extended his country beyond even visible things. Perhaps he would not have spoken so well as Demosthenes or Cicero in the public place; but he would have acted better than these two orators at Chæronea and in Sicily. Socrates did not once mount to the tribune to discuss public affairs, as he himself said, but he refused at the peril of his life to obey the orders of the thirty tyrants who oppressed Athens and died so as not to violate her laws.

Socrates and the philosopher of whom I have spoken first were providential men; Demosthenes was a volitive man, as was Cicero; Philip of Macedon and Cæsar, dictator of Rome, were prophetic men. Considered as members of a political society, the men who are something can be placed in one of these three classes, and, according to the amount of enthusiasm, force, or talents, in the first rank of these classes; or indeed in the lower rank, in descending to the crowd which is grouped around them and follows their movements. Sometimes the opinions of these men are decisive and their colours pronounced; at other times, they mitigate them, they adopt a middle course, and thus place themselves between the different classes. When the opinions of these men are pronounced, the first are called *Theocrats*, the second *Republicans*, and the third *Monarchists*. Hence, three principal forms of government, in which dominate exclusively the three great powers that rule the Universe: Providence, the Will of Man, and Destiny. These forms, when they are pure, constitute pure Theocracy, pure Republic, and pure Monarchy.

The Will of Man is properly animistic and free, and its seat is in the universal or the particular soul, according as the man whom it moves is considered universal or particular; but this Will can as well be placed in the intelligence as in the instinct, usurping there the place of Providence or ruling Destiny there; and then Theocracy is corrupted and the Republic takes aristocratic or emporocratic forms.

Providence is properly spiritual and inspiring, and its seat is in the intelligence; but although it has laid down the laws of liberty and necessity which rule the Will and Destiny, and although it has imposed upon itself the obligation of never violating them, it can, nevertheless, by means which are its proper means, ever new, ever unknown, which it never divulges and which no one can penetrate beforehand, determine these laws towards the end which it has proposed, in such a way that, whatever the causes, whose existence the Will freely calls forth, and the necessary and forced effects, which Destiny brings about, this end is always attained. Providence, evoked by one or the other of these powers, consolidates their creations and communicates to them the principle of life which nothing but it could possess.

Destiny, which resides in the universal or particular instinct, is properly instinctive and necessary. The Will, which dreads it, constantly produces it and augments its strength in proportion as it exasperates its own. If it mingles with the Will and dominates it, it creates a military empire; if it is dominated by the Will, on the contrary, it produces a demagogic tyranny. When, with the aid of the Will.which it has subjugated, it succeeds in usurping the place of Providence, it produces the most terrible of governments, absolute despotism.

After having stated these principles, which are only a résumé of what we already know, we shall enter upon their developments.

CHAPTER II

A MODERN writer who is believed to have genius because he has *l'esprit*, and much wisdom, whereas he has only science and talent, has said that the principle of republican government was *virtue*. Forced to explain what he understood by *virtue*, he said that it was the *love of country*. This love of country does not resemble, in his opinion, that of the Greek philosopher of whom I have spoken; it was a much narrower sentiment, much more exclusive, in which there was more pride than anything else; but, however that may be, it is not true that the love of country, considered as a virtue, is the principle of any government; it can be the mainstay, no doubt, when this government is established; but it is not a question here of knowing whether one prefers a republican country to a monarchical or theocratic country; each can have his own opinion in this respect, as Montesquieu had his; the question is of knowing what will cause this love. Now I say that it will be the Will of Man, when abandoned to its free will and rejecting all other dominion than its own, that will declare itself sovereign in the Republic and will dedicate to itself its self-esteem. Rousseau has felt this truth strongly; he has seen that the general Will constitutes the essence of the republican government, and

463

it is this that has made him proclaim the sovereignty of the people as the sole principle of political right and the only foundation of the Social State. But this is an error received from the cradle and nourished by its prejudices; for, in admitting the sovereignty of the people as a result of the general Will, it is not this sovereignty which is the principle but the Will which creates it; and if this Will is declared the principle, who will dare say that this principle is the only one in the Universe? If this was so, whence would have come the obstacles which arrest it at every step and which break it? Can a unique principle have opposites?

The mistake of Rousseau has been stating as a fact what was a question and saying that the Social State has only one principle, whereas it has three. It is true that one of these principles which he has seen sanctions the sovereignty of the people and its absolute liberty; this is the Will of Man, irrefutable and free in its essence; but also Destiny equally irrefutable and always compelled draws forced submission from this same people; and Providence, irresistible in its course, commands its voluntary submission and shows it, that it is only by means of this submission, that it can evade subjugation. It is therefore not a question of saying only that the people is sovereign, it is a question of saying it is inclined to become so and is always prevented from being so.

The Will of Man has conceived republics to realize the illusory phantom of this sovereignty of the people.

In order that the establishment of a republic may take place, it is necessary for a co-operation of circumstances to favour it. It would certainly be in vain if some volitive men, dreaming in their study of Utopian republics, should foolishly imagine that any time is fitting for the execution of their designs. There are times when a similar enterprise is impossible. In order that it may be effected, it is always needful that Destiny be vanquished, and it can never be so except it is abandoned by Providence.

The history of the world proves that the most favourable

moment for the foundation of a republic is that wherein the colonies, driven away from their mother cities, separate themselves, or when states, having become subjugated by others, succeed in throwing off the yoke of their viceroys or their governors. In this situation Destiny which dominates the colony or the subjugated state, being only secondary, is naturally more feeble and yields more readily to the Will. It was under similar conditions that the republics of Greece were formed, after that the Thracians were separated from the Phœnicians, the Greeks separated themselves from the Thracians. Carthage was at first a colony of the Tyrians and Rome a colony of the Etruscans. We have seen in our day the Swiss throwing off the yoke of the Austrians and Holland that of Spain. More recently still the American colonies of England have abandoned their mother country and declared themselves independent. In all these occasions the Will has triumphed over Destiny and has been able to a certain point to enjoy its triumph.

But men who, deceived by these events, the conditions of which they have not penetrated deeply, have imagined themselves able to take them, for example to bring forth similar ones not only in the colonies or in the subjugated states, but in radical monarchies, have committed the gravest errors and occasioned the greatest evils. This is one of the capital faults of the Will. This fault has depended principally upon the ignorance of historians and politicians who have never known how to go back to causes or establish the principles. The revolution attempted in England under the veil of religion has not succeeded better than that which has been consummated in France under the veil of philosophy. The two republics founded with the most formidable apparatus, cemented by the blood of two unfortunate monarchs, have not for a moment sustained the breath of Destiny; they have been crushed by two prophetic men who used them as steps to reach the throne. I seriously recommend volitive men to reflect upon these two

30

events. If there are still any who regret a form of government which flatters their passions, let them learn by these two experiences that this absolute liberty after which they sigh is absolutely impossible in the actual state of things and that a republic, such as the Americans have at present, cannot belong to Europe unless Europe consents to become the conquest of America and to be one of its dependencies.

I do not believe that there exists a single European who would wish to be called a republican at this price, but supposing that there were one whose pride was exalted enough to conform to such a humiliation, I must say to these men, preoccupied with a fixed idea, that the American Republic, founded upon shifting sands, lacks a basis and owes its apparent stability only to the extreme weakness of its destiny, which does not yet permit it to make foreign conquests; and which, when it will be strong enough to permit this, will surely be overthrown. I hope that this republic will find occasion to found its institutions and its laws upon better bases; but I am forced by the nature of this work to say to it that the only thing which can give them stability, that is, providential assent, is not there. It is in vain that the Will of Man, always prompt to deify itself, should persuade its despotic followers that its force is sufficient for everything; this assertion would be contradicted by the history of all ages.

Hear what Plato said in proposing his laws. He said it was necessary to obtain the sanction of the oracle of Delphi. Sparta, Athens, none of the Greek republics was constituted without having the Divinity intervene in their constitution. Rome had a sovereign pontiff whose influence was very great in the beginning of this republic, since he could by a word break up the assemblies of the people, suspend agricultural societies, and arrest the most important affairs. It is true that this influence diminished much afterwards; but when it no longer existed the country of Cincinnatus had become that of Sulla.

Do not forget that the republican germs scattered in America are the fruits of a political schism whose principal aim has been to destroy sacerdotal authority.   No sovereign pontiff exists in the United States and cannot exist there, unless one considers, according to the doctrine of the Quakers, each member of the church capable of serving in it; a doctrine so absurd that even today it is abandoned by its own followers.   So that, by quite a strange inversion, it is possible in this republic that all the citizens are religious without the government having the least religion; that they are all pious, even devout, virtuous, scrupulously upright, without the government having the least piety, the least devotion, the least virtue, the least probity.   For the government is a purely political being, which adopts the sentiments of none of its members, and which above all, in point of religion, affects an absolute indifference.   Now, as this government has above it no spiritual power to which it owes account of its conduct, and that even God does not exist for it,[1] although it may exist in different ways for each of its members, it follows from this that it is really without religion in its political constitution and that the law which constitutes it and which emanates from it is atheistic, as one of the most orthodox writers among the Catholics has judiciously observed.

It is possible that there are men who find this state of things exceedingly good, and who, profoundly imbued with that maxim of vulgar politics that religion is made for the people, regard as the masterpiece of governments the one where that maxim is not only received in theory but in practice; not only as followed in secret but adopted openly; however, let them moderate a little their enthusiasm; for I declare to them that such a government is a sterile government incapable of ever producing anything great and destined

[1] I say that God does not exist for such a government, speaking politically always, because this government does not make the idea of God enter into any of its political acts.

to pass on earth without leaving there the least trace of its existence. But, they will say to me, what matters it that a state is religious provided the citizens have a religion? Does it not suffice that each citizen is pious? Does not the piety of each make the piety of all? No, it does not; and this is why. It is because the state is not only a physical being depending upon this relation of the physical existence of its members, but an intellectual being besides, enjoying a general intellectual existence, which is right for it, which does not depend upon the particular intellectual existence for its members, but upon its constitutive laws; and if these laws are atheistic they can only give him atheism for principle even when those who would have made them should be the most pious of men.

Vulgar politics commit in this respect a grievous fault. They imagine that the religion, which is individually scattered among the mass of the people, suffices the nation, without thinking that there is no essence of light arising above from below, but, on the contrary, it must descend below from above. If there were a choice between these two alternatives, putting the force of religion either in the government or in the people, one should not hesitate to put it in the government; for religion is a principle of life and a light.

The two chapters where Montesquieu and Rousseau have spoken of religion are the most false and the worst of all their works. One sees, through the perplexities of their diction and the obscurity of their thought, that they feel alike that this is the point where their systems collapse. They cannot entirely repel Truth which cries out to them that no government can exist without religion; and nevertheless they deceive themselves and they deceive their readers as much as they can, in order that the volitive or republican law, which they have evidently put above all others, may remain atheistic as they have made it. What a contradiction! what a fatal error! they both wish the republic and they do not feel that this form of government, being incessantly menaced by dissolution, would need, more than another, a superior power which would hold it in unity. But religion not being able to enter into the republican government without restricting there the sovereignty of the people, their favourite idol, they like better to leave this idol intact and run all the other risks, founding this government on a purely volitive law.

So be assured of one thing: the ancient republics, such as those of Athens, Carthage, and Rome have been able, by favour of the vital principle which they have received from their origin, to live five or six centuries; but that political life, already very short, will be greatly shortened in the modern republics where this principle is not admitted.

CHAPTER III

THE Will of Man, which has made so many efforts to remain absolute master of the universe, has finally estranged Providence completely from the form of government which belongs to it. The modern republics which are founded or which have tried to be founded under its influence have not only thrown off the yoke of sacerdotal authority, but have even reduced this authority to being considered no more than an ordinary institution, whose members, subjected to the sovereignty of the people and dependent on it as all its agents, ought to receive a recompense similar to other civil or military officers; so that the delegates of Providence have become those of the people and have been paid to continue certain ceremonies of the cult to which it was accustomed. In the states where one has wished to admit priests to the number of representatives of the nation, which has been often very difficult on account of the conditions of fortune which have been demanded, these priests no longer being admitted as priests, but only as citizens on account of one of the consequences of the volitive law which has given place to this singular maxim: that a man is a citizen before being a priest, which is assuredly not true, taking the name of citizen in the sense which Rousseau gives it, for one is man before being citizen; and since a man, following the reasoning process of this writer, can never be bound by a contract to what he has not given his approval, he can just as well choose to be a priest before being a citizen as a citizen before being a priest.

But this passed in modern republics for a maxim so irrefutable that even in the case of Geneva, whose constitutions ought to have been theocratic if it had aimed to be anything, this maxim showed its full import. The ministers, outside of their consistories, had an influence no different from that of the lowliest artisans; and when they were members of the great or petty council they were associated with linen drapers or watchmakers. This confusion of powers was called equality of rights. At Venice, where the spirit was wholly opposed to that of Geneva, opinion has not differed on this point; which proves that it was neither the diversity of the aristocratic or democratic forms, nor that of opposed cults, which operated upon this, but the Will of Man alone. This Will having wished to dominate Providence had apparently dominated it easily enough.

It remained only to dominate Destiny; but this was a little more difficult because the submission which Providence demands before being free can be easily refused; whereas the subjugation which Destiny threatens, being forced, cannot so easily be eluded.

The ancient republics exhausted themselves in contrivances more or less strong, more or less ingenious, to escape from the fatality of Destiny; while, on the contrary, they had left a comparatively easy access to the action of Providence, in according much influence to the oracles of the gods. Nothing more is necessary to give a high idea of their knowledge and to prove that they recognized, at least in a confused manner, the action of the three great powers of the Universe. It is remarkable that the moderns have acted in an inverse manner in this respect. One would say in reading their republican constitutions that, wholly imbued with their power, they have believed themselves above all fatality and have directed their efforts only to guarantee religious influences. A priest seemed to them more formidable than a hundred soldiers, and a prophetess, as Mother Theos, more pernicious than all the *tricoteuses* of the Jacobins.

The strongest guarantee that the ancients had found to assure the stability of the republics was the slavery of a part of the people. The free men, called *citizens* were served by the enslaved part of the people who cultivated the lands for them and performed other hard duties. This terrible means had a great hidden efficacy: slavery, in dividing the population of a state into two parts, broke the course of Destiny, and by this division deprived it of half of its forces; for one feels that if a helot in Lacedæmon were endowed with any animistic faculties he could never disturb the liberty of that city. The Will of Man, in creating this factitious Destiny called *slavery*, had then taken possession of a part of the power of Destiny which it had turned against it. All men whom fate caused to be born among slaves, or whom the Will forced there by its laws or by its ruses, were so many victims whose sum of lost liberty was turned to the profit of those who enjoyed it. The moderns who have not this resource can only supply it by the great inequality of fortunes, which creates misery and domestic service. But the course of Destiny, far from being broken by this inequality, is only arrested a moment to be rendered more impetuous afterwards; because republican laws sanctioning the equality of rights, the poor men, whom nature has endowed with audacious characters, seeing poverty the only obstacle to their ambition, seek by all imaginable means to get out of it and present to the factionists instruments as sure as docile.

One should draw from what I have said this important conclusion, that slavery is neither the work of Destiny nor that of Providence; but assuredly the work of the Will alone, which, as I have said, creates an artificial Destiny to oppose it to a real Destiny; and, having only a certain amount of liberty to dispose of, deprives some men whom it abandons to enrich some others whom it protects. It is therefore in republics that slavery has been for the first time established systematically and rendered legal by the laws which have founded it. Before this time it was only the result of war, and the vanquished enemy groaned under it. It had no other law than that of the force which sanctioned it; so it could not be called legal, as I have called that which had existed in the republics. If one will reflect here, one will see that the difference which existed between these two conditions of slavery was enormous.

In military slavery, he whom the fate of arms submitted to his enemy came under the yoke of force, obeyed by constraint, and took care not to make his obedience a duty, and his duty a virtue. His master was obviously his enemy. Force had subjected him, force could deliver him. Only a victory of his compatriots was necessary to put him at liberty. He did not form a particular caste; or when this did happen, as in great conquests when entire nations were subjected, then the feudal system was established and with it the serfdom of the lands; but this was slavery of a certain form which had no relation with domestic slavery. A serf was not a slave properly speaking; he was a man who, having been deprived of his rights of property by the fate of arms, recognized a territorial master and found himself forced to devote to him a more or less considerable part of his labour. At the time when the Goths invaded the Roman Empire, domestic slavery which they found established there modified somewhat the ancient feudalism of the Celts and caused something of that slavery to enter there; but notwithstanding this mixture, it was always easy to distinguish a slave, properly speaking, from a serf and a serf from a captive. Captivity was the result of war pure and

simple; it had no other guarantee than force. Serfdom was
the consequence of an agreement made between the victor
and the vanquished after which the vanquished consented
to abandon a part of his property to preserve the other.
Slavery was the effect of a law which man decreed upon
himself, and regulated when and how a citizen should be
deprived of his liberty, when and how he could sell himself
or be sold. In this sort of slavery, peculiar to republics,
the law which sanctioned the principle of it made a duty of
obedience and obedience became a virtue. A slave could
not without crime seek to recover his liberty by other means
than those authorized by the laws. The morals which from
childhood were inculcated in him were respect and even
love for his chains. One went so far as to tell him that
slavery was ennobled by the virtues of a slave; and that this
state had singular sweetness, all drawn from that internal
satisfaction which depends upon the accomplishment of his
duties; and, safe from cares and alarms which the exercise
of liberty draws with itself, a slave was often happier than
his master. Thus, by a bizarre inconsistency, it was necessary in such a state of things that the legislator should
inspire both respect for the chains that one bore and horror
for those that one did not bear. He was obliged to do this
by the singular relationship which existed between slavery
and liberty and the inevitable force which drew from one
state to another. It is difficult to cite in Greece a man who
has not been a slave or who has not run the risk of becoming
one. Originally in the Roman Republic a father had the
right to sell his children three times. The insolvent debtor
became the slave of his creditor. At Athens the least de-
fault of payment of the tax involved the loss of liberty.
One knows that Xenocrates the successor of Plato, head of
the Academy, was sold in the public place and bought by
Demetrius of Phalerum. In this Greece, so proud of her
liberty, one could not pass from one city to another, sail
a moment on the seas which washed her shores, without

the risk of becoming a slave.   The celebrated Diogenes experienced this difficulty as well as a host of others.

It should be seen after these examples, that I could greatly extend if I did not believe it useless to repeat things that all the world knows, that the domestic slavery of republics must not be confused with the military slavery of empires, nor with the territorial serfdom of feudal states.   Nothing resembles it less.   Domestic slavery was, I repeat, the effect of a fundamental law without which veritable republican government would not have been able to exist.   I say veritable because one is accustomed to confuse it with modern emporocracy which differs essentially from it.   This fundamental law not having been able to be renewed in Europe since Christianity was established there, the absence of domestic slavery has prevented and will always prevent the consolidation of republics.   One has seen that the consolidation of England and that of France, to which their founders had vowed eternity, has not attained a second five years.

It is after all by a favour of Providence that every kind of slavery has disappeared.   It would have been in vain to wish to recall its principle in London as well as in Paris; it would have been impossible.   Something stronger than the Will of Man would have opposed it.   This Will, however, acted in different times and armed itself with diverse means. At London, it was adorned with the colours of religion and pushed zeal to fanaticism; at Paris, it embraced the philosophism of the century and carried incredulity to atheism. One would have thought that what it did not dare on one side it would dare on the other.   Not at all.   Religious fanaticism and cynical philosophism meet upon this point, that neither one nor the other has been able to call back the principle of domestic slavery, which was, however, indispensable to their designs.

If a reader is found whose sight is sufficiently resolute to attain certain depths, here is an occasion for him to see how Providence acts upon the Will of Man without in the least checking the law of liberty which it has been given. He needs only to seek to discover the secret and powerful motive which prevented the Puritans of England and the Jacobins of France, so opposite in religious systems, from throwing the chains of domestic slavery upon their enemies instead of sending them to the scaffold; it was not force which they lacked. Death was indeed at their orders; why not slavery? The ancients would not have hesitated. The reason why they did not do it is very difficult to explain. It can nevertheless be expressed in this logical formula: there are things which the Will of Man, being able to will, does not wish to will. The opposition which this Will experiences in its own essence belongs to the course of universal things which changes their character and which, for example, causes captives to be only prisoners of war for us, serfs only farmers, and slaves, domestics. Endeavour to reflect upon this point, politicians imbued with the prejudices of Montesquieu or of Rousseau, and understand that where it is an impossibility to wish for slaves, it is impossible to make pure republics.

CHAPTER IV

OTHER MEASURES WHICH THE WILL TAKES TO DOMINATE
OVER DESTINY IN REPUBLICS: HOW THEY FAIL—AMAL-
GAMATION ATTEMPTED BETWEEN THE WILL AND DESTINY
IN MODERN REPUBLICS—ORIGIN OF EMPOROCRACY—
WHAT ITS MAINSPRING IS

BUT this law of domestic slavery, this terrible law which
would have forced Plato himself to restrain all his
republican virtues in the accomplishment of his duties of a
slave if he had not been ransomed by Nicetès, this law which
dictated the manual of Epictetus, was not yet the only
means which the Will of Man had conceived to counter-
balance the fatality of Destiny always opposed to its action.
Athens had its famous law of ostracism by virtue of which
the one who arose above the others through too great talent
or celebrity was condemned to banishment. At Rome there
were rigid censors who forced each citizen to remain in his
rank and who chastised as breach of custom all demonstra-
tions of fortune or talent which could wound the common
people. As in this last republic the Will had not been able
to prevent Destiny from manifesting itself in the establishment of a sort of senatorial aristocracy; they created tribunes
of the people to arrest any encroachments. The ephors of
Sparta had likewise been appointed to examine the conduct
of the two kings, or rather the two generals of that republic,
and to control all their acts. These precautions and many
others too long to mention did not prevent these republics

from devouring each other and succumbing, before their time, under the blows of Destiny. Notwithstanding the laws of ostracism Athens experienced the tyranny of Pisistratus; and Rome, often stained with blood by her tribunes, did not escape the proscriptions of Sulla. The institution of the dictator, which assured her safety as long as the Will dominated Destiny, caused her downfall as soon as that domination ceased.

In general, all the efforts of the ancients in the establishment of the republican system tended to break everywhere the influence of Destiny, that is, to arrange that nothing sufficiently powerful could be presented whether in the fatality of things or in the fatality of men, in order that the Will should not have ready and sufficient means to destroy it instantly. The legislators flattered themselves that they constantly sustained that superiority of the Will over Destiny; but they were mistaken on this point, that they had counted on a permanence of unity in the action of the Will which is not found there. It would be necessary, in order that the republican system should last, that the volitive power which founds it should not be divided; but, as it is the essence of that power to divide itself, genius consists in finding means which would prevent this division or which would at least greatly retard it.

Although the moderns have acted in a manner opposed to the ancients and although they judge themselves wiser, they are, however, far from seeing where the difficulty really is. They have believed that it was not so much the question of dominating Destiny by opposing constantly its progress, as by adroitly getting possession of its effects to dominate it. They have conceived, without suspecting, perhaps, the singular idea of forming a sort of fusion of the Will and Destiny, an amalgamation of the liberty of the one with the necessity of the other, so as to obtain an *ensemble* which would be neither wholly prophetic nor wholly volitive, but which would hold the essence of both. This idea, which has been realized in many ways, has appeared the great work of politics, and some liberal minds, too much preoccupied to see the defect of such a government, have cried out, Miracle!

I have already remarked that among the extraordinary things which took place in Europe at the time when the political overthrow, caused by the downfall of the Empire of Charlemagne, left to all the feudal members of this great body the possibility of making themselves sovereigns in their domains, there was a certain number of cities which, not having any military chiefs in position to seize the authority, fell into the hands of their ecclesiastical or civil chiefs and formed under the laws of their bishops or their municipal magistrates sorts of petty states, whose unusual government without model in antiquity could not be compared to anything. These cities, which were entitled imperial and which wished to be protected by the emperors, pretended by an inconceivable whim to depend in no way upon these monarchs. They finally withdrew completely from their jurisdiction and took the name of *republics*.[1] These so-called republics which had nothing republican but their name were at first feudal municipalities, and later real emporocracies[2]; that is to say, states where commerce, considered as one of the motives of the government, is the leading factor in it. The union of the Hanseatic cities effected in the middle of the thirteenth century offered even a sort of grandeur; and these cities should have claimed some sort of celebrity, if it had been the essence of commerce to give other than riches without *éclat*.

The greatest effort of emporocracy was made in Holland when that country, having thrown off the yoke of the Spaniards, offered the singular spectacle of a company of traders, who, subjects on one hand and sovereigns on the other, were reputed as receiving laws whereas they were giving them;

[1] By the Treaty of Constance in 1183.
[2] See note which terminates Chapter IV., Book Fifth.

and who, constituting a state within the state, displayed a
considerable maritime power, maintaining troops on land
and sea, declaring war or peace in their own name, and sending afar their diplomatic agents, military and civil officers.
This institution imitated in England has succeeded perfectly there; whereas it has had no success in France. Some
political writers, among whom is Raynal, have bemoaned
loudly regarding the downfall of the French Company of the
Indies; but they have not seen that this institution did not
at all agree with the national spirit of the French which is
not mercantile, as I believe I have already said, but agricultural. England has been able, by her East India Company,
to give to her government the extraordinary form which
it has, that form where the principal elements of monarchy
and of republic seem *confondus* whereas they are only
mêlés and in which they had claimed to draw into the same
vortex Necessity and Liberty, Destiny and the Will of Man.

This is what I call an Emporocracy. It is the sort of
government of which I spoke just now, an object of the
admiration of some writers preoccupied with a fixed idea,
whose weakness they have not perceived. Montesquieu
is the first in France who has led the fashion on this point
and unfortunately Madame de Staël has followed him. I
am sorry for her in this. She was susceptible, through the
high faculties of her intelligence, of raising herself to nobler
conceptions. Rousseau has not been the dupe of appearances; he has felt that this government so much lauded
did not realize any of the hopes which he had cherished. If
he considered it as republican, he saw the people without
liberty, without power, without consideration, without voice
in its own affairs, turbulent without object, servile without
need, delivered to a misery increasing more and more, which,
devouring the little virtue which was left, made it by turn
factious or venal. If he regarded it as monarchical he
saw a king without force, without authority, without grandeur, obliged to follow even in the interior of his palace the

movement of his ministry, itself subordinate to that of a parliament composed of the most heterogeneous elements which, always floating between the fear of opinion and the attraction of favour, never knew if it would want on the morrow what it had wanted the day before.

But perhaps this government is aristocratic. Then if one searches this aristocratic body, whose power, raised above that of the people and of the king, is presented to the imagination as a colossus, one sees with astonishment that it is not thus. The House of Peers, which this body should be, constrained by its equivocal position to follow the movement of the ministry, gives it a force which it does not share; for if it is the House of Peers which sustains it, it does not create it; this prerogative belongs to the House of Commons which, formed under the influence of the ministry, cannot abandon it without exposing the state and without exposing itself to the most violent catastrophes. One would say, after this, that the government residing entirely in the ministry, this ministry ought to be vested with an immense power; and that if by chance it is conducted by an able prime minister, this prime minister ought to be the most powerful potentate in the world; but, not at all. This prime minister staggering under an enormous burden, always exposed to the darts of violent opposition which he is obliged to respect, although it does not respect him, only progresses with extreme fatigue towards an end which he could not fail without shame and which he attains without glory. With whatever genius he may be endowed, he cannot offer resistance to a lowering of the public funds, which he has not foreseen. Bankruptcy, occurring in the court, shakes his credit; a most important transaction miscarries through the incapacity of a banker. Accustomed to believe every man has his price, to traffic with talent and even virtue, he lets himself be penetrated with a profound distrust of humanity; and as he sees nothing great about him he makes no effort to become so himself.

In the meantime, where is the force hidden then that

31

makes this maritime colossus move?   This force is concealed in its credit, and this is the magical mainspring which executes these formidable movements which have astonished the world. This is the commercial mainspring of which the ancients had not the least idea; this is the marvellous invention of which I have spoken and in which the contrivances of modern genius are exhausted.   Its sole presence announces an emporocracy.   It is the principle of this sort of government, as the Will is that of republics and Destiny that of monarchies. It is in credit that Liberty and Necessity are supposed to be united.   Its name, which signifies a thing to which one adds faith upon the testimony of others, expresses perfectly the sense which should be attached to it.[1]   This law which rests upon material and physical objects, and which causes a fictitious existence when it does not even exist, has also its superstition and its fanaticism.   Its superstition, in that it admits for certain facts positive nullities, as when it attaches a value to that which has none, or that it receives as indubitable that which is more than hypothetical; its fanaticism, in that it dissimulates to itself the emptiness of its fantastic doctrines and that in its terror of ceasing to believe that which would reduce it to nothingness it makes more and more violent efforts to appear to believe what it doubts and to force others to believe it.

This physical mainspring, which in all emporocratic governments takes the place of intellectual principles which

[1] Notice that the sense given to the word *credit* is here more extended than this word ordinarily is.   I do not understand by the word *credit* merely the power which a government can have to borrow sums of money more or less considerable, but that sort of security which it inspires on account of its foreign supports and resources, which one can see or believes he can see in it. The credit of the English Government does not come from itself, but is received from the commercial power which is outside of it.   An interior credit, as that of a constitutional monarchy, France for example, cannot serve as mainspring for this monarchy, for the reason that the thing moved and the thing moving cannot be the same.   Emporocratic credit must then be exterior and must come to the government from a power, independent in some way of it, that it supports and by which it is supported.

are lacking there, makes up only indifferently for their action. It is the work of the Will and brings about in these governments, constituted by the hand of man, the same effect that the mainspring of a watch brings about on this sort of clock; it makes all the machinery go and causes an artificial movement which, at first glance, appears that of Providence or that of Destiny; but this movement is anything but that; it must, on the contrary, constantly fight against them and oppose its artificial strength and be limited to their essential strength without limit; which cannot be done without necessitating at some time or other a new tension, a winding up of the mainspring by which this machine is more or less set in motion and which finally wears it out and destroys it.

What pleases the volitive man above all in this artificial government is his work; he admires himself in the work of his hands and, without foreseeing the disadvantages in it, proclaims its advantages. When he is made to observe that Destiny there is forced and that Providence is absent, he responds with pride: what matters that? everything proceeds none the less. No doubt everything proceeds, but everything proceeds as in a machine where a skilful artist might have copied the movements of the Universe. You have a clock very well made, by which for a certain time in the absence of the sun itself you can calculate the height of that celestial body above the horizon, and knowing very nearly what time it is, regulate your domestic affairs. But tell me, is there a man ignorant enough to prefer this copy, however perfect it may be, to the Universe itself and not to feel that such a machine is admirable only by comparison, and that its very existence proves another by which it must be regulated? What would you say of a clockmaker, who would calmly assure you because he had made a good watch that one can henceforth do without the sun for measuring time and determining the return of the seasons? You would laugh him to scorn no doubt and send him to the madhouse. The language of the haughty mechanician would not differ, however, from that of the insensate politician who, seeing with admiration a mechanical government with which one has succeeded in supplying for a time the action of Providence and in constraining that of Destiny, would propose to you to do without these two powers forever and establish a similar government everywhere.

But it would be in vain for you to wish to follow the ideas of this politician by voluntarily closing your eyes to the evidence; you could not do it. The mainspring of emporocratic government, the credit, is not of a nature to be forged everywhere, nor indifferently placed. A nation essentially mercantile must furnish the elements of it and the maritime power must strengthen it or wind it up when it is run down. The places where this mainspring is shown with the greatest force and advantage have always availed themselves of this double prerogative. The cities of Italy which have possessed it, those of Flanders, Holland, England, and finally the United States of America, have been or are still commercial and maritime states. When one is content to consider France superficially, and when one sees her only under certain geographical relations, one can believe that she is also susceptible of admitting this mainspring and of becoming an emporocracy as Holland has been or as England and the United States still are; but if one wishes to examine further the nature of her territory and above all penetrate the particular mind of her inhabitants, one will see that she is agricultural on the one side and warlike on the other, which gives the alternatives of repose and movement, which striking the eyes of the observer have often caused the French to be taxed with inconstancy. Although agriculture leads to commerce and warlike habit to marine force, neither commerce nor marine force can ever be the aim of the French, but only their means either of augmenting the products of their agriculture, or extending their conquests so as to attain either the repose which fortune gives or the glory which victory procures. Of all the European peoples there is not one which cherishes so much pleasure or glory. These tendencies which could make her adopt the emporocratic mainspring, if this mainspring was of the nature to present itself all made, have prevented and will eternally prevent her from having sufficient perseverance to create it. Credit, such as I understand it,[1] is not a thing which springs up suddenly in the midst of a nation; it is not the fruition of a transitory enthusiasm; it is the product of a slow and deliberate calculation of which the French people are incapable. This people can certainly be infatuated for a moment with the system of Law and give to a trifling bit of paper the nominal value of coin; but the chances to which it is exposed must be rapid. If it has time to reflect, all illusion is destroyed. Reflection shatters belief in it; and in that which has relation to emporocratic credit, on the contrary, it must strengthen it.

An agricultural and military state inclines necessarily towards Destiny, which monarchy calls there. A violent effort of the Will is necessary that the republic may be established. If it is established as among the Greeks and Romans it is always under the form of a pure republic, in favourable circumstances, and with the conditions which I have indicated. If, in such a state, one wished suddenly to create an emporocracy, the mainspring which one would put there to move the machinery, exposed to the attacks of Destiny, would be broken in a short time.

[1] See preceding note.

CHAPTER V

PRINCIPLE OF MONARCHICAL GOVERNMENT—DESTINY DOMI-
NATES THERE THE WILL—THIS GOVERNMENT IS NATURAL
TO MAN, ESPECIALLY TO MAN OF YELLOW COLOUR—
WHITE RACE INCLINES TOWARDS THE REPUBLIC: WHY—
ORIGIN OF THE IMPERIAL AND FEUDAL GOVERNMENT
—PRINCIPLE OF THEOCRATIC GOVERNMENT—MOVEMENT
OF THE THREE POWERS

MONTESQUIEU, who had established *Virtue* as a
principle of republics, wishes that of monarchies to
be *Honour;* so that the duties that a citizen fulfils in one of
these governments through love of country, in another a
subject accomplishes them by a certain sentiment of self-
esteem which makes him find glory in his obedience. All
this is somewhat vague; and, as I have already remarked,
does not touch the principle which creates the government,
but certainly the consequence which follows. Republics
have their principle in the Will of Man which dominates
Destiny; monarchies have theirs in Destiny which dominates
the Will of Man.

When the Will absolutely dominates Destiny, the sovereignty of the people is recognized and with it the liberty and
equality of the citizens. No one has the right to invoke the
past to create a future; all the offices are elective; there
exists no rank, no distinction, no privilege outside of those
which the office gives. The Will which disposes of everything can build everything and destroy everything; it brings

all its force, so that Destiny may be nothing and that all its political consequences may be nullified.

When, on the contrary, it is Destiny which absolutely dominates the Will, men are born what they ought to be, masters or subjects, unequal in rights, in fortune as in power. Their future is always a consequence of the past. Heredity of the throne is the first law of Destiny, that from which all others receive their form. The lines of demarcation which divide men by castes are firmer as Destiny is stronger. Those who command are born to command; those who obey are born to obey. Destiny which dispenses ranks never suffers the Will of Man to invert them. All the institutions which it creates are directed towards this unique end, of preventing this Will from changing in any way the established order and of being anything by itself.

Such would be the general forms of pure republics and monarchies if it were possible for the Will to dominate absolutely Destiny or for Destiny to dominate absolutely the Will. But this absolute dominion of one power over another is impossible. Providence which guards the maintenance of the Universe never permits it, because, if on the one hand the Will remained quite triumphant, it would throw all in confusion by too much movement; and on the other hand if Destiny remained alone victorious, it would make all things retrograde by too much repose. Therefore these two principles must be mingled to modify each other and correct what would be too vehement or too stationary in their action if it were abandoned to its own nature.

Now that we understand the principles of these two principal forms of government, republic and monarchy, we must draw from this knowledge a simple and natural induction; which is, that the republic which depends upon the Will of Man has always need of an effort to establish itself, while the monarchy which follows from Destiny, being a result of the force of things, establishes itself alone and has only need of the development of the Social State to be developed with it. I beg you to observe and consider that the history of the world confirms it. A republic is always the work of a revolution. The Will of Man which has created it cannot abandon it an instant to itself lest it perish or fall back into the monarchy whence it originated. Monarchy is therefore the natural government for man, the prophetic government which Destiny gives to him.

When the Western Hemisphere was discovered,—to which I have given the name of *Columbian* on account of Columbus who was the first to land there—royalty was established wherever civilization had advanced sufficiently to bring it about. There were the Caciques at Haiti, the Incas in Peru, and a sort of Emperor in Mexico. The only two regular governments which were constituted on the continent were monarchies. That of Peru had received from Asia its theocratic forms and that of Mexico, its imperial and feudal forms from Europe.

It is noticeable that the peoples of Asia have been from all time governed by kings, and that it is only with great difficulty that the republican forms have been admitted among them; which indicates in the Yellow Race, the first that has inhabited this part of the earth, a tranquil social development, purely prophetic and exempt from the violent shocks which have agitated that of the White Race in Europe; for we must not forget what we have seen in the commencement of this work. The Borean Race, placed at the dawn of its civilization in eminently difficult circumstances, attacked by the Sudeen Race, warlike and powerful, had to display extraordinary means and a force of Will which could only save it from destruction by giving it an irresistible ascendancy over the fatality of Destiny. This ascendancy, which it then took and which it has preserved with more or less energy among the different peoples which have issued from it, has stamped them with a distinct character, more or less decisive, but always indelible. If this race could have been developed without inconsistency as happened undoubtedly to the Yellow Race; if it had entered into the Social State and if it had slowly passed through the diverse phases, it is certain that it would not have differed essentially from the other races in its social forms, and the pure monarchical government would have been its natural government; but the too precocious exasperation which was given to its Will, by the dangers to which it was exposed, changed this direction and forced Destiny to give way in all its consequences. Instead of a monarchical government it had an imperial government in which free will manifested its force by the election of chiefs. Castes were formed in its midst; but whereas they were formed in consequence of an extraordinary mixture of prophetic Necessity and volitive Liberty, they participated in these two principles and were not purely monarchical but imperial and gave rise to that mixed government which has been named feudal. It is useless for me to repeat in this respect all that I have said. It is well known how the Borean Race, after having been oppressed for some time by the Sudeen, took the upper hand and spread afar over all the earth and principally in Asia, where, by the influence of Providence which it recognized, it founded under the leadership of Rama the last Universal Empire. I have shown sufficiently that such an empire could be only theocratic. I have indicated the simple and majestic forms of this admirable social edifice, as much as the obscurity and remoteness of the ages have permitted me; I have related with what great splendour it had shone before reaching the epoch of its decadence; I have described this epoch and I have shown first the singular causes which had brought about its downfall. In exposing its retrograde movement and dissolution, I have not failed to repeat many times that the three principles united in it had become separated, and that each of them had retaken its own movement. Now Destiny, which was found to be the strongest in Asia during the first development of the Yellow Race, had returned to its first monarchical forms; and the Will of Man, which was exasper-

ated in Europe from the beginning of its civilization to preserve the White Race there, after having passed through the
republican forms which belonged exclusively to it, had
fallen again into the imperial and feudal forms which are a
fusion of the two principles. But at last, after an infinite
number of vicissitudes, of which I have briefly indicated
the principal ones, the Universal Empire, entirely dissolved
and reduced to its primitive elements, tended to become
reformed, and Destiny and the Will of Man laboured each
on his own side at this great work: Destiny in reconstructing
monarchies, and the Will of Man in organizing republics.
Each of these principles strove, by means of prophetic or volitive men whom it influenced, to remove as far as it could the
contrary principle, so as to obtain entire dominion; and this
tended on the side of Destiny to establish absolute despotism,
and on the side of the Will, absolute democracy, with all
the difficulties which are attached to these two extreme
governments and which draw with them always anarchy
whether military or civil.

In the meanwhile, Providence was not idle; in the midst
of the two other contending principles and without openly
thwarting the laws of Necessity and Liberty to which it is
submissive, it tempered their asperity by invisible means,
which, notwithstanding their apparent weakness, were
neither less efficacious, nor less strong. Men, whom it
inspired and whom it threw into the midst of the volitive
or prophetic vortex, abated its vehemence and according to
their position gave rise to opposed institutions which now
offered powerful barriers to the usurpation of democracy
and then arrested the disastrous effects of despotism. I
have named several of these providential men and have
entered as much as the subject of this work has permitted
me into details of their character and their doctrine. I
have by no means named them all. A great number of
them has remained even unknown. Some of them, for
reward of the services which they rendered to humanity,

have received from the men whom they have annoyed, mistrust, outrage, and even death; but these passing evils often came under the notice of Providence, which well knew how to find for its envoys recompenses worthy of their labours, their sufferings, and their virtues.

Providence which proceeds always towards unity is the principle of theocracies as Destiny is of monarchies and the Will of Man of republics. It gives all religious ideas and presides at the foundation of all cults. There is nothing intellectual which does not come from it. It is the life of all. Destiny gives the form and the consequence of all principles. There is nothing legitimate outside of it. The Will possesses the movement which gives progression. Without it nothing would be perfected. The aim of Providence is, in politics, the Universal Empire; that of Destiny, the triumph of Necessity and the consolidation of what is; that of the Will, the triumph of Liberty and the realization of what can be. Among these three principles, two have been for a long time engaged in violent combat. Destiny and the Will, exasperating by turn the men who depend upon them, have displayed the most formidable forces against each other. Providence, long unrecognized in their midst, has always softened their blows and prevented any from being mortal. The greatest triumphs which these two powers have gained over each other have been transitory and have not brought about the results that each expected. After one of the greatest shocks of which the history of the world makes mention, the men enveloped in the two vortexes find themselves face to face for the first time since long ago and are plainly classified in setting up the colours which have made them easily recognized. The men of Destiny and those of the Will are there. Some demand to stop at what is necessary and legitimate; others tend towards what is possible and legal. The obscurity of these words which they do not define permits them to confuse them, and in their ignorance of the underlying principles they are astonished at not being comprehended. A few providential men placed in their midst speak to them without being understood. A great number keep silence and await the issue. Since I have made myself the interpreter of these men who are silent, I will say to those who give themselves to cruel dissensions, that the only means of bringing peace among them and of attaining the end which they no doubt alike propose, is the general good; that is, by recognizing Providence, and instead of making one sole principle dominate, as they pretend, to consent, on the contrary, to their being blended in the providential ternary. I will indicate shortly how this can be done, after having examined with impartiality if this can be avoided.

CHAPTER VI

THERE is this notable difference between the actual epoch and ancient time, that knowledge being increased by the inevitable effect of the universal progress of things, these things, although respectively the same, being found more enlightened, appear to change their nature; and that the Will of Man which has sought them and which finds itself facing them, being able to wish them, does not wish them, however, on account of the consequences which these things bring about; consequences which formerly this Will would not have seen and which it sees clearly today. This reflection that I have already made when discussing domestic slavery, which, having been able to establish itself recently among us, is not, however, established there, applies to many other things equally important.

To continue: if the establishment of the pure republic brings about necessarily, as I have shown, domestic slavery of a part of the citizens, and if the Will of Man, which unceasingly tends towards that republic, can not or will not desire this slavery, the result will be that this Will will be found in contradiction with itself; it will become divided and will not attain the aim of its desires. And if the estab-

lishment of the absolute monarchy which is called Despotism
exacts certain necessary severities towards which Destiny
inevitably pushes, and if these severities encounter a violent
opposition in opinion which does not permit them to be fulfilled, then Destiny, provoked by itself, will be broken and
the prophetic establishment will not take place. Open, I
pray you, Machiavelli, and see what he counsels his despotic
prince. He principally advises cruelty. When he conquers
a new empire, he wishes that the blood of its former masters
be entirely drained; that no proud head be allowed to dominate, and in the manner of Tarquin he passes a bloody scythe
over all that has risen above the vulgar; and as for the mass
of people who could have enjoyed republican liberty, he
wishes that it be dispersed or destroyed. "The surest way,"
he said, "is to destroy it; for the republican peoples, naturally
spiteful, are inclined to vengeance and never lose the memory
of their ancient liberty."

Thus, no republic without slavery, no despotic state
without murder. The republicans who cannot make slaves
and the despots who cannot sacrifice their rivals, were they
their dearest friends and their brothers, will never obtain
either the pure Republic or absolute Despotism. Liberty
must give chains and autocracy command death. There,
it is the misery of a part of the people which assures the
prosperity of the other; here, it is the terror of the nobles
which makes the surety of the monarchs. If a political
conqueror enters upon a career with fortune equal to courage,
let him dare as Ninus or Cyrus, Attila or Timour, to deliver
to death the royal families which he has dethroned; let him
understand how to send the flame of incendiarism throughout
the provinces, overthrow the capital cities, and drench the
débris and ashes in the blood of their inhabitants; then he
can reign as despot. But, you say that such a conqueror
will not dare in our day to commit such atrocities; that his
nobler ideas will dissuade him from it; and that even if he
cherished such cruelty in his heart, to abandon himself to

such furors, he would lack instruments for his crimes. Very well! I know all that as you do, because I have known the opinion of the century and because I have appreciated its force; but I also know that a conqueror who will obey this opinion will betray his destiny, will connive with his eternal enemy which is the Will, and will lose all the results of his conquests. He could not do otherwise, no doubt; but then, to what good to undertake conquests, if it is to lose them inevitably? To what good, to incline towards pure Republic, towards absolute Despotism, if opinion, to which the republicans, as the despots are obliged to submit, makes them impossible?

Here is precisely what I wished to make you understand in commencing this chapter. That, someone will reply to me, is all understood; besides experience has just shown it in such a manner that it is not permitted any one to doubt it; it is even the reason for which one no longer seeks anywhere to realize the idea of a simple government, whether republican or monarchical; but there is a tendency, on the contrary, to seek mixed governments, which present the advantages of these two kinds of government without having any of their disadvantages. This is, as I have already said, the great work of politics; it is a question of uniting two extremes and of making, as the alchemistic adepts pretend to teach, fire and water become friends. However, the proof that one has not yet found the means of uniting them, and that the old enmity of the two principles manifests itself as strongly as that of the two elements, is, that the men called liberals, who are those whom I call volitive, and the men who are designated as royalists, whom I call prophetic, can agree to nothing between them, although they all appear to be asking for the same thing: a constitutional monarchy.

They cannot agree among themselves and this is why: it is because the volitive liberals wish that everything be *de facto* and legal in this constitutional monarchy, and the prophetic royalists, that everything be legitimate and *de jure*.

Now what is *de facto* and legal is composed of a Destiny subject to the Will; and what is legitimate and *de jure* announces a Will subject to Destiny. Let us try to determine what should be understood by these words which are applied less in determining than in confusing.

The men of Will, volitive or liberal, consider things only as isolated facts without any connection, seeing in man only man, in a king only a king, in a magistrate only a magistrate, without admitting as a thing existing by itself, either humanity or royalty or magistracy. These terms offer them only an abstract idea which is not attached to real existence. If they utter the word royalty, for example, they do not understand a thing pre-existent to a king, determining it to be a royal potentiality, but only a thing which issues from this being and which is designated as the dignity, pure and simple. Thus for them the king exists before royalty and creates it. Royalty is therefore only an abstraction and the king a fact, which when it is recognized as such by the people, in whatever manner, becomes legal.

But the prophetic men see all this in another manner: they admit universals, which the volitive men reject; and consider things not as isolated facts, but as links of a chain, which, without being the chain itself, yet constitute it. For them humanity, royalty, magistracy are things which they conceive as pre-existent to men, kings, magistrates, and placed by Destiny to determine the necessary existence. In the same manner, for example, as one can conceive that an army, when it is decreed with power of being, will necessarily involve the existence of a certain number of soldiers. These soldiers will not be isolated facts considered as soldiers, but facts co-ordinated to this end, of forming a whole which results from them if one wishes it, but from which also results, if one considers it as one ought, the primordial and creative idea which has decreed the army. Now that royalty, for example, may be a thing decreed beforehand by Destiny or by quite a different superior power, even by

God, put here in place of Destiny, it is that which no really prophetic man, no pure royalist can doubt, without being a contradiction to himself. This man will always put royalty before the king and will only consider as legitimate the king born in royalty. It will be in vain for a king born outside of royalty to be legal, according to the volitive men; the prophetic will always regard him as illegitimate and will distinguish *de jure* from *de facto;* the former will always be for him the order of Destiny and the necessary consequence of an anterior universal law; whereas he will see in the latter only the usurpation of the Will, and the consequence of a particular posterior law.

If what I have just said is well understood, it will be seen clearly what distinguishes a prophetic man from a volitive, and a monarchist from a republican; the difference will be made between what is legitimate according to some, and legal according to others; and it will be seen that they can never be agreed upon anything. Let us suppose that in the constitutional monarchy, where they appear to be united, there may be question of establishing a nobility as intermediary body between the monarch and the people, prophetic men will see this institution all established if it exists, and impossible in its establishment if it does not exist. They will conceive that one may, if strictly necessary, augment it in mass but not create it in principle; for although they may accord to the king the faculty of making a noble, they will never accord to him that of making a nobility. The volitives, on the contrary, will believe it easier to create a nobility than to make a noble; for they will confuse nobility with aristocracy and will believe that it is by abstraction that the generic name is given to all men who possess the offices. According to them, the king will be the highest noble and the mayor of the village the lowest. They will be able to see legality in the titles but they will never see legitimacy. A noble who relies only upon the legitimacy of his nobility will be nothing in their eyes, if he does not join to it legality of fact, that is to say, employment. The prophetic men will think quite the contrary upon this point and mock the noble *de facto*, who will not be it *de jure;* that is to say who will be legal without being legitimate.

And if, by a condescendence commanded by imperious circumstances, the men of Will, the liberals, proclaim the legitimacy of the throne as the conservative principle· of monarchies, as in truth it is when it is understood, they will know better than to see it where it really is, in the royalty which makes the king, as nobility makes the noble; but they will place it in its simple positive demonstration—in heredity so that the people being able to see it can seize and render it legal by the adhesion of its will; that which is always to destroy on one side what is built on the other, by submitting to a power that which belongs to the opposed power. It is not heredity which makes legitimacy; it is legitimacy which sanctions heredity. If legitimacy depended upon heredity, the people could indeed submit it to their examinations and render it legal by regulating the mode of this heredity; but as it results solely from royalty and from birth in this royalty, according to the order of time, the people have nothing to see there; for royalty is one and time has not two ways of proceeding.

So then, men of Will and of Destiny, or as they are called today, liberals and royalists, are found drawn along by the universal progress of things to the singular situation, which neither of them can absolutely triumph over, by arriving at the end determined by their nature, nor be united together to constitute a permanent mixed government; for in order that both triumph absolutely, it is necessary that they should be able to bring about a pure democracy or an absolute despotism, which is rendered impossible by the opinion which repels the only means of attaining this result: the slavery of some or the murder of the others; and for them to be united, a median line would be necessary, of which neither wishes to admit the action nor recognize its efficacy.

They prefer in confusing the sense of some doubtful words, to deceive themselves, to use stratagem with their adversaries, and to recommence a hundred times the ever useless attempts. They do not perceive that, notwithstanding the disguise of their discourse, the substance of their thoughts is always shown; because this substance is indelible and because Destiny or the Will, which unwittingly influences them, makes them receive as fundamental truths these opposed axioms,—to the royalists: *Si veut le Roi, si veut la loi;* and to the liberals: *La voix du Peuple est la voix de Dieu.*

CHAPTER VII

IMPORTANT DISTINCTION BETWEEN THE ESSENCE OF RELIGION
AND ITS FORMS—THE FORMS WHICH CONSTITUTE THE
CULTS CAN BELONG TO DESTINY AS TO THE WILL: THE
ESSENCE IS ALWAYS PROVIDENTIAL AND LEADS TO THE-
OCRACY—CAUSES OF RELIGIOUS QUARRELS AND SCHISMS

IT will doubtless be understood that I mean by the median line, of which I spoke in the preceding chapter, the providential action which must be admitted into the government to consolidate there the union of the other two principles, which, without this means, will never be united, because these principles are extremes, and two extremes under any relations which one considers can never be united except by a medium which touches them equally. But, perhaps, some of my readers will say, if by providential action you mean religion, this action, already admitted into many governments, has not produced the effect that you appear to expect; experience has proved, on the contrary, that it has divided the minds instead of uniting them; and that, far from producing good results, either it has not produced any or it has produced bad ones.

I must make an important distinction here.

This providential action is manifested in principle in all religion, as the prophetic action in all monarchical institutions and the volitive action in all republican institutions; but the cult that consecrates this religion is only one of its forms, and this form can as well become monarchical as republican, according as Destiny or the Will of Man succeeds in taking possession of it. The cult never remains providential only as far as it is theocratic, that is to say, as far as it makes an integral part of the government and as it bears in it not so much the form as the essence of its principle. Understand this well, I beg you, and do not look for examples in ancient times and far away from what is happening before our eyes; consider the difference there is between a Greek archimandrite and a minister of the Holy Gospel among the Quakers; these two men call themselves Christians and Christians *par excellence*, and profess nevertheless opposed maxims. They both hold to the providential action by the religion to which they belong; but the forms of the cult have become with the one prophetic and with the other volitive. Both of them schismatic, they could only become again providential by becoming orthodox, supposing that orthodoxy might be recognized as a universal theocracy, which it certainly has wished to be, but which it never has been.

When the distinction which I have just attempted is well established in the minds of my readers, I can go a step further. It is said that religion has often produced evil results by dividing the minds which it ought to unite and precipitating into bloody dissensions the peoples whom it should maintain in concord and in peace. I reply, that it is a mistake to say this; religion is not to blame for these calamitous effects. Issued from Providence, which is the principle of all good, it has never been able of itself to cause any evil. It is the forms of the cults which have been the occasion of these deplorable ravages, when these forms, invaded by the Will of Man or by Destiny, are found in contradiction with the forms of government given by an opposed principle. Europe, it is well known, has been the theatre, more than any other part of the world, of these cruel dissensions which have served as pretext to the enemies of Providence to slander the means; but the principle of these dissensions was not in

Providence; it was either in the free action of the Will or in the fatality of Destiny. What were called religious quarrels were only political quarrels in which the prophetic or volitive men armed themselves with forms of cult, to fight and deal harder and deeper blows. Providence, submitted to its own laws, could change neither the essence of liberty nor that of necessity, which caused these attacks; it has only lessened the vehemence and prevented the two powers while triumphing completely one over the other from being reciprocally destroyed.

If one would go quite deeply into the causes of these fatal dissensions by which Europe has been agitated, he must believe that the Christian religion which dominates there is not of European origin, but Asiatic; that it holds even by its primordial roots to Africa, since the Sepher of Moses containing all the Atlantean traditions and all the Egyptian mysteries serves as its basis, and that in consequence the forms of its cult are all of the domain of Destiny, which has been able easily to take possession of it. The rigidity of its dogmas, their obscurity, their prophetic concatenation, which leaves it no liberty, no unfolding possible to human reason, all in this religion has therefore served the movement of Destiny, which must arrest the too petulant impetus of the Will. The cult of Odin, entirely volitive, has happily been restrained after the effect which it had to make has been attained; the barbarians surprised in the forms of a a new cult have seen their audacity expire there; and the downfall of the Roman Empire, which had to bring about the total ruin of the Social State in Europe and the annihilation of the Borean Race by itself, has not had the fatal consequences that it ought to have. After several centuries of stupor and of gloom, this race has come out of its lethargy and begun anew its ascending movement; it has wished to retake the dominion over Asia that it had had there, and without doubt, with the aid of its Asiatic cult, it would have done so, if this cult had not been found divided by that of

Mohammed whose forms more prophetic still have forced it to recede.

If the Christian religion had been able to become theocratic at the time of the Crusades as it ought, none of the evils which have happened since would have taken place. It would have been able, by exercising a just influence over governments, to reveal a legitimate power which following the increase of knowledge would have continued to modify its forms in such a way as to be always in harmony with exterior things; but the reasons, that I have developed at length, prevented it from reaching this height of prosperity, and the constantly renewed struggles which have sprung up since between the Priesthood and the Empire, the Pope and the Emperors, have forever removed the possibility.

The Christian religion not having become theocratic and consequently not having entered the governments as an integral part, these governments have been delivered over to the interminable divisions of these two rival powers, the Will of Man and Destiny, which have both aspired to dominate there exclusively, and which, taking possession of the forms of cult, have sought by turn points of support favourable to their designs. These forms entirely prophetic in orthodoxy and very fitting to serve the pretensions of the pure monarchists have offered a singular contrast with the morals of Christianity, which from another side, preaching humility to the great ones and even more than equality to all men since it declares that the first shall be last, favoured completely republican demagogues; so that in opposing only forms to morals, the two parties have been able to find in the Christian cult political weapons which they have unfortunately used too dexterously.

But these arms although already very strong have not sufficed for them. The prophetic men in attaching themselves to the forms of cult and feeling what a solid force they were putting into their hands to move all the political machine have wished to co-ordinate the morals which vex them and thence has come the Greek schism; whereas the volitive men, in taking possession of the morals whose fundamental principle offered them a powerful lever to move the multitude, have sought to make the forms follow from it, and they have succeeded and thence arose the German and English schism.   Thus the divisions in the Christian cult have not been religious as one has believed without examination; they have been political.   It is not religion, it is politics which has always stained Europe with blood.   Religion was there only as a pretext; politics was the real cause.   Providence, a stranger to all the calamitous divisions, left the Will and Destiny to fight; and not being able to arrest their opposed movements, inherent in the essence of things, has tempered at least the fury of it, never ceasing in the midst of war to offer to both parties the means of making peace.

Be assured, that if the Catholics have suffered so much in England and in the north of Germany, and if the Protestants have been so cruelly persecuted in France, it is not as religious men but as political men.   The forms of the Catholic cult could not agree with republican liberty; nor those of the Protestant cult with monarchical necessity. Wherever this discord exists, there is an open or secret struggle between the government and the cult.   There are persecutions whenever forms can be opposed to forms; that is to say, whenever political men whose secret intention is to make the Will or Destiny, the republican or monarchical principles, triumph, are able to take possession of the forms of cult to represent their adversaries not only as rebels but as ungodly men, infidels, or reprobates.   The individuals who suffer from these persecutions do not ordinarily attribute them to their real causes; they believe themselves to be victims of their beliefs, when they are only thus by their opposition to a political system.   Involved by the force of things they do not realize to what vortex they are obedient; often they are even in opposition with themselves; this happens whenever a Catholic protests in England that the king is not king by the grace of God, or when in France a Protestant affirms that the sovereignty is not in the people. This Catholic or this Protestant can speak truly for himself; he can really believe this as an individual, but private belief has no bearing on the general system. No one gives credit to his discourse, and it is one more evil for him in time of trouble, when driven by uncontrollable forces into movements to which he does not consent.

If religion had been powerful, if it had been able to make the voice of Providence understood in the midst of the tumult of ardent or indifferent passions which have agitated the men of Will and of Destiny, it would have stopped their ravages; but where was its strength? Where was the sanctuary from which it might send forth its oracles? Did the diverse governments receive the divine influence? Did it enter as theocratic power into the constitution of these governments? Not at all; admitted simply for the salvation of the individuals it did not appear that the salvation of the states might depend on it. It is, however, in the salvation of the states that it would manifest its force if it were invoked. But does one think even in the midst of evils which the European population has experienced of invoking it there? No; one still dreams of forms of cult, and the most subtle politicians are those who seek the means of employing them with the greatest skill. The greater part nevertheless, and they are the so-called liberals, do not wish it at all. According to them it is better to place religion outside of governments and leave to each the liberty of following the cult which is his by heritage from his fathers and which he keeps by domestic custom, or that to which he gives preference by conviction or by interest. The prophetic politicians, on the contrary, wish to assure the dominion of an exclusive cult, but only over the people and without being obliged, on their own account, to give the slightest credit to it, or to receive from it the least influence in the *ensemble* of the Social State; all that they can do, is to allow themselves to be inconvenienced temporarily by exterior ceremonies and to throw over their scoffing and inattentive glances a hypocritical veil which they well know how to lay aside at the proper time.

But it is not thus that religion can attain its end and scatter over human societies the benefits of Providence, whether one pretends to isolate it in the manner of the volitive men called *Ultra-Liberals* or in making a political force of it, as the prophetic men called *Ultra-Royalists* imagine. Providence could never enter into these chimerical projects. Again my pen reiterates this truth, that Providence must be all or nothing in a state, as in an individual. Those who isolate it lose it; those who hope to make it an instrument turn it against them by changing its nature, which, from the good which it would have been in its divine liberty, becomes bad in its prophetic necessity.

CHAPTER VIII

NEW CONSIDERATIONS OF THE SOCIAL STATE—WHAT ITS UNI-
VERSAL TYPE IS—HOW THE THREE POWERS DETERMINE
THE THREE FORMS OF GOVERNMENT—THESE THREE
UNITED FORMS GIVE BIRTH TO THEOCRACY — DIF-
FERENCE BETWEEN EMPOROCRACY AND CONSTITUTIONAL
MONARCHY

L ET us try to retrace our steps, and after having recalled
to memory the constitution of Man, such as I have
explained in my Introductory Dissertation, and after having
carefully considered this truth, so often repeated by the
ancient sages, that Nature alike in all things is the same in
every place, let us sum up by saying that the Social State,
being only Man himself developed, should represent to us
an image, as Man himself represents to us an image of the
Universe and the Universe an image of *God*.

Now, we know that Man contains in his volitive unity
three different spheres, whose perfect harmony constitutes
the perfection of his being. Man can only be perfect as far
as these three spheres are not only entirely developed, but
all three determined towards a unique end by the Will which
moves them; that is, as far as instinctive life, animistic life,
and intellectual life, resulting from these three spheres, form
only one sole and same life. If one of these lives fails, the
human being is as much more imperfect as the life which
fails is more elevated; and if, between the lives which remain,
one seeks to dominate to the detriment of the other, this

being is a prey to disorder.　More or less tormented by confused and incongruous thoughts, and more or less inclined towards the weakness which drags it to nothingness, or the blind force which precipitates it towards crime, it inclines likewise towards destruction.

Such then is Man and such is the Social State.　The three spheres of which I have just spoken: the intellectual, the animistic, and the instinctive are represented in this state by three forms of government which issue from the three great powers by which the Universe is governed: Providence, the Will, and Destiny.　The theocratic form is providential and intellectual; the republican, animistic and volitive; the monarchical, prophetic and instinctive.　This last form belongs to *Nature naturée ;* it issues from the very force of things and the Social State inclines to it unceasingly.　The first belongs to *Nature naturante ;* it is brought about by the perfectibility of things and the Social State aspires to it. The median form, which is the republican, belongs to *Nature transitive*, that is to say, to that nature which unites *la naturante* to *la naturée* and transforms without cessation one into the other; it results from the movement of things which brings about their fermentation, their dissolution, or their regeneration; the Social State falls into it according to circumstances to be purified or to be destroyed.

These three forms of government, of which I have just shown the principle and the aim, incline all three to become dominant and exclusive in the social order; but although good in themselves, their absolute domination, which can exist only by the exclusion of the other two, becomes bad whenever it is too prolonged; because it counteracts the tripleform nature of man and hinders harmony from being established there.　This domination therefore is to be feared, as in reality man does fear it; but not to such an extent, however, that the fear which it inspires can stifle all desire of the union of these three forms into a single one, whatever name this union may bear.

I beg you to observe that it is in the application of this name that the greatest difficulty lies, and in the idea that men form of it that the greatest danger is encountered; for it is in vain that one would, in this elementary life in whose depths men are plunged, evade the influence of names. The name is to the idea what the body is to the soul. One obtains knowledge of the soul only by the body; one can attain any of these rational or intellectual things only by the name which contains the idea of it. Now, the name given to the form of government which unites the three forms in a single one is ordinarily that of theocracy; and this name is incomplete, in that it represents only the idea of the providential form dominating alone, because men, too far away from *God* to understand Him, confuse Him with Providence, which is only one of His laws. But a real theocracy is not only providential, it is volitive and prophetic to the same degree, that is to say, it contains the action of the three universal powers equally balanced, and it reflects the harmony of the three spheres of the life of the Kingdom of Man.

At the sole name of theocracy, however, the volitive and prophetic men rebel, imagining that it is a question of taking away from some the action of the Will, whence results civil liberty, and from others that of Destiny, whence issues political property. This chimerical danger which they consider as imminent unites them, notwithstanding their opposed nature, and renders them strong enough to resist providential men; to counteract their efforts and nearly always makes them incomplete or useless. This unusual union is that which retards most the Social State in its development and which causes the greatest evils there. It would be better that the two powers, unreservedly separated, as in republics or in pure monarchies, should watch each other or combat openly, than to devour one another in secret as in emporocracies or in constitutional monarchies. I shall relate why. It is because in pure republics where the Will of Man reigns without obstacles, or in absolute monarchies where Destiny dominates, Providence can find its place, by making a sort of alliance with the exclusive principle against the excluded principle; whereas in emporocracies or in constitutional monarchies where a sort of pact binds momentarily the Will and Destiny, Providence can be admitted only as an impotent form and always more harmful than useful.

But, one will say, if this pact which binds momentarily Destiny and the Will, whether in emporocracies or in constitutional monarchies, procures tranquillity and welfare to the people, what more could one ask for the governments? Indeed if welfare and tranquillity resulted from these sorts of governments, that would be more than sufficient for the people, jealous of these advantages, to close their ears to the advice of providential men of all countries, who have not ceased to tell them that these short moments of apparent prosperity would be dearly paid for by the real calamities which would follow; but it is more than doubtful that in these sorts of mixed governments, even the best organized, these benefits are really enjoyed. This faint *éclat* which is seen in emporocracies, and which is considered as welfare, is only a false disguise with which commercial luxury colours for a moment the cheeks of the moribund. The excessive misery of a greater part of the people and the profound immorality which torments the rest, nourish in the heart of the nation the ferments of hatred and impiety, which cannot fail to destroy it. As to the kind of tranquillity which one believes to attain in constitutional monarchies, it is a political phantom, a vain shadow which escapes the very moment when one expects to seize it. These vain institutions which are constantly recommended, this mass of ordinances which are decorated with the name of laws, these mainsprings which break at the least shock, these frivolous counter-weights where constitutional genius exhausts itself, all this proves sufficiently that the great work is not yet found and that this golden age so much promised by our modern Solons has not stood the test.

In speaking with regard to the republic, I have explained what I meant by this kind of government which I call emporocratic; it is a government where the republican principle which constitutes it is found mitigated by monarchical institutions where the opposed principle dominates. This government in which commerce plays the principal rôle has for its mainspring national credit, a modern invention whose nature I have sufficiently explained. Constitutional monarchy which injudicious publicists confuse with emporocracy has other bases. It results also from a *mélange* of the two principles; but whereas the republican principle is mitigated by the monarchical, as in emporocracy, and whereas liberty passes before necessity, here it is quite the contrary: necessity passes before liberty and the monarchical principle is here mitigated by the republican. In the first of these governments it is forbidden to say that the king, considered as a representative of the people, is king by the grace of God, even if he were to fulfil the functions of sovereign pontiff. The people, to whom one accords the supreme sovereignty, is put by this sole fact above even God. There, religion is isolated from law; and whereas it is invoked for the private individual with a sort of severity, and whereas it is wished that individuals should have a cult, it is entirely dispensed with for the government, whose sole cult is commerce and sole providence, national credit.

In the second of these governments, on the contrary, the king is declared such by the grace of God and in virtue of the constitutions of the state. It is supposed that the people who 'ecognize him as legitimate and by divine right, accord to him this title of supreme sovereignty, and only preserve in the legislation the right to discuss the law, in order to admit it or reject it. The law here is the result of two powers, one which proposes it and the other which sanctions it; but whereas this proposition and this sanction appear simple they are not so. The king, declared inviolable and incapable of doing evil, is, as a consequence of this inviolability, reduced to doing nothing, or what amounts to the same, reputed as never having done anything, not even having improvised the formal speeches which he pronounces. It is a ministry which passes everything as though suggested by him. This ministry is responsible not only for the laws which it proposes in the name of the king, but even for all administrative acts which result from these laws, the execution of which is confided to it. Here, therefore, is a complex proposition made in the name of a monarch not responsible, irresponsible in his royal acts by a ministry responsible and capable of being accused on account of these very acts. The sanction given to the law is equally complex; for the power which sanctions is no longer the people, properly speaking, but a part of this people, called the national representation, and this national representation is divided into two chambers, the one permanent, composed of hereditary members called peers of the realm, named originally by the king, and the other removable, composed of members elected for a certain time by the electoral colleges assembled in different districts according to forms fixed by a law. These two chambers give or refuse their sanction and co-operate thus in the completion of the law which could not be perfect unless vested with two sanctions: the one independent of the people and the king, since it emanates from the permanent body; and the other dependent on the people and always influenced by the king, since it depends upon a removable assembly whose members are elected by the electoral college where the popular and royal action makes itself felt by the way in which these colleges are assembled and by that in which they are directed by the president, who is by appointment of the king.

Here, without doubt, is a government which offers the complication of the most ingenious political machinery that one can find; it is a machine of the most wonderful conception; which if it moved would astonish the world by its boldness. What more admirable, indeed, than to see a monarch, whose power appears to emanate from the Divinity itself, since he is entitled king by the grace of God, recognize the liberty of the people and divide with them his legislative authority? What more noble than this inviolability, which places him beyond the attacks of factions, in the happy impotency of doing evil, whilst one attributes to him all the good which is done under his paternal administration? What better could be imagined than that this national representation which, without being subject to any of the blind passions of the people, yet feels its salutary influence in everything related to its real interest? This division into two chambers, one hereditary and the other elective, is it not the fruit of a most felicitous combination since it offers the possibility of resisting opinion or of submitting opportunely? Do not these peers of the kingdom form a nobility exempt from all danger? Can any ambition exist for them other than that of the public good; any rivalry other than that of national glory which reflects upon them? Are not the representatives of the people the organs of public opinion? Do they not see the career of eloquence opening before them? Is not this tribune, where their manly voices cause to be heard either the felicitations of the people, its fears, hopes, or energetic protestations, the aim of all generous desires, the maintenance of all virtues, the motive of all talents? All this is admirable; why then does so worthy a political machine not move? Precisely because it is a machine; it does not move for the same reason that the statue of the Pythian Apollo, masterpiece of art, notwithstanding the immense talent of him who made it, does not move either. It should have had either a mainspring to make it move or it should not have been a statue.

Where then is the mainspring of constitutional monarchy? It has none; when it moves it is the ministry which pushes it and which makes it move; it is the ministry which impresses it with movements by which it is afterwards frightened itself; for a great machine which moves by impulse, a colossus which, deprived of life is about to be moved, is something terrible. If the ministry, fatigued or frightened, suppresses its efforts, all is arrested, and then this is what happens: a sort of fermentation is established in the national representation, all of whose members aspire to be ministers of the king, and according as this fermentation is either in the chamber of peers or in that of the commons, it produces a slight movement of the prophetic or volitive life, whose commotion the monarch feels and it acts upon him according to his character. If it continues in its ministry indolent or unskilful it is exposed; if it does not continue and if it chooses other ministers, the same impulse begins afresh in the machine and lasts until the new ministry allows the government to fall again from fatigue or alarm.

But could not a mainspring be found for constitutional monarchy as has been found for monarchical or emporocratic republics? Yes, but not of the same nature; because a monarchy cannot be commercial in the same manner as a republic, and because national credit could never become sufficiently powerful to serve as a mainspring; for, consider this once more, in a constitutional monarchy, it is not commerce that can be placed in the first rank, as in an emporocracy; because the throne, although constitutional, holds always by its basis to a prophetic origin which, notwithstanding the volitive force which repulses it, calls for an aristocratic or noble order whose brilliancy, independent of all other consideration, surrounds it. This order, which always depends upon birth to be in harmony with the legitimacy of the throne, can in no way be founded upon commerce, where the *éclat* which birth gives, is useless and even harmful. Its true bases are either territorial possession, that is, agriculture, or the profession of arms, that is, military glory. The existence of this order depends upon the very essence of monarchy, and there is no constitution

possible that can annihilate it, when monarchy is not annihilated; now, constitutional monarchy differs in this very
thing from emporocracy, that the monarchy exists there,
modified by the republic; whereas in emporocracy it is the
contrary, the republic is modified by the monarchy; so that
the commerce, which one finds here in the first rank and
which still gives to agriculture its means of growth and of
activity, is there, only in second or even third rank and
only follows agriculture, from which it draws its greatest
resources. In an emporocracy entirely developed, it is
commerce which dominates; it forms a state within the state;
it arms in its own defence; it supports land and sea forces;
it commands subjected peoples and becomes powerful
enough to put the state itself under its dependence, by
furnishing the magic mainspring which makes it move.
But nothing of all this can take place in a monarchy where
commerce, however flourishing it may be, can never give
glory, at least directly. Any attempt made to affect the
sovereignty, to raise armies, to maintain a warlike and conquering navy, would be illusory, so long as the state of
which it was a part was not constituted as a republic; because the noble or aristocratic order of which I spoke would
not obey it and would have to destroy it in order to rule it.

The action of a mainspring in any machine depends for
its superior force on that of the machine. A watch would
not go if its works opposed to the detention of its mainspring
a force superior to its own. The action of the commercial
mainspring, which is credit, is not powerful enough to move
a monarchy, on account of the too great resistances which
it finds in the institutions. It is necessary to search elsewhere for this action; but at the same time that I indicate
where this action is and consequently where it should be
taken, God forbid my advising ever to make use of it! The
mainspring which gives it is too strong for the very reason
that it must be in proportion with the mass to be moved,
so that its use will not be eminently dangerous.

CHAPTER IX

WHAT THE POLITICAL MAINSPRING OF THE CONSTITUTIONAL
MONARCHY SHOULD BE—DANGERS OF THIS MONARCHY
DEPRIVED OF MAINSPRING—NEW CONSIDERATIONS UPON
THE THREE FORMS OF GOVERNMENT AND UPON THEIR
DIVERSE KINDS

IN the preceding chapter, I have said that one should always seek the mainspring of any machine whatsoever in a thing whose force is evidently superior to that of the machine, so as to overcome by its means the resistance of the masses which are opposed to its movement. In explaining here what this mainspring is that one might employ to move a constitutional monarchy, I must declare again that the use of this mainspring would be dangerous and so much the more dangerous as the state to which one would apply it would be more extended in mass and more firm of institution.

Considering therefore a constitutional monarchy as a political machine made by the hand of man, and from the government of which the action of Providence would be removed in so far as political theocracy is concerned, here is the mainspring that one could apply to it.

One should not take this mainspring either from the essence of the monarchy or from that of the republic, because it would give too much force to one or the other, and break the equilibrium which blends them; but it should be sought in the very thing which has caused this blending and from which constitutional monarchy itself has received its existence; now this thing is the Law. Therefore, place the Law above all the institutions which emanate from it, and, without any exception, submit them all to it, and one will see that in displaying its superior force, it will cause them to move; this is the way. Law, by which I mean here political law, is a being of reason which has no movement by itself, and which cannot raise its voice when it is abandoned, eluded, or infringed; but, give it an organ which is independent of all other authority whose eye watches over both people and king, and whose hand restrains both the power of the Will and that of Destiny; establish by a momentary co-operation of these two powers a mixed power represented by the judiciary body; name a Supreme Arbiter and cause the sovereign courts over which he will preside to be sovereign not only in name but *de facto;* and you will see what a terrible mainspring they will display under his orders. Justice will be in the hands of this Supreme Arbiter and all heads will bend before him. This supreme magistrate, independent of any other magistrate, permanent but elective according to certain forms, can have nothing outside his jurisdiction, and his duties will be only to represent the Law and to see that it is executed. By means of its existence there should be three powers in constitutional monarchy: the prophetic and royal power represented by the king, his nobility, his ministry, his councils and his administrative agents; the volitive and popular, represented by the legislative body divided into two chambers; the mixed power of magistracy, independent of the other two, represented by the Supreme Arbiter, president of all the sovereign courts. This last power, veritable creation of the human reason, will make the political work advance and will give it the duration which the force of its institutions would promise it.

This mainspring, as I have said, is dangerous, because it is susceptible of giving too strong an impulse; but it is the only one which may be adapted to the political machine, which is called a constitutional monarchy, and which is capable of maintaining it upright and of making its various works move. In its absence, this machine although of a matchless form is too weak to resist the least shock. The men who do not see this are the blind in politics. In order that a constitutional monarchy may preserve its mixed constitution a long time, deprived of all mainspring, it should be isolated from all other political powers; it should never be harmed, and the governed and the governors equally content should not seek to dominate except by law and by agreement. In the contrary case, the least pure monarchy, if it is governed by an ambitious prince, the least emporocracy, if it has an interest to submit, will suffice to make it tremble. At the lightest shock it will fall. If the constitutional king is endowed with military talents, if his character carries him towards a certain glory whose brilliancy always dazzles young monarchs, he will easily break the badly tied knot which unites the royal power to the popular, he will subjugate the latter, and giving the former the power towards which it inclines by its nature, will make of it a pure monarchy, more or less strongly constituted according to his force and talent. But if, on the contrary, the constitutional king finds himself in difficult circumstances, reduced to his civil virtues alone, and if there exists among the people a man endowed with great force of will, whose position in the legislative body or in the army renders him formidable, this man obtaining possession of the popular power will easily crush his rival and will establish a pure republic.

In the meantime, as pure monarchy and republic have both become impossible among us, on account of the indispensable consequences which they bring about, and as opinion repulses absolutely slavery or murder, it will happen that neither prophetic man nor volitive man will attain to the absolute end towards which they will tend, and that they will be obliged to fall into the military or emporocratic government according to the circumstances and the means which they will have employed. It is in vain that they will seek to deceive themselves upon the nature of these means, and that they will believe, as Robespierre or Bonaparte, to make up for slavery by murder, and for murder by servitude; neither servitude nor murder will serve them for anything, and they will finally be the victims themselves of their own means and be massacred or enslaved; for one can never prevent indefinitely the effect from following its cause. All that one can do is to retard it.

As to the military empire, or the emporocracy, which will irresistibly result from a constitutional monarchy deprived of its mainspring: as these two governments possess for mainspring the very force which constitutes them, military or commercial, they can subsist much longer according as they are favoured by exterior circumstances; but their existence will always be very much limited in comparison with that of simple governments, and above all in comparison with that of Unitarian governments, which are the only perfect ones.

Now that I have stated, although with some difficulty on account of the danger which it involves, what the mainspring of the constitutional monarchy is, and as I have sufficiently explained what I mean by simple and mixed governments, I shall without more delay pass on to Unitarian governments; yet before reaching that point, I believe it useful, in such a new matter, and in which it has been impossible for me to bring as much method as I would wish, to state clearly the difference between the three kinds of government of which I now speak, and the three forms of which I have spoken. This difference consists principally in the fact that the three forms of government, which depend upon three distinct principles and issue from the action of the three great Powers which rule the Universe, can be considered as simple, mixed, or unitarian; and consequently can produce three kinds of government in each of these forms. Let us examine this.

Providence, the Will of Man, or Destiny in exercising their action upon the Social State, determine potentially three forms of government, which pass into action as soon as the exterior circumstances favour their development. These three forms are in general: theocracy for Providence, republic for the Will, and monarchy for Destiny. I call them pure when that which dominates offers no fusion with the other two. Theocracy, for example, was pure among the Hebrews; the republic, pure among the Athenians; monarchy pure among the Assyrians. Among these peoples the government was simple. In Palestine, it was in the hands of a sovereign pontiff established by Moses to rule the people in the name of *God* alone; in Athens, it depended upon a certain number of magistrates, named *Archons*, established to guide the people in the name of the people themselves. At Nineveh, it rested completely in the hands of an absolute monarch, heir of Ninus, and commanding the people in his own name. After having considered the principle of these three forms of pure government, we should consider the consequences and the means, which are: for pure theocracy, faith and absolute devotion to the Divinity; for the republic, love of country transformed into virtue and horror of servitude; for the monarchy, self-esteem and pride transformed into honour, and fear of pain or of ignominy which accompanies death.

These pure forms become the species in comparing them to mixed forms which can result from their blending; and then I call them simple forms. Mixed forms result from the amalgamation which is made of the two simple forms. The union of theocracy to the Republic, for example, constituted the legislation of Orpheus among the ancient Greeks; that of theocracy to monarchy expressed the mission of Krishna to India, or Zoroaster in Persia, of Numa among the Etruscans. Odin among the Scandinavians united theocracy to feudalism, which was already a fusion, made by force of arms of the monarchy in the republic. Wherever theocracy is found, whether mixed with the republic, with monarchy, or with feudalism, it gives political life to the states and serves as means of making them move. These states have no need of other mainspring. But when theocracy is wanting in the mixed forms, that is to say, when the providential action is put outside of the governments, whatever they may be, then these governments have need of a political mainspring, which serves them as means to set going the diverse works. This mainspring is, in the simple forms, the result of their principle, and then I call it the means of life; it is again in the mixed forms, where theocracy is found in action, a consequence of the providential action which is felt there; but in those where Providence is absent, this mainspring, which should be called political, is the very work of the legislation. It must always draw itself from the primal cause which has determined the *mélange* or fusion of the two principles. Thus the military empire and feudalism which is the consequence of it, founded by force of arms and by conquest, receive their mainspring from the same force; thus all aristocracies, oligarchies, or emporocracies borrow theirs from the primal cause which has raised the aristocrats, the oligarchs, or the emporocrats, and it is always a sort of political illusion, a faith given to the birth, the wisdom, or the fortune of those governing; a credit finally, which rests upon whatever may be, most often upon nothing.

All the constitutional monarchies, however they may be constituted, have equal need of a political mainspring; and this mainspring can be found only where it exists, that is to say, in the primal cause of their constitutions. The European monarchies, whose forms have never been simple on account of the volitive movement acting in Europe since the origin of society in the Borean Race, have employed, according to the time and circumstances, diverse mainsprings to continue them. In Aragon, the Supreme Arbiter; in Castile, the Santa Hermandad; in England and in France, the

Parliaments which are called tutors of the kings; in Germany, the order of Teutonic Knights, etc.; all these political institutions, nearly always produced by the state of things and without premeditation for the object which was devolved upon them, have held the place of political mainspring, according as the true means of life or of existence became extinct or worn out; that is to say, according as the providential action was withdrawn from the governments or as the force of arms was without power there.

At the epoch when social order commenced to emerge in Europe from the depths of the gloom into which the downfall of the Roman Empire had dragged it, politics and legislation developed, so to speak, all alone in the darkness; the force of things stood for much in all the institutions, which often took quite another direction and quite another place than their founders had intended; but today, as knowledge acquires an ever-increasing *éclat*, instinct is of no further use to the legislator and he is no longer permitted to ignore the end for which he works. He should know, if he wishes to found a military and feudal empire, that he has need of force of arms and that without conquest he can do nothing. If he dreams of a pure republic, he must examine where or how he will find slaves. If he wishes an absolute monarchy, he must consider that he will need instruments of death. But a superior force prevents him from wishing slavery or murder; he must cease then wishing for democracy or despotism. His attention is fixed upon aristocracy; where is the illusion with which he will surround his aristocrats? Who will believe them greater or wiser than himself? But his aristocrats will be the oligarchs whose fortune, and principally great territorial possession, will constitute the merit. I say that if oligarchs are noble as well as rich, they will wish a monarchy; and that if they are only rich without being noble, they will wish a republic. I say that never will fortune alone serve either as bond or mainspring to a state, because it is too fickle and changes hands too often. It will be fixed by *majorats* or right of primogeniture; yes but, then it is a phantom of nobility that will be created, to which they will attach all the difficulties of real nobility without one of its advantages. Well, the legislator will incline the State towards emporocracy; but has he at his disposal an immense commerce which covering both hemispheres with its pavilions can change into a two-edged sword the caduceus of Mercury? If he has not, let him seek another form of government; for emporocracy demands for mainspring a national credit that such a commerce alone can give him. This is why the legislator stops at a constitutional monarchy, half monarchy and half republic; it presents the model which he has meditated in the calm of all his passions. This model is very beautiful; it will become a statue of most happy proportions; it is too bad that it will not move. He will place a mainspring in it; he will do well; but he would do still better if he tried to put life in it. How! life into a statue! Yes, life into a statue. Ah! Who will be the protecting Divinity who will hear this political Pygmalion? A Divinity who will never refuse assistance to those who invoke it with a pure heart and in the interest of universal good: Providence.

CHAPTER X

REAL CONDITION OF THINGS IN EUROPE—COMBAT BETWEEN
MEN OF WILL AND THOSE OF DESTINY, THE LIBERALS
AND THE ROYALISTS—WHAT THE MIXED MEN CALLED
MINISTERIAL ARE—DANGER IN WHICH THE SOCIAL
ORDER FINDS ITSELF—MEANS OF EVADING THIS DANGER

PROVIDENCE is in all things wherever its presence is
recognized. It is in the fetish of the African savage, as
in the Tables of the Law presented by Moses. Like the
universal life which emanates from it and shines both in the
eye of the gnat and in that of the elephant, it differs only by
the grandeur, merit, or importance of the objects. As divine
faith is the moral fruit that it bears, it is also this fruit which
produces it. Wherever divine faith is, there also, in potential existence, is the intellectual power which dominates
the Universe. Outside of this faith are only transitory
productions; for everything that volitive liberty or prophetic
necessity produces is transitory. Providential productions
alone have the right to immortality.

I believe I can openly announce this truth. Providence
can be called into all the governments and all could owe
life to it; but in order that this life should be complete, it is
necessary that the three powers should be united in a single
one. This union, when it is possible, constitutes what I
call a Unitary government. This government can take
place whenever two powers are already united in a mixed

form. To make it perfect, one needs only to add the power which is lacking.

If one will but reflect upon what I have just said, one will feel that the moment is extremely favourable for constituting a military government in Europe; and that if the men, called by Destiny or by the Will to be legislators there, do not feel the enormous advantage given them by the shock which has just agitated this part of the world, they will miss one of the most excellent opportunities that could be offered to their labours. I know well that at first, drawn on by appearances, these men will tell me that far from seeing things tending towards the Unity that I indicate, it seems, on the contrary, that everything is making efforts to divide itself more and more. I do not deny these appearances; I find them even quite natural and very fitting to prove what I have said.

And let one recall how the Will of Man has made attempts in Europe to seize the power. What labours! what marvellously woven plots! what long and painful efforts! At last it was about to succeed; an unexpected obstacle has presented itself. The pure republic twice established and twice cemented with the blood of two unfortunate monarchs has not been able to resist the first shock of Destiny. It has fallen upon the bloody ruins which it has heaped up. In the meantime a prophetic man has presented himself; he has enveloped in his vortex this terrible European Will and has told it that this vortex was his. It has believed him even long after it no longer could believe him. But finally when this man, repulsed by a Destiny more powerful than his own, has fallen, ought it still to sustain him? Yes, because it had no other hope than to deceive him, as he had deceived it. Astonished at its defeat but not discouraged, this proud Will struggles again against events. It tries its last resources and agitates everything that it can agitate. From the Tagus to the Don its voice is heard. It shakes Spain and Italy, it troubles England and Germany; it intimi-

dates France; it moves the dust of ancient Greece, where
formerly it ruled; Turkey and Russia having sprung into the
arena will strike blows of which it is difficult to foretell the
result. Whatever it may be, it always hopes to derive
advantage, at least, by the enfeeblement of its most formidable enemies.

Meanwhile Destiny, still trembling from the risk it has
run, excites its defenders. The prophetic men which it
animates oppose themselves with all their strength to the
volitive ones. Under the names of royalists and liberals,
both urge the Social State in contrary directions, and seem
to wish to destroy it. The former, who only aspire to the
re-establishment of the overthrown institutions, are accused
of wishing to retard civilization; the latter, who only strive
to realize their ideas of improvement, are accused of wishing
to ruin it by urging it ahead into the whirlpools of revolutions. These two accusations, which are not devoid of
foundation, cause a multitude of defences and explanations
which exonerate no one and explain nothing. However,
some mixed governments being formed and having operated
by means of the interest of the moment, a sort of union
among several of these men, have succeeded in mitigating
their ideas and in producing among them a sort of intermediate party, which is called the party of the centre. The
men who compose it are not of the party, properly speaking:
they are moderators, arbitrators, supporters of the government, and these names, which ought to be an honour and
make their strength, are precisely what ruins them in the
public opinion and which takes all means from them.

If one had need of a new reason after all these I have
given, or which have issued naturally from announced facts,
this one will be more than sufficient to make it understood,
that these mixed governments, in which is wasted the genius
of modern legislators, lack still the two most powerful political motives, love of country and honour, since the royalists and the liberals wish to put there neither the one nor

the other. It appears in these governments that there is a sort of shame to be of the opinion of the ministers and to sustain them. The mind which animates them, however pure and disinterested it may be, carries always with it a character of obscurity and of ruse which arms beforehand against it. One cannot enter there without making concessions which wound self-esteem, and this could not be otherwise. The mixed governments are mixed, precisely because they are not simple and because nothing pure or simple could agree with them. The royalists would have the ministers, royalists, and the liberals would have them liberals; but that cannot be without involving instantly the overthrow of the constitutional edifice; because this edifice is not composed of homogeneous elements, but of elements participating of two opposed principles—the monarchical and the republican. If the ministers were pure liberals or royalists, they would not be the ministers of a constitutional monarchy, but those of a republic or of an absolute monarchy; and because they are in the spirit of their institution, in the real constitutional character which is a blending of the republic and the monarchy, they are accused of duplicity. One pours out more than ridicule and less than blame upon them and upon the intermediate party by which they are surrounded; one reproaches them with living by corruption; one is on the point of telling this government, which one has chosen, that it can have agents and friends only at the price of the lowest interests and that there exists for it in the hearts of the people neither love, nor honour, nor zeal which excites them outside of sordid passions that it knows how to inspire.

Suppose, in a similar state of affairs, such a government in a great danger, you will see that it cannot sustain itself a moment by its own force. It will be obliged to seek support among its most decided enemies, the pure liberals or royalists, from whom it will find it only on condition of ceasing to be itself to become them; which not being able to do, it will see the necessity of deceiving them and of sinking deeper than ever into that path of stratagem and of corruption for which it is so much reproached. It will be able thus for some time to stir alternatively the love of country or honour by appealing to liberty or necessity; but this see-saw play will end soon by finding dupes no longer; the mainsprings which it will employ will be worn out; its means of corruption will be exhausted; it will have no more allurements sufficiently powerful at its disposal; party hatred, fatigued, will no longer be open to the conspiracies which it will form to frighten the one by the other; only the masses moving themselves will clash and be broken and annihilate each other if the exterior enemy does not triumph by conquest.

This is the actual condition of a great part of Europe: on the one side a violent movement towards a pure republic; on the other a movement none the less strong towards absolute monarchy; in the middle some mixed governments, emporocratic or constitutional, alternately drawn by one or the other tendency, and by turn forced to follow their opposed vortexes. This condition is difficult and if it lasts long, it menaces the social order in Europe with an entire subversion. There exists only one means of saving it, and this means I have clearly indicated: it is to call Providence into the governments and to bring into Unity what is mixed and divided. Make therefore the schism of religion disappear; efface all the differences of cult; have a European sovereign pontiff, who will be both recognized and respected by all the peoples; let this sovereign pontiff dominate over an enlightened priesthood, wise and powerful, whose voice will be heard in your councils; let these councils, instead of admitting only two principles and of being in consequence the arena of an eternal combat, receive three, represented thus: Providence, by the sovereign pontiff and the priesthood; Destiny, by the monarch, the peers of the kingdom, his ministry, and his nobility; the Will of Man, by the electoral colleges and the deputies of the departments; and you will see that that Unity so much sought for will be formed of itself, for three powers or three principles united produce always, in amalgamating, a fourth power or a fourth principle, whence results the sole Unity possible on earth.

But you will object, that I propose, to heal an actual and positive evil, a remedy contingent and almost illusory; you will say that it is impossible to bring religion to the uniformity of a cult and to create a sovereign pontiff who may unite in him the assent and the veneration of all the peoples of Europe. I reply to this objection, the only one indeed which you can make, that the proposed remedy appears to you eventual and almost illusory only because you do not conceive its physical and moral reality, and that this reality escapes you only because you regard as impossible, things that are the easiest when they are veritably desired. Desire then only these things and you will see the obstacles which you loved to believe insurmountable smooth away before you. Dare to make a movement towards Providence; it awaits it to help you. Nevertheless do not be deceived in it; yes, no doubt, it would be impossible to remove from religion the schisms which disfigure and dishonour it; it would be impossible to arrive at the uniformity of the cult that Providence demands, if you would try again to obtain these admirable results either by oblique *détours* of strategy or by the odious means of force. Neither strategy nor force would succeed for you. Do not forget this axiom which I have so often repeated in the course of this work: that universal things, dependent on a universal principle, are only destroyed by themselves or are changed only by the interior labour of their own principle. Now, of all the things that one can place in the category of those which depend on a universal principle, religion is assuredly of the first rank. It can therefore never be changed or modified but by itself; all other change, all other modification would be useless or harmful. All the exterior means which one could take to arrive at this end would be dangerous and without effect. Providence can restrain neither the liberty of the Will nor the necessity of Destiny; but also it can never be restrained by either. When one wishes it to change or to modify its productions one must know how to interest it for that purpose.

If, therefore, the Protestants find that, relative to the enlightenment of the century, the Catholic cult continues to offer in its dogmas too great an obscurity and in its doctrines too great a stiffness; if, on the other hand, the Catholics and the Protestants themselves agree to regard the reformed cult as insignificant and cold, incoherent and versatile; if the schismatic Greeks refuse less their assent to certain dogmas as they fear the papal influence; if the Jews themselves, long enough persecuted for a fatal error, suffer from living isolated in the midst of European nations, it would assuredly be very possible to obviate all these difficulties. The obstacles formerly insurmountable are no longer so today.

Everything wears away with time and the forms of cult efface themselves as all other things. They lose their asperity; their principal signs disappear and soon they can no longer distinguish outwardly men who belong to the different sects, even the most opposed. A Catholic, a Protestant, a Schismatic Greek, and even a Jew can meet in the same hostelry and live there for months without perceiving today that they follow different rites. Not a century or two ago on the first Saturday in the week which had assembled them at the same table, all four would have been struck with an unquestionable impression; they would have separated instantly. Now they do not separate; because at first they are not recognized, and they would see no reason for separating even though they should recognize each other; for their different habits are merged in the same habits, which is to behave in the world as all the world. It is not because all four do not hold to their own cult and because they would not give themselves over to violent movements if one wished to force them to change it. But be certain that it is by political motives that they hold to it, and that opinion or self-esteem, necessity or liberty are there to take the place of their religious zeal. This is the reason; manage these political motives; act in the interior and not upon the exterior; make Religion influence the cults and not the cults Religion and doubt not the success.

One appears to dread the influence of a sovereign pontiff; one recalls with terror the disastrous epochs of which I have sketched the history; but these epochs were the inevitable crises of the decadence of the Social State in Europe; they were produced by the darkness which the barbarians had drawn with them; this darkness is dissipated; it can renew itself no more.

Besides, has there been in Europe a veritable sovereign pontiff? I have taken enough pains to show that there has not been. There is no reason why there should not be one, even the one who occupies the place today, provided he is providentially recognized and he himself recognizes the supreme power from which he will take his authority.

CHAPTER XI

APPEAL OF PROVIDENCE IN THE MIXED GOVERNMENTS TO RENDER THEM UNITARY

PROFOUNDLY penetrated by this truth, that the salvation of Europe and that of the world which it draws into the vortex of its will can come only from Providence, and assuming that in the absence even of all intellectual inspiration the physical reality has spoken clearly enough by the voice of experience, to peoples and kings, to engage them to turn at last their attention towards a superior power which only awaits their appeal to fly to their succour, I had shown in this chapter what the forms of this appeal should be and by what means as simple as easy one could attain the accomplishment of all the things of which I have spoken. But after having written with deep feeling this important chapter, the one perhaps for which the others have been conceived and co-ordinated in a primal thought, having reread it coldly and with a calm mind, I have seen that it ought not to be published; for it is not here a question of setting forth principles, but of showing the consequences of them in the future, in giving them legal forms; which was submitting inevitably one power to the other and leaving the Will master to stifle the productions of Destiny before they had acquired enough stability to resist it.

It is with a keen regret, I confess, that I am obliged to suppress that part of my labour, which I regarded as the newest and most necessary; but prudence and reason have commanded this sacrifice. A scheme of theocratic legislation, of the nature of that which I have laid down, could not be confided to the public without imminent danger; for the public, not being called to realize it, can take possession of it only to destroy it by opposing its consequences or by depreciating beforehand all its advantages. Only a statesman placed in most fortunate circumstances, a monarch, a minister of the Church vested with an august character, can assure its immense results by giving successively to its diverse parties a force and stability which they can receive only from laws.

An obscure and simple writer, I have indeed been able to show the power that men should invoke if they would recall into their midst the peace which they have banished; but when the moment has come to establish the forms of this invocation I have felt my weakness and my inability; and, forced to keep silent for fear of profaning them, I hold my tongue. The chapter, wherein I have written down these forms, exists it is true, but I will keep it to communicate it only when a favourable opportunity presents itself. If during the course of my life this occasion does not present itself, I have taken care that it will at least survive me, for the very sacrifice that I make proves sufficiently that I attach to it quite a different importance from that which springs ordinarily from the self-esteem or vanity of an author.

CHAPTER XII

GENERAL RECAPITULATION

I FIND myself at the close of my work with a satisfaction mingled with some uneasiness; I have done what I wished, without doubt, but not exactly as I would have wished to do; I feel that in many passages I have fallen short of my subject; and that, notwithstanding all the trouble I have taken to be clear, many things remain obscure. In the unusual course that I have taken, determined to sketch in a few pages the history of the Kingdom of Man in one of its races during the space of twelve thousand years, innumerable events are presented to me. Nearly all of these appear worthy to be rewritten, nevertheless it was necessary to make a choice, for my intention was not to compose a too long work, at a time when the small number of readers who seek still to instruct themselves, surrounded by a mass of political pamphlets and of ephemeral sheets, has but little time to give to prolix works. In making this indispensable choice, I have at times seen, but too late, that I could have made a better choice; at other times, when my choice has seemed fortunate I have recognized that I had not entered into all the developments which the importance of my subject should have demanded. I have often reproached myself and I will perhaps be reproached, but it was inevitable. I could not, while I was still occupied in outlining the most shadowy plans of my historical picture, design all the aspects, nor determine all the masses: if I had endeavoured

534

to do it, I would have produced a picture without perspective or I would have been forced to give it a distance out of all proportion.

Perhaps one will believe that it would have been possible at the commencement of my work to enter into greater details upon each of the races which compose the Kingdom of Man, and that I should have indicated more clearly their origin; to say, for example, why these races had not appeared simultaneously on the earth and by what reasons they were born upon one part of the globe rather than upon the other. I admit that this would have been worthy of being presented to the curiosity of the reader; but as I have given it to be understood, the origin of the races and their position on the earth holds too closely to the origin of the Kingdom of Man itself to be able to be separated from the science which treats especially of it; this science, which is by its elevation outside of history, properly speaking, is called *Cosmogony*. Our hierographic writer, Moses, has treated particularly of it, not in an obvious manner, it is true, for the vulgar grasp, but in a manner clear enough, nevertheless, so that the veil by which he has covered the origin of all things can be raised by a learned hand. I have given first the chief means of raising this veil, by restoring the Hebraic tongue, and by rendering thus to the terms of the original text the veritable sense which they should have. I hope later to make use of these means to establish in all its splendour the thought of one of the greatest men who has ever appeared upon earth.

After this first difficulty, many others will successively arise, none the less important. One will ask if love should be the principle of sociability and of civilization in man, as I have declared it to be; why this need, transformed into passion, does not manifest itself in the two sexes in the same manner; whence comes this difference in the transformation of sensation into sentiment; and urging the curiosity as far as it can go, why two sexes exist in nature. To this I will reply that this existence of two sexes, of which one asks the cause, belongs again to cosmogony, as well as the very difference which constitutes them.　This existence and this difference must be received by history as certain facts, from which all others issue and beyond which it cannot go without leaving its domain.　And as to what are the consequences of this existence and of this difference, of which the most important is marriage, basis of the social edifice, if one insisted that I should enter into all the details, of which a subject of this nature could admit, one would ask me with all the more reason to explain at greater length as regards the origin of speech and the establishment of the languages.

But does one not feel that each of these subjects, if I had wished to go deeply into them, would have necessitated a book to each alone?　I could only indicate in mine, the principles and choose among the consequences the principal ones, those which could throw the most light upon that which was to follow, leaving to the sagacity of the reader the care of finding others.　I know well that an attentive reader could ask me many questions upon these commencements of the Borean civilization; for example, why marriage, which I give as the basis of the social edifice, was not felicitous. This question and many others which I have sketched designedly must find their solution in the *ensemble* of the work. The history of Mankind offers unceasingly the striking proof of this truth: that a particular evil is often necessary in order to bring forth a general good.　Here, moreover, is the reply to the difficulties which one suggests; it will serve to clear up many difficulties of the same nature.　Marriage— the inevitable consequence of the existence of the two sexes, and the necessary difference between their manner of thinking after having felt—marriage was not entirely happy, because if it had been it would have limited there the course of the Borean civilization; Man, satisfied with his lot, would have desired nothing, sought nothing beyond it, provided that he could not desire or seek anything beyond happiness;

he would have bent himself to the yoke of the woman, would have become effeminate as she, and his race would have been inevitably destroyed before having passed through any of the more elevated phases of the social order.   If woman was unfortunate at this first epoch of civilization, it was principally in accordance with her nature, that does not permit her to give birth to anything without pain, either in the physical order or in the moral order.   It is true that her faults aggravated her evils; but her faults were then a consequence of an anterior fault, the knowledge of which depends upon cosmogony.

It has been seen how war, always inevitable between the two races, because the races all strive for the dominion and usurpation of the earth, had developed much useful knowledge in the White Race, and had put it in condition to struggle advantageously against the Black Race.   I have on this occasion shown the origin of a number of institutions and usages, whose principle, plunged in the obscurity of centuries, had escaped the researches of the savants.   No doubt one has observed with interest that first organization of the Celtic people, whose indelible imprint is found more or less strong among the nations which hold to the same stock.   I venture to flatter myself that one will excuse certain hypotheses of detail, in favour of the striking truth of the whole.   If the situation of Voluspa, for example, has appeared too poetic, one ought at least to agree that she was not beyond probability, since all the civil and religious usages preserved by our ancestors confirmed the possibility. It was impossible that a picture of this dimension, exposed to so many storms and lasting so long a space of time, should not offer some gaps to be filled and some features to be restored.

At the close of the First Book, the intellectual sphere was already developed in the Borean Race and the cult was born.   The Second Book has showed the consequences of this first development.   Let us consider here, how politics, at first influenced by religion, has reacted upon it; let us observe that the first schism which was manifested among the Celts, that which gave birth to the nomad peoples, has been purely political; and let us remember what I said in this last book, that all the quarrels which one has inappropriately called religious, all the schisms, have not drawn their principle from the very essence of religion, but only from the forms of cult, of which politics had taken possession. An observation none the less important, relative to superstition and fanaticism, can be made in this Second Book. It can be seen how often one has been mistaken in accusing religion of these excesses to which it was a stranger, and above all how one is wrong in believing that theocracy could have led to them. It is, on the contrary, theocracy which puts an end to it. Superstition and fanaticism reign only where the forms of cult, in which Destiny or the Will of Man have seized the dominion, have succeeded in usurping the place of Religion and in stifling the voice of Providence. As soon as Providence finds an organ capable of making its voice heard, a prophet, a theocrat, a sovereign pontiff, an envoy worthy of it, all superstition disappears and human blood no longer inundates the altars.

It is useless for me to review the foundation of the Universal Empire by that extraordinary man whose glory filled the universe under the name of Rama, the Ram; Scander of the two horns; Osiris, chief of men; Dionysus, the divine intelligence; Giam-shyd the dominator of the Universe, etc. I have said almost all that I could say, without falling into details foreign to this work. But let us notice again that it is only in admitting the existence of this empire that one can account for a multitude of usages common to all the peoples; as, for example, giving a crown to the king, and a mitre to the pontiff; of elevating their thrones a certain number of degrees and of placing a sceptre in the hand of the one, and a pastoral crook in the hand of the other. The certain form of the altars, the manner of prostrating oneself while invoking the Divinity, all bespeaks a universal rite whose impress is not effaced through the infinite variations which the cults have undergone. Can the wise philologists see without admiration that the essential forms of language are the same everywhere and that the general grammar, resting on the same bases, attests the existence of a universal tongue of which one finds remnants spread about in all places? If it is a question of poetry, can one doubt that the rhyme admitted by the Chinese and by the Arabs, and the rhythm known by the Hindus, as by the Scandinavians, partake of the same origin? Look at music; does not this admirable art, wherever it is known, receive seven notes from one octave to another, divided into five tones and two half-tones? How will one explain all these things and an infinity of others of which it would be too long to speak, if one does not consider them the relics of a religious and political unity which has become divided? One must believe on this point the sacred books of the Hindus and admit as an incontestable verity the existence of the Universal Empire of Rama. It is from these sacred books that I have drawn the greater part of the things that I relate concerning the dismemberment of this empire, and concerning the cause of the political schisms, which brought about its downfall. In general, it is in the sacerdotal archives of the ancient nations that I have searched for the necessary documents to compose my Third Book, and to conduct the history of Mankind from the appearance of Rama to that of Pythagoras. This first part of my work can therefore be considered as more particular, rational, and philosophical than the second, which is supported by more positive documents and does not deviate any more, as to chronology of facts, from the ordinary history.

This then, is why I have purposely divided my work into two parts, so that the second, composed of stronger material, should give a support to the first, through the connection of ideas and the chain of events. I do not believe that an observant reader has failed to recognize this chain, nor that he has been able to consider as simple hypotheses, things generally unknown, it is true, but of which the known things are presented to the mind only as quite simple consequences.

The first part, although less voluminous than the second, contains however a much greater quantity of important facts and includes a lapse of time much more considerable. One can observe three principal epochs: the first extends from the dawn of civilization in the Borean Race to the appearance of the Divine Envoy among the Celts; it is the ascending movement. The second includes the appearance of this Envoy and the establishment of the Universal Empire, to the first symptoms of its decline announced by the political schism of the Phœnician Shepherds; it is the social order, stationary in its greatest splendour. The third, contains the entire duration of this decline from the first weakening of the moral knowledge to the first approach of the darkness; it is the descending movement. The second part includes also three epochs, but much more limited: that of the twilight, where one observes a sort of combat between the light and the gloom; that of complete darkness, and that of the ascending movement which recommences. These three epochs, which are not equivalent in duration to one of the ancient ones, represent only an interval of about three thousand years. One can date the first of these last epochs from the taking of Troy by the Greeks; the second, from the downfall of the Roman Empire; and the third from the commencement of the Crusades. This last epoch is not terminated, and although all may augur, by the increase of knowledge, that it ought to be for us the morning of a fine day, we cannot deceive ourselves, nevertheless, that this morning of the rebeginning of our Social State has been disturbed by many storms.

If one would take the trouble to reflect upon the causes of the most violent of these storms, called French Revolution, one will see that they hold to the first forms of civilization that the Borean Race has received at its origin. One can unravel the traces by going back over the flood of centuries and be convinced that it is to the precocious and extraordinary development which the Will received in this race, that the shocks, more or less strong which it has experienced at various times, should be attributed. This volitive development, indispensable in order that the White Race, exposed early to the attacks of the Black Race, should be preserved, struck it with an indelible character which has followed it in all the phases of its Social State, and has insinuated into all its political institutions, civil as well as religious, these extraordinary forms, which the Black Race or the Yellow Race, called before it to bear the sceptre of the earth, had never known. In these two races, the Will, early submissive to Destiny, had supported its yoke, scarcely ever feeling its weight and without seeking to throw it off; whilst, on the contrary, in the Borean Race, the Will has always submitted with difficulty to this yoke of Necessity and has freed itself whenever it was possible from it. This is the origin of the difference, which is always noticeable between the peoples of Asia and those of Europe, notwithstanding the fusion which has many times been effected between the Oriental blood and the Borean, and even in spite of the Universal Empire that the Celts of Borean origin have exercised over the whole hemisphere. The people of the Yellow Race, although they had to submit many times, now to those of the Black Race and then to those of the White, have always preserved their spirit of necessity and stability, whose force has finally, at least in Asia, enchained in the long run the spirit of liberty and of revolution, with which the Celts have always been imbued.

Europe, veritable seat of the White Race, place of its origin, and principal hearth where its force is concentrated and preserved, has been particularly the theatre where this spirit has displayed all its vehemence; it is there that the

Will of Man has manifested its greatest power. If this Will, less proud, could have recognized the action of Providence, at the same time as she opposed hers to that of Destiny, it would, without doubt, have produced magnificent results; for liberty, which it made its idol, constitutes its intimate essence and emerges from the Divinity itself; but it has never appeared to fight the necessity of Destiny and attempt to overthrow its productions, except to raise itself upon their débris, and place itself by their means above Providence. This could not be; because its greatest efforts tended to produce only political storms, by which the Social State has experienced violent disturbances rather than progress, and received rapid flashes rather than lasting light. I agree, however, with volitive men, that these storms have often had their usefulness. No doubt, as in the elementary world tempests which trouble for a moment the planes of the air, heaping up the clouds to deliver them to the fires of lightning, have the incontestable advantage of purifying them; political storms have also the advantage of purging the social world and can by their very disorder re-establish harmony; but it would be foolish to desire these unseasonable tempests and unbounded storms and to consider these formidable movements as spectacles worthy of admiration and sacrifice thus the hope of agriculturers and the welfare of the nations to the pleasure of contemplating its terrible effects and sanctioning its ravages.

I have expressed my opinion regarding the French Revolution. To be useful, it must be stopped, and to stop it, the only power which can do this must be invoked. The Will of Man was the motive in it; I have said it often; I have proved it in all ways. Destiny, which it had vanquished, has again the advantage, not because it has been stronger, but because it is divided by an inevitable effect of its nature, and of the universal progress of things. But prophetic men would be greatly deceived if they believe this triumph of Destiny assured: it is not at all; its absolute reign

in monarchy has become impossible, for the reasons that I
have clearly indicated. The fusion of the Will which has
been tried in emporocracies and in constitutional monarchies
cannot last; because Necessity and Liberty which are two
extremes can unite only by a medium which is lacking in
these two kinds of governments. Engaged in seeking this
medium in purely political things, I have sought it frankly
but in vain; I have seen only mainsprings more or less ingenious, more or less strong, which for a certain time can
make these political machines which are called mixed governments, move. I have indicated these mainsprings, but I admit, disapproving of the usage; for as ingenious as a machine
may be, admirable as a mechanically moving statue may be,
an organized being, animated by life, would always be worth
much more.

Now, what is this life which these governments lack and
that one can summon there? What is this means, alone
capable of uniting two powers as opposed as the Will and
Destiny, Movement and Repose, Liberty and Necessity? I
have said it boldly; it is Providence. That I may have had
the pleasure of showing by what manner this divine power
could be called into political institutions, is what the experiment alone should have the right to demonstrate; and an
experiment of this nature is not in the hand of any ordinary
man. The people themselves are not likely to have it; and
it is on account of this, as I have explained, that I ought not
to expose to light the chapter which enclosed its elements. I
can but hope that a man exalted enough might present himself, a monarch powerful enough, a legislator placed in favourable enough circumstances, to attempt this experiment and
succeed there; his glory, above all glories, should then have
limits as extended only as that of the Universe, and for
duration a term similar to that of the last century where the
last people of the Borean Race lived.

But what is the ultimate question? For what purpose
are all the preparatory forms indicated in the suppressed

chapter? It is a question of coming to the nomination of a
Supreme Pontiff, whose sacerdotal authority all Europe may
recognize; it is a question of finding the simple but secret
ways, which lead to this important act; finally it is a question
of making the forms which will be employed, participate at
once with those of Providence, the Will of Man, and Destiny.
This Supreme Pontiff, who, according to what I have already
said, could be that very one who exists today, provided he
had recognized the authority which will appoint him, would
be by the very fact of his appointment vested with an august
and holy character, and with a veritable sacerdotal power.
He would extend his pastoral staff over entire Europe and
over all the nations which would participate in his cult;
his moral influence would not be illusory or of no value as
it is today, because it would no longer be the fruit of ignorance or of usurpation, with which one has perhaps too justly
reproached it, but the fruit of learning and the legitimate
result of a general assent, of a sworn alliance between peoples
and kings, the Will of Man and Destiny. This Sovereign
Pontiff would then become the organ of Providence and its
representative on earth; he would hold in his hands the bond
so much desired, which would unite the three powers in
one and which would hold the Universe for a long time in
permanent peace. As representative of Providence and
its sensible organ, he would not only dominate over the
diverse cults which would follow the nations subject to his
august priesthood, but over the very essence of religion from
which the cults would draw their force. He could, according to the needs of the peoples and the kings, according to
the increase of knowledge, the advancement of the sciences,
and the progress of civilization, modify the dogmas of religion, enlighten its mysteries, and carry in Truth the progressive development, which is in all things. Religion no longer
stationary in the midst of the general government, far from
troubling this movement, would regulate its march by favouring it. Schisms would become impossible so long as the

Unity would not be broken; and the cults, in order to reform themselves, would no more have occasion to excite any storm in the governments. They would be in the hands of the Supreme Pontiff and the other sacerdotal chiefs, who would dispose of the forms according to the character of the peoples and the climatic positions. Thus men would nowhere be encumbered with these inflexible chains which are repugnant to their nature. Truth, ever more brilliant, would become more and more dear to them; and Virtue, which would be their happiness, would no more be a vain phantom doubted by the oppressed.

A Supreme Pontiff, thus constituted, thus vested with the force of the three great powers of the Universe, would become without doubt the highest person of the world. Emperors and kings who would reign under the shadow of his moral influence would exercise over all civil things a temperate but steadfast power. Never would revolt or sedition approach their throne; never would they be a butt for the furies of the factions or the plots of the ambitious, because the factions would have no issue, and the ambitious would find success only in the way admitted by honour. These dreaded shocks, which one calls revolutions, would be unknown because the Will of Man, freely exercised and daily satisfied, being able to make its voice heard at any time, and besides, seeing that it was well represented and sustained, would have no interest to risk losing all its advantages by struggling against two powers which would inevitably crush it in uniting together against it. The position of the Will would be exactly that of Destiny and even that of Providence. Neither of the two powers could usurp absolute dominion, even if it tried, because it would always meet, at the least movement that its own representatives would attempt in their own interest, an insurmountable object in the spontaneous union of the other power with the Will.

The wars of nation with nation could never take place by motives of ambition or personal interest, because these motives, at the instant divulged, would attract upon the turbulent nation all the united forces of the other nations. Besides the morality and immorality of things being in the hands of the Supreme Pontiff, it would suffice that a war should be only declared by him immoral, that, in the very nation which would undertake it, the instruments which might serve it, should not be found. The only wars possible, if Europe could have any, would be those which foreign enemies might necessitate, or the perjured nations, so insensate as to welcome the revolt, or sanction the crimes of a usurper or a tyrant. Thus would be realized a very beautiful idea, which has been lately conceived, and which one has believed possible to be contained in what has been called the *Holy Alliance;* this idea, worthy by its grandeur of the august monarch who had welcomed it, has not been able to be contained in the diplomatic frame given it, for the reason that politics alone had fashioned this frame, that the Will of Man was not there, and that Destiny alone, although acting in the name of Providence, could not replace the two powers which had likewise refused its support.

Calling Providence into these governments, by admitting three principles and consequently three chambers instead of two, one would see reborn, as by enchantment, those three states of the ancient Celts, of which the fierce followers of Odin, the Goths, had seated upon the débris of the Roman Empire only an image, grossly outlined and deprived of life. The three chambers would enclose actually the States-General of the nation, and would offer expression of the three universal powers, whose unity of force would reflect itself upon the inviolable and sacred person of the king. Above this united political power the Supreme Pontiff would be raised, enveloping a great number of these political unities in his intellectual unity, and residing in a holy city, that all the nations submissive to his pontifical authority would swear to respect. The violation of this holy city and that of its determined territory would be regarded as most odious impiety and a most enormous crime. He who would dare, armed and with hostile designs, to cross its pacific limits, would be doomed with anathema and given over to the execration of mankind. It is upon the veneration, which the sacerdotal chief inspires as representative of Providence, that all the social order is founded. The respect which one bears to the king and the obedience which one owes to the magistrates speaking in the name of the civil law comes only afterwards. If this veneration fails in an empire, all fails; the respect for the prince is soon effaced and obedience is withdrawn and evaded. Force is then obliged to show itself; but force is a two-edged sword which inevitably wounds those whom it serves.

After the appointment of the Supreme Pontiff, the most important act would no doubt be the choice of the city that this august chief of religion should inhabit. This city must be by unanimous consent declared holy and inviolable, so that Providence might be able to make its voice heard without the fatality of Destiny, or the liberty of the Will ever being able in any way to disturb its influence. A Supreme Pontiff who can fear anything whatever is of no importance; it is despicable when he can say that he has fear of anything except *God*, or Providence which emanates from Him. A monarch himself ought never to be restrained in anything. He ought never to say that he has been, because that can never be. If he finds himself in such violent circumstances that the Will of Man crushes Destiny in him he ought to die and not to flinch. Let him be aware especially not to recognize judges; he has none outside of the Supreme Pontiff. With whatever name other personages, sacerdotal or laymen are adorned, with whatever authority they say themselves to be momentarily vested, they are never anything but his highest subjects. Besides, their persons are not inviolable, whereas that of the king is. They are not inviolable because they do not constitute by themselves alone a unity, whereas the king constitutes one.

The unity which has constituted a Supreme Pontiff, being still more elevated, the person of this august representative of Providence would be not only inviolable, but would communicate also the inviolability to all that it wished to render inviolable.

As soon as the sacred alliance, whose possibility I have shown without divulging the means, would be effected among the European nations; as soon as Providence, called into their governments, would have made these mixed governments unitarian; as soon as the Supreme Pontiff would be elected and able to exercise his providential influence over all the peoples, a thing would happen which, in the actual state of things would be impossible, or could not take place without costing torrents of blood and tears; it would be done without the least shock, in the midst of most perfect tranquillity.   Europe, which for a long time inclines to form a sole empire, would form it; and the one who would be called to dominate over kings, under the name of Emperor or Sovereign King, respected by kings, as much as the Supreme Pontiff, would proceed by the sole force of things to the conquest of the world.   Then the Borean Race would have attained its highest destinies; the entire earth would offer the same spectacle which has already been offered in the time of Rama; but with this remarkable difference, that the pontifical and royal seat would be in Europe instead of being in Asia; men united under the same cult and under the same laws would recognize only a same *God*, a same Supreme Pontiff, and a same Sovereign King; they would speak the same tongue; would treat each other as brothers and enjoy a felicity as great as their mortal nature would admit, during a long term of centuries and until the end fixed by the Eternal Wisdom.

Printed in the USA
CPSIA information can be obtained
at www.ICGtesting.com
LVHW042057261023
762248LV00023B/289